Christianity and Capitalism in China

Ottavio Palombaro

Christianity and Capitalism in China

A Case Study from the Diaspora

palgrave
macmillan

Ottavio Palombaro
Department of Social and Political
Sciences
University of Milano
Milan, Italy

ISBN 978-981-97-3548-8 ISBN 978-981-97-3549-5 (eBook)
https://doi.org/10.1007/978-981-97-3549-5

This Palgrave Macmillan imprint is published by the registered company Springer Nature Singapore Pte Ltd.
The registered company address is: 152 Beach Road, #21-01/04 Gateway East, Singapore 189721, Singapore

Contents

List of Tables

CHAPTER 1

Introduction

Since its inception, the discipline of Sociology sought to eliminate the possibility of metaphysics. Few since then have sought to ascertain how someone's beliefs about life can change the way reality is shaped. This happens when the view of self leads someone to become a social agent of change. Objects, like in optical illusions, can be perceived in differing ways, when a face becomes a glass or a rabbit becomes a duck. The reality stays the same, but the perception of the individual makes all the difference in the world. Back in 1928, sociologists (see the Thomas theorem in Merton, 1995) conceived what became known as the Thomas theorem, which states: '*If men define situations as real, they are real in their consequences*'. It is possible to put it this way: if someone believes that little green goblins are hiding in the woods and he changes his route to avoid them, then his idea of reality has affected his actions. This is more than a psychological cliché, especially when the social power of those mechanism is taken into consideration. Adam Smith's economic idea of the invisible hand embraced at large, changed the whole direction and shape of modern society. The power of ideas, someone's view about self, as immaterial as they are, tend to go beyond the naturalistic realm and still influence individuals, societies and economies.

Someone may ask at this point: what difference does it makes to take those aspects into consideration when entering the field of economics and sociology? For endless decades scholars have tried to come up with an

O. Palombaro, *Christianity and Capitalism in China*,
https://doi.org/10.1007/978-981-97-3549-5_1

answer on what could the determinants for economic success be. Some relied only on economic formulas, some pushed on the sociological side and pointed out the role of innovation, some just relied on the influence of personality, some listed culture or networking, others simply trusted that chance will do its work. Yet despite the fact that all those contributions may be instructive and important, they never seem to grasp the power of ideas in shaping economic success for individuals and then at large for the whole society. Are those factors listed in and of themselves able to pass the test of empiric validity? Success, as I will show in this study, is to be defined in relation with its opposite: failure and crisis. And that's where certain beliefs can come into the picture and really make the difference.

The concept of self-esteem to start with, has some clear significance for the achievement of economic success. Surprisingly, even to the social actors themselves, this success finds its origin in certain beliefs. Among Christian teachings for example, ideas such as 'feeling loved', self-worth, seeing oneself as 'uniquely wonderful' and 'intrinsically valuable' do have a powerful influence in shaping the daily life of an individual. Those self-worth teachings based on the idea of man as made in the 'image of God', lead the individual under this influence to perceive an infinite worth in himself, becoming 'glorious', 'dignified', full of 'beauty' (Adams, 1986). Despite these ideas may be debated within 'religious' entourages, I argue here that those ideas can in fact powerfully influence and shape the life of the individuals, including their work-life.

The purpose of this book is to seek to build a closer bridge between the disciplines of economics, sociology and religion. This will be done through an explorative analysis on the relationship between capitalism and Christianity, particularly Calvinism. This will be a study between economic behavior and a peculiar set of religious beliefs. Entrepreneurship will here be treated in its sociological significance for the relationship between an etherogeneous set of forms of religiosity. When I refer to religiosity, I refer to something far broader than religious affiliation or church attendance. Since this study intends to be more in-depth than a description of nominal religious adherence, one may question the legitimacy of such undertaking. Can a study that intends to reach a certain degree of objectivity appeal at all to a set of ideas of religious connotation? Such question challenged my study from the primary stages of this research to its conclusions. In fact, the scientific study of religion has a way to represent a challenge, due to the many different ramifications of the discipline of sociology from its positivistic beginnings, to biologism, Marxism, neoclassical economics, structural functionalism, world system theories, rational choice theory, etc. … I argue here that there are many practical reasons why the discipline of sociology needs to confirm its efforts in the topic of religion. Chief among these reasons is the central relevance of an individual set of religious beliefs for the formation of a specific economic behavior that indirectly is able to affect the presence or absence of economic success.

The modern and secular worldview of today has neglected the centrality of certain of these concepts, simply because they are connected to the idea of the supernatural. To introduce such dimension would force the discipline of sociology to rethink the very foundations of how somebody looks at human behavior. Many sociological approaches to this topic were undertaken with a load of assumptions, mainly on how somebody must view science. The task of any science and discipline is said to be to observe and analyze all phenomena objectively, without making 'religious assumptions'. But if reference to the supernatural is left out in the foundation of any theory, this will limit the possible conclusions. This bias should force scholars to rethink sociology, its foundational assumptions and the effects of such bias for the free progress of the discipline as a whole. Even if today the majority of scholars would tend to dissociate themselves from many of the positivist claims of the ancient sociology, people would still indirectly agree with its naturalistic and empiricist claims. Religion as a result of this is 'disqualified' from the possibility of having any sociological relevance. How are we to give account however for the myriads of social phenomena of extreme significance today for the foundations of Western civilization, which still have their roots in religion? Among the many examples I here focus on the economic, political, cultural and sociological benefits that the spread of the Protestant Reformation had for the progress of Western civilization. This case was notoriously defined by a main theoretical inspiration to this study: the Dutch politician, journalist, statesman and Neo-Calvinist theologian Abraham Kuyper in his *Lectures on Calvinism* (Kuyper, 1931). Reading through those lectures should lead anyone to recognize how certain ideas (mainly the belief in Calvinism), regardless of their spiritual origin, are able to transform the way people act as individuals in society, exercising an influence that extends to every area of life: religion, politics, science and art (Bratt, 1998, pp. 279–322).

But the present status of humanities and social sciences seems to be quite allergic to the inclusion of non-material terminology such as 'spirit'

(*Geist*) of capitalism. In this respect it is remarkable to ponder Vern Sheridian Poythress's description of the fallacies of modern approaches to societies:

> In the twentieth century sociological and anthropological study of human societies has assumed, as a foundation for the discipline that God can be left out of the account. Sociology and anthropology may of course study 'religion' as one aspect of society. But this study focuses on human practice of religion not on God himself. Why this exclusion of God? One response would be that only by such an exclusion could these disciplines hope to be scientific. But the aspiration to be scientific is itself loaded. To begin with it may be loaded with the assumption that somehow human beings can be treated exactly as if they were on the same level as animals or rocks or other creatures [...][1]

Beyond metaphysics and beyond my personal view as the author of this book, here lies a crucial perennial problem in the discipline of sociology, when seeking to establish how certain ideas unavoidably connected with the supernatural can or cannot be legitimately analyzed. The broad discipline of religious studies, and within it the field of sociology of religion, in the past century has, with few exceptions,[2] undermined the factual determinants of religious beliefs as an aspect worthy of intentional study. The positivist roots of this attitude have instead labeled beliefs as 'illusion', opposing the study of beliefs not from purely scientific motives but because those scholars themselves entertain other 'convictions' (paraphrased but still forms of beliefs), which they replaced with the previous (Bavinck, 2003, Vol. I, pp. 51–52). Later on Vern Sheridian Poythress continues to point out the intellectual fallacy of this prevailing interpretation:

> [...] But even more seriously the label scientific ignores the possibility that our modern conception of science, taken from the existing state of the natural sciences, has already been distorted by a systematic human flight from recognizing the presence of God in science. The aspiration to

[1] Poythress V. S., 2011, *Redeeming Sociology. A God-Centered Approach*, Wheaton, CROSSWAY, p. 47.

[2] For our case of Protestant migrants, see for example: Light, Ivan, and Edna Bonacich, 1991, *Immigrant Entrepreneurs. Koreans in Los Angeles. 1965–1982*, Los Angeles, University of California Press.

> be scientific may already have introduced biases. [...] But from a biblical point of view, the move to exclude God ignores the single most important fact about communication and the most weighty ontological fact about language. When we exclude God we distort the subject matter that we study, so we can anticipate a multitude of repercussions when it comes to the detailed analysis of the subject.[3]

By saying this, I am not suggesting an outright re-introduction of theology in humanistic sciences in the Medieval steps, but I am only pointing out a logical problematic biased conclusion coming out of this drastic separation. In the same way an approach of outright 'religious defense' of a certain topic is to be discouraged in the scientific study of religion, a complete rejection of religious explanations in the name of objectivity is also to be avoided. The point made by Poythress apart from its rhetoric is that, first through the humanistic view centered on man, then with the positivist shift that gave birth to sociology, man so far was not able to give a final fundamental solution to the problems of society by intentionally replacing God from any objective sociological discussion. It is possible to conclude that from both sides of the debate no determinism whatsoever is compatible with the scientific study of religion. As the reader will go through the pages of this work, it will be clearer why this methodological point is so crucial and what type of problematic repercussions there are when somebody ventures the analysis of such topic.

Having set this premise in the outset and coming to the heart of the matter, the area of research of the following book has to do mainly with the economic and sociological relevance of religious elements. To better comprehend what this means, we have to go back to the classics of sociology that understood well what is at stake here, what today is the big 'elephant in the room' for our contemporary society. The starting point of this study is the famous work of Max Weber on the *Protestant Ethic and the Spirit of Capitalism* (Weber, 1930 [1905]). Together with subsequent analysis, this seminal work set the foundations for the analysis of the role of religion for the economy and society. Weber identifies a specific set of religious beliefs proper of Protestantism as the spark able to ignite the fire of modern capitalism. The Protestant ethic has nothing to do with love

[3] Poythress V. S., 2011, *Redeeming Sociology. A God-Centered Approach*, Wheaton, CROSSWAY, p. 47.

of money or desire to be rich common to all ages and men. The function of those religious beliefs, sometimes even accidentally, was the one of shaping a specific conduct and a way of life that resulted in successful economic behaviors, crucial for the advent of modern capitalism. It must immediately be clarified that Weber was not equating the spirit of capitalism with capitalism itself, nor did he intend to say that Protestantism was the ultimate cause for capitalism.

This conduct and way of life is what later I will better describe as *ethos*,[4] a variety of individual systems of values different according to time and space. Among them I focus on a specific economic *ethos* that lies behind what even Adam Smith perceived as a turning point in the worldview of modern economy. At the heart of Weber's thesis was the centrality of the Calvinistic belief in predestination as an element that in his view was causing anxiety about eternal salvation in the believer and therefore leading people to find a solution through economic success as a sign of their personal election. As I was noting the popularity of such thesis in every manual and book of introduction to the matter, I was surprised of the absolute neglect of the original sources from the side of scholarly studies. Entering the study of the works of John Calvin as well as successive expressions of Calvinism, mainly in Puritanism, it is possible to see no presence of such anxiety about salvation but rather the very opposite: a state of complete and perpetual assurance as the chief countercurrent to the Roman Catholic view of salvation. After Max Weber's intriguing thesis, a quite intricate field of studies has developed around this matter (McKinnon, 2010; Barbalet, 2008; Schaefer, 2007; Cohen, 2002; Delacroix and Nielsen, 2001; Kalberg, 1996; Treiber, 1993; Giorgi and Marsh, 1990; Marshall, 1980; Collins, 1980; Razzel, 1977; Kim, 1977; Bouma, 1973; Mirels and Garrett, 1971; Bendix, 1967; Means, 1966). For the most part those critics were not able to deny the validity of Weber's thesis, also due to their sometimes superficial understanding of concepts and historical facts or their lack of substantial alternative explanations.

My book therefore has the intent to redirect those theoretical conclusions on the basic of documentary theological studies on the sources of such thought, pointing out their sociological significance. I argue that the belief in Perpetual Assurance of Salvation together with other

[4] From the Greek word: ἔθος, ους, τό '*custom*', '*habit*', '*character*' used to describe the guiding beliefs or ideals that characterize a community, nation or ideology.

beliefs already identified by Weber is the core of the revolutionary change introduced by Calvinism which was and is still able to impact indirectly economic success. Economic success, among other qualities, has been said by literature to be already connected with the principle of self-efficacy, mainly someone's belief in his ability to achieve a certain goal (Bandura, 2001; Zhao and Seibert, 2006; Laguna, 2013; Rauch and Frese, 2007). Giving the fact that some studies already have shown that certain religious beliefs leads to self-efficacy, the question remains on how to check the presence of such correlation between the belief in Perpetual Assurance of Salvation (which I will call throughout the book PAS) and self-efficacy. This can be done only by searching for any contemporary case of what Weber described when referring to the Protestant Reformation and the genesis of the Spirit of modern Capitalism.

I am not referring to a thing of the past, no longer part of a secularized society, but to a very active principle that can be traced only by considering the economic changes in today's world equilibrium. Some studies showed the possibility of the validity of Weber's thesis still in today's world, but within different contexts and conditions (Merton, 1957; Lenski, 1961; Willems, 1968; Crowley and Ballweg, 1971; Kim, 1977; Barker and Carman, 2000; Feldmann, 2007; Barro and McCleary, 2003, 2006). This evolution must be taken into account, if someone desires to explore any re-actualization of the thesis. It consists in the crucial passage of Protestantism from Western Europe in the sixteenth to seventeenth century to North America. In this respect, particularly notorious was the sociological study of another classic: Robert K. Merton's study of Puritanism (Cohen, 1990). Although Merton focuses more on the impact of Puritanism on modern science, this and many other studies point out to the survival of the Protestant ethic in American Puritanism, for the evolution and growth of such spirit of capitalism. Puritanism, Calvinistic in almost all its constituencies as a religious movement, was accompanied by a pervasive ethos that worked as a crucial sociological factor for the rise of modern science, technology as well as for the economic development of New England. Yet today such Puritan heritage seems almost lost, or substituted by a consumeristic society or a 'prosperity Gospel' that announces the death of such ethos, or perhaps its further evolution into another geographical and historical context.

I am strongly persuaded that with the current fall of the Western civilization, we are also experiencing the rise of the east. With the fall of the Protestant ethic in the West, I bring here to the attention of the reader the specific case in the far East, which saw recently the 'genesis' or rapid growth of capitalism. Now it is true that capitalism saw some setback in China in the short term, yet that was due to the draconian measures from the communist government and not from what I will describe in this book. For this reason, the case of contemporary China and how this country is changing the economic equilibrium of the relationship traditionally viewed between east and west, between the Western world and Asia is extremely relevant. Particularly after the economic reforms of the 1970s, China has witnessed the advent of capitalism, while remaining surprisingly on paper a communist nation. Paralleling the economic shift, a consistent Protestant religious revival is taking place in the rice fields as well as in the modern eastern cities of China such as Wenzhou. Among all other religions Protestant Christianity plays a leading role in such context of religious revival, at the same time as this economic boom. Some scholars already pointed out that Wenzhou, also called China's Jerusalem, because of its growing population of Christian Protestants, is also one of the richest cities of China, with a very high rate of entrepreneurship. Wenzhou has also witnessed the presence of a 'Boss-Christian phenomenon' where many Protestant believers are also strongly involved in business entrepreneurship (Hefner, 2010; Cao, 2008; Wenger, 2004; Bays, 2003; Fried, 1987; Masland, 1952). As I was approaching the literature on this interesting case (Yang, 2006), I've found that many ideas present on Weber's treatise about Western Europe during the times following the Protestant Reformation were surprisingly 'resurrected' among those contemporary Chinese businessmen of Wenzhou. At the same time of this birth of capitalism, China today is interestingly witnessing the presence of an ethos from a variety of influences that could include Protestantism as a crucial factor. This was then leading me to elaborate a research question that flows from the pages and years spent investigating the roots, characteristics and economic influence of such Chinese economic ethos, reflecting and overlapping the ideal-types described by Weber (*Yi Xiang, Boss-Christian phenomenon, House Churches*, etc.). This initial connection is what gave a starting point to my quest for the understanding of how this theoretical argument that affected the discipline of sociology from its early stages could find an evident interplay in today's real life.

As I was listening to stories from my Chinese friends, it became apparent that it was not something just confined to the borders of the Public Republic of China but it was transported in many country of the

Western world including my own. Italy like much of Western Europe has witnessed a massive Chinese migration that is contributing consistently to the advancement of economy. In Italy big cities like Milan or Prato as well as many other European cases like Paris, London and other Western countries experienced in the past decades a strong involvement in business among Chinese entrepreneurs migrating, mainly from the Chinese city of Wenzhou. Having found this theoretical connection between the system of beliefs described by Weber and the contemporary case of Protestant China's spirit of capitalism, I decided to apply the theoretical verification of Weber's model to this specific sociologically relevant case. With the contacts I had and the context I was living in the city of Milan, this was enough to begin an ethnographic investigation. If under the constraint of a heavy and long economic crisis in Italy, the Chinese community was doing exceedingly well in their business, above many other migrant communities, then there was a need to discover an explanation.

Because of the nature of the subject (religious beliefs and social behaviors in the workplace), I decided to proceed with a case-control comparative holistic qualitative design in the shape of an ethnography. The study presented here was done among Chinese entrepreneurs migrated from Wenzhou and involved as part of the Chinese Diaspora in different ways in small business activities in Milan, Italy. The research that I present here is the result of two primary tolls: first the submission of interviews and questionnaires to 85 Chinese entrepreneurs in Milan, Italy. The group was etherogeneous, composed by both Chinese Protestant and non-Protestant entrepreneurs to check the validity of my original theoretical framework. The intention was to identify the presence and role in business of the set of beliefs among the Protestant entrepreneurs and to compare those results with non-Christian entrepreneurs to see the difference through a series of potential alternative explanations to the religious ones for the presence of economic success. The study however was also open toward different interpretations not necessarily connected with the original theoretical framework as they arose from the field.

At the same time, I was contacting Chinese entrepreneurs and having interviews with them as well. I also started a more focused qualitative analysis of repeated participatory observation through the technique of job-shadowing. I was basically following weekly a group of six entrepreneurs in their daily work-life, observing their behavior at work in an informal setting and following after them in the less invasive way possible. The group was composed by two separate samples: one made of Chinese Protestant entrepreneurs and the other made of Chinese entrepreneurs with no relationship at all with the Protestant faith. This was done in order to guarantee a somehow reliable comparison between the two samples, and in order to observe the features of this economic ethos. As it will be further explained in the methodological section, access to the field was particularly challenging and not without problematics even in applying the findings to the initial theory of the study.

The main questions that the following study tries to answer can be expressed in the following ways: how can we define properly and understand the practical significance of concepts such as the 'spirit of capitalism' or economic 'ethos'? What are the specific features and historical origins of the relationship between religious belief and economic success? Why is the case of Wenzhou relevant for the understanding of this relationship and how can the theoretical model of the Protestant ethic relate to our contemporary societies? What significance religion has for contemporary economics and sociology? The objectives of this book can be outlined as follows:

- Identify and define the relationship between Protestantism and the spirit of capitalism in a contemporary setting.
- Identify and analyze the economic, psychological and sociological significance of the concepts of beliefs, ethos, values, ideas, rituals, etc.
- Establish their determinants for economic success among Chinese small businesses in the Diaspora.
- Analyze the historical origins of the theoretical debate in light of the more contemporary religious evolutions.
- Produce an exhaustive ethnography of Wenzhou's entrepreneurship model overseas in the specific migratory contextual environment of Milan, Italy.;
- Promote a case of entrepreneurial success among migratory communities in the contemporary world.
- Promote and develop the centrality of a scientific study of religion in sociology of religion and contemporary economic sociology.

Concerning the first point, which is the central objective of this study, the method and the practical steps in the road through which I attempt to achieve such objective and the expected foreshadowed results, can be listed as follows:

- Check the presence of the model as reformulated here on the basis of Weber's original argument among Chinese Wenzhouren Protestant entrepreneurs today.
  - (a) Survival of the Weber's thesis, and acknowledgment of its validity still in today's contemporary societies.
  - (b) Necessary adjustment of Weber's original claims in light of this fieldwork and other contemporary findings that go in a different direction.
  - (c) Possible inclusion, or even complete replacement, by other intervening factors.

In the following pages the reader will find the recollection and fruit of hard labor during the years I spent among Chinese entrepreneurs and small businesses in the area of Milan, Italy. The observations of the qualitative research here are preceded and accompanied by the theoretical framework that originated such investigation. My aim is that at the end of this sociological journey, the reader will at least have an idea of the reasons why successful entrepreneurship involves specific social and cultural aspects that move beyond mere business strategies. This study furthermore demonstrates the reality of a lesson: economic success in a situation of economic crisis like today is for the one creatively exploiting it, not for the one desperately fleeing it.

References

Adams J. E., 1986, *The Biblical View of Self-Esteem, Self-Love, Self-Image*, Oregon, Harvest House Publishers.

Bandura A., 'Social Cognitive Theory: An Agentic Perspective', in *Annual Review of Psychology*, Vol. 52 (2001), pp. 1–26.

Barbalet J. M., 2008, *Weber, Passion and Profits: The Protestant Ethic and the Spirit of Capitalism in Context*, Paris, Lavoisier.

Barker J. E., and Carman J. C., 'The Spirit of Capitalism? Religious Doctrine, Values and Economic Attitude Constructs', in *Political Behavior*, Vol. 22, No. 1, (2000), pp. 1–27.

Barro J. R., McCleary R. M., 'Religion and Economic Growth Across Countries', from American Sociological Review, Vol. 68, No. 5, (Oct. 2003), pp. 760–781.

Barro J. R., McCleary R. M., 'Religion and Economy', from *The Journal of Economic Perspectives*, Vol. 20, No. 2 (Spring 2006), pp. 49–72.

Bavinck H., 2003, *Reformed Dogmatics*, Vol. I–IV, Grand Rapids, Baker Academic.

Bays D. H., 'Chinese Protestant Christianity Today', from *The China Quarterly*, No. 174 (Jun. 2003), pp. 488–504.

Bendix R., 'The Protestant Ethic—Revisited', in *Comparative Studies in Society and History*, Vol. 9, No. 3 (Apr., 1967), pp. 266–273.

Bouma G. D., 'A Critical Review of Recent Protestant Ethic Research', in *Journal for the Scientific Study of Religion*, Vol. 12, No. 2 (Jun., 1973), pp. 141–155.

Bratt J. D. (Eds.), 1998, *Abraham Kuyper. A Centennial Reader*, Grand Rapids, Eerdmans.

Cao N., 'Boss Christians: the business of religion in the "Wenzhou Model" of Christian Revival', from *The China Journal*, Vol. 59, (Jan. 2008), pp. 63-87.

Cohen B. I. (Eds.), 1990, *Puritanism and The Rise of Modern Science. The Merton Thesis*, London, Rutgers University Press.

Cohen J., 2002, *Protestantism and Capitalism: The Mechanisms of Influence*, California, CJS.

Collins R., 'Weber's Last Theory of Capitalism: A Systematization', in *American Sociological Review*, Vol. 45 (1980), pp. 925–942.

Crowley J. W., Ballweg J. A., 1971, 'Religious Preference and Worldly Success', in *Sociological Analysis*, Vol. 32 (Summer), pp. 71–80.

Delacroix J., Nielsen F., 2001, 'The Beloved Myth: Protestantism and the Rise of Industrial Capitalism in Nineteenth-Century Europe', in *Social Forces*, Oxford.

Feldmann H., 'Protestantism, Labor Force Participation, and Employment Across Countries', from *American Journal of Economics and Sociology*, Vol. 66, No. 4 (Oct. 2007), pp. 795–816.

Fried H. M., 'Reflections on Christianity in China', from *American Ethnologist*, Vol. 14, No. 1 (Feb. 1987), pp. 94–106.

Giorgi L., Marsh C., 1990, 'The Protestant Work Ethic as a Cultural Phenomenon', from *European Journal of Social Psychology*, London.

Hefner R. W., 'Religious Resurgence in Contemporary Asia: South-East Asian Perspectives on Capitalism, the State and the New Piety', from *The Journal of Asian Studies*, Vol. 69, No. 4 (Nov. 2010), pp. 1031–1047.

Kalberg S., 'On the Neglect of Weber's Protestant Ethic as a Theoretical Treatise: Demarcating the Parameters of Postwar American Sociological Theory', in *Sociological Theory*, Vol. 14, No. 1 (Mar., 1996), pp. 49–70.

Kim H. C., 'The Relationship of Protestant Ethic Beliefs and Values to Achievement', in *Journal for the Scientific Study of Religion*, Vol. 16, No. 3 (Sep., 1977), pp. 255–262.

Kuyper A., 1931, *Lectures on Calvinism*, Grand Rapids, Eerdmans.

Laguna M., 'Self-efficacy, self-Esteem, and Entrepreneurship Among the Unemployed', in *Journal of Applied Social Psychology*, Vol. 43 (2013), pp. 253–262.

Lenski G. E., 1961, *The Religious Factor*, Garden City, New York, Doubleday.

Marshall G 'The Dark Side of the Weber Thesis: The Case of Scotland', in *The British Journal of Sociology*, Vol. 31, No. 3, Special Issue, Aspects of Weberian Scholarship, (Sep., 1980), pp. 419–440.

Masland J. W., 'Communism and Christianity in China', from *The Journal of Religion*, Vol. 32, No. 3, (Jul. 1952), pp. 198–206.

McKinnon A. M., 'Elective Affinities of the Protestant Ethic: Weber and the Chemistry of Capitalism', in *Sociological Theory*, Vol. 28, No. 1 (March 2010), pp. 108–126.

Means R. L., 1966, 'Protestantism and American Sociology: Problems of Analysis', in *Sociological Analysis*, Vol. 27 (Fall), pp. 128–137.

Merton R. K., 'The Thomas Theorem and The Matthew Effect', in *Social Forces*, Vol. 74, No. 2 (Dec., 1995), pp. 379-424.

Merton R. K., 1957, *Social Theory and Social Structure* (Revised ed.), New York, Free Press.

Mirels H. L., Garrett J. B., 1971, 'The Protestant ethic as a personality variable', from *Journal of Consulting and Clinical PSYCOLOGY*, London.

Rauch A., Frese M., 'Let's Put the Person Back into Entrepreneurship Research: A Meta-Analysis on the Relationship Between Business Owners' Personality Traits, Business Creation, and Success', in *European Journal of Work and Organizational Psychology* (Nov., 2007).

Razzel P., 'The Protestant Ethic and the Spirit of Capitalism: A Natural Scientific Critique', in *The British Journal of Sociology*, Vol. 28, No. 1 (Mar., 1977), pp. 17–37.

Schaefer R., 'Infallibility and Intentionality: Franz Brentano's Diagnosis of German Catholicism', from *Journal of the History of Ideas*, University of Pennsylvania Press Vol. 68, No. 3 (Jul., 2007), pp. 477–499.

Treiber H., (eds.), 1993, *Per leggere Max Weber*, Padova, CEDAM.

Weber, 1930, *The Protestant Ethic and the Spirit of Capitalism*, Unwin Hyman, London [ed. orig. 1905, *Die protestantische Ethik und der Geist des Kapitalismus*].

Wenger J. E., 'Official vs. Underground Protestant Churches in China. Challenges for Reconciliation and Social Influence', from *Review of Religious Research*, Vol. 46, No. 2 (Dec., 2004), pp. 169–182.

Willems E., 1968, 'Culture Change and the Rise of Protestantism in Brazil and Chile', in *The Protestant Ethic and Modernization: A Comparative View*, Basic Books, pp. 184–200.

Yang F., 'The Red, Black, and Gray Markets of Religion in China', from *The Sociological Quarterly*, Vol. 47, No. 1 (Winter, 2006), pp. 93–122.

Zhao H., Seibert S. E., 'The Big Five Personality Dimensions and Entrepreneurial Status: A Meta-Analytical Review', in *Journal of Applied Psychology*, Vol. 91, No. 2 (2006), 259–271.

CHAPTER 2

Sociology and Capitalism

> You were designed for accomplishment, engineered for success and endowed with the seeds of greatness.
>
> —Zig Ziglar

2.1 Entrepreneurship from a Sociological Standpoint

2.1.1 Classic Perspectives

Dealing with capitalism today requires us to begin with entrepreneurship. When faced with the question on how to become a successful entrepreneur, no one is able to avoid the consideration of a large amount of principles that are in their nature, still inherently social. Entrepreneurship can be defined as the *creation of new organizations, which occurs as a context-dependent social and economic process* (Thornton, 1999, p. 20). Entrepreneurs provide the capitalist economy with new ideas, products and ways of doing things (Iyigun and Owen, 1998). But apart from their features and characteristics, what are the determinants of their eventual economic success? Is it dependent on family background? Environment? Cognitive skills? Level of education? Ethnicity? Personality? I define here economic success on a personal level (not company or national level) in the sense of an accomplishment of an aim or purpose from the side of

O. Palombaro, *Christianity and Capitalism in China*,
https://doi.org/10.1007/978-981-97-3549-5_2

the entrepreneur related with the attainment of a profit (Halsey, 1982). The Oxford dictionary simply defines it as the accomplishment of an aim or purpose, in particular as the attainment by the individual of fame, wealth or social status (Soanes and Stevenson, 2010). In this sense from the side of successful entrepreneurship in the twenty-first century, success means the achievement of the results wanted or hoped for, mainly the making of profit. Therefore, the measurement of economic success is not just dependent upon GDP, overall profit or economic growth of whole enterprises as traditionally considered in capitalism. It is the case of relatively small businesses that today has come into the scene as a key player in the quest for economic success in the twenty-first century. Economic success is always related with the measurement of several indicators such as number of employees, profit, turnover, working capital, capacity utilization, years of operation, etc. The definition of economic success can also vary depending on the context of reference and the surrounding standard of economic life. Among the many aspects able to bring an entrepreneur to achieve economic success, it is my intention to emphasize here the social aspects. By doing so I am not neglecting the centrality of other aspects for the achievement of economic success in entrepreneurship, starting with economics, reaching to any other aspect such as technological, environmental and more. This will open the door in the next chapters to evaluations concerning the role of business ethics in economic success. I am not necessarily referring to success on a mere social level, a success which substitutes the quest for profit with the benefits to the community (like NGOs), nor am I denying the possibility of economic influence coming from ethics different than those that will be considered in the next chapters. To better understand this, it is crucial to reflect first on the main suggestions that have been proposed in the field of sociology about entrepreneurship, and in particular its connection with economic success.

The field of studies on entrepreneurship in sociology has focused mainly on two dimensions: willingness to take risk and ability to promote innovation. Risk-taking, the willingness to accept the risk and uncertainty involved in entrepreneurship has been a defining aspect of the study of entrepreneurship since the first reflections on this matter by Adam Smith and John Stuart Mill. Capitalism from its beginning involves economic activities where profit is under constant threats, especially because of competition. Therefore this creates a dynamic of constant anxiety. Apart from some circumstantial reflections by Karl Marx on the historical pattern that led merchants to transform into entrepreneurs through the advent of the industrial capitalism, no classical sociologist has analyzed deeply entrepreneurship in cultural and social terms as Max Weber did.

Later on, with Joseph Schumpeter the second element of innovativeness was introduced as defining the dynamic quality of successful entrepreneurship. Schumpeter is considered as the theorist of entrepreneurship *par excellence*. Schumpeter defines innovation as a *combination of factors of production that when combined with credit, breaks into the static equilibrium of the circular flow of economic life and raises it to a new level* (Schumpeter, 2010 [ed. orig. 1947]). The entrepreneur has in his DNA a revolutionary character, a specific function of innovating through an ability to change, to combine elements and to create new production functions. The role of the entrepreneur is to reform or revolutionize the routine of production through the exploitation of an invention or in a broader sense through the introduction of a novel technical possibility (Breton, 1984).

According to Schumpeter the entrepreneur is a deviant that develops non-rational attitudes in a rational environment and through his anticonformism, he brings innovation into the picture (Stark, 2011). Another interesting contribution from Schumpeter was the idea that the entrepreneur holds a specific type of personality, specific traits: he has will to power (*wille zur macht*), desire for action in order to build, to create, to gain, as well as flair, intuition, creativity, boldness in leadership, strong will, he breaks social resistance in his own sphere of action, etc. This entrepreneurial type must face strong and multiple social, political and psychological resistances, and with all those different elements combined he can be crowned with economic success (Breton, 1984).

2.1.2 Some Factors

Applying the reflections of Schumpeter, several studies on social psychology have focused on the psychological traits of the entrepreneurial personalities, their background characteristics or cognitive schemas (Åstebro et al., 2014; AA. VV., 1990). Those studies of the supply-side school focused on the individual characteristics of entrepreneurs, their potential for agency and change as well as the social context that affects their behavior (Thornton, 1999). There is a specific type of personality and conduct that according to this view surprisingly differs from the simple, rational conduct of the economic man. Entrepreneurship is permeated with an ideological element of passionate individualism, independence, laissez-faire competition and even a moral evaluation of someone's work. According to these scholars, special types of individuals create entrepreneurship. These are individuals with high need for achievement, clear locus of control, strong risk-taking and risk-seeking propensity, problem-solving, innovativeness, evident leadership style, socialization experience as well as strong values. An entrepreneur in his quest to venture new activities must display tolerance of failure, flexible planning in order to manage uncertainty and ability to hold a good reaction to changes (Thornton, 1999). Entrepreneurs enter and persist for long periods of time in their business despite low returns. First of all, the entrepreneur values the non-pecuniary benefits of being self-employed, even if this sometimes means lower earnings. Because of this motivation, entrepreneurs work longer hours than the average employee, in autonomy and independence, with no pressure of being interfered by other parties, or having to rely on others. The entrepreneur enjoys having control over his life and over the decision-making process. He tends to have also a sense of purpose for his life.

Added to this, the entrepreneur achieves economic success because he is constantly looking for new challenges. He is ready to manage challenges when they involve his business. This once again is linked to the entrepreneur's affection for risk, being risk-tolerant, getting utility out of risk itself. The element of risk and relative return is essential for successful entrepreneurship because in its nature entrepreneurship is risky, characterized by activities that probably can result in failure. The pay-off of skills and investments, as high and consistent as they can be, remains always uncertain and possibly can lead to zero returns (Iyigun and Owen, 1998). For these reasons, skills, human capital, economic resources are really not the focus. Even the most brilliant entrepreneur, if with all those prerequisites he misses this element of risk-taking and risk-management, the economic success of his business remains unreachable.

What is therefore the motivation and the originating source that enables somebody to become a risk-taker? The management of risk is strictly correlated with an attitude of overconfidence and endemic optimism (Åstebro et al., 2014). Concerning overconfidence, it is important to consider the tripartite difference between: (i) *over-estimation* of one's ability or performance, (ii) *over-placement*, too high assessment of one's skill relative to other competitors and (iii) *over-precision*, the excessive certainty regarding the accuracy of one's belief (Åstebro et al., 2014, p. 58). It is precisely this last element that, as I will point out in the next chapters, is a crucial force for the enhancement of economic success. Optimism on the other hand in entrepreneurship tends to increase the probability of favorable events. When this optimism is led to the extreme by forces that I will later on describe, the entrepreneur is more likely to make risky and even imprudent financial choices. Those are the features of the persisting vitality of entrepreneurship without which entrepreneurship loses the propensity toward economic success. Following this interpretation other studies pursued a more situational approach to entrepreneurship, focusing on what an individual actually does as an entrepreneur. An entrepreneur has the unique ability to recognize new opportunities and to take advantage of them. However, many studies on the individual traits of entrepreneurs fail to provide information on the environment and surrounding context within which the entrepreneur interprets and makes sense of his actions (Thornton, 1999). What is the source that causes the presence of his personality traits? Is it just dependent on the single individual or are there certain contextual, social or cultural inputs able to generate such propensity and to favor economic success?

In order to respond to this question, emphasis must be given on a more socio-cultural level to other dimensions interesting when examining entrepreneurship: ethnic groups, social classes, economic sectors and cultural logics. Other sociological studies on entrepreneurship have been focusing therefore, like the following study, on the formation of entrepreneurship among specific social groups, classes or ethnicities. Contrary to a traditional approach to capitalism where family-based economy was supposed to leave room to industrial and managerial forms of business, today small business is growing and is a field of studies largely undeveloped. Markets are developing in countries and continents previously thought to have non-entrepreneurial cultures, as in the case of Asia. According to those scholars the reason why someone gets involved with entrepreneurship is also due to their social group of origin.

The fact of being a minority group in a certain society, mainly a group that is deviant from the cultural norms of the larger society, that tends to suffer from a withdrawal of status, pushes the individuals of those social groups to get involved in entrepreneurship. Usually according to those theories, whether in the case of ethnic or religious minorities, the purposes and values of those minorities are not respected by groups in the society where they live as migrants. Those groups on the other hand, usually respect and esteem the values of the society around them. The desire to be accepted leads those people to seek the approval of the community through achievement of economic success in their business. For this reason, many of those minorities tend to foster individualism and the development of a creative self-reliant personality. They tend to create bounded solidarity with their migrant customers, workers and even investors, because they are treated as foreigners.

Scholars have noticed how migrants within metropolitan areas tend to locate in ethnic 'enclaves' as they were evaluating the effect of living inside ethnic enclaves for the labor market (Edin et al., 2003). Once arrived in a big city, those migrants tend to be spatially concentrated in a state of semi-segregation. There are economic consequences of living inside those enclaves. In the case of some entrepreneurs of those enclaves, this leads them toward high or low benefits. This is depending also on their position in the enclaves: being rich or poor, being part of a high- or low-quality enclave. For example, entrepreneurs with high earning and self-employed individuals have larger benefits through the identification with the enclaves (Edin et al., 2003). Other studies however (McAllister, 1995) go in the opposite direction, pointing out how the condition of being a migrant entrepreneur has negative effects on economic success. Migrants perform far worse economically than individuals born in the country, because of economic disadvantages caused by the act of migrating itself. This is true especially in the case of migrants from a drastically different cultural and linguistic context. Such disadvantage may often result in persisting and lifelong inferiority (McAllister, 1995). Immigrants in fact very often are discriminated within the labor market because of their ethnicity, resulting in the long term to a labor market segmentation and other structural major disadvantages. Moreover, those disadvantages deriving from the fact of being migrant (difficulty on the language, problems in the recognition of academic titles, low access to information…) must be distinguished from the disadvantages deriving from discrimination itself (statistical vs. ethnic discrimination).

Another branch of studies in line with this perspective considers how economic environments are embedded in specific social and structural relationships. This approach underlines in particular the centrality of family as a social network source in entrepreneurship. The connection between work and family with economic success among small business owners has been interestingly investigated by some. In this picture, gender and the family background results in having a decisive impact for the owner's business success. Family characteristics have different effects on the earnings and business revenues and even in work-related attitudes such as commitment, which ultimately affects economic success. Commitment to one's business, willingness to work long hours, seeing business as an important part of life are all crucial elements to achieve success (Loscocco and Leicht, 1993). The greater is the economic need in the family, the greater the entrepreneur tends to work harder, especially in the case of men. This study shows that the difference in how hard the entrepreneur wants to push sales growth depends also on the presence of children, the fact to be a man (breadwinner) and the presence of certain family responsibilities. More and more small businesses are funded informally through personal savings, family or network of friends, as primary sources for the establishment of new ventures (Thornton, 1999).

Some studies on the growth of entrepreneurship firms in China considered, for example, how family members or close friends were of great importance, especially to new entrepreneurs (Zhao and Aram, 1995). Family background in fact is a significant predisposing factor to entrepreneurship. Individuals are more likely to become entrepreneurs if somebody in their family has previously been an entrepreneur (Åstebro et al., 2014). In this case it is also of particular interest to consider the succession of businesses among those families of entrepreneurs in second, third and fourth generations of entrepreneurship. The extended family however not only can have positive effects on entrepreneurship, but it is often a burden, because of the financial needs that come with the extended family.

Social networks, not to be confounded with professional networks (interfirm cooperation or business linkage), do hold a role in entrepreneurship. Most of the existing literature on this matter tried to point out the role of networking in achieving economic success. Scholars have shown how Asian cultures have a better standing for entering and thriving in business due to group cohesion, mobility and level of education (Kristiansen, 2004, p. 1149). High-quality social networks and not any kind of networks, are more able to provide the needed motivation, ideas, information, capital and trust. These are the necessary resources in terms of social capital for business start-up, growth and success. Such resources are important especially in the first phase of business start-up where high risk is involved. During this period, the entrepreneur is able to reduce the transaction costs and risks as well as receiving useful information for new learning skills.

The subculture within those networks is also important for the development of value systems, motivation, taking initiative, generating ideas for business expansion and trust (Kristiansen, 2004). The lack of trust in fact, clearly hinders cooperation between entrepreneurs and increases transaction costs. Other scholars challenged this one-sided view which sees social networks as an essential factor for economic success in and of themselves (Egbert, 2009). More often than not, social networks have a negative or restrictive effect on success. Social networks according to this opposite perspective may be considered as institutions, which are not cost-free. Sometimes they prove to be a constraint to entrepreneurial success. This view still agrees that social networks at particular stages of the development process can provide essential resources in the form of communities, circle of friends or co-ethnicity. However, in and of themselves social networks can in the long term hinder market development and also constitute a constraint to success, through social obligations or boundaries of mutual responsibilities overseeding profit calculations.

Few times a network can cause serious problems to the economic growth or can even lead to a business failure, becoming a clear impediment to the economic success (Egbert, 2009). Because of their exclusive nature, networks tend to be self-enforcing, preventing market structures from establishing themselves. This has negative effects on the economy as a whole that should not be ignored. Sometimes even what may look like a positive effect from the side of the entrepreneur, can act as corruption, since access to the network is a privilege only for members.

2.2 The Role of Ethics

2.2.1 Contemporary Amnesia Toward Ethics

Since all those sociological and economic variables can only partially count for the presence of economic success, where does the ultimate motivational source of success lies? Few studies have explored what is the place of values, in the sense of personal virtues, subjective principles and ideals, in the achievement of successful entrepreneurship. Those interested in the economic behavior often have no particular interest in this. Yet economic behavior is an analytic dimension of virtually all social behavior, including values. Values, ethics, are able to create meaning, order and they even influence and channel economic behavior along certain tracks. Values continue to provide internalized sets of moral assumptions about human behavior that add a sense of rationality and order to the economic relations, which remain inherently uncertain left to themselves.

The market system, in other words, is embedded within a cultural sphere of which values are a significant part. Few scholars have pointed out the role of business ethics and the social approval of economic activities (AA. VV., 1990). What really interests me here is the need to point out that entrepreneurship is in and of itself deeply embedded in certain societies and cultures. Certain tools of rationalization, which are so crucial in entrepreneurship, don't simply generate out of business models; they are strictly embedded in specific traditions, cultural, and, even religious, traits. These traits continue to shape the economic growth and social modernization of capitalism. Therefore, the cultural norms and the related role of expectations and social sanctions can either favor or hinder the innovation I've described above.

Economic categories must be subjected to cultural constructions and not exclusively to utilities. Even elements such as beliefs or trust, as well as marginality status or motivation for achievement have all a central role. The inculcation of an achievement, a standard of excellence and self-reliance, all go far beyond the mere economic activity or other external structural influences. As crucial as they may be, these aspects are not able to exhaust all the possible options. In particular, values in entrepreneurship play a therapeutic role, helping the individual to feel better about himself, his work and his wealth. Values provide several important contributions, especially in allowing economic success. Values among other things are able to provide:

- legitimation for the ways in which economic resources are distributed;
- maintenance of norms on which ordinary economic relations constantly depend;
- encode and preserve knowledge useful for technical adaptation to a specific environment;
- explanations and comfort in face of economic activities that fall short or produce unexpected consequences.

In the coming chapters I will show how all those principles find detailed and specific examples. The burden of this present study therefore is to follow the following theoretical argument: culture, as well as values, and even religion, should not be seen as separate entities with a reality of their own. What is sociologically relevant for me is to observe the interaction of those dimensions in a specific social context and how they lead to distinctive ambitions and behaviors. Sadly economic sociology, perhaps under suspicion, with few exceptions (Light et al., 1991), has paid very little attention to the relationship between economic life and values, or religious beliefs. Some have argued that values and religious beliefs in a secularized context find functional alternatives and therefore can exert only a passive and reactive role in the economic life.

According to this view, values and religion are only epi-phenomenal to the economic activity. The latter is said to operate according to its own laws, rather than being significantly affected by anything like personal values or even a religious beliefs. Market behaviors in economics traditionally have been, in the words of John Stuart Mill, operating according to their own laws and have been considered therefore as a domain separate from ethical considerations. Yet the fundamental question remains: how the economic action is constructed and what interaction there is among the different spheres of actions? This process inevitably involves cultural, psychological as well as ethical dimensions. It is crucial therefore once again to reintegrate the ethical concerns into the economic realm.

2.2.2 *Some Examples*

Just to give an example of the role that religious networks can still have on business, some scholars found that among various social groups, the ethnic-religious communities of migrants in a new area play a leading role in business success. Closely knit networks based on religious sectarianism and ethnicity offer financial support to their members fostering a form of business where the entire community contributes directly to entrepreneurial success. In those cases alone, rather than networks in general, a form of strict social control limits deviant behavior in private as well as in intra-community business affairs. Also, the identification with those ethnic-religious communities provides an interest-free loan scheme that allows taking credit for business investments (Egbert, 2009).

Ethical systems are proven to provide still today moral restraints to economic affairs and are central to the understanding of the socio-economic action of the individual. It is important therefore to bring more directly in the picture social, institutional as well as ethical and normative questions in order to advance the study of the economic behavior in our present society. I am not advocating a perfect harmony in such matter. In fact, many times, general religious beliefs can come into conflict with economic action. However, as Durkheim pointed out, there are social sources and functions of religion even toward economic action that should never be considered in isolation from a consideration of ends. Sometimes those tensions unexpectedly resolve in greater advancements (Durkheim, 2005 [ed. orig 1912]). In the next section I will introduce one of the most famous examples in sociology where that connection has been discovered, and it will be possible to identify what can be precisely the role of beliefs from a sociology perspective.

References

AA. VV., 1990, *Economy and Society: Overviews in Economic Sociology*, London, Sage Publications.

Åstebro T., Herz H., Nanda R., Weber R., 'Seeking the Roots of Entrepreneurship: Insights from Behavioral Economics', in *The Journal of Economic Perspectives*, Vol. 28, No. 3 (Summer, 2014), pp. 49–69.

Breton Y., 'La théorie schumpétérienne de l'entrepreneur ou le problème de la connaissance économique', in *Revue économique*, Vol. 35, No. 2 (Mar., 1984), pp. 247–266.

Durkheim E., 2005, *Le forme elementari della vita religiosa*, Meltemi, Roma [Ed. orig 1912].

Edin P. A., Fredriksson P., Åslund O., 'Ethnic Enclaves and the Economic Success of Immigrants: Evidence from a Natural Experiment', in *The Quarterly Journal of Economics*, Vol. 118, No. 1 (Feb., 2003), pp. 329–357.

Egbert H., 'Business Success Through Social Networks? A Comment on Social Networks and Business Success', in *The American Journal of Economics and Sociology*, Vol. 68, No. 3 (Jul., 2009), pp. 665–678.

Halsey A. H., 'Who Gets Ahead? Determinants of Economic Success in America', in *American Journal of Sociology*, Vol. 87, No. 4 (Jan., 1982), pp. 965–967.

Iyigun M. F., Owen A. L., 'Risk, Entrepreneurship, and Human-Capital Accumulation', in *The American Economic Review*, Vol. 88, No. 2, Papers and Proceedings of the Hundred and Tenth Annual Meeting of the American Economic Association (May, 1998), pp. 454–457.

Kristiansen S., 'Social Networks and Business Success: The Role of Subcultures in an African Context', in *The American Journal of Economics and Sociology*, Vol. 63, No. 5 (Nov., 2004), pp. 1149–1171.

Light, Ivan, and Edna Bonacich, 1991, *Immigrant Entrepreneurs. Koreans in Los Angeles. 1965–1982*, Los Angeles, University of California Press.

McAllister I., 'Occupational Mobility among Immigrants: The Impact of Migration on Economic Success in Australia', in *The International Migration Review*, Vol. 29, No. 2 (Summer, 1995), pp. 441–468.

Schumpeter J. A., 2010, *Capitalism, Socialism and Democracy*, Kessinger LCL [ed. orig. 1947].

Soanes C., Stevenson A., 2010, *Oxford Dictionary of English*. Oxford University Press.

Stark D., 2011, *The Sense of Dissonance: Accounts of Worth in Economic Life*, Princeton University Press.

Thornton P. H., 'The Sociology of Entrepreneurship', in *Annual Review of Sociology*, Vol. 25 (1999), pp. 19–46

Zhao L., Aram J. D., 'Networking and Growth of Young Technology-Intensive Ventures in China', in *Journal of Business Venturing*, Vol. 10, No. 5 (1995), pp. 349–370.

CHAPTER 3

Protestantism and Capitalism

> Lastly, there was another most pestilential error, which not only occupied the minds of men, but was regarded as one of the principal articles of faith, of which it was impious to doubt: that is, that believers ought to be perpetually in suspense and uncertainty as to their interest in the divine favor. By this suggestion of the devil, the power of faith was completely extinguished, the benefits of Christ's purchase destroyed, and the salvation of men overthrown.
>
> —John Calvin

3.1 The Case for a Protestant Ethic

3.1.1 Weber Under Scrutiny

Several efforts have been made in the past to try to define the relationship between economy and religion. My major starting point for the discipline of sociology remains the classic work by Max Weber on *the Protestant Ethic and the Spirit of Capitalism* (Weber, 1930 [1905]). The study starts with the question on why in Western civilization alone, cultural phenomena attained universal significance and value (Weber, 1930 [1905], see author's introduction, n. xxviii). The study then provides statistical evidence of the impact of the Protestant religious affiliation on social stratification. It must be remembered that despite his

O. Palombaro, *Christianity and Capitalism in China*,
https://doi.org/10.1007/978-981-97-3549-5_3

notoriety, Weber was not the first author who made a reflection on such matter (Laveleye [ed. orig. 1889]; Bendix, 1967).

What makes Weber so unique is that through a historical-scientific method, he explained how a non-economic element such as a specific religious belief was able to influence the birth of what he calls the spirit (*Geist*) of modern capitalism. This was done in clear opposition with the dominant interpretations of the time, where positivism, Marxism, neoclassical economy theory, structural functionalism and biologism reigned supreme. The 'spirit of capitalism' is defined by Weber not as mere economic accumulation, but as an economic *ethos* that appeared at the birth-stage of modern capitalism, both in Western Europe and New England (Weber, 1976 [ed. orig. 1905], p. 132). The concept of 'spirit of capitalism' can be understood only in light of the complex of elements associated in modern history. In this sense, this spirit can be conceived into a conceptual whole only from the standpoint of its cultural significance, as Weber states:

> [...] The peculiarity of this philosophy of avarice appears to be the ideal of the honest man of recognized credit, and above all the idea of a duty of the individual toward the increase of his capital, which is assumed as an end in itself. Truly what is here preached is not simply a means of making one's way in the world, but a peculiar ethic. The infraction of its rules is treated not as foolishness but as forgetfulness of duty. That is the essence of the matter. It is not mere business astuteness, that sort of thing is common enough, it is an ethos. This is the quality which interests us [...]. (Weber, 1930 [ed. orig. 1905], pp. 16–17)

The spirit of capitalism therefore can be defined as an individual's system of values (*ethos*) able to generate an attitude toward life which sees profit as an end to itself, the incessant pursuit of economic gain as an ultimate end to human existence. Such attitude, not to be confused with the mere utilitarian attitude common to all men, is based on a source of spiritual satisfaction able to provide real purpose in all that someone says and does, including his economic action. This spirit of capitalism is the opposite of traditionalism and was historically present primarily in Northwestern European and North American capitalism at the time of Weber. He argued that widespread forms of what he defines as 'ascetic' Protestantism inadvertently legitimated the rise of acquisitive capitalism (AA. VV., 1990). The spirit of capitalism was directly generated by several beliefs proper of the Protestant ethic, and developed later even in contexts that were not necessarily religious. Such religious beliefs can become an explanatory factor because according to Weber's sociology of religion, even economic actions, must be understood from the idea of the individual and his system of values (*ethos*).

In order to understand the cultural causes, not just technical or economic, for the advent of modern capitalism it is extremely important to identify the 'ethic of conviction', of which the Protestant beliefs are a direct manifestation. Among the many options, the actor decides which kind of actions to display: rational with respect to the purpose, affective or rational with respect to the value. The intriguing element for Weber was that Protestantism and capitalism came to be compatible despite their conflicting ends. Protestant beliefs are able to push the individual to act according to his conscience and sometimes even with unexpected or unwanted outcomes from the perspective of the doers (Weber, 2003 [1923]).

Weber tries to identify the components, not necessarily economic in nature, that led to the formation of what he calls the 'spirit of capitalism', the ethical premise to the advent of modern capitalism (Weber, 1993 [1920]). This doesn't mean that the ethical premise plays a deterministic role for the advent of modern capitalism. In his lessons on economic history Weber makes an important distinction between 'speculative capitalism', which was present long before modernity, and 'rational capitalism', a product proper only to the modern era. Weber does not neglect the role that technical conditions, trade, rational organization of work, the advent of the modern state, a mercantile political economy, played in the formation of 'rational capitalism'. On the other hand, he does not reduce to those elements the advent of modern capitalism. Through his study of Sociology of Religion Weber tries to explore the cultural conditions, mainly the core ethic impulse, that contributed to the advent of 'rational capitalism' (Weber, 2003 [1923]).

Weber pointed out the presence of a correlation, not a causal relationship, between several religious beliefs peculiar to Protestantism, that here I will call *preconditions*, and the genesis of a specific economic ethos, the spirit of capitalism. The first precondition that he identifies is the *Beruf*, a calling from God for someone's life, precisely in the field of worldly work. This concept, fully elaborated in the Protestant faith, was very crucial in the attribution of purpose and meaning for any type of work. In the following centuries, even in contexts with no relation at all with the Protestant faith, such idea was the background for the development of professions. This concept of *Beruf* is the starting point in Weber's analysis. This was the breaking point with the traditional society of the time that Martin Luther, as a seminal figure of the Protestant Reformation, promoted in his theology. This concept can be extrapolated from Luther's writings and sermons had an antecedent already in the Catholic concept of *vocatio*. But in this last case the calling in terms of a *vocatio* was considered appropriate and active only within the realm of the religious structure (mainly the *vocatio* to priesthood or monasticism), inside the framework of the church hierarchy. Luther on the other hand, believing in an 'universal priesthood' of all believers, applied this concept to any aspect of life and to the specific call that each Christian must discover, discern and pursue, whether to become a pastor as well as any specific secular job. This view not only addresses the 'soul arena' of someone's life but also sees work in and of itself as a form of service to God. Such revolutionary use of the term had a profound impact in all future aspects of society, especially how the common people viewed and performed their work.

Another precondition strictly related to the first one is the *Inner-worldly asceticism* (*Inner-weltliche Askese*). To be 'ascetic' is defined by Weber as an attitude characterized by a methodical procedure to achieve religious salvation. Such view was applied in Catholicism mainly to the world-rejecting form of monkish asceticism (*Weltablehnende Askese*). The issue can be better understood considering Weber's distinction between asceticism and mysticism. Mysticism differs from asceticism in the sense of being the content of salvation. This is not an active quality of the conduct when having executed the divine will, but a subjective condition in a state of illumination. In this sense it would be more appropriate to talk about a Protestant 'inner-worldly active mysticism' as opposed to the Catholic 'world-rejecting asceticism'. According to this Protestant belief, men can live pleasing God, not through monkish asceticism as in the Catholic tradition, but through the fulfillment of worldly duties (Weber, 2003 [1923], p. 176). This view pushed people to understand their work in strict connection with their spiritual life as something with intrinsic value, as a 'service to Christ'. The very work someone does becomes then part of 'service' and 'ministry'.

Such view promoted by the Protestant Reformers was going openly against the hierarchical importance of social roles so common during the Middle Ages and inherited by Aristotelic philosophy. According to this ancient perspective, those that were engaged in contemplative life were to be considered at the top of all the social classes. Luther and all the Protestant Reformers, after their delusion and secession with the traditional order, rejected plainly this idea that monastic life ought to be considered as the highest level of 'Christian service'. On the contrary work in all of its forms was to be considered as a 'service to Christ' in the world. Work had an eternal significance tied to it in the same way, and level, of a preacher ministering in the church. Protestantism in this way restrained people from behaving in an irrational or unsystematic manner, disciplining themselves in order to consider carefully the relationships among their various social activities (AA. VV., 1990). Among the features of such restraint generated by this inner-worldly asceticism in the workplace, the crucial restriction from frivolous expenditure of money or from too much dependence on one's kin, consuming alcohol, disordered conduct, taking constant breaks from work or walking off a job, all resulted in a saving mentality.

Before the advent of the Protestant Reformation, a principle of this kind was almost unconceivable. The Greek-Roman culture, promoted often a direct exaltation of *otium*, accompanied with the value of a daily life devoted to the intellectual and philosophical quest. Manual work was considered a matter for the slaves or the illiterate, something to be ashamed of and to be relegated among the lowest classes of society. With the advent of Christianity, the widespread diffusion of monasticism, the common mindset of people for centuries was to think that the only way to fully please God, to really live up to the spiritual demands, was to separate oneself from the world (pleasure, marriage, riches, secular offices, work, etc.) and live one's lives in isolated places to practice abstinence, self-denial and quiet meditation. Such tendency was compensated by a period of transition during which the monks gradually began to be involved in the world (like the *ora et labora* introduced by Benedict), but such system was always confined in the realm and boundaries of the church. Even if the majority of the people did not pursue such drastic choices, everyone else still embraced the idea behind them and work or worldly duties were perceived more as an obstacle to their spiritual life, looming affairs which alienated them from the more important task of the contemplative pursuit of God.

When many of the Reformers that were part of such system left the priesthood or the monastery, they almost immediately promoted the counter-idea that the participation within the institutions of the world and the use of personal qualifications through work became the primary arena for the quest to please God. In contrast with the Catholic mystics that supported the view that the believer needed to be passive in order to receive God, the Protestant believer needed to be active in serving God and his work and professional life became the primary divine instrument to make sure he was pleasing God. This cultural transformation obviously did not happen overnight, but nevertheless it traces back its roots at the origin of Protestantism and later it was developed in many contexts outside Protestantism.

The third precondition, formalized by Weber in another of his successive writings (Weber, 1977 [ed. orig. 1906]) is the *role of sects*. Such precondition is not only successive in terms of when it was formulated by Weber, but also in terms of its timeframe, that must here be considered (see the shorter arrow in Table 3.1). We refer here to a period much later than Luther and Calvin or the early stages of the Protestant Reformation. In this second writing, Weber is considering observations done by him during his lifetime among North American Protestant sects. The sect, differently from the official church, is a voluntary-based congregation where the access is possible only after a long period of examinations and tests on the ethical qualification of the individual. Such element has more been defined in sociology as the core of the ritual action of 'disciplines', where whoever fits measures and standards dictated by the scheme is recognized as a member of the discipline (Barbera and Negri, 2015). This religious context was able to foster auto-affirmation, search for quality, charisma and strive for rewards. For those reasons, being part of a sect is profitable for someone's reputation and often used as a business card of the ethical and commercial qualities of the individual. This doesn't mean that the sect is important only because it is able to activate a social network between the entrepreneurs. Although this may had been the case and the network had its delimited role, Weber was more interested on how the process of selection peculiar of the Protestant sect generated reputation of a good character from the eyes of the outside context and therefore was particularly fruitful in business.

What was the main element on the micro level about Protestantism able to push, according to Weber, the individual's economic propensity generated by the preconditions toward economic success? The heart of Weber's theory lies on the Calvinistic belief in the doctrine of *predestination*. This doctrine championed by John Calvin and his followers (2009 [ed. orig. 1559]) in the sense of 'double predestination', stated that God

Table 3.1 Relationship between Protestant beliefs and economic ethos according to Max Weber theory

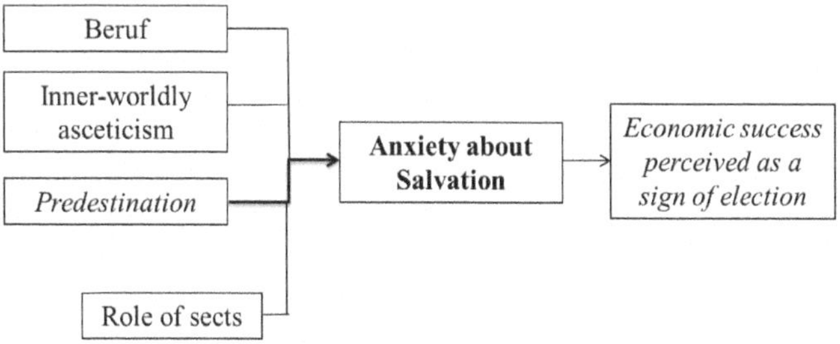

before the foundation of the world predestined some men to eternal life and foreordained others to eternal death (Romans 9, 14–24). The Calvinist believer then, according to Weber, faces the perpetual question on his own eternal destiny: 'Am I elected or am I damned?' This creates a vicious cycle of anxiety that indirectly was actually extremely beneficial in daily life, generating the propensity to work and strive for success. Working for the glory of God, and receiving God's approval through economic success, was, according to Weber, the instrument through which the Calvinist believer looked for a sign of his status as elect and predestined:

> [...] "But since Calvin viewed all pure feelings and emotions, no matter how exalted they might seem to be, with suspicion, faith had to be proved by its objective results in order to provide a firm foundation for the certitudo salutis. It must be a fides efficax [...]. Especially by comparing the condition of one's own soul with that of the elect, for instance the patriarchs, according to the Bible, could the state of one's own grace be known. Only one of the elect really has the fides efficax [...]. It was through the consciousness that his conduct, at least in its fundamental character and constant ideal (propositum oboedientiæ), rested on a power within himself working for the glory of God; that it is not only willed of God but rather done by God that he attained the highest good towards which this religion strove, the certainty of salvation". (Weber, 1930 [1905], pp. 67–69)

And later on Weber continues:

> [...] So then, although good works are absolutely incapable to serve as means to obtain the eternal beatitude [...] yet they are essential as sign

of election. They are the technical mean not to buy salvation, but to be free from the anxiety of not obtaining salvation. (Weber, 1930 [1905], pp. 67–69)

Weber defines here his crucial idea. The Calvinist believer creates his own certainty of salvation through good works, by his continuous working for the glory of God, trying to find an answer to the persistent question of his own election or damnation. A more definitive emphasis upon this anxiety came with the successors of Calvin's thought within Puritanism, like with Richard Baxter or William Perkins. According to the Weberian interpretation of those theologians, it is especially through an exam of one's professional work, through the achievement of an effective economic success, as a sign of possessing the *fides efficax* and being in a state of grace, that the believer can establish his eternal state (Weber, 1930 [1905], p. 220). Even though good works (i.e. good deeds) are not useful for salvation in Calvinism, they are still necessary to ascertain the state of the true elect. The believer then, according to Weber, has an internal obligation to strive for professional success in order to avoid this anxiety and be sure of his state of grace.

Right after the first publication of the text, first as an article (Weber, 1904, pp. 176–202; 1905, pp. 554–599), then later on in his comprehensive monograph (Weber, 1920), Weber's thesis generated a great debate. Several important sociologists where motivated to develop further analyses (Troeltsch, 1906; Brentano, 1916; Tawney, 1922; Groethuysen, 1964 [1927]; Sombart, 1928) and a specific field of studies developed through the critics and suggestions of many scholars (McKinnon A. M., 2010; Barbalet J. M., 2008; Schaefer R., 2007; Cohen J., 2002; Delacroix J., Nielsen F., 2001; Kalberg S., 1996; Treiber H., 1993; Giorgi and Marsh, 1990; Marshall, 1980; Collins R., 1980; Razzell P., 1977; Kim H. C., 1977; Bouma G. D., 1973; Mirels and Garrett, 1971; Bendix, 1967; Means, 1966). The approach of these scholars toward the validity of Weber's theory on the correlation between the Protestant ethic and the spirit of modern capitalism tends to vary. I sum up here my personal meta-analysis of four main types of approaches in criticizing the validity of Max Weber's theory:

- *Endogenous* approach;
- *Historical materialistic* approach;
- *Methodological* approach;
- *Revisionist* approach.

The first approach refers to those scholars who deny the validity of Weber's theoretical argument, basing their critique on their personal belief or identity claims (Brentano, 1916; Tawney, 1922; Groethuysen, 1964 [1927]; Robertson, 1933; George and George, 1961; Swanson, 1967; Winckelmann, 1968; Luthy, 1970; Marshall, 1982; Martello, 1992; Zaret, 1992; Novak, 1993; Burgos, 1996). Those authors tend to conceive Weber's intention as if he was claiming the superiority of a certain religious belief over the other. Max Weber's thesis on the Protestant ethic must be understood however in light of his comprehensive attempt to re-construct universal economic history. Weber had many cultural interests, and his inter-disciplinary approach was always directed by an objective intellectual purpose. Nothing is more ridiculous than isolating the thesis from its original descriptive, explanatory and interpretative role and giving the impression as if Weber was expressing a judgment of value over religious affiliations. The critic stands here upon a wrong and simplified interpretation of the theoretical argument as if, in light of Weber's opinion, capitalism is a product of the Reformation or as if only a Protestant mentality can relate to the development of capitalism. That was not Weber's intent.

Those scholars seek to counter-argue with the economic role of the Catholic Europe in the Middle Ages, the reception of the Roman Law, the Renaissance, the counter-Reformation or the doctrinal contribution of Erasmus of Rotterdam, as if the key factor can be found ultimately in an alternative 'spiritual' cause for capitalism, either Catholicism or some secular spirit. An example of this is the critique by Sombart, that finds a different preceding origin of the spirit of capitalism. I refer here to his particular emphasis on the role of Jews on an international scale for the birth of modern capitalism, their involvement on credit and their crucial contribution for the birth of entrepreneurship (Sombart, 1962 [ed. orig. 1911]).

Judaism, grounded in history and Scriptures (particularly the Torah of the Old Testament), had the ability to stimulate the economic performance through a rational, active, self-aware and self-restrained ethos. Sombart considers rabbinic Judaism as the source of this spirit in an evident correlation between the religious ethos and the economic performance (Fishman, 1989). Sombart made this investigation in light of Karl Marx, who already pointed out before the role of Judaism in capitalism. Marx, even though with a negative outlook, talked about the individualistic religious ethic of Judaism as centered on the marketplace and making monetary gain as an ultimate substantially rational goal. The 'practical Jewish spirit' according to Marx's historical materialistic approach, conceives religiosity as being composed by merely formal ceremonies encompassing the world of self-interest (Fishman, 1989). This diffuse world-transformative ethos, rather than a specific economic ethos, was according to this perspective able to generate economic success. It's interesting to notice that many elements of Calvinism are in tune with the previous Jewish economic ethic. However, these systems of belief were already in action long time before the genesis of modern capitalism and played an ethnic-based role that resulted to be inevitably limited compared with the Calvinist Reformation that took place on the Western world in sixteenth to seventeenth centuries.

The case of the Jews nevertheless remains central in understanding how entrepreneurship in its antecedent pre-modern forms of mercantilism was more frequent among members of certain minorities, not completely accepted in the societies where they lived, permeated by an acute sense of diversity, living in a marginal status and able to contrast the prevailing attitudes of the society around them against innovation. This point will be crucial as I will consider on a more contemporary level the role of marginal groups as the Chinese migrants (Benton and Pieke, 1998; Ziegert Van, 2006) specifically in the diaspora. Not all minority groups are able to display such propensity to develop genuine innovations in their social behavior. The Chinese Protestant entrepreneurs from Wenzhou, baptized by the public opinion as 'Jews of China', are particularly suited.

Another primary example of this approach remains Tawney in his study of religion and the genesis of capitalism. The author starts by defending the economic inheritance of the Middle Ages, then he arrives to question the role of the Reformation, especially that of Calvinism and later Puritanism, for the genesis of capitalism, exalting the contributions of the Church of England which however itself was very impacted (though not without controversies) by both those elements of Calvinism and Puritanism. This approach, largely ideological, remains in general unable to provide explanations that can be valid in the academic arena.

The historical materialistic approach, on the other hand, involves those scholars who embrace the Marxist's claim that all human institutions, including religion, are based on economic foundations (Robertson, 1933; Gordon Walker, 1937; Lowy, 1989; Grossman, 2006; Clark, 2009; Hirschman, 2013). This approach does not refer uniquely to scholars that hold a Marxist view. For example, I find in this category also some evolutionary theorists (Razzell, 1977; Blum and Dudley, 2001). However, they have in common the interpretation of modern capitalism simply as a consequence of gradually increasing economic exchange and they deny therefore that any kind of religion can have a crucial influence in the formation of the capitalistic system. Modern Capitalism then is born uniquely out of economic reasons and social norms are always determined by productive structures.

The absolutization of the material dimension can clearly be seen in the effort of those authors to explain the birth of capitalism by only referring to political and economic conditions. For example they mention the price revolution, the pre-existence of usury and speculative practices or some comprehensive geographical and biological explanations. Even the Reformation, according to them, is just the result of needs created by the advances in the means of production. What those authors often misunderstand is that Weber's 'spirit of capitalism' is something very different from acquisitive greed. It is an *ethos* with internalized rules of conduct for which profit maximization is only a by-product (Rimlinger, 1976). This leads those authors to an equally reductive and erroneous conclusion, as if Weber's first objective was to define the causes of the birth of the modern capitalistic economy. Weber's objective instead was to show how a specific religious belief can influence the formation of an economic ethos that led to the foundation of the spirit of modern capitalism. This approach is biased, tainted by an economic determinism that is equally questionable in his conclusions as the first approach.

Then there is the methodological approach that involves a larger number of scholars. This approach refers to scholars who, rather than focusing on religious or economic aspects, criticize Weber's methodology in his formulation of the theory (Green, 1959; Hudson, 1961; McClelland, 1961; Hagen, 1962; Nelson, 1969; Warner, 1970; Giddens, 1973; Glock and Hammond, 1973; Collins, 1980; Laitin, 1986; Lehmann and Roth, 1995; Kalberg, 1996; Chalcraft and Harrington, 2001; Gerhardt, 2007; McKinnon, 2010). Some of those scholars, for example, criticize Weber for the use of 'ideal-types', his concept of rationality, misunderstandings related to the translation of German concepts, the Weberian difference between 'capitalism in general' and 'modern capitalism' or the fact that Calvinist doctrine is only a fragment of Weber's full theory, which in their view led to the neglect of his diverse theoretical contributions.

One of the main concerns of those critics was the alleged neglect of the social aspects in Weber's religious analysis (Stark, 2005).

According to this critical position social networks between people of the same religion might more clearly explain the economic success rather than the particular religious belief on salvation. If this was the case, I then wonder why the strong social network related to the adherence of faith equally present between other religious minority groups in European past history, such as Quietist, Mystics of sixteenth and seventeenth centuries, never led to an economic tendency as for the case of Huguenots or other Protestant sects, but pushed them either toward hedonism and radical anti-modern positions. Once again, contrary to the opinion of Boudon, it appears to me that the beliefs of Calvinism tend to play a major role over any social network explanation on the constitution of the spirit of capitalism. Those authors underline also the fact that some of the entrepreneurs in sixteenth century were not the product of Calvinistic societies as Holland or Switzerland, but immigrants. What they forget to mention is that those immigrants embraced anyway the Calvinist belief and even though Köln, Antwerp or Liege had their own Catholic entrepreneurs, they were an exception compared to the regularities documented by Weber in the ranks of the Protestant economic elite. Critics then frequently refer to the exception of Scotland. Even though Scotland was a Calvinist state church from 1560, it remained economically backward until the nineteenth century. Some recent analysis again shows the superficial interpretation of that position based on the strength of largely irrelevant evidence for the case of Scotland. The relative lowness of the Scottish capitalist development tells us nothing about the modern capitalist ethos that Weber intended to point out. According to Marshall the case of Scotland, examining different data, may in the end go against the established opinion and actually be well consistent with Weber's argument.

Another example can be found in using Weber for the explanation of the 'endogeneity problem' (Laitin, 1986). According to this interpretation the Europeans who already had an interest in breaking the bonds of a pre-capitalist spirit left the church precisely for that purpose. Those scholars, tend to emphasize the role of political and economic circumstances such as decline of the imperial legitimacy or the emerging of new mundane obligations already pushing society toward a transformation (Jepperson and Meyer, 2011). The fact overlooked by those authors is that those who embraced Calvinism did it often under strict persecution apart from any economic interest and guided by motivations that go beyond the simplistic economic considerations. Also, as Weber already pointed out, often the effect of the Reformation on the economic ethic was unintended. All of those scholars in their critics have not been able to deny the validity of the core of Weber's theory.

Finally, the revisionist approach includes some scholars who are not directly referring to Max Weber or his thesis. These authors may come from different disciplines and collateral fields of interests such as cultural anthropology or sociology of religion and they may embrace different schools of thought such as the post-modernist or post-colonial perspective. From their perspective, it is possible to identify one main logical conclusion that undermines any role that the Western society may have had in past history, compared with other cultures and societies. What those authors have in common is an anti-ethnocentric perspective and a deconstruction of the concept of modernity as is known in Western societies (Goody, 1996; Schluchter, 1996, 1989, 1985, 1979). The direct consequence of such approach is the inevitable denial of the validity of Weber's theory. As fascinating as it may sound however, the authors that held such a position don't provide facts and compelling evidence for their position.

Summing up, it is possible to see that those variegated post-Weberian critics are still not able to deny the validity of Weber's main theoretical argument, the facts and evidence that he provided in his articulated historic, cultural and economic study of religion. Another element that I've noticed with many of those critics is their superficial understanding both of the conceptual background of Weber and of the historical, theological and documental framework of the phenomenon.

This is to say that many critics of Weber's theory do not refer to the original writings of Weber or simply do not hold a knowledge of the historical sources that Weber was referring to in his analysis.[1] For

[1] To better understand Max Weber is also important to consider the fact that his life and work were deeply affected by his family traditions. Weber's mother had strong religious Calvinistic convictions that led Max to the decision of doing serious inquiries into religious subjects early in his life (Swatos and Kivisto, 1991). From those elements I can deduce the personal interest and intellectual tension of the German sociologist. This doesn't mean that someone can objectively identify some sort of secret religious intention in his sociological work counting his declared breakdown with religion and his strive as a social scientist to always describe, explain and interpret rather than evaluate.

Table 3.2 Critical approaches to Weber's thesis on Protestant ethic and the genesis of the spirit of capitalism

Critical approach	*Main features*	*Critical points*	*Author's*
Endogenous	Alternative "spiritual" cause for Capitalism	*Ideological arguments based on determinism of values*	Tawney, Groethuysen, Fanfani, Fischoff, Novak, Burgos...
Historical materialistic	Unilateral economic cause for Capitalism	*Ideological arguments based on economic determinism*	Robertson, Gordon Walker, Baechler, Lowy, Grossman, Razzell...
Methodological	Mixed complex of causes for Capitalism	*Formed arguments without any alternative interpretation*	Parsons, Roper, Giddens, Boudon, Laitin, McKinnon...
Revisionist	Elimination of the concept of Capitalism	*Denied of historical evidences without any valid support*	Goody Schluchter...

this reason, the efforts of falsification mentioned above led very often to misunderstanding and blatant errors. Therefore, at least from a sociological point of view, they fail to provide an alternative scientific valid description to Weber's theory. Even after examining all those critics, contrary to the established opinion in social sciences, the core of Weber's thesis on the Protestant ethic remains valid. As it will be analyzed in the next section, I'm not suggesting that Weber thesis could not undergo any falsification, a process that according to the Popperian criteria of scientific investigation is indispensable. I'm just pointing out the fact that the critics fail to give a valid alternative interpretation according to the sociological criteria. An investigation that seems to be already partial or incorrect and that is utilized in solving a sociological problem through its elimination as an end in itself should never be considered as reliable (Table 3.2).

3.2 European Calvinism and Capitalism

3.2.1 Anxiety and Predestination

Two dimensions are involved in Weber's analysis, on one side the history of sociological thought and on the other side the characteristics of the Protestant Reformation. If someone wants to have a clear understanding of this sociological topic however, it is not possible to remain just on the side of sociological thought. The subject involves something else behind the sociological component: a particular theological impetus paving the way for a moral one (*ethos*), which in return is able to influence the conduct and social actions. I must now necessarily consider the characteristics and dynamics of this particular system of beliefs: Calvinism. In analyzing the facts, I can notice several points where Weber's description of Calvinism diverges consistently from my own interpretation of it as well as that of other experts in the topic. What is interesting to notice is that the doctrine of predestination already was embraced in the history of Christianity long before Calvin.

When John Calvin, Martin Luther or Huldrych Zwingli during the Reformation refer to such doctrine, they were relating to a concept that was already deeply rooted in the history of Christianity. In particular, Augustine of Hippo (354 a. C.–430 a. C.) already upheld the idea of predestination, and the Roman Catholic church all the way to Thomas Aquinas acknowledged the validity of such doctrine. The reformers then were conforming themselves to a long tradition of thought that already believed in the doctrine of predestination: Lucid and Gottshalck of Orbais already upheld double predestination and, more generally, Thomas Aquinas, Duns Scoto, William of Ockham, Gregory of Rimini as well dealt extensively with the topic in medieval times. Many believed and preached this doctrine, even in its more radical implications such as the 'double predestination' long before the Reformation. To claim therefore, as Weber gives the impression of, that Calvin's doctrine was somehow uniquely notable for being totally pre-ordained and completely beyond anything that human can do, doesn't do justice to its multiple and continuous examples in church history that were the basis of Calvin's legitimacy.

Even after the Reformation such doctrine continued to exist in both Catholic and Protestant traditions: Jansenius, Pasquier Quesnel or even Karl Barth, all the way to the second Vatican council speak of it. Not only the doctrine of predestination, despite the frequent debates that generated it, is rooted into the history of Christianity but it finds its ultimate origin into the Sacred Scriptures, the Bible. Particularly Paul of Tarsus in the New Testament clearly defines the doctrine of predestination (Romans 8:29,30; Ephesians 1:5–11). Although not so elaborated as in the New Testament, the doctrine of Predestination is indirectly present in the Old Testament concept of 'election' both on a national Israel and on the individual level (Jeremiah 49:20 50:45; Micah 4:12; Isaiah 14:24 26–27 19:12 23:9). Therefore the Jewish tradition, long before the advent of Christianity held these beliefs. Judaism was always characterized by the awareness of the state of election of Israel, according to which only the Jewish people were God's people, chosen and separated from this world. Christianity carried that idea forward expounding it beyond ethnic identity to anyone who embraces the Christian faith.

When the Apostle Paul spoke of predestination in his writings, he was defining a concept that was understandable and not foreign to his Jewish audience. The same belief in predestination can also be found in the Muslim faith, in the Quran, an element that with some exceptions (Abbas, 1988; Turner, 1974; Tyler, 1966) scholars never noticed. This therefore seems to challenge the central idea of Max Weber, that predestination played a central role in the genesis of the spirit of capitalism. What was new in the history of Christianity from Reformation and specially with John Calvin is not anxiety about salvation of which the medieval church was full of, but the opposite belief in assurance of salvation. Assurance is a Christian doctrine present only in Protestantism, and chiefly in Calvinism, which states that the inner witness of the Holy Spirit allows the justified disciple to know that he or she is saved (based on Romans 8, 16). This doctrine was important in Methodism, Lutheranism but chiefly in Reformed Calvinistic churches and Puritanism. It is in Calvin's idea of a perpetual assurance of salvation that this doctrine reached its highest implications (taken from a literal reading of John 10, 28–29):

> [...] but the grace granted to the members of Jesus Christ has a strong pre-eminence of dignity, because, being united to their head, they are never cut off from their salvation. (Calvin, 2009 [1559]; Vol. III, C. XXI, p. 1105)

For many centuries Christians believed with few exceptions in the fact that salvation can rarely be fully achieved and it only comes through faith and good works. What was new, or rather a return back to the original Scriptural emphasis, in the Reformation was that man could be justified before God and receive this salvation by faith alone, without good works and that he can have absolute assurance in this life of his eternal salvation. All the main reformers, such as Luther or Zwingli before their conversion were Catholic priests while Calvin was an educated scholar of law and humanism. This element surely led his systematic theology to explore the deepest implications of salvation as an eternal state of the soul which nothing in this life can change (Adamo et al., 1994). Particularly Calvin, more than the other reformers, places the emphasis of assurance on the fact that the doctrine of predestination should leave no room for anxiety:

> The most serious and dangerous temptation that the devil has to hit the believers, is to leave them restlessness questioning their election and prompting them to look with absurd lust outside of the Way. [...] This inner turmoil is the most appropriate element able to show how perverse is to imagine predestination in that way. As the spirit of man cannot be infected with something more harmful than this mistake that may distract the conscience from the calm and rest which he should have in God. (Calvin, 2009 [1559]; Vol. III, C. XIV, pp. 1147–1148)

In open contrast with the previous Catholic theology that for centuries was characterized by a 'dangerous' and 'anxious' struggle for achieving salvation through all sort of human efforts in order to be freed from a state of perpetual anxiety, Calvin proclaims here an opposite message of 'calm' and 'rest' in a perpetual assurance of salvation received by faith, championed also by the following Protestant generations. It is evident then that this Calvinistic doctrine does not imply a continuous state of anxiety, but an opposite state of peace and confidence caused by the awareness of being forever saved. Although Weber states the presence of a distortion in this doctrine in subsequent developments of Calvinism, there's no trace of such a distortion either in Calvin's theology, or in subsequent developments of Calvinism (with the exception of few hyper-Calvinistic cases). On the contrary, Calvinism more than any other reformed traditions believed in the total depravity of men, and in the impossibility for a man to come to salvation by any kind of effort, even if it were the effort to control his state of grace, like Weber had stated (Miegge, 2010). Faith is a gift from God, sovereignly given by God's grace and dissociated from any meritorious element. Any effort to gain God's favor through human efforts, according to Calvinism, is therefore in vain.

3.2.2 Alternative Views on Assurance of Salvation

The research question here instead of anxiety then becomes: is this belief in a 'perpetual assurance of salvation' that led the Calvinist believer to have a positive psychological attitude, therefore capable to enable him to contribute to economic success? This doctrine stated by Calvin, as a completion of Luther's *Sola Fide*, was the real novelty, or the return to the original scriptural intent, in the history of Christianity. Perpetual assurance of salvation implies that once a person comes to faith in Christ he is forever sure of his eternal salvation and totally aware of being among the elects. This is not because of works or merits but because of a sovereign call from God. The believer then, instead of living in a state of anxiety about his eternal condition is completely sure of his salvation. The person believes that it is impossible to lose salvation.

It is this perpetual state of assurance, proper of those Calvinistic branches of Protestantism, that we now want to switch our focus back to the realm of capitalism. Such belief is able to enhance confidence, a confidence that even in modern Psychology has been identified as *self-efficacy* (Bandura, 2001; Zhao and Seibert, 2006; Laguna, 2013; Rauch and Frese, 2007). Self-efficacy has been defined as the extent or strength of one's belief in one's own ability to complete tasks and reach goals. This represents a psychological attitude that, interestingly enough, has been proved to be highly correlated with economic success. Particularly, self-efficacy is a very crucial quality for success in what I defined in the previous chapter as entrepreneurial successful attitudes: (a) intention to engage in new firm creation, (b) personal choice of the specific entrepreneurial activity, (c) actual business start-up, (d) propensity toward planned behavior, (e) ability to perform various tasks effectively, (f) strive for implementation regardless of the obstacles, (g) perception of difficult tasks as challenges rather than threats, (h) need for achievement, (i) stress tolerance, (j) proactive personality, (k) risk-taking, (l) propensity toward perseverance and (m) openness to new experiences (Laguna, 2013; Rauch and Frese, 2007; Zhao and Seibert, 2006). What scholars point out here is that the main element that is able to generate those attitudes is what a person thinks about himself, the person's belief, his consciousness. As the belief tends to be more specific and perpetual, self-efficacy enhances more easily economic success (Bandura, 2001). Some literature has shown how self-efficacy plays a crucial role in situations of risk and uncertainty (Kahneman, 2003; McLain and Hackman, 1999; Tversky, 1995).

What is interesting to notice is that for the case of Calvinism the belief in the perpetual assurance of one's eternal salvation could generate in the individual a perpetual state of peace and trust. From my point of view this condition results, together with other elements proper to Calvinism, in the display of all the attitudes proper of self-efficacy. The believer, through perpetual assurance of salvation, can take risks, tolerate stress, reach new experiences, embrace difficulties as good challenges rather than threats, strive for his spiritual growth regardless of the obstacles that he faces, because he knows that everything, even difficulties, work for his good and he is sure that one day he is going to heaven. Of course, that belief alone does not explain all the economic propensity, yet it results in being the foundational principle toward it. Adding to this element, the Protestant idea of calling (*Beruf*) helps the believer to choose a specific entrepreneurial activity as well.

If we look carefully to other elements of Calvin's theology, I find that the Calvinistic vision of the glory of God as the ultimate purpose in life enhances such need for achievement. Achievement in this particular case is not intended for the individual but for a much higher cause: God. The believer knows that every single task has an eternal purpose higher than himself. Also, the Calvinistic belief in the perseverance of the saints, enhances planned behavior and a general propensity to persevere. This can be, in my opinion, the main element, together with all the other *preconditions*, bringing Calvinism to develop a particular economic ethos. Perpetual assurance of salvation plays a central role under situations of risk where the believer achieves economic success, because of his state of self-efficacy related to this belief despite the challenges. It is the peculiar belief in eternal salvation, and not the anxiety, that could explain the correlation generating self-efficacy.

There are also several Calvinist doctrines, apart from predestination, that have been overlooked or only partially analyzed by Weber, which still need some attention. I will include them in the model as 'assistants' to the *preconditions*. In introducing them in the model I will not consider them in a strict causal relationship toward my theoretical question, as if they are generating the belief in PAS (an acronym for perpetual assurance of salvation I'll use often from now on). Instead, they are the preconditions without which it is impossible to rightly understand how the belief in PAS generates self-efficacy and therefore favors economic success. For example, it would be interesting to analyze the negative impact of religious traditionalism for the economic ethos. For this case I will refer to Calvin's *anti-superstition* approach. This can be seen clearly in Calvin's treatise on relics (Calvin, 2010 [ed. orig. 1543]) and in his strong attack on superstition and idolatry proper of many Catholic rituals. Also, very important is Calvin's strong attack toward superstitious views of the sacraments even within the Protestant tradition (Calvin, 2009 [ed.

orig. 1559], Vol. IV, Cp. XIV, pp. 1490–1519, Cp. XVII, 1578–1652). While Luther was supportive of a 'sacramental union' of the believer with Christ in the Last Supper, Calvin was challenging this view, and together with others in the Reformed camp like Zwingli, while still emphasizing spiritual communion, leaned more toward the symbolic function of that rite. Other medieval practices such as private confession disappeared in Calvinism.

Such anti-traditionalism and anti-superstitious moral stand denies the utility of any kind of religious means to free the individual from the guilty sense apart from Christ. This change had a huge impact on the daily ethical praxis of the individual (Weber, 1976 [ed. orig. 1905], p. 210). Superstition can be identified as an irrational belief maintained by ignorance of the laws of nature that an object, an action or a circumstance not logically related to a course of events influences its outcome. It seems that a belief, such as the anti-superstitious moral stand of Calvinism, is the opposite of superstition, which was so important in the eyes of Weber's search for the religious disciplinarism of Calvinism (Op. Cit., Vol. IV, Cp XV–XVI, pp. 1519–1578).

Another crucial aspect in Calvinism is the *role of the Sacred Scriptures*. More than any other reformed traditions, Calvinism exalted the Bible as the only infallible rule of faith and conduct, the only source for the knowledge of God. This view not only was crucial for the successive development of society, fostering writings, rationalization and the scientific inquiry, but it exalted even the principles of business. The Scriptures command every men to work and consider each other as responsible before God of their high accomplishments. Financial success is seen here as a result of 'doing the right thing' and obeying the Biblical principles of business. The *role of Sacred Scriptures* will refer here therefore to the series of principles and teachings contained in the Bible (especially wisdom literature of the Old Testament) concerning business. Protestantism more than any other religious group placed the emphasis on the strict application of those principles in order to have a prosperous business. Among other things the Scripture gives no tolerance to idleness, to carelessness and instead it emphasizes the importance of respecting worldly concerns. Industry is considered as the duty and true happiness of man. The surest means for the increase of one's property according to the Scriptures requires a wise economy of personal resources rather than rapid gains, in order to promote the greatest promise for long-term success.

Such an economic attitude finds its antecedent only in the Jewish tradition. The Jews or the Armenians are ethnic religious groups of whose role in economic history has already been clearly explained (Sombart, 1962 [ed. orig. 1911]). Those minorities like the Protestants were highly involved in the European business across the centuries. They find a correspondence in the Eastern tradition of the Samurais in Japan or the Parsees in India. Those minorities, above others, display a more frequent involvement in entrepreneurship according to Sombart. Due to the lack of acceptance in societies and their subsequent avoidance of traditional values and norms proper of that society these minorities develop an acute sense of diversity and a propensity to innovate in order to survive. Although the Jewish religious tradition, at least after the advent of Christianity, doesn't provide any belief such as the perpetual assurance of salvation, it is still characterized by the faith in the promises of God contained in the Bible able to give the strength to persevere in trials and situations of risk. It is primarily their status of ethnic minority however, as well as other cases mentioned above, that results in them playing a major role in enhancing entrepreneurial activities.

An equally crucial belief of Calvinism that explains much of Weber's misinterpretation around anxiety is the doctrine of the *perseverance of the saints*. Such doctrine states that only those who persevere are true believers. This doesn't mean, as Weber misinterpreted, that is perseverance that ensures salvation, but it means that true believers are kept by the power of God through a firm faith. Perseverance promises that any person who comes to true faith is forever preserved by God from perdition. It is in this sense that perseverance and assurance are strictly correlated. On one side assurance promotes perseverance through God's mighty hand preserving and enabling the believer, and on the other side perseverance is the evidence of genuine salvation leading the believer who is saved by grace to a process of intense vigilance and rigorous discipline. This doesn't mean that perseverance is a pre-requisite for salvation however, since in Calvinism men are totally depraved and incapable to do anything good. Perseverance is rather a consequence of salvation. It can be illustrated as a race to run. Salvation is the goal of the race and the true believer has already won, being already saved by grace through faith. The warnings and admonitions given in the Calvinist call are meant for retrospective and introspective self-examination to assess whether one is already saved or not.

In critical moments of life the individual is called to go back to the basic teaching of salvation through faith alone and, as a consequence, to make fruits worthy of repentance. To abandon the race on the other hand proves one was never saved (Schreiner and Caneday, 2001). Here's what in Reformed theology is called the 'practical syllogism', upheld by Theodore Beza. According to this principle one can gain assurance of salvation by observing evidence of faith in his life. Beza denied any use of material riches as a sign of justification or election (Muller, 2008). Also, according to Reformed theology, good works are the epistemological ground of faith and justification, rather than the ontological. In other words, the evidence of faith only makes faith apparent: it does not create faith. John Calvin particularly warns against inferring election from such signs (Beeke, 2011, p. 273).

Of great importance for the theoretical argument on the perpetual assurance of salvation and the display of self-efficacy is also the doctrine of the *sovereignty of God*. This doctrine states that every single event is under the control of God and responds only to His will. Although Reformed theology tried to reconcile such view with human responsibility, the original Calvinistic belief placed all the emphasis on God's purpose. This auxiliary aspect, if related to the perpetual assurance of salvation, can explain even more strongly the psychological impact of the system of beliefs on self-efficacy. A man under situation of risk and stress has the certainty that God has the complete control over every circumstance of his life and that everything, even bad experiences, work for his good.

All those auxiliary aspects cannot be understood completely if they are not incorporated within a crucial precondition. Such precondition that cooperates with *inner-worldly asceticism*, *Beruf*, and *role of sects*, is able to prevent the shift of the perpetual assurance of salvation into a mere state of unproductive contentment. This precondition refers to the pursuit of the *glory of God as the ultimate purpose* of life. All aspects of life, especially work and worldly duties, contain therefore a greater spiritual purpose that is able to push the individual to strive for excellence. In this sense every working activity, even the more despised, has its internal dignity, it can be 'sanctified' into a legitimate 'act of worship' and it contains therefore its spiritual purpose also in light of a common good that is lacking in the individualistic reconstruction of Weber (Beeke, 2009, pp. 360–361). Therefore, both in the theologians and the consequences of their thoughts for the common believer, it is possible to trace the absence of anxiety, if not even the presence of its opposite () (Table 3.3).

Table 3.3 Dynamics of the relationship between the Protestant beliefs and the economic ethos according to the theoretical argument

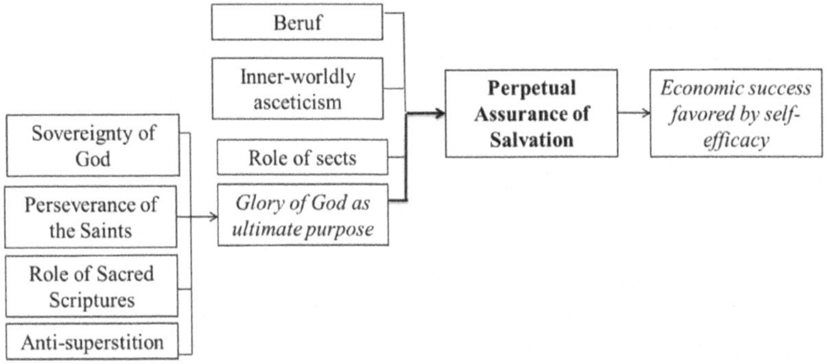

Weber's intuition must be also understood in light of the influence of the neo-Kantian German school, especially through the theological and intellectual clues received from his contemporary Ernst Troeltsch (1865–1923) who put a strong emphasis on the definition of the 'spirit' of thought and the 'forces' of history (see in particular Adair-Toteff, 2015; Graf, 2013). Troeltsch emphasized particularly the mystical orientation in Western religion and how the ascetic orientation so evident in modern Protestantism is fundamentally compatible with the economic life (AA. VV., 1990). Trying to understand the roots of individualism and instrumental rationality, Troeltsch, points out the role of Protestantism in its different branches (Calvinism, ...) and throughout its different times (paleo-Protestantism, new Protestantism). But Troeltsch also acknowledges the crucial role of the doctrine of perpetual assurance of salvation, and the absence of any form of anxiety in such belief. His more accurate interpretation stresses the fact that, in contrast with Lutheranism where grace was revocable, the Calvinist believer possesses an assurance and serenity due to their belief in PAS and his irreversible election to salvation (Troeltsch, 1987 [Ed. orig. 1906]).

References

AA. VV., 1990, *Economy and Society: Overviews in Economic Sociology*, London, Sage Publications.

Abbas A., 1988, 'Scaling an Islamic Work Ethic', in *Journal of Social Psychology*, No. 128, pp. 575–583.

Adair-Toteff C., 2015, *Fundamental Concepts in Max Weber's Sociology of Religion*, London, Palgrave Macmillan.

Adamo P., et al., 1994, *Modernità, politica e protestantesimo*, Torino, Claudiana.

Bandura A., 'Social Cognitive Theory: An Agentic Perspective', in *Annual Review of Psychology*, No. 52 (2001), pp. 1–26.

Barbalet J.M., 2008, *Weber, Passion and Profits: The Protestant Ethic and the Spirit of Capitalism in Context*, Paris, Lavoisier.

Barbera F., Negri N., 2015, 'Rituals as Mechanisms', in P*aradoxes, Mechanisms, Consequences: Essay in Honor of Mohamed Cherkaoui*, edited by G.L. Manzo, Oxford, Bardwell Press.

Beeke J. R., 2009, *Living for God's Glory. An Introduction to Calvinism*, Lane Mary, Reformation Trust Publishing.

Beeke J.R., 2011, 'The Assurance Debate', in *Drawn into Controversie: Reformed Theological Diversity and Debates Within Seventeenth-Century British Puritanism*, Göttingen, Vandenhoeck & Ruprecht, p. 273.

Bendix R., 'The Protestant Ethic—Revisited', in *Comparative Studies in Society and History*, Vol. 9, No. 3 (Apr., 1967), pp. 266–273.

Benton G., Pieke F. N., 1998, *The Chinese in Europe*, London, MacMillan Press.

Blum U., Dudley L., 'Religion and Economic Growth: Was Weber Right?' in *Journal of Evolutionary Economics*, No. 11 (2001), pp. 207–230.

Bouma G. D., 'A Critical Review of Recent Protestant Ethic Research', in *Journal for the Scientific Study of Religion*, Vol. 12, No. 2 (Jun., 1973), pp. 141–155.

Brentano L., 1916, *Die Anfdnge des modernen Kapitalismus*, Munich.

Burgos J. M., 1996, *Weber e lo spirito del capitalismo. Storia di un problema e nuove prospettive*, ACTA PHILOSOPHICA, vol. 5, fasc. 2—pp. 197–220.

Calvin J., 2009, *Institutes of the Christian Religion*, Grand Rapids, B. Eerdmans Publishing Co., [ed. orig. 1559, *Institutio Christianae religionis*].

Calvin J., 2010, *A treatise on Relics*, Edinburgh, Johnstone, Hunter & Co [ed. orig. 1543, *Traité des reliques*, Genève].

Chalcraft D. J., Harrington A., 2001, *The Protestant Ethic Debate*, Liverpool University Press.

Clark G., 2009, *A Farewell to Alms: A Brief Economic History of the World*, Princeton University Press.

Cohen J., 2002, *Protestantism and Capitalism: The Mechanisms of Influence*, California, CJS.

Collins R., 'Weber's Last Theory of Capitalism: A Systematization', in *American Sociological Review* No. 45 (1980), pp. 925–942.

De Laveleye E., 1889, *Elements of Political Economy*, New York, G. P. Putnam's Sons, p. 44.

Delacroix J., Nielsen F., 2001, 'The Beloved Myth: Protestantism and the Rise of Industrial Capitalism in Nineteenth-Century Europe', in *Social Forces*, Oxford.

Fishman A., 1989, 'The Religious Kibbutz: A Note on the Theories of Marx, Sombart and Weber on Weber and Economic Success', in *Sociological Analysis*, No. 5 (1989), pp. 281–290.

George C. H., George K., 1961, *The Protestant Mind and the English Reformation, 1570–1640*, Princeton University Press.

Gerhardt U., 'Much More than a Mere Translation: Talcott Parsons's Translation into English of Max Weber's "Die protestantische Ethik und der Geist des Kapitalismus": An Essay in Intellectual History', in *The Canadian Journal of Sociology/Cahiers canadiens de sociologie*, Vol. 32, No. 1 (Winter, 2007), pp. 41–62.

Giddens A., 1973, *Capitalism and Modern Social Theory: An Analysis of the Writings of Marx, Durkheim and Max Weber*, Cambridge University Press.

Giorgi L., Marsh C., 1990, 'The Protestant Work Ethic as a Cultural Phenomenon', in *European Journal of Social Psychology*, London.

Glock C. Y., Hammond P. E., 1973, *Beyond the Classics: Essays in the Scientific Study of Religion*, Iowa City, Prairie Book Cellar.

Goody, J., 1996, *The East in the West*, Cambridge, Cambridge University Press.

Graf F. W., 2013, *Fachmenschenfreundschaft: Studien Zu Weber Und Troeltsch*, Berlin, Walter De Gruyter Inc.

Green R. W. (ed.), 1959, *Protestantism and Capitalism: The Weber Thesis and Its Critics*, Boston, Heath.

Groethuysen B., 1964, *Le origini dello spirito borghese in Francia*, il Saggiatore, Milano [ed. orig. 1927, *Die Entstehung der bürgerlichen Welt- und Lebensanschauung in Frankreich*].

Grossman H., 'The Beginnings of Capitalism and the New Mass Morality', in *Journal of Classical Sociology* Vol. 6, No. 2 (July 2006).

Hagen, E. E., 1962, *On the Theory of Social Change*, Dorsey Press.

Hirschman A. O., 2013, *The Passions and the Interests: Political Arguments for Capitalism before Its Triumph*, Princeton University Press.

Hudson W. S., 'The Weber Thesis Re-examined', in *Church History*, No. 30 (1961), pp. 88–99.

Jepperson, R. Meyer, J., 'Multiple Levels of Analysis and the Limitations of Methodological Individualisms', in *Sociological Theory*, Vol. 29, No. 1 (2011), pp. 54–73.

Kahneman D., 'A Psychological Perspective on Economics', in *The American Economic Review*, Vol. 93, No. 2 (May 2003).

Kalberg S., 'On the Neglect of Weber's Protestant Ethic as a Theoretical Treatise: Demarcating the Parameters of Postwar American Sociological Theory', in *Sociological Theory*, Vol. 14, No. 1 (Mar., 1996), pp. 49–70.

Kim H. C., 'The Relationship of Protestant Ethic Beliefs and Values to Achievement', in *Journal for the Scientific Study of Religion*, Vol. 16, No. 3 (Sep., 1977), pp. 255–262.

Laguna M., 'Self-efficacy, Self-esteem, and Entrepreneurship Among the Unemployed', in *Journal of Applied Social Psychology*, No. 43 (2013), pp. 253–262.

Laitin, David D., 1986. *Hegemony and Culture: Politics and Religious Change among the Yoruba*. Chicago, University of Chicago Press.

Lehmann H., Roth G., 1995, *Weber's Protestant Ethic: Origin, Evidence, Contexts*, Washington, DC, German Historical Institute.

Lowy M., 1989, *Marxism and Christianity in Latin America*, Scribd.

Luthy H., 1970, *From Calvin to Rousseau: Tradition and Modernity in Socio-Political Thought from the Reformation to the French Revolution*, Basic Books.

Marshall G., 1982, *In Search of the Spirit of Capitalism*, New York, Columbia.

Marshall G., 'The Dark Side of the Weber Thesis: The Case of Scotland', in *The British Journal of Sociology*, Vol. 31, No. 3, Special Issue, Aspects of Weberian Scholarship, (Sep., 1980), pp. 419–440.

Martello L., (eds.), 1992, *Sulla genesi del capitalismo*, Rome, Armando.

McClelland D. C., 1961, *The Achievement Society*, Boston University Press.

McKinnon A. M., 'Elective Affinities of the Protestant Ethic: Weber and the Chemistry of Capitalism', in Sociological Theory, Vol. 28, No. 1 (March 2010), pp. 108–126.

McLain D. L., Hackman K., 'Trust, Risk and Decision-Making in Organizational Change', in *Public Administration Quarterly*, Vol. 23, No. 2 (Summer 1999).

Means R. L., 1966, 'Protestantism and American Sociology: Problems of Analysis', in *Sociological Analysis*, No. 27 (Fall), pp. 128–137.

Miegge M., 2010, *Vocazione e lavoro*, Torino, Claudiana.

Mirels H. L., Garrett J. B., 1971, 'The Protestant Ethic as a Personality Variable', in *Journal of Consulting and Clinical Psycology*, London.

Muller R. A., 2008, *Christ and the Decree: Christology and Predestination in Reformed Theology from Calvin to Perkins*, Ada, Baker Academic.

Nelson B., 1969, 'Conscience and the Making of Early Modern Cultures: The Protestant Ethic Ethic Beyond Max Weber', in *Social Research*, No. 36 (1969), pp. 4–21.

Novak M., 1993, *The Catholic Ethic and the Spirit of Capitalism*, Free Press, New York.

Rauch A., Frese M., 'Let's Put the Person Back into Entrepreneurship Research: A Meta-analysis on the Relationship Between Business Owners' Personality Traits, Business Creation, and Success', in *European Journal of Work and Organizational Psychology* (Nov. 2007).

Razzel P., 'The Protestant Ethic and the Spirit of Capitalism: A Natural Scientific Critique', in *The British Journal of Sociology*, Vol. 28, No. 1 (Mar., 1977), pp. 17–37.

Rimlinger G. V., 'Max Weber on the Spirit of Capitalism', in *The Journal of Economic History*, Vol. 36, No. 4 (Dec., 1976), p. 990.

Robertson H. M., 1933, *Aspects of the Rise of Economic Individualism: A Criticism of Max Weber and His School*, Cambridge University Press.

Schaefer R., 'Infallibility and Intentionality: Franz Brentano's Diagnosis of German Catholicism', in *Journal of the History of Ideas*, University of Pennsylvania Press Vol. 68, No. 3 (Jul., 2007), pp. 477–499.

Schluchter, W., 1979, *Max Weber's Vision of History. Ethics and Methods*, Berkeley, University of California Press.

Schluchter, W., 1985, *The Rise of Western Rationalism: Max Weber's Developmental History*, Berkeley, University of California Press.

Schluchter, W., 1989, *Rationalism, Religion, and Domination. A Weberian Perspective*, Berkeley, University of California Press.

Schluchter, W., 1996, *Paradoxes of Modernity. Culture and Conduct in the Theory of Max Weber*, Stanford, Stanford University Press.

Schreiner T. R., Caneday A. B., 2001, *The Race Set Before Us. A Biblical Theology of Perseverance & Assurance*, Downers Grove, Inter Varsity Press.

Simmel G., 1994, *La religione*, Bulzoni Editore, Roma [ed. orig. 1906, *Die Religion*, Frankfurt am Main, Rütten & Loening].

Sombart W., 1928, *Der moderne Kapitalismus. Historisch-systematische Darstellung des gesamteuropäischen Wirtschaftslebens von seinen Anfängen bis zur Gegenwart*, Paperback ed., 3 vol., Munich.

Sombart W., 1962, *The Jews and Modern Capitalism*, New York [ed. orig. 1911, *Die Juden und das Wirtschaftsleben*, Leipzig].

Stark R., 2005, *The Victory of Reason. How Christianity Led to Freedom, Capitalism, and Western Success*, New York, Random House.

Swanson G. E., 1967, *Religion and Regime: A Sociological account of the Reformation*, University of Michigan Press.

Swatos W. H. Jr., Kivisto P., 'Max Weber as Christian Sociologist', in *Journal for the Scientific Study of Religion*, Vol. 30, No. 4 (Dec. 1991), pp. 347–362.

Tawney, R. H., 1967 [ed. orig. 1922], *La religione e l'origine del capitalismo*, Milano, Feltrinelli.

Treiber H., (eds.), 1993, *Per leggere Max Weber*, Padova, CEDAM.

Troeltsch E., 1987 [Ed. orig. 1906], *Protestantism and Progress: The Significance of Protestantism for the Rise of the Modern World*, Toronto, Fortress Press.

Turner B. S., 'Islam, Capitalism and the Weber theses', in *The British Journal of Sociology*, Vol. 25, No. 2 (Jun. 1974), pp. 230–243.

Tversky A., 'Ambiguity Aversion and Comparative Ignorance', in *Quarterly Journal of Economics*, Vol. 110, No. 3 (1995), pp. 585–603.

Tyler L. L., 'The Protestant Ethic Among the Black Muslims', in *Phylon*, Vol 27, No. 1 (1966).
Walker G. P. C., 'Capitalism and the Reformation', in *The Economic History Review*, Vol. 8, No. 1 (Nov., 1937), pp. 1–19.
Warner, R. S., 1970, 'The Role of Religious Ideas and the Use of Models in Max Weber's Comparative Studies of Non-capitalist Societies', in *Journal of Economic History*, No. 3, pp. 74–99.
Weber M., 1930, *The Protestant Ethic and the Spirit of Capitalism*, London, Unwin Hyman [ed. orig. 1905, *Die protestantische Ethik und der Geist des Kapitalismus*].
Weber M., 1993, *The Sociology of Religion*, Vol. I–IV, Boston, Beacon Press [ed. orig. 1920, *Gesammelte Aufsätze zur Religionssoziologie*].
Weber M., 2003, *General Economic History*, Dover, New York [ed. orig. 1923, Wirtschaftsgeschichte].
Winckelmann J., (eds.), 1968, *Die protestantische Ethik II: Kritiken und Antikritiken*, Siebenstern, München.
Zaret D., 1992, 'Calvin Covenant Theology and the Weber Thesis', in *British Journal of Sociology*, No. 43 (1992), pp. 369–391.
Zhao H., Seibert S. E., 'The Big Five Personality Dimensions and Entrepreneurial Status: A Meta-Analytical Review', in *Journal of Applied Psychology*, Vol. 91, No. 2 (2006), pp. 259–271.
Ziegert Van S., 2006, *Global Spaces of Chinese Culture. Diasporic Chinese Communities in the United States and Germany*, New York, Routledge.

CHAPTER 4

From History to the Present

> Men are wont to set the highest value on those things upon which they are sensible their interest chiefly depends. And this renders time so exceedingly precious, because our eternal welfare depends on the improvement of it.
>
> —Jonathan Edwards

4.1 North American Puritanism and Capitalism

4.1.1 Evolution into Modernity

This chapter opens the way to my second main concern: could Weber's theory still be valid today? Obviously, this question was not behind Weber's intention. His primary aim was to show which role the Protestant ethic played for the genesis of the spirit of capitalism during sixteenth to seventeenth centuries, as he looked at the first stages of modern capitalism. However, despite his claims, many of the assertions and conclusions contained in his subsequent study on Puritanism, the Protestant sects and the spirit of capitalism, were made on the basis of contemporary observations among American Protestants during the early twentieth century. Yet, both Weber and Tawney were very pessimistic about the role that a 'ghost' of the Protestant professional ethic could play in advanced stages of capitalism where religious motivations tend to disappear and work finds no other meaning than the mere satisfaction of

O. Palombaro, *Christianity and Capitalism in China*,
https://doi.org/10.1007/978-981-97-3549-5_4

personal needs (Weber, 2002 [ed. orig. 1905], p. 185). This view assumes that modern capitalism, once set in motion, functions largely without any continuing influence from religion.

It must be clarified however, in tune with all the neo-Weberian approach and the social attitude models, that even if the theological basis disappeared, the ethos generated by such beliefs can still exert its influence in places and periods with no relation at all with its inception. The tension toward making profit tends to prevail even to the present, through a dynamic relationship between ethical systems and economic life. Scholars are usually very skeptical about any effort to actualize Weber's theory (Bouma, 1973; Delacroix and Nielsen, 2001). Through a quantitative and comparative study of the early accurate data available from the late nineteenth century, those authors state that industrial capitalism was not facilitated more in Protestant countries. One of their first mistakes however is trying to invalidate Weber's thesis by only focusing on Europe and basing their conclusions on evidence dated from two to three hundred years after the period of time when the Protestant ethic influenced the genesis of the spirit of capitalism. Such spirit was an ethic and attitudinal ideal-type that, once again, has nothing to do with industrial capitalism or any sort of economic development.

Other scholars (Cantoni, 2012; 2014) based only on quantitative indicators, not entirely congruent with the thesis that they want to falsify,[1] lacking a clear understanding of Weber's terminology, incurred in serious issues of misinterpretation. Even if one were to take their conclusions on the impossibility of actualizing Weber's theory, the features of what they call the 'common interpretation' of Weber's theory are a total misunderstanding of his sociological argument. The attitudes and mental predispositions that Weber associates positively with certain behaviors

[1] Cantoni tries to measure the impact of Protestant religious affiliation on economic growth through population figures such as city sizes, city growth or fertility. I am not denying the importance of quantitative methods. Weber, for example, used quantitative indicator in his introductory stage of the book but, according to my point of view, those dimensions cited by Cantoni have little to do with the core thesis of Weber. The German sociologist looked primarily to a specific Calvinistic belief and how such belief impacted the economic ethos. I suggest that, together with appropriate quantitative indicators, including for the United States, such as working hours, employment rates, labor force participation, such dynamic may be observable mainly through a critic of the historical evidence provided by Weber and on a micro level primarily through a qualitative research design more appropriate to the objective (Cantoni, 2014, 2012).

were not common to all Protestant branches. That's why some authors (Kim, 1977) correctly address the fact that religious affiliation is a less adequate measure than the particular religious belief, when assessing religion's effect on behavior. Also, many scholars completely leave out the case of United States, a case that by the late nineteenth century was already the center of reflections rotating around the Protestant ethic and the fast rise of capitalism.

Starting from other presuppositions, many quantitative and qualitative findings (Merton, 1957; Lenski, 1961; Willems, 1968; Cowley and Ballweg, 1971; Kim, 1977; Verba et al. 1993; Barker and Carman, 2000) show that the actualization of Weber's theory is still supportable. It has been clearly observed on a macro level by some scholar (Feldmann, 2007) that countries in which the largest portion of the population practices Protestant religion have substantially higher labor force participation and higher employment rates. Other studies on religion and economy tell that the particular case of Calvinist Protestantism confirms to have a dynamic influence on honesty, work ethic and economic performance (McCleary and Barro, 2006; 2003). This then certainly means that, although historical changes and conflicting evidences must be taken into consideration, Weber's theory still has an area of authenticity. What those studies fail to identify is the central element of such theory. This, in my view, can be better understood through a clear explanation of the beliefs under my investigation, their evolution in history (Miegge, 2010) and their impact in the spirit of capitalism that has become global, rather than relying on mere economic indicators.

4.1.2 Protestantism Becomes 'Americanized'

This evolution concerns primarily the historical passage that gradually led large portions of Protestantism to emigrate from continental Europe to the United States. Weber's interest on the American evolution of Protestantism was marginal, since his primary purpose was to identify the role of the Protestant ethic in the early stages of the Reformation in Western Europe. However, several scholars after him pointed out the absolute relevance of the Protestant ethic for the case of North America, from the Puritan era onward (Bottum, 2014; Harrison, 2012; Huntington, 2001; Landes, 1998). The historical passage of Protestantism into the New World was responsible for two major transformations that occurred in Protestantism: (i) its de-institutionalization through the breaking of dissident Protestantism with the mainly institutional and national European churches toward the New World seen as a fresh 'Promised Land'; (ii) its syncretic development, the inevitable progressive mix of the different branches of the Reformation into a heterogeneous scale of beliefs even inside the same single Calvinistic branch (Durston and Eales, 1996).

As it was the case with Protestantism spreading in countries of Western Europe, like the Netherlands, England, part of France or the Scandinavian countries, so it was for the pilgrim fathers and Puritans that came in New England. They came both for economic and religious reasons, to build a 'wilderness Zion' a 'New American Israel'. Puritanism was almost in its entirety strongly Calvinistic. One of the main elements that characterized Puritanism as a religious movement was the submission of every aspect of life, including work and money, under the higher purpose of bringing glory to God. Puritanism developed first in England through the efforts to reform the official Church of England. Having experienced dramatic conversions, the Puritans felt the need to separate themselves from the mass of the unregenerate members of the high Church of England to reform human history. Their zeal was displayed into standardized patterns of behavior intended to revive religion into every aspect of life (Simpson, 1955). Puritanism was characterized by great influential preachers and theologians like Isaac Watts, John Owen, Richard Sibbes, Thomas Brooks, John Bunyan, John Flavel, Thomas Goodwin, Matthew Henry, Thomas Watson, William Perkins, Richard Baxter, Samuel Rutherford, John Winthrop, etc.... Those were brilliant intellectual minds that influenced the Anglo-Saxon world for generations. Their movement spread abroad also through the influence of Dutch and Scottish diviners from a Calvinist and Reformed background. Yet the king of England and the authorities of the national Church of England responded with persecution to the efforts of Puritans, which culminated with the Uniformity Act of 1662, when many puritans were expelled from their posts or forced to compile with the directions of the national church.

Through this began the great exodus of the Pilgrim Fathers toward the New World. The Pilgrims and Puritans that migrated at Plymouth and the Massachusetts Bay would set about to order their lives in a way that fostered the practice of piety in all that they did. They were zealots who envisioned a theocratic society based on the Bible. Their austere heritage is a vital part of the American history and heritage to this day. A good Puritan could have been identified as industrious, thrifty, practicing inflexible integrity in his business dealings, brought up in the pursue of a calling with sober living and purpose, where temperance was considered a Christian duty, having a propensity to link religious faithfulness with economic prosperity, virtues that were bound to bring about plenty in an abundant promised land (Lambert, 2003). Hard work perceived and promoted as a duty to be accomplished was a religiously based value toward God. Weber and a vast number of scholars after him up until today (Barlow, 2015; Klein, 2013; Burg, 2012; Hewett, 2012; AA. VV., 2011; Tipson, 2010; Le Beau, 2008; Shulevitz, 2001; Beder, 2000; Mulder, 1976; Foster, 1972; Little, 1966) identified in this type of Puritan religious experience the historical survival of the Calvinist work ethic in the New World.

One example of the endurance of the difference between world-rejecting asceticism and inner-worldly asceticism can be found in the change from the external to the internal 'spiritual resolutions' of Puritanism. In this sense someone could compare two religious authors that use the same word, such as: 'spiritual resolution' but they intend it in a totally different way. In the first case of the Catholic monk Brother Lawrence, the term refers to exterior practices that a man can display in his life as a monk to be closer to God. In the second case of the American Puritan preacher Jonathan Edwards, exponent of the 'new light Calvinism', the same term refers to internal practices of self-examination and commitment that any person can embrace in order to pursue the glory of God in every aspect of the mundane (Piper, 1974, pp. 59–69). Being among the chief exponents of this Puritan ethic, Jonathan Edwards often put special emphasis on hard work in his sermons like '*The Preciousness Of Time And The Importance Of Redeeming It*' (Edwards, 2003 [ed. orig. 1734]).

> Consider what hath been said of the preciousness of time, how much depends upon it, how short and uncertain it is, how irrecoverable it will be when gone. If you have a right conception of these things, you will be more choice of your time than of the most fine gold. Every hour and moment will seem precious to you.[2]

Puritans were pursuing an orderly organized life, an ascetic work, a zeal and diligence against any kind of idleness (Cohen, 2002). It is enough to

[2] Edwards J., 2003, [ed. orig. 1734] *The Preciousness Of Time And The Importance Of Redeeming It*, A Puritan Mind, Yale.

go through the pages of treatises by William Perkins on the particular calling to see the centrality of the theoretical model of Weber concerning the *Beruf* even several centuries after the Protestant Reformation:

> A vocation or calling is a certain kind of life, ordained and imposed on man by God. [...] God is the General, appointing to every man his particular post. God Himself is the author and beginning of callings. [...] There is ambition and envy when we see others placed in better callings and conditions than ourselves. [...] Must we not labor in our callings to maintain our families? I answer: This must be done: but it is not the scope and end of our lives. The true end of our lives is to do service to God in serving man.[3]

It is possible to see here the practicalization of the Weberian *Beruf* in every aspect of worldly duties through a strong Calvinistic emphasis. In the same way another Puritan, Cotton Mather argues:

> A Christian should follow his occupation with contentment. Contentment is no little part of your homage to that God who hath placed you where you are. [...] When God hath called me to a place, He would have His gifts improved to their best advantage. [...] A Christian should not be too ready to fall out with his calling. Many a man, merely from covetousness and discontent, throws up his business. A man ought to pursue a calling so that he may glorify God. [...] We may not aim only at our own, but at the public good. Therefore, faith will not think it hath a comfortable calling unless it will serve, not only its own turn, but the turn of other men. [...] In our occupations, we spread the nets, but it is God who brings into our nets all that come into them.[4]

Again many elements proper of Calvinism (*Inner-worldly Asceticism, Beruf, Glory of God, Perseverance of the Saints, Role of Sacred Scriptures*, etc.) became the practical guidance and pressure toward working hard and pursuing business success. Particularly interesting are also the intellectual reflections of another Puritan, Richard Baxter, on the search for the common welfare by the Christian:

[3] Perkins W., 1603, *Treatise of the Vocations or Callings*, Princeton, New Jersey, p. 56.

[4] Mather C., 1825, *Essays to Do Good*, Chalmers and Collins, Glasgow.

> The public welfare, or the good of the many is to be valued above our own. Every man, therefore, is bound to do all he can for others, especially for the church and commonwealth. [...] Choose that employment or calling in which you may be most serviceable to God. Choose not that in which you may be most rich or honorable in the world, but that in which you may do most good. [...] In choosing a trade or calling, the first consideration should be the service of God and the public good, and therefore, that calling that most conduceth to the public good is to be preferred.[5]

In a similar direction Thomas Watson's invitations on diligence, in addition to many other Puritans like John Preston or Robert Crowley, help us to single out their strong emphasis on hard work:

> Religion does not seal warrants to idleness. God sets all His children to work. God will bless our diligence, not our laziness. [...] Neither covetousness nor hard work can make men rich, since God alone blesses with success. [...] We must labor, not for our own good, but for the good of others.[6]

All those principles were derived directly from the *Sacred Scriptures*, particularly from the continuous practical exhortations for business contained in the Old Testament (see, for example, Proverbs 14, 23 18, 9 19, 15 23, 21). Much of what is now recognized as distinctively American in thought, culture and tradition, is actually derived from the Puritan temper of the sixteenth and seventeenth centuries here displayed. Being Calvinist, Scripturally oriented, seeing themselves as the chosen people, the Puritans continually struggled in a fight against any kind of sinfulness, including laziness and work (Gaer and Siegel, 1964).

In fact idleness, luxury and extravagance were considered evil threats that needed to be overcome through hard work (Pointer, 1988). Individual success and social prosperity were extremely dependent upon virtue, whereas national sins were leading America as well as the individuals to experience punishment and economic crisis. Religious contentment here did not mean inactivity or passive acceptance of the status quo. Rather the Puritan had to exhibit economic ambition and economic satisfaction, simultaneously avoiding all forms of luxury. Their piety was

[5] AA. VV., 2000, *The Practical Works of Richard Baxter*, Vol. I-IV, Soli Deo Gloria Publications, Morgan, p. 585.

[6] Phillips M., 2001, *Puritan View of Work*, Grace Baptist, Fremont.

considered essential to man's temporal prosperity, enhancing rather than undermining their chances for a happy successful life (Pointer, 1988). Yet those Puritans, contrary to Weber's thought, denied that wealth was a sign of individual salvation, instead it was viewed as God's blessing for their lives.

For example, the Puritan preacher Richard Baxter, contrary to Weber's own interpretation of him, in his *Christian Directory* never relates work to the doctrine of salvation nor does he conceive hard work and economic success as a way to be sure of someone's state of election. On the other hand, Baxter opposed work to 'idleness' and underlined how diligence puts off the dangerous temptations or confusions of a life without the orientation of a calling (Baxter, R., *Christian Directory*, in Miegge M., pp. 144–146). This message represents an important example for the precondition of the inner-worldly asceticism, but it has nothing to do with predestination or anxiety. An open invitation to embrace inner-worldly asceticism then is the only intention of Baxter when he talks about the 'moral misery' of men that needs to be removed through work. He does not connect then this invitation to the topic of salvation, which supposedly causes a state of anxiety about their eternal destiny among listeners. The believer could come to salvation only through faith in Jesus Christ apart from any human effort or good works. The good works of a redeemed person are possible only because of the grace of God and they are not the foundation of his eternal salvation, rather they are a consequence of his salvation. The only solution for men, in the words of another important Puritan, was the establishment of a 'personal relationship with God' (Bunyan, 2003 [1668]).

It is true that many times prominence in the business world was the primary prerequisite for leadership in the church, encouraging an attachment to business by Puritan believers in a wholehearted but tempered manner. Those principles find their roots in Calvinist theology and can be clearly observed in the collection of Puritan prayers: their emphasis on self-discipline, self-restraint, frugality, diligence and freedom from anxiety in the realm of work (Bennett, 1975). The Congregationalists and Puritans who founded the Plymouth colony and the Massachusetts Bay colony were mainly English Calvinists and even the radical Whigs of the American Revolution were inspired by ideals that find their ultimate root in Calvinist theology. Without a theological understanding of Puritanism, there's no understanding of America. Sociological studies of Puritanism like the classic of Robert King Merton on the role of Puritanism for the establishment of modern science show how pervasive and successful such disciplined way of life was in every aspect of society (Cohen, 1990 [ed. orig. 1936]).

But what was the main element in the beliefs of the Puritans able to promote such strong work ethic? According to Max Weber such work ethic was due to a series of religious beliefs such as the belief in someone's calling for his life (*Beruf*) or the inner-worldly asceticism clearly emphasized in many sermons of Puritans such as William Perkins or Richard Baxter (Miegge, 2010). But the main element that according to Weber is able to generate such economic action is once again the anxiety about someone's salvation derived by the belief in predestination proper of Calvinism and internalized even more strongly by the Puritans compared to their forefather John Calvin. It is true that a core of the Puritan creed was for the individual to work out his own salvation, marshaled as a whole society of regenerated people into one united array. It did not merely regulate misconduct but inspired and directed all the conduct of individuals (Waller, 1973). Yet Puritans, being Calvinist, remained champions of the doctrines of grace by which man can be saved only by grace alone through faith alone. All those efforts were not exerted in order to find assurance of salvation but in order to 'work out someone's salvation' according to a specific Calvinist doctrine already mentioned: perseverance of the saints.

In this picture there seem to be no trace of Weber's anxiety about eternal salvation. Weber was led to focus on this aspect possibly because of some hyper-Calvinistic fringes or Quaker recollections of the time written in diaries. But it remains a misunderstanding. The case has been made by Weber and some subsequent scholars that some puritan writings (for example Bunyan, 2013 [ed. orig. 1666]) displayed the presence of such strong anxiety. But those scholars forget to mention that Bunyan is giving an autobiography of his life before embracing the Protestant faith. The state of anxiety therefore is precisely the absence of such identification with the Puritan faith but once the individual becomes a Puritan, he then experiences after his conversion a perpetual state of assurance as the second part of the book testifies.

Furthermore, when using some of those Puritan writings for his argument, Weber was mistaken in not considering the Puritan distinction between 'assurance of faith', obtainable only believing in Jesus and not through any actions or feelings, and the 'way of faith', the invitation to listen to the Word of God and to seek God. The 'way of faith' by itself never provides the 'assurance of faith' because, as I've already said, evidence of faith cannot create assurance, as Weber wrongly assumed. To give an illustration, according to this Puritan perspective, in a family only God can provide assurance of faith in a son. Parents can address their child to the way of faith, but this does not create saving faith in the child. When Puritans exhort the use of the 'means of grace', they never meant that those means 'gave the right' to believe. Once again, this issue refers to the doctrine of the *perseverance of the saints*, in confirming one's salvation and not to the general matter of obtaining salvation (Hulse, 2000; part III, C. 6). Contrary to Weber's view, throughout almost all expressions of Puritanism, more than in any other Protestant tradition, there always has been a predominant attention to the work of the Holy Spirit, and not in the efforts of men in their total depravity, in order to produce the obedience to faith (McNeill, 1957).

The cycle of self-examination, repentance, exaltation and good works mentioned often in Puritan writings, could strengthen assurance but it was not for this purpose that such set of practices was followed, since the elects already had their assurance through regeneration (Simpson, 1955). Not only such evidence of anxiety about someone's salvation is lacking throughout Calvinism but even Puritanism, if exception is made for few hyper-Calvinist fringes, never held such belief. On the other hand, what was really unique about Puritanism was the strong stress on the doctrine of the *Perseverance of the Saints*. Puritans, in accord with Calvinism, believed that salvation was a work of God, obtained by grace through faith in Christ's sacrifice at the cross for the forgiveness of sins. Yet true faith in Christ is necessarily followed by good works, through a repenting soul, as a result, and not a precondition, of salvation. In order to avoid easy commitments and false conversions often Puritan preachers were pointing out that those who claimed to have put their faith in Christ for salvation but lived in a lifestyle of constant sin were never truly converted in the first place. For this reason, the doctrine of the perseverance of the saints led unconverted people to self-examination and the people inside the community to a constant control of their personal conduct, to a diligent and severe display of their faith in every aspect of life. The discipline of self-trial, the perpetual self-accusation so common in Puritan diaries and poems came out of this belief. This was done not in order to achieve salvation but as a result of their belief in the perseverance of the saints.

All those principles in Puritan interpretations came increasingly to imply an active commitment to one's career as a service to God, in a progressive practicalization of Calvinism in the New World (AA. VV., 1990, p. 630). It is possible to find some clear example of this in the daily life of those Puritans in the colonies, where the religious activity and economic activity were not opposites but significantly overlapping. The Puritan merchants in their counting houses were able to make a handsome profit as well as receiving through it an assurance of their divine calling (AA. VV., 1990). America was also the land of arrival for all the religious groups of radical Protestantism such as Independents, Separatists, Quakers, Baptists, Huguenots, Methodists and many dissident groups coming from the Protestant Reformation which acted as levelers of the old system of society. They composed the wide spectrum of the new Protestant wave and were guided by the search for religious freedom in the New England.

Hard work, frugality and diligence found their complete and deeper expression in the case of what was becoming the United States of America. Particularly interesting was the concept of impersonality according to which the ethical orientations of the Puritans, Baptists, German and Dutch Pietists were more compatible with the rational economic action than Catholicism, Islam or other religious groups that migrated later on to the New World. This was because those Protestant merchants thought that it was ethically virtuous to treat all customers the same. No partiality was to be shown on the basis of personal characteristics, other than those dictated by the marketplace (AA. VV., 1990). They developed a work ethic that again was chiefly derived strongly from Calvin's own ideas (Bernbaum and Steer, 1986). All the features today so central and common to the American capitalistic spirit: economic rationality, requiring equal and fair treatment according to market principles, find their roots in this religious historical background. Through the revivals and evangelistic preaching of Jonathan Edwards and George Whitefield (both Calvinists) the thirteen colonies experienced unprecedented cases of mass conversion (Latourette, 1975) that gradually led to the first great awakening (1731–1755), which preceded the political revolution that gave birth to the United States. The leading force of those awakenings were the religious sects that in less than one hundred years passed from a thousand to billion members (Finke and Stark, 2005). In later chapters I will show why such Protestant revivals are crucial in understanding the economic uprising also for the case of China.

Many studies focusing on the case of the United States show clearly that the mixture between religious orientations and economic growth were recurrent and widespread (AA. VV., 1990; p. 629). This ethical premise didn't stop with the Puritan movement but it involved even the future development of the enlightenment in personalities more prone to Deism like Benjamin Franklin or Thomas Jefferson. Having been raised in this Puritan context, they both were debtors to this specific religious set of beliefs for their economic propensity and outlook on life. Both the Puritan work ethic and Benjamin Franklin's plan of moral perfection were characterized by an emphasis on industry, thrift, frugality, sobriety, honesty and charitableness. The impact of the Puritan ethic on the American society flourished also indirectly from founding fathers of America such as Patrick Henry, George Washington, James Madison, John Adams, Alexander Hamilton, Noah Webster, John Hancock, Francis Scott Key, Andrew Jackson, Abraham Lincoln and many other influential figures that had explicit Protestant aspirations and where not shy about connecting their ethics to their belief and their ultimate origin in the Protestant faith (Lambert, 2003).

These were the distinctive qualities of a man in the workplace which gave him readiness for success. Opposite concepts such as: idleness, intemperance, prodigality, sloth, extravagance were believed to lead to economic ruin and poverty (Pointer, 1988). Puritan figures like Thomas Hooker, John Winthrop, William Bradford, Roger Williams or even William Penn are just few examples among those Bible-believers that influenced predominantly the religious, economical and institutional foundations of the United States of America. Such all-encompassing influence of the American religiosity was very important for the shaping of the politics of a '*nation under God*' and an economy based on the motto: '*in God we trust*' (Moore, 2005; Kosmin and Lachman, 1993). The positive separation between church and state, the absence of an official religious institution, coupled with the general tolerance toward all religious minorities, and the public expression of religion in all the aspects of life (Shriver, 2011), fostered liberal tendencies in trade, commerce and low taxation. These were all unprecedented examples of how far the Protestant ethic was able to provide the good soil for the development of the American nation (Wagner, 1964). Calvinism among many frameworks, first in Europe then in America, provided models of social discipline and executive administration. The institutionalization of religious pluralism contributed also to the conventionalization of intellectual pluralism (Jepperson and Meyer, 2011).

Such heritage guided America up until its emerging as the main global economic power throughout all the nineteenth and twentieth centuries. Frank Chodorov argues that the Protestant ethic was considered for a long time as a crucial element for the success in the campaign of any American political figure. Politicians had to measure up with the standard of a 'self-made man' that made his way up the ladder through sheer ability, self-reliance, perseverance in the face of hardship and responsibility (Chodorov, 2011; Duncan, 2014). The influence of the Protestant ethic in America was not only active in the political realm (Mocombe, 2012; Stevens, 2010), but it had also an impact in the general work ethic of the American population. Interestingly, some scholar (Pointer, 1988) focused on the example of Philadelphia Presbyterians and their quest for morality, capitalism and economic success during the eighteenth century. Many pastors from that same area frequently preached that it was a Christian duty to increase one's and one's neighbor's worldly prosperity choosing the right calling and pursuing it diligently. The image of the quite orderly and prosperous man with a successful family life and work, was promoted through the correct application of the Bible and its demands on ethics. Pointer shows the spread of Calvinistic ideas in those Presbyterian circles such as Christian's duty to prosper, self-help as the way to wealth, Christian piety as an asset to temporal success, the ordering and disciplining effects of Christian morality, etc. ... There, a convergence between Protestant and middle-class values was possible. Philadelphia, back then the most Presbyterian-Calvinist of any of America's major cities, was permeated with the 'true' path to economic success: honest, persistence and toil.

Niall Ferguson, looking to the data of working hours and employment by country from the Organization for Economic Co-operation and Development (OECD), confirmed that the experience of North America in the past quarter-century offers an unexpected confirmation of the Protestant ethic. At the same time, according to Ferguson, during the nineteenth and twentieth centuries there has been a decline of the Protestant work ethic in Europe. Together with the triumph of secularization in Western Europe, the author points out the simultaneous decline of Protestantism. A steady decline of working hours and employment rates can reveal some of the misunderstandings of the critics to Weber's thesis. Those critics neglected the evolution of the spirit of capitalism in its transmigration to the industrious context of the United States, where the Protestant work ethic was alive and well throughout all the twentieth century (Ferguson,

2003; Mccloud and Mirola, 2009). Other scholars stressed this strong relationship between socioeconomic factors and denominational preferences for the American case. They pointed out the compatibility between the religious ethic of America and capitalism, suggesting a positive relationship between religious faith and such economic measures (Berger, 1969) (Table 4.1).

4.1.3 Impact on Beliefs

In this American landscape, Calvinism did play a unique role in shaping the Protestant ethic. Calvin's concepts of God, purpose and duty, with its elements of freedom were crucial in the development of American liberalism and democracy. Some scholars pointed out that even today among the different religious denominations the Presbyterians, one of the main Calvinist denominations, tend to be considerably wealthier. This is because they are usually better educated, in terms of degrees pro capita, than most of the religious group in America, disproportionately represented in the upper classes of American business and politics (Drummond, 2011). However, fewer of the general populace if compared to America's beginnings belongs today to religious denominations properly identified as part of the Calvinistic tradition (Rauscher, 1997). Calvinism has suffered from several fragmentations, due also to the fight between liberal theology and conservatives. Such is the case among the Presbyterian Church in America, the Dutch Reformed Church and other Calvinistic denominations, both in Europe and then in parts of United States.

Between the eighteenth and nineteenth centuries, historic Calvinistic denominations became unable to break free from all forms of traditionalism. The influence of Baptists, Methodists and other churches was very crucial as well. Although those groups initially faced persecution in the thirteen colonies, forbidden to preach by the state church, their social impact during the First and Second Great Awakenings surpassed both the Anglican state church as well as the Congregational and Presbyterians, forcing traditional churches to keep in step with religious liberty during the revolutionary era, and experience syncretistic developments. The advent of separation between church and state, together with the voluntary-based adherence to religious practice, represented the strength of an American competitive and fervent religiosity (Finke and Stark, 2005). An interesting case is the one of Charles Grandison Finney (1792–1875) that although being a Presbyterian minister, left the denomination

Table 4.1 Timeline that summarize the evolution of the spirit of capitalism according to the analysis

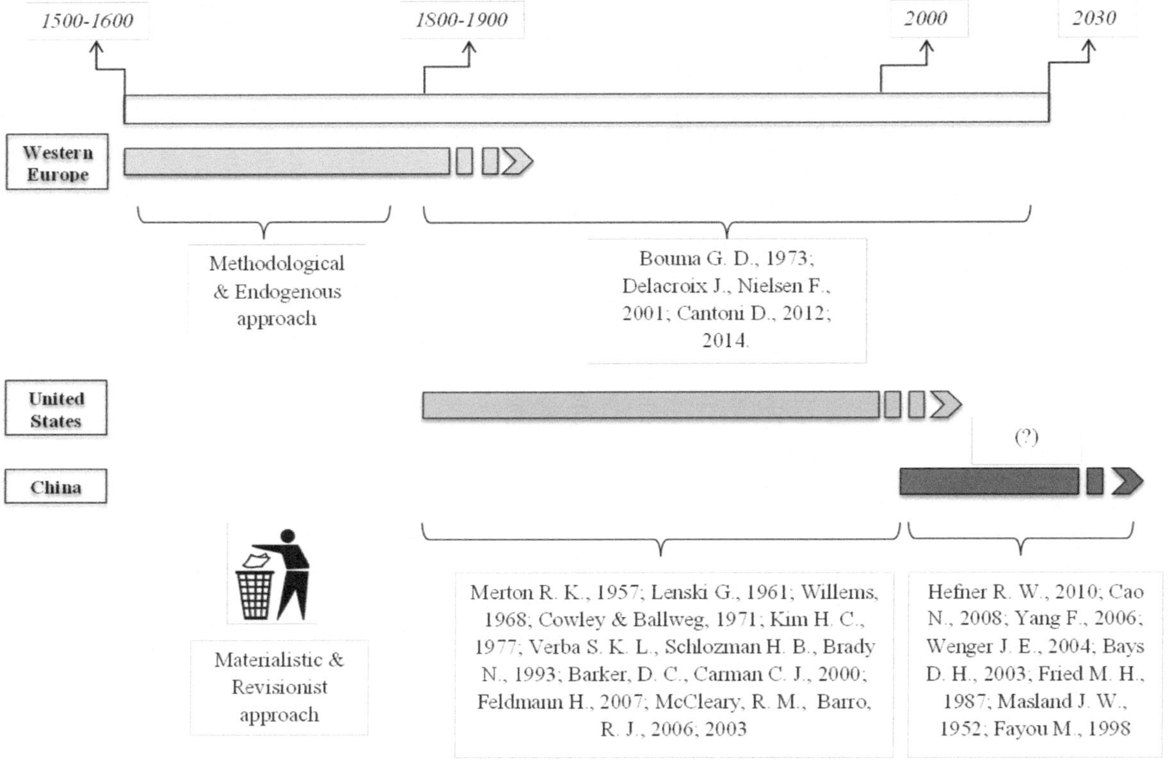

and led a revival that is known as the Second Great Awakening. While facing some setbacks, Calvinistic beliefs and values were still very diffused among Protestant denominations and sects in America (Kim, 1977).

Still to this day religion in United States remains an important source of guidance in the ways individuals make even their economic choices. The belief of calling survived, displaying itself an intrinsic commitment to work, a desire to make work a meaningful experience. Approximately 30% of US citizens say they feel that God has called them to their particular kind of work, 25% say that religious values influence their choice of a career (AA. VV., 1990, p. 635). The foundation for such legitimation of hard work finds its root in the Judeo-Christian tradition. People are in this case seeing themselves as 'stewards of the world', with individual responsibility, even in their own budgeting and spending, seeking to use their talents wisely and responsibly. Having a Protestant religious majority, many in United States pursue such considerations still to this day, being a nation still permeated by this cultural influence.

Calvinism is still strongly active today. It is possible to find a clear inheritance of the Calvinistic beliefs in many of today's evangelical and reformed preaching: from J. I. Packer, to R.C. Sproul R. C., or Timothy Keller, Alister McGrath and Michael Horton. Calvinistic doctrines such as the Perseverance of the Saints, for example, recently came back into the scene of popular mainstream American evangelical churches. The popular preaching of men like John Piper, Paul Washer, Steve Lawson or John MacArthur, in their emphasis on assurance as well as true repentance, holiness, self-examination and sanctification, speaks for itself (Washer, 2008).

From the United States the influence of such values has gradually opened to a more global focus. Yet it was from the United States that in the nineteenth century Christianity, particularly Protestantism, had its greatest numerical growth. With the advent of the industrial revolution all the different minorities that arrived in the United States in their migration were pressured to act and behave like the Protestant majority. This created a particular type for the case of United States, where the Protestant ethic can be observed even outside the borders of Protestantism, since those elements have become part of the 'cultural' traits of society as a whole. I find some examples of such ethic in the universalization of work as a 'religious duty' for the entire American middle class, including for family life, homeschooling and patriotism. Another example is individualism. In the American context individualism has often been conceived as a moral virtue, contrary to the traditional European portrait of individualism usually as a sign of incivility and chaos. Nevertheless, it remains difficult to isolate the American Protestant ethic into specific borders (McClosky, 1984).

Another consequence of the syncretistic development of American Protestantism, is that it is no longer as easy to isolate the Weberian preconditions that I've mentioned before in a clear way. The only option is to seek to systematize the different religious traditions, through the use of ideal-types. With this procedure it is possible to at least identify the inheritance of Calvinism, not just in the concept of predestination, but also in the perpetual assurance of salvation. What is interesting to notice from such ideal-types, is that all the religious branches holding the belief in the perpetual assurance of salvation are the same branches that generally have higher political participation, support free-market principles and display attitudes of acceptance toward economic individualism (Means, 1966; Verba et al. 1993; Barker, 2000). Those contemporary American evangelicals are doctrinally conservative and while they are not always Calvinistic in the strictest sense of the word, still share much of its assumptions. The explanatory table in the previous pages gives a synthetic view of the evolution of the spirit of capitalism as well as the different ecclesiastical contexts where it is observed. My starting point was the suggestion of a scholar concerning the reality of such phenomenon (Means, 1966). Not every single denomination necessarily fits into one category. An interesting case in this regard is the one of the Southern Baptists, one of the largest Protestant branches in America, a blend from different traditions. It is easy to identify churches where the belief in the perpetual assurance of salvation is still held, as it is the case for most of the churches of the groups b) and some of the groups c).

It is also true that there are churches where the perpetual assurance of salvation is not universally held, such as the case of many Anglicans, Pentecostal and progressive churches. The case d), in the example of the Methodists or the Congregationalists, also represent an interesting case, which once again might be able to explain Weber's misunderstanding of the anxiety about salvation. John Wesley, founder of Methodism, believed in assurance (although with some caveat) as well as Lutherans or Congregationalists, but in many of those cases assurance is not something as perpetual as it is for the peculiar case of Calvinism.

Another matter not accounted for by Weber, is the role of Anabaptism and other streams of Christianity, which apart from Calvinism have exercised a role in shaping democracy in America. The formation of liberal democracy in United States was indeed possible through a union between the spirit of freedom and the spirit of religion (Tocqueville A., *Democracy in America*, [ed. orig. 1835–1840], in Aron, 1996). This union, together with equality of conditions and abolition of traditional class distinctions, were largely inherited from beliefs peculiar to the Anabaptist tradition and other more radical dissident Protestant movements. While those radical groups often willingly avoided involvement in politics or worldly professions, their influence in the strive for freedom of religion, separation between church and state, a general distrust toward the state and many other aspects so deeply rooted in the American mindset are connected (Adamo P. [et alii], 1994).

Another element underlined by Weber in his study of sects which will be very important for my research on Chinese Protestantism in coming chapters has to do with the role of a religious belief as a 'business card' of the quality of the individual to develop trust. This was a very crucial element for the success and development of a capitalistic spirit (Fukuyama, 1995). To say this does not mean that sects were important simply due to their ability to activate a social network, but also due to their process of selection, which created reputation from the eyes of outsiders and trust.

In United States the connection between free economy and religious liberty can be clearly observed by having a closer rook to contemporary popular literature on business. Notions such as 'spiritual capital', virtuously successful business, or faith-based trust are all considered proper tools for any 'spiritual enterprise', in order to pursue business as a purpose (Roosevelt Malloch, 2008). Virtues often promoted by American Protestants such as leadership, courage, perseverance, discipline, justice, are more than a set of rules. They here become the basis of a successful spiritual enterprise (Roosevelt Malloch, 2008).

Several authors have underlined the economic impact of religious beliefs in the field of business ethics (Fox, 1987; Quinney, 1981; Wayne, 1989). The majority of these kind of writings are directed at American business owners, offering a practical approach on how to achieve a successful business (Maxwell, 2003). Ethic dilemmas and moral principles such as the 'golden rule' are applied to specific business practices, in order to promote economic success. A growing number of those writings, which are often from a Protestant background, stress the centrality of doing business by being ruled by Biblical principles (Tam, 1969). Applying this perspective to someone's life defines the realm of work for a Christian as a 'way–station of spiritual witness and service', a 'sacred stewardship' with its own special dignity (Henry, 1964). There is a 'theological view of work' at work here. Work is no longer seen as a 'necessary evil' or a 'product of the human curse' but as a good thing entrusted to humankind. Work is understood as a 'calling' and as a 'ministry opportunity' for Christians. Within this perspective, work is seen as a moral duty and an ethical responsibility to be fulfilled with excellency, in order to guard someone's spiritual and material status (Witherington, 2011).

Terms as vocation, calling, working for the kingdom of God, excellence, savings, transforming the world of business, dismantling the divide between 'sacred' and 'secular', are constantly emphasized by this literature of business ethics. Labor is more than a tool. It has strong value and purpose, it implies being a 'steward of the world, from the hands of the highest Boss: the Creator' (Bernbaum and Steer, 1986). The way by which this ethical premise shapes the conduct of readers involves motivation, which in turn results into a unique workstyle, unique methods, attitudes, strategies utilized to achieve results. Within this perspective the worker must have a good character and maniacal integrity, respecting authorities, taking responsibilities. He must see work as a service and a ministry to be done in excellence and with motivation. The worker must utilize his beliefs in order to face risk, crisis and failures (Sherman and Hendricks, 1987). At the same time sobriety, self-discipline, a sense of 'separation from the world', even if 'being involved in the world', gives a crucial balance to the conduct of those that follow this ethical premise (Peabody, 1974). Many of those popular American concepts are once again echoing Weber's literature and draw a strict connection between the workplace and a series of ethical pre-requisites such as justice, abiding with the law, honesty, agency between contrasting interests, ethical employer-employee relations, etc. ... All this set of ethical guidelines becomes necessary in order to achieve economic success (Hill, 1997).

Such findings are also confirmed by several studies in the field of sociology (Harrison, 1992, Fishman, 1989; Mayer and Sharp, 1962; Veroff et al. 1962). Those scholars point out the difference between the traditional Protestant beliefs and our contemporary work ethic, given the secular evolution of society. Yet these same authors still witness a survival of such influence, as these ideas are paralleled by beliefs proper of Protestantism, that influenced the emerging of free-market liberal ideas. One explanatory example of this survival is the economic and monetary theorization of Calvinistic principles such as *sovereignty of God*, financing the kingdom of God, the *role of Sacred Scriptures*. Gary North has provided an interesting analysis in this regard (North, 1973). It is possible to notice the inheritance of Benjamin Franklin's wisdom in business, for example in American business literature intended for the general public (Bland, 1972; Burkett, 1990; Cook, 1974; Covey, 1990; Devine, 1977; Egli and Hoerr, 1984).

In order to sum up this articulated mixture of religious beliefs, I present here a table that synthetizes the evolution of the Protestant ethic in the American context. Although this classification is useful for the explanatory purposes, it is still an approximation and it may not be completely in step with the far more syncretic nature of American Protestantism. A clear example of this is the case of infant baptism, which even though was part of Calvin's and Luther's theology, it is abandoned by many evangelical churches today. I observe the same trend for the case of branches coming from the Swiss Reformed tradition. On the other hand, Baptists and Southern Baptist traditions, at least historically, embraced much of the Calvinistic theology.

A clear example of the heterogeneous set of theological positions within American Protestantism today is the gradual mixture between what is known as Covenant theology, inherited from the Reformed theological tradition, and Dispensational theology, a more recent phenomenon (Scofield, 1999 [ed. orig. 1909]). Not all the beliefs proper of Calvinist, particularly the doctrines of grace, also known in the acronym T.U.L.I.P., survived inside those who would identify themselves as Calvinism, particularly for the case of the belief in limited atonement. This shows how doctrinal positions are far more fragmented today, between Amyraldism, hyper-Calvinism, New-Calvinism, five point Calvinism, four point Calvinism, etc. This development involves also the Anglicans, historically strongly divided between the national state church and other dissident groups within it (Bainton, 1958; Schorn-Schütte, 2001) (Table 4.2).

It is also true that materialism in American society today is also widespread. Some scholars argue that American capitalism encountered major difficulties at the end of the 1960s as a result of a growing tension between ways of relating to work based on Protestant asceticism and the blossoming of a mode of existence based on immediate consumer pleasure stimulated by credit and mass production. Materialism has come to coexist side by side with the traditional Puritan ethic. One can think of tele-evangelists or mega-churches, where the 'prosperity Gospel' or

Table 4.2 Evolution of Protestantism in the United States and their contribution to the American capitalist spirit

Reformation tradition	*German Lutheran*	*Swiss Reformed*	*Swiss Anabaptist*	*British Anglican*	*Mixed*	*Pentecostals*
Branches	Lutheranism, Evangelical Lutheran Churches, Missouri Synod, Wisconsin council of churches	Presbyterian, Presbyterian Church in America, Reformed, Huguenots, Waldensians, Boer Calvinism, Neo-orthodoxy, Paleo-orthodoxy	Congregationalism, Mennonites, Amish, Hutterites, Brethren, Baptists. Southern Baptists, Quakers	Church of England, Methodists, English Puritans, Episcopal	Modernism, Liberalism	Pentecostalism, Assemblies of God, church of God, Holiness movement, Church of the Nazarene, Adventists
Main beliefs and type of Leadership	a) Sola Scripture b) Sola Fide c) Sola Gratia d) Solus Christus e) Soli Deo Gloria *Centralized leadership*	a) Total depravity: b) Unconditional election; c) Limited Atonement: d) Irresistible grace; e) Perseverance of the saints *Centralized leadership*	Separation of powers, opposition to institutional churches, religious freedom, horizontal leadership, mystic spiritualism, *horizontal leadership*	National church, largely institutional, *traditional leadership*	Weak doctrinal Stand, adaptation to modern culture, *Intellectual leadership*	Charismatic manifestations, *Charismatic leadership*

(continued)

Table 4.2 (continued)

Reformation tradition	*German Lutheran*	*Swiss Reformed*	*Swiss Anabaptist*	*British Anglican*	*Mixed*	*Pentecostals*
Contributions to the American Capitalist Spirit	Beruf, professional work. Inner-worldly asceticism, universal education	Predestination, individualism, saving mentality, laissez-faire, universal literacy, bookkeeping, natural sciences, political constitutionalism	Freedom of conscience, revolutionary spirit, tolerance, subjectivism, enlightenment, women suffrage, distrust towards the state, democracy, minority status, break traditions, human rights	British empiricism, Universities, experimental science		
Perpetual assurance of Salvation	no	yes	yes/no	no	no	no

'Gospel of wealth' has spread. A famous example is Lakewood Church led by Joel Osteen. This church claims more that forty thousand members and it counts today as the largest church in America. A strong emphasis is made within these type of churches toward economic success.

Scholars believe that in United States, the Protestant ethic has lately declined. It has lost its ascetic frugality, being under the pressure of an ever-growing consumeristic society (Wisman and Davis, 2013). Modern Capitalism functions well under underlying restraints that for long time were embraced in Western societies but that now are fading. With the example of the prosperity Gospel today, controlling one's conduct or work ethic, leaves the place to the desire for quick money. Such love of money is common to all ages, and it is not what the spirit capitalism consists of: a control of the conduct, a saving mentality, a frugality, which mainly Calvinism had been able to provide with. We may wonder then, whether this phantomatic 'spirit of capitalism' has suddenly died or whether, as I will explore in the coming pages it might have once again changed locality.

4.2 Chinese Christianity and Capitalism

4.2.1 Religious Growth and the Advent of Capitalism

It is at this point that China finds its place in the analysis. It might come as a surprise to some to think of the People's Republic of China of being in anyway the next arena where Protestantism might play a central role in the development of Capitalism. Recently some studies have shed light on a large-scale unprecedented upsurge in religious attendance and religious association in East Asia as a whole (Hefner, 2010). The link between religious resurgence and economic development has already been investigated in the case of Taiwan (Lu et al. 2008). Other nations have experienced spiritual revivals as South Korea, Indonesia, Malaysia. One must however compare those cases with Hong Kong or Japan, where economic development took place without any major spiritual resurgence (Constable, 1994). Yet what is more surprising is how Asia's revitalizations has been taking place more recently in China, where the flourishing of neoliberal economic tendencies is taking place together with an underground spiritual renewal.

The reason why this book focuses on China therefore as a contemporary candidate for the Protestant ethic is the wide revival, taking place together with the rise of capitalism. It should surprise us that such religious revitalization is taking place in a country like China where historically monotheism has never been important (Fried, 1987), and secularism was the predominant voice through the Chinese Marxism of the recent past (Masland, 1952). Despite harsh persecution coming from the Chinese Communist Party, instead of decrease in religion data shows a substantial growth of religion. Christianity in China today is spreading more than any other religious affiliation. In particular the exponential growth of Protestantism stands out as the most prominent and fastest example of growth in Communist China. From only 700.000 Christians in 1949, before the Cultural Revolution even started, China counts today more than one hundred million Protestants. Some sources report that between 130 and 170 million of Protestant Christians exist in China (Robertson, 2009). More modest estimates talk about from 50 to 80 million Protestants in China (Bays, 2003). This estimate however underestimates the enormous amount of Christians belonging to underground churches. Even if we were to consider the most prudent estimations, the growth is still dramatic: Protestantism grew from 0.2% to 5.7% of the total population, whereas other forms of Christianity like Catholicism stay well below 2%.

For the case of Wenzhou under focus here, the estimates go well beyond 12%. China is home to more evangelical believers than any other nation (Baugus, 2014). Some say that by 2030 China could become the biggest Christian nation in the world, despite the persecution coming from the Communist Party (Yiwu, 2011; Yang, 2005). Control from the government and its ideological removal of religions, created a vacuum that actually led many to search answers in Christianity. More interesting in this case is also how together with the spreading of Christianity, it is possible to observe the growth of a particular form of capitalism in clear contradiction with the Marxist values upheld by the government (Guthrie, 1999, 2003; Krug, 2004; Knight and Song, 2005). Ever since the famous 'economic reforms' implemented from 1978, the Chinese Communist Party (CCP) decided to move toward market-oriented policies. Such move meant a drastic change of paradigm, a fundamental shift which 'will not be altered for a hundred years' (Hou, 2011). Out of such shift, China's economic success came to the surface. China experienced a promising average of 8% in economic growth for more than three decades. The country already exceeds the United States in domestic consumption, in both imports and exports. China is today the world's fastest-growing economy (Huenemann, 2015; Kennedy, 2011). This success through the international trade was surely due to economic and structural features (Finnane, 2005). What is not clear, beyond preliminary considerations, is why such major economic development took place under the particular institutional constraints of communism and socialism.

China is the product of a Cultural Revolution where every effort was made to destroy any form of capitalism. Yet today the majority of Chinese people no longer recognize themselves in the ideology of Communism (Dorn, 1999; Huang, 1971). China had a monetary system in decadence, a general economic, political and cultural traditionalism as well as an environment of perceived segregation. Chinese society was not able in past centuries to systematize its achievements into an elaborated technology and industrial system, such as what materialized in the West. These barriers were often paralleled by religious beliefs such as occultism, *feng shui*, which forced people to act on the basis of how water and wind were moving (Mooneyham, 2014).

From Weber's own contribution on the study of sociology of religion, China was in the past apart from the Western world (Weber, 1976 [ed. orig. 1920]; pp. 377–592). Confucianism and Taoism, main beliefs in China for centuries, always held a vision of society ranked into classes and ruled by aristocracy. When the Catholic missionary Matteo Ricci (1552–1610) went to China, it took him 18 years to enter Beijing. This was also the difficulty that many Protestant missionaries met, such as Hudson Taylor (1832–1905) or Charles Thomas Studd (1860–1931) (Austin, 2007). For example, William Edward Soothill (1861–1935), a Methodist missionary to China, spent 29 years in Wenzhou. He started more than 150 churches and witnessed ten thousand conversions. It is not therefore that China did not have Christianity prior to the present situation (Dunch, 2001). John Sung Shang Chieh played an instrumental role in the revival movement among the Chinese Christians during the 1920s and 1930s. Yet the proportions of the religious awakenings in China today are far more widespread. They permeate every aspect of Chinese society, including as I argue here its economy.

The events that occurred with the two opium wars or later on with the boxer rebellion show how the relation of China with the outside world and particularly with the West was often tumultuous. Meanwhile, during past centuries Confucianism as religion of the elite did not make many effort to integrate and organize the religion of the common people (Taoism) as part of a unified religious identity. According to Weber the goal of Confucianism was 'a cultured status and position', a humanistic project of good living and contemplation. Protestantism's goal instead is to create individuals who are 'tools of God' in every aspect of society. The intensity of belief are rare in Confucianism, yet common in Protestantism. Actively working for wealth is perceived as wrong in the eyes of any devout Confucian. Taoism for its own part promoted quietism and passivity, not so beneficial for professional accomplishments. The 'third way' of Chinese Buddhism, arrived in China since the third century a. C. Yet Buddhism holds within it a world-rejecting asceticism similar to Catholicism. Weber states that it was this set of differences in social attitudes and mindset, shaped by religion, that contributed to the absence of capitalism in China (Weber, 1951 [1916]).

It is only in this sense that the advent of Communism is somehow in step with the history of China. Even with its radical break with the past, Communism ended up supporting a traditionalist anti-capitalistic approach. The state-oriented socialist project promoted by Mao Tse-tung was always guided by the ideal of a future abolition of capitalism. Mao destroyed the structure of technicians and economic experts, closed the universities and promoted the idea of a proletariat man living with few dollars a day. Individualism during Communist as well as in Chinese's past history was never appreciated, and rarely thoughts about one's private life were allowed. This anti-innovative ideology of the status quo still promoted in the educational, cultural and social system in China is very far from the Weberian spirit of capitalism. Such ideological baggage leaves today a great void that does not attract anymore the Chinese masses.

Paradoxically American capitalism, often condemned as 'decadent' by the regime seems to be the element that is making the difference in China. The remarkable success after China's economic reforms against all expectation was made possible without any governmental change. The government penalizing successful enterprises, the absence of security for property rights and many other negative factors, meant that the expectations of experts toward Chinese economic boom were very low (Montinola et al. 1995). Particularly interesting here is the case of the city of Wenzhou. From being a little village of fishermen, in the last decades years have experimented an incredible development, becoming a modern center of business for all China. Wenzhou three generations ago was a very poor city. Many people were forced to migrate due to the state of misery. This is quite different from the hard-working people and modern city that can be observed today.

The question remains then on where does this profit-oriented mentality comes from, which stands out today among Chinese entrepreneurs (Dunch, 2001). The current uncertainty in passing from communism to the market economy has also rendered Christianity attractive to the young generations of Chinese people. The drastic changes of the Cultural Revolution, added to heavy urbanization led to the shattering of all traditional social norms over a relatively short period of time. People began to search for support and meaning. Under Western influence, the Protestant ethic has its place in China as a potential explanatory component, though not being an exhaustive one. The current Chinese generation, grown up without attachments toward the ancient Chinese traditions removed by Communism, is searching for a lifestyle able to make one: 'happy all the time', that: 'gives you the peace of mind among many difficulties', able to aid even in the pursuit of: 'worldly profession' (Mooneyham, 2014, p. 155). The generation of the 1980s, under the 'one child policy', grew up without siblings, without the needed support. So it makes sense that they crave for an environment like the church, where a community and a family of 'brothers and sisters' is able to offer a life that other social structures are unable to provide. Anomy and globalization, which affected China ended playing in favor of the growth of Christianity. Global Christianity seems to be more compatible with the values of modernity and democracy, if compared with Communism, Confucianism or other traditional Chinese sets of values.

Protestantism is not a sufficient condition for the genesis of a possible spirit of capitalism in China, yet it could still be a necessary one. If we were to subtract the current revival of Protestantism in China, then the passage from a socialist and anti-capitalistic project into a market economy could not have taken place with the same degree of impact upon society. Chinese capitalism is not a direct consequence of Protestantism. Such phenomenon is due to many different institutional and technological dimensions. I am also aware that the cultural features of Protestantism during sixteenth-century Europe are totally different than those of the China during the twenty-first century. I'm not suggesting either that wherever capitalism emerged, it was always because of Protestantism. However, it must follow from Weber that, even though the spirit of capitalism is not a universal phenomenon, everywhere it emerges it should at least emerge for similar reasons. We will deal here with few pieces of a far more complex mosaic. Yet I argue that there are enough pieces of evidence to suggest that Protestant revival in China is currently playing a non-marginal role for the genesis of the spirit of capitalism there.

4.2.2 *Wenzhou: China's Jerusalem*

Moving our investigation on a micro level, we can observe that an increasing number of converts to Protestantism today are well-educated young people living in urban China (Yang, 2005). Coming out of a historical context adverse toward the Western civilization, Christianity stands in open contrast with traditional Chinese religions as Taoism, Confucianism or ancestral veneration. Christianity is often perceived as progressive, liberating, modern and universal. In this post-Mao transition to market economy, the coastal city of Wenzhou in the south east is playing a major role. Wenzhou is today one of the richest cities of China in terms of per capita income and is also known as 'China's Jerusalem', the largest urban Christian center in China (Cao, 2008). Historically Wenzhou was also the stronghold of the national Chinese party (*Guomindang*), in opposition toward Maoist China. This in part favored the fortune of Christianity in this area.

In Wenzhou, Protestant Christianity with its over one million Protestants and more than 1.200 churches (Yang, 2005), has accompanied the economic development of the city. Wenzhou moved from an impoverished rural town into a dynamic regional center of global capitalism. Wenzhou became a pioneer city in developing China's current market economy (Cao, 2007). For the particular context of Wenzhou, evidence demonstrates a combination of rapid economic growth and high rate of adherence to Protestantism. In this turmoil a new entrepreneurial class emerged known as 'Boss Christians'. They are rich successful private entrepreneurs who also are influential Christian leaders, able to provide funds for church initiatives. One-third of Wenzhou's entrepreneurs today is considered to be affiliated somehow with the Protestant faith. Protestantism is a system of beliefs that interferes with the status quo. The CCP makes a continuous effort to control and suppress it. Wenzhou Protestant entrepreneurs do represent a 'religious risk' to the Communist government.

The mobility and commercialism of these so-called Jews of China is a success which represents a positive contribution to the economy of China. Attracted by Western civilization, Chinese Christianity took many elements from mainstream Protestantism, applying them in a syncretistic way to their own context. Many beliefs, such as the Beruf, inner-worldly asceticism, the role of sects, the glory of God as the ultimate purpose in life, are present, as well as other important beliefs such as ***millenarianism, dramatic conversion, literal reading of the Bible*** or the presence of a ***charismatic leader***. Many churches in the area of Wenzhou are Calvinistic churches. The majority of Chinese Protestants today lives in rural areas, outside of the cities and far away from the economic hubs of China (Bays, 2003). Yet if someone were to look more closely, it would become evident that converts are not just individuals who are marginalized, deprived of material and social resources.

An increasing proportion of converts are actually well-educated young people, living in the urban city of Wenzhou (Yang, 2005). Evidence shows (Bays, 2003; Wenger, 2004; Yang, 2005; Cao, 2008) that a growing number of them is involved in economic activity. Wenzhou is full of cases of entrepreneurs who instead of fearing the local government as an enemy to their faith, takes the state as a potential partner to facilitate their mission. Boss Christians represent today a dominant feature in the development of Wenzhou and hold some measure of political influence in their local society (Cao, 2007). Research recently studied the effects of religious beliefs on political preference, human capital, work ethic and economic growth, using data from 2001 to 2011 (Wang and Lin, 2014). Among the different religions Protestant Christianity remains the more numerous and it has a significant effect on economic growth. Studies on Protestants entrepreneurs have shown the presence of many elements of Weber's theory such as the *Beruf*. When those entrepreneurs are been asked about their success, they acknowledge having been 'blessed by God' in their business success and they have little fear of revealing their religious identity in the public arena. Those entrepreneurs have a clear view of their life as a 'calling' (*Yi Xiang*,[7] the Chinese version of the *Beruf*) stating to have:

> [...] the special vision from God. [...] God's power to go ahead in the emerging market economy. [...] (Cao N., 2007; p. 53).

Everything they do, they say, they do it:

[7] 异象 yì xiàng here means 'vision', but yi xiang for the purpose of this analysis also encloses the idea of 意向 yì xiàng, 'intention', 'purpose', 'disposition', and is associated also with the word 异想天开 yì xiǎng tiān kāi in the sense of 'imagine', 'indulge in fantasy'. From: Manser M. (Eds.), 1999, *Concise Chinese-English, English-Chinese Dictionary*, Oxford University Press.

[...] for the glory of God and the love of Christ. [...] (*Ibidem*)

Business is perceived by them as a way of serving God. Their job is 'arranged by God' and everything they do is seen as 'God's special calling' (Cao, 2007, p. 58). Hard work is seen as a calling and high economic status as God's blessing. This becomes a crucial motivation to ambition among new adepts who embraces this faith. Although the traditional Chinese religion of this region may have played a certain influence, this economic outcome is unprecedented.

The second interesting aspect for my analysis concerns the characteristics of Christian communities in China. The bipartition between the Christian Three-Self Patriotic Movement (TSPM) and the 'house churches', is similar to the distinction between the official church and the sects as defined by Max Weber. Protestant Christianity in China on one side has the Christian Three-Self Patriotic Movement (TSPM) and the government-related offices of ecumenical churches affiliated to the China Christian Council (CCC). Together they form the only state-sanctioned Protestant church in mainland China. On the other side we have what is commonly known as 'house churches', Protestants not registered by the government (Bays, 2003). Originally the TSPM was established as a government arm of the Communist Party. Many Chinese Christians are distrustful of the TSPM/CCC because of the government control over these churches (Wenger, 2004). A 'Christian Manifesto' was written with the attempt to control the Protestant churches.

Since 1979 the TSPM was re-established and in response several leaders left the 'official church', due to disagreement over the control over worship practices, preaching and behavior. These Christians then began to meet in 'underground churches' and acted independently from the official church, refusing to compromise with the Communist government. While house churches are not under the CCP, they are constantly under watch by the government. Despite the strong opposition, more than half of Protestant believers are part of those autonomous Christian communities (Bays, 2003). Estimates coming from TSPM include only the Christians registered by the government. They speak of 15 to 20 million of Protestants in China, while it is obvious that the number is way higher (Yang, 2006). A scholar (Yang, 2006) proposed the idea of a triple-market model of religion in China: a red market (officially permitted religions), a black market (officially banned religions) and a gray market (religions with an ambiguous legal/illegal status). The author points out how despite the suppression of religion from the government the opposite took place (Yang, 2012). The focus of this study will be the gray and black religious markets with their non-institutionalized religiosity. With the exception of the TSPM, the gray and black market are the main component of Protestantism in China today.

What organizational factor within this context is able to explain in Weberian terms the economic development of those Chinese Christians? An interesting case is Taiwan where, after the deregulation of the late 1980s, governmental suppression of sectarian minorities weakened organized religion while enhancing unchurched religions (Lu et al. 2008). Economic deregulation was associated with the rise of religious groups, while state control had a negative impact on economic competition. China is not so different in this regard. The house church model, very critical of any form of hierarchy, led to the flourishing of an entire spectrum of sectarian groups which became the main target of religious persecution. Those religious groups tend to stress a dramatic conversion, a literal reading of the Bible. They have a strong emphasis on millenarianism and a charismatic leader (Bays, 2003). These sectarian groups have the ability to supply the necessary confidence (*self-efficacy*), community and direction which is largely lacking in China (Wenger, 2004). As among the sects identified by Weber, the house churches in China are better able to stimulate the believer to the achievement of an economic success.

In other words, there seems to be a link between Max Weber's thesis and the Protestant revival that is taking place in China (Tong, 2013). The features of the Protestant ethic, such as inner-worldly asceticism, Beruf, the role of sects, the glory of God as the ultimate purpose of life, all seem to be fading in the Western world, yet they find an example in today's Chinese Protestant revival. Chinese Protestant revival goes beyond the local level to the national and even global level. Success among these Chinese entrepreneurs is also related to their massive involvement in the migratory process. Particularly interesting for me is the case of Italy, where the majority of Chinese immigrants, 80% of all Chinese immigrants (Lisci, 2011), come from the Wenzhou area. One-third of Wenzhou people actually live outside of China, the Jews of China in the diaspora and involved into all sort of businesses. It is also from Wenzhou that comes the majority of the products that China exports to the West. My task therefore is to check empirically the validity of my thesis on the impact of the belief on perpetual assurance of salvation on self-efficacy, a cognitive process that has been proved as an element able to favor economic success.

References

AA. VV., 'Milano, ogni giorno nascono due imprese cinesi', su *Il Giorno*, (Dicembre 2012), Camera di Commercio, Milano

AA. VV., 1990, *Economy and Society: Overviews in Economic Sociology*. Sage Publications.

Adamo, P. (et alii. 1994), *Modernità, politica e protestantesimo*. Claudiana.

Aron R., 1996, *Le tappe del pensiero sociologico*, Milano, Mondadori.

Austin A., 2007, *China's Millions: The China Inland Mission and Late Qing Society, 1832–1905*, Grand Rapids, Michigan, Eerdman's.

Bainton, H. R. 1958, *La riforma protestante*. Einaudi.

Barker J. E., & Carman J. C., 'The Spirit of Capitalism? Religious Doctrine, Values and Economic Attitude Constructs', in *Political Behavior*, Vol. 22, No. 1, (2000), pp. 1–27.

Barlow, A. J. 2015, 'Puritanism and Modernist Novels: From Moral Character to the Ethical Self', in *Current Reviews for Academic Libraries*, Vol. 53, No. 1 (Sept., 2015), p. 68.

Barro J. R., McCleary R. M., 'Religion and Economy', from The Journal of Economic Perspectives, Vol. 20, No. 2 (Spring. 2006), pp. 49–72

Barro J. R., McCleary R. M., 'Religion and Economic Growth Across Countries', from American Sociological Review, Vol. 68, No. 5, (Oct. 2003), pp. 760–781.

Baugus B. P., 2014, *China's Reforming Churches. Mission, Polity and ministry in the next Christendom*, Reformation Heritage Books, Grand Rapids.

Bays, D. H, 'Chinese Protestant Christianity Today', from *The China Quarterly*. No. 174 (Jun., 2003), pp. 488–504.

Beder S., 'Selling the Work Ethic: From Puritan Pulpit to Corporate PR', in *Zed*, New York, (2000), pp. 410–411.

Bennet A., 1975, *The Valley of Vision. A Collection of Puritan Prayers and Devotions*, Edinburgh, The Banner of Truth.

Berger P., 1969, *The Sacred Canopy: Elements of a Sociological Theory of Religion*, New York, Anchor, Garden City.

Bernbaum J. A., & Steer S. M., 1986, *Why Work? Careers and Employment in Biblical Perspective*, Grand Rapids, Baker Book House.

Bland, G. 1972, *Success!* Wheaton, Living Books.

Bottum J., 2014, *An Anxious Age: The Post-Protestant Ethic and the Spirit of America*, Victoria, Image.

Bouma G. D., 'A Critical Review of Recent Protestant Ethic Research', in *Journal for the Scientific Study of Religion*, Vol. 12, No. 2 (Jun., 1973), pp. 141–155.

Bunyan J., 2003, *Pilgrim's Progress*, Bridge Logos, Alachua [ed. orig. 1668].

Bunyan J., 2013, *Grace Abounding to the Chief of Sinners*, Chapel Library [ed. orig. 1666].

Burg B. R., 'Godly Republicanism: Puritans, Pilgrims, and a City on a Hill', in *Current Reviews for Academic Libraries*, Vol. 50, No. 2 (Oct. 2012), p. 350.

Burkett L., 1990, *Business by the Book. The Complete Guide of Biblical Principles for Business Men and Women*, Thomas Nelson, Nashville.

Cantoni D., 'The Economic Effects of the Protestant Reformation: Testing the Weber Hypothesis in the German Lands', in *Journal of the European Economic Association*, (May 2014).

Cao, N., 'Boss Christians: The Business of Religion in the "Wenzhou Model" of Christian Revival', from *The China Journal*, No. 59 (Jan., 2008), pp. 63–87.

Cao, N., 'Christian Entrepreneurs and the Post-Mao State: An Ethnographic Account of Church-state Relations in China's Economic Transition', from *Sociology of Religion*, Vol. 68, No. 1, (Spring. 2007), pp. 45–66.

Cantoni, D., Adopting a New Religion: The Case of Protestantism in 16th Century Germany. *Economic Journal,* Vol. 122, No. 560 (May 2012), pp. 502–531.

Chodorov F., 2011, *The Radical Rich*, Ludwig von Mises Institute, Auburn.

Cohen B. I. (Eds.), 1990, *Puritanism and The Rise of Modern Science. The Merton Thesis*, London, Rutgers University Press.

Cohen J., 2002, *Protestantism and Capitalism: The Mechanisms of Influence*, California, CJS.

Constable, N. 1994, *Christian Souls and Chinese Spirits: A Hakka Community in Hong Kong*. University of California Press.

Cook, W. H. 1974, *Success*. Nashville, Broadman Press.

Covey, S. R. 1990, *The Seven Habits of Highly Effective People*. Simon & Schuster.

Crowley, J. W., & Ballweg, J. A., Religious Preference and Worldly Success. *Sociological Analysis*, No. 32 (Summer 1971), pp. 71–80.

Delacroix, J., & Nielsen, F. 2001, 'The Beloved Myth: Protestantism and the Rise of Industrial Capitalism in Nineteenth- Century Europe', in *Social Forces*.

Devine, J. D. 1977, *Find God's will for you*. Regal Books.

Dorn J. A., 'The death of Communism in China', in *The Journal of Commerce*, (March 5, 1999), CATO Institute.

Drummond A. B. Jr., 'The Episcopalians: an American Elite with Roots going back to Jamestown', *New York Times* (Aug., 2012).

Duncan, A., Reimagining the Self-Made Man: Myth, Risk, and the Pokerization of America. *Western Journal of Communication,* Vol. 78 (2014), pp. 39–57.

Dunch, R. 2001, *Fuzhou Protestants and the Making of a Modern China 1857–1927*. Yale University Press.

Durston, C., & Eales, J. 1996, *The Culture of English Puritanism, 1560–1700*. Palgrave MacMillian.

Edwards J., 2003, [ed. orig. 1734], *The Preciousness Of Time And The Importance Of Redeeming It*, Yale, A Puritan Mind.

Egli J., Hoerr B., 1984, *The I factor. How to influence your world*, Urbana, North Star Strategies.

Feldmann H., 'Protestantism, Labor Force Participation, and Employment across Countries', from *American Journal of Economics and Sociology*, Vol. 66, No. 4, (Oct. 2007), pp. 795–816.

Ferguson N., 'Why America Outpaces Europe. The God Factor', New York Times, (June 2003).

Finnane A., 'China on the Catwalk: Between Economic Success and Nationalist Anxiety', in *The China Quarterly*, No. 183, Culture in the Contemporary PRC (Sep., 2005), pp. 587–608.

Fishman, A., 'The Religious Kibbutz: A Note on the Theories of Marx. Sombart and Weber on Weber and Economic Success', in *Sociological Analysis*, No. 5 (1989), pp. 281–290.

Foster, S., Their Solitary Way: The Puritan Social Ethic in the First Century of Settlement in New England. *Yale Historical Publications Miscellany*, No. 94 (Jan.1972), pp. 200–214.

Fox R., 'The Liberal Ethic and the Spirit of Capitalism', in *Center Magazine*, (Sept./Oct., 1987), pp. 4–11.

Fried H. M., 'Reflections on Christianity in China', from *American Ethnologist*, Vol. 14, No. 1, (Feb., 1987), pp. 94- 106.

Fukuyama, F. 1995, *Trust: The social virtues and the creation of prosperity*. Free Press.

Gaer J., Siegel B., 1964, *The Puritan Heritage. America's Roots in the Bible*, New American Library, New York.

Guthrie D., 'The Quiet Revolution: The Emergence of Capitalism. China', in *Harvard International Review*, Vol. 25, No. 2, (Summer 2003).

Guthrie, D. 1999, *Dragon in a Three-Piece Suit: The Emergence of Capitalism in China*. Princeton University Press.

Harrison, L. E. 2012, *Jews, Confucians, and Protestants: Cultural Capital and the End of Multiculturalism*. Rowman & Littlefield Publishers.

Harrison, L. E. 1992, *Who Prospers? How Cultural Values Shape Economic and Political Success*, Basic Books.

Hefner R. W., 'Religious Resurgence in Contemporary Asia: South-east Asian Perspectives on Capitalism, the State and the New Piety', from *The Journal of Asian Studies*, Vol. 69, No. 4, (Nov. 2010), pp. 1031–1047.

Henry C. F. H., 1964, *Aspects of Christian Social Ethics*, Baker, Michigan.

Hewett R. S., 'Thrift and Thriving in America: Capitalism and Moral Order from the Puritans to the Present', in *Current Reviews for Academic Libraries*, Vol. 49, No. 7 (Mar. 2012), p. 1319.

Hill, A. 1997, *Just Business*. InterVarsity Press, Madison.

Hou, J. W., Economic Reform of China: Cause and Effects. *The Social Science Journal*,, No. 48 (June 2011), pp. 419–434.

Huang L. J., 'The role of religion in Communist Chinese Society', from *Asian Survey*, Vol. 11, No. 7 (Jul., 1971), pp. 693–708.

Huenemann R. W., 'Economic Reforms, 1978-Present', in *Oxford Bibliographies*, (18 May 2015).

Hulse, E. 2000, *Who are the Puritans? And what do they teach?* Evangelical Press.

Huntington, S. P., & Harrison, L. E. 2001, *Culture Matters, How Values Shape Human Progress*. Basic Books.

Jepperson, R., & Meyer, J., 'Multiple Levels of Analysis and the Limitations of Methodological Individualisms', *Sociological Theory*, Vol. 29, No. 1 (2011),pp. 54–73.

Kennedy, S. 2011, *Beyond the Middle Kingdom: Comparative Perspectives on China's Capitalist Transformation*. Stanford University Press.

Kim H. C., 'The Relationship of Protestant Ethic Beliefs and Values to Achievement', in *Journal for the Scientific Study of Religion*, Vol. 16, No. 3 (Sep., 1977), pp. 255–262.

Klein S., 'First founders: American Puritans and Puritanism in an Atlantic world', in *Current Reviews for Academic Libraries*, Vol. 50, No. 5 (Jan., 2013), p. 942.

Knight J., Song L., 2005, *Towards a Labour Market in China*, Oxford University Press.

Kosmin, B. A., Lachman, S. P., 1993, *One Nation Under God*. Religion in Contemporary American Society.

Krug, B. 2004, *China's Rational Entrepreneurs: The Development of the New Private Business Sector*. Routledge.

Lambert, F. 2003, *The Founding Fathers and the Place of Religion in America*. Princeton University Press.

Landes, D. S. 1998, *The Wealth and Poverty of Nations: Why Some Are So Rich and Some So Poor*. Norton.

Latourette K. S., 1975, *A History of Christianity. Reformation to the Present*, New York, Harper Collins Publishers, Vol II.

Le Beau, B. F., The Puritan Origins of American Patriotism. *Current Reviews for Academic Libraries,* Vol. 45, No. 9 (May 2008), pp. 1602–1603.

Lenski G. E., 1961, *The Religious Factor*, Garden City, New York, Doubleday.

Lisci, A. 2011, *Wenzhou, la Patria dei Cinesi d'Italia*. Gruppo Editoriale L'Espresso.

Little, D., 'Max Weber Revisited. The Protestant Ethic and the Puritan Experience of Order', in *Harvard Theological Review,* No. 59 (1996), pp. 415–428.

Lu Y., (*et alii*), 'Deregulation and the Religious Market in Taiwan: A Research Note', from *The Sociological Quarterly*, Vol. 49, No. 1 (Winter, 2008), pp. 139–153.

Masland J. W., 'Communism and Christianity in China', from *The Journal of Religion*, Vol. 32, No. 3, (Jul. 1952), pp. 198–206.

Mather C., 1825, *Essays to Do Good*, Glasgow, Chalmers and Collins.
Maxwell, J. C. 2003, *There's no Such Thing as Business Ethics*. Warner Business Books.
Mayer, A. J., & Sharp, H., Religious Preference and Worldly Success. *American Sociological Re-View*, No. 27 (April 1962), pp. 218–227.
McClosky, Z. 1984, *'The American Ethos', in Cambridge Journals*. Harvard University Press.
Mccloud S., Mirola W. A., 2009, *Religion and Class in America: Culture, History, and Politics*, Brill, Leiden.
McNeill, J. T. 1957, *The History and Character of Calvinism*. Oxford University Press.
Means, R. L., Protestantism and American Sociology: Problems of Analysis. *Sociological Analysis*, No. 27 (Fall 1966), pp. 128–137.
Merton, R. K. 1957, *Social Theory and Social Structure* (Revised). Free Press.
Miegge, M. 2010, *Vocazione e lavoro*. Claudiana.
Mocombe, P. 2012, *Liberal Bourgeois Protestantism the Metaphysics of Globalization*. Ebrary Inc.
Montinola G., Qian Y., Weingast B. R., 'Federalism, Chinese Style: The Political Basis for Economic Success in China', in *World Politics*, Vol. 48, No. 1 (Oct., 1995), pp. 50–81.
Mooneyham, W. S. 2014, *China, a New Day*. Logos International.
Moore, R. L. 2005, *L'intreccio di Sacro e Profano nella Storia Americana*. Claudiana.
Mulder, J. M., 'Pursuing the Puritan Ethic', in *Theology Today*, Vol. XXXII, No. 4 (Jan., 1976), pp. 341–344.
North, G., 1973, *An Introduction To Christian Economics*, Craig Press.
Peabody L., 1974, *Secular Work is Full-Time Service*, CLC, Fort Washington.
Perkins W., 1603, *Treatise of the Vocations or Callings*, New Jersey, Princeton.
Phillips M., 2001, *Puritan View of Work*, Fremont, Grace Baptist.
Piper J., (eds.), 1974, *Resolutions. Works of Jonathan Edwards*, Banner of Truth, Vol. 1, Eidinburgh.
Pointer R. W., 'Philadelphia Presbyterians, Capitalism, and the Morality of Economic Success 1825–1855', in *The Pennsylvania Magazine of History and Biography*, Vol. 112, No. 3 (Jul., 1988), pp. 349–374.
Quinney R., 'Religion and the Spirit of Capitalism', in *Morality and Capitalism*, (Sept., 1981), pp. 55–58.
Rauscher M., 'Protestant Ethic, Status Seeking and Economic Growth', in *Universität Rostock*, (1997), Working Paper No. 9.
Robertson L., 'Could China's Underground Churches Soon Meet Openly ?', in *CBN—Christian Broadcasting Network*, (Jan., 2009), Virginia Beach.
Roosevelt, M. T. 2008, *Spiritual Enterprise*, New York, Encounter Books.
Schorn-Schütte, L. 2001, *La riforma protestante*. Il Mulino.

Scofield C. I., 1999, *The Study Bible*, Oxford University Press.

Sherman, D., & Hendricks, W. 1987, *Your Work Matters to God*. NavPress.

Shriver, G. H., 'The Protestant Ethic and the Spirit of Sport: How Calvinism and Capitalism Shaped America's Games', in *Current Reviews for Academic Libraries*, Vol. 48 (Aug., 2011), p. 2354.

Shulevitz, J. 2001, *The Puritan Ethic*. Times.

Simpson, A. 1955, *Puritanism in Old and New England*. University of Chicago Press.

Stark R., 2005, *The Victory of Reason. How Christianity Led to Freedom, Capitalism, and Western Success*, New York, Random House.

Stevens J. W., 2010, *God-fearing and Free: A Spiritual History of America's Cold War*, Harvard College.

Tam, S. 1969, *God Owns my Business*. Wordbooks.

Tipson Jr. L. B., 'Heavenly Merchandize: How Religion Shaped Commerce in Puritan America', in *Current Reviews for Academic Libraries*, Vol. 48, No. 4 (Dec., 2010), p. 704.

Tong, K. J. 2013, *Overseas Chinese Christian Entrepreneurs in Modern China: A Case Study of the Influence of Christian Ethics on Business Life*. Anthem Press.

Verba, S., King G., Keohane R. O., 1994, *Designing Social Inquiry. Scientific inference in Qualitative Research*, New Jersey, Princeton University Press.

Veroff, J., Feld, S., & Gurin, G., Achievement Motivation and Religious Background. *American Sociological Review*, No. 27 (Apr., 1962), pp. 205–217.

Wagner H., 'The Protestant Ethic: A Mid-Twentieth Century View', in *Sociological Analysis*, Vol. 25, (1 April 1964), pp. 34–40.

Waller G. M., 1973, (Eds.), *Puritanism in Early America*, Lexington, D. C. Heat and Company,.

Wang Q., Lin X., 'Does Religious Beliefs Affect Economic Growth? Evidence from Provincial-level Panel Data in China', in *Chinese Economic Review*, (Dec., 2014), pp. 277–287.

Warren R., 2002, *The Purpose Driven Life. What on earth am I here for?* Grand Rapids, Zondervan.

Washer P., 2008, *Ten Indictments against the Modern Church*, Pensacola, Chapel Library.

Wayne S. F., 'An Instrument to Measure Adherence to the Protestant Ethic and Contemporary Work Values', *Journal of Business Ethics*, No. 8 (1989), pp. 793–806.

Weber, M., 1951 [ed. orig. 1916], *The Religion of China*, Translated by Hans H. Gerth. Glencoe, Ill., Free Press.

Wenger J. E., 'Official vs. Underground Protestant Churches in China. Challenges for Reconciliation and Social Influence', from *Review of Religious Research*, Vol. 46, No. 2, (Dec., 2004), pp. 169–182.

Willems E., 1968, 'Culture Change and the Rise of Protestantism in Brazil and Chile', in *The Protestant Ethic and Modernization: A Comparative View*, Basic Books, pp. 184–200.

Wisman J. D., Davis M. E., 'Degraded Work, Declining Community, Rising Inequality, and the Transformation of the Protestant Ethic in America: 1870–1930', in *The American Journal of Economics and Sociology*, Vol. 72, (Nov., 2013), p.1075.

Witherington, B., III. 2011, *Work, A Kingdom Perspective on Labor*. Grand Rapids, Eerdmans Publishing.

Yang, F., 2012, *Religion in China. Survival & Revival under Communist Rule*, New York, Oxford University Press.

Yang, F., 'Lost in the Market, Saved at McDonald's: Conversion to Christianity in urban China', from *Journal for the Scientific study of Religion*, Vol. 44, No. 4, (Dec., 2005), pp. 423–441.

Yang, F., 'The Red, Black, and Gray Markets of Religion in China', from *The Sociological Quarterly*, Vol. 47, No. 1 (Winter, 2006), pp. 93–122.

Yiwu L., 2011, *God is Red. The secret story of how Christianity survived and flourished in Communist China*, New York, Harper Collins.

CHAPTER 5

From Theory to the Fieldwork

> When a truth is necessary, the reason for it can be found by analysis, that is, by resolving it into simpler ideas and truths until the primary ones are reached.
>
> —Gottfried Wilhelm Leibniz

5.1 Qualitative Research Among the Chinese of the Diaspora

5.1.1 Chinese Small Businesses in Milan

After having explained the theoretical relevance of the study and before moving on to the empirical level of analysis, I first must make a methodological note. Immanuel Kant wrote his famous essay: 'prolegomena to any future of metaphysics'. When the discipline of sociology came into the picture and up until now metaphysics, theology and religion were marginalized or simply forced to silence. The goal of this chapter is to shed clarity and avoid any idealism. No determinism whatsoever is compatible with the scientific study of religion. In order to be objective, a study as the one presented here must not to be conceived as a mere acritical defense of any set of beliefs. At the same time, this study must be free from the other extreme of a secularized determinism that excludes a priori any explanation that involves religious explanations.

O. Palombaro, *Christianity and Capitalism in China*,
https://doi.org/10.1007/978-981-97-3549-5_5

This book is the fruit a comparative qualitative study in the shape of an ethnography. The reason why I chose this specific technique is due to the nature of the object of analysis. Studying the behavior of entrepreneurs requires prolonged observations of their daily life. This is something that escapes the eye of mere quantification. This study contains the observation of practices, meetings, roles and social types as well as social relations, groups, organizations, environments and subcultures as observed during three years among Chinese migrants involved in various forms of entrepreneurship in the diaspora, in the city of Milan, Italy.

In order to understand how this entrepreneurial propensity pushes toward economic success, it is important to have a 'bottom-up' approach. Any social action, including the economic action, according to my perspective acts like a cultural artifact, shaped by the meaning ascribed to these actions by those who engage in them. My aim will not be to merely observe the actions of individuals but to go beyond them and understand the meaning given by them, regardless of the judgment of value that they may give to them. The subjective perspective of the actor must still be taken into account. It is crucial to treat entrepreneurs as ordinary people, to examine their variety of goals, activities, practices, habits and ideas. Then it is also important to mediate between those micro-level elements and the more large-scale structures of society. My methodological approach in analyzing the social action of individuals will go beyond exclusively utilitarian considerations.

Conceiving of entrepreneurs as ordinary people, with all their subjective perspective, I followed in this study the methodological suggestions of other ethnographers (Duneier, 1999). In examining the entrepreneurs in their behaviors and interactions, I considered their role as ideal-types, their functioning as a 'public character', the symbolic role of their places, framing them into a narrative describing their social life as well as their business. Like Duneier I approached the field with a research design that came before the access to the field. My focus however was not as much the social position of people (Duneier, 1999), but the economic behavior of the individual as well as his social interactions. In connecting the macro and micro dimensions, I also did not go from case to case through a multi-sited ethnography, but I instead focused on the same case of Chinese entrepreneurs, part of the same network. Then I enlarged it to other cases even in their motherland of Wenzhou. The role of places was very crucial in my study, considering how I immersed myself in cafes, workplaces, stores and shops of Chinatown. Those locations were investigated as a social world in and of itself, with the lives of its people, their relationships, their different ways in which they interpret and defined community, how they relate with the boss. In this the setting worked for me as a 'laboratory'. I saw places in the city as objects of investigation yet I placed a greater emphasis on the behavior of individuals (Ocejo, 2013). My approach to their work life was interested in aspects proper of 'conventional economy', highlighting the role of social rules and the moral dimensions of economic action (Chicchi, 2006).

My role was of being a passive observer. Yet at times I was actively participating in the daily life of entrepreneurs. I made clear from the beginning to any person that asked me that my intention of being there was to be a researcher. Surely this, especially in the initial stages led to the problem of reactivity in the individuals being observed, as they tended to modify their behavior, their way of speaking, due to my presence. This was a problem I was willing to bear with, giving the time to immerse myself in their point of view until a level of trust and authenticity was achieved. Furthermore, once the social acceptance of such role was achieved, I decided to follow on. In terms of reliability, the field went through ups and downs. In the first group of entrepreneurs a complete identification with the point of view of the social actors was possible due to my own identification with their religious beliefs and practices. In this case I was able to display what in qualitative research is defined as the 'emic perspective' (Babbie, 2015) as opposed to 'etic' and disembodied relationship with the point of view of the social actors. Yet the cultural distance between me and them was often forcing me to dissociate myself from their interpretation with disenchantment, especially in the last part of my research. Another aspect of methodology that is important to take into account is what in literature is defined as 'reflexivity' issue (Babbie, 2015). During my time as an observer in the field, the negative effect that my presence was having in the surrounding environment was at times felt. For example, my presence or words at times were changing the type of answers given to my questions or the specific behavior of the entrepreneur. I was able to notice this at times, yet in most cases this issue was compensated by the fact that I was deeply involved in the life of the people I was observing. I was able to verify therefore almost always when they were faking or being spontaneous.

The ethnography took place mainly into the urban area of the Chinatown of Milan, in Italy. The study therefore borrows also from several methodological suggestions coming from urban anthropology, with a special focus on the ethnic community living in the territory of the chinatown and other residential areas of migrants (Hannerz, 1980). Even though this study is more focused on the cultures of work among Chinese entrepreneurs, it still needs to take into consideration the methodology followed by those urban studies. For example, many of the interactions and circles of relations that I observed on the field may properly be considered as what is referred to as 'urban villages'. Urban villages are cultural realities with their specific features inside a broader urban context. The study will try to point out those islands of entrepreneurship in the big city that follows traditional and cultural patterns and possess unique features. Instead of thinking of the entrepreneur therefore as an aseptic figure shaped by the economy and with no specific features apart from their profession, I try to point out here the role of their cultural and social dimensions in shaping their business. Differently from the majority of the sociology of culture, this study still follows the more factual or functionalist suggestions of the classic theoretical approach to the subject of analysis. Yet, I will not apply a mere constructivist interpretation to the matter. In my view, when approaching the field, objects are still to be considered as objects independently from the perception of the single observer. Even though I took those contributions into account in my research, I don't identify necessarily with a naturalistic approach to social research held by those classical methodologists.

This research took the shape of a case study, or multiple case study, focusing on a specific social phenomenon: Chinese entrepreneurs in the city of Milan in Italy and their economic behavior. In many ways what I observed there is very similar to other realities of Chinese migrant communities from Wenzhou living in other big cities of Western Europe. The purpose of this study is not just descriptive but explicatory. It tries to discover the role of values in the life of entrepreneurs. Differently from the grounded theory, my field was approached already with theoretical questions a priori and re-elaborated a posteriori in light of the empirical results (Babbie, 2015). An empirical case was later identified deductively, to satisfy the theoretical requirements of analytical categories. Through this book I explored the relationship between a case study and a theory according to extended-case method (Burawoy, 1991). My fieldwork also will confront gaps in the theory, addressing the need for modifications as needed. It is impossible to enter any field without expectations on what will be discovered. On the other hand, many expectations were also often challenged by the field (Babbie, 2015). Some of the theories that I've listed in previous chapters at times crushed with the bare observations in the field, yet overall surprisingly they found a positive validation. My research started with an in-depth analysis of existing literature, with the specific purpose to go into the field with a clear theoretical question. Certain interpretations not necessarily part of the original theoretical framework were later added to the study.

Systems of relationships were a crucial part in approaching the field. From the very beginning of my entrance into the field, I tried to gather the entire spectrum of the social relationships of these entrepreneurs: their ethnic, social, laborial, religious as well as recreational environment (Babbie, 2015). Like the Chicago School, I held the importance of considering the 'definition of the situation' as well as the impact of social rules on groups of work, or the impact of cultural segregation, as well as the transient character of relationships from formal to informal. The study of the Ghetto's in Europe by Louis Wirth (Hannerz, 1980) almost paralleled the Chinatown who migrated in Milan from Wenzhou. The institutionalization of an ethnic border in those areas, together with oppositions by the surrounding society, was followed by an identification and a quest for success which slowly seemed to lead entrepreneurs toward upward mobility. This in second or third generations of migrants led to a break, a move from adaptation to assimilation, leaving traditional values in favor of economic competition (Hannerz, 1980).

In terms of *network analysis*, I followed the perspective according to which the individual is to be considered on the basis of the different roles he undertakes. Actions were considered on the basis of the social purposes, on the basis of the different levels of connections, with a specific focus on the individual (Hannerz, 1980). The findings in the field connected to the role of network were under my constant investigation, particularly whether the specific network under my investigation had few or more connections. Many times these networks were driven by business, but as I will point out later, they had their cultural and even religious components. When I was shadowing on a closer-level entrepreneurs in their contexts of action, their role as catalysts for the ramification of several businesses was my focus. During the whole period of my observations, it was also crucial to observe the evolution of these networks in the way their participants, purposes and places of influence interacted.

5.2 Summary of the Research

5.2.1 Presenting Results

Applying what I've outlined previously about Weber's theory, the next table gives a synthetic overview of the dynamics of my model applied to the empirical context of Protestant China. The first challenge that I had to face was how to identify the presence and role of something not as tangible, such as a religious belief. How can someone use observation to investigate an un-observable thing such as religious beliefs? Ever since the birth of sociology, the discipline has been characterized by a radical refusal of metaphysics. Such approach however neglects the importance of analyzing how phenomena are produced, even how certain beliefs (what the actor thinks he can do) give meaning to their social action, through intentionality, recognition and social identity. Such approach also neglects how individuals often see themselves as 'moral agents', as in Durkheimian terms the 'sacred' does indeed give birth to social interactions which begin to be seen as 'rituals'. Actions, even economic actions, do have a symbolic, intrinsic and ritual aspect (Barbera & Negri, 2015).

According to this perspective beliefs, understood as internal states of mind, define the cause of the action, expressing themselves in observable behaviors. In order to ascertain the influence of those beliefs objectively, it is important to remember that ideas, framework, meaning and values seem to all have an endogenous transformative power which does transform behavior over time. This theme of the influence of beliefs and values toward economic action, will be pursued through induction, in the same way someone might investigate other invisible things: by observing their effects in practices, rhetorical discourses, norms and relationships which do weight in toward economic involvement. From those effects, I will then make an inference concerning the existence of sociological relationships. The presence of several beliefs (which I call here *preconditions*) has already been pointed out by some studies in the case of Protestant China (Cao, 2007). Some of the beliefs that were crucial in Calvinism, especially among what I call here the *assistants to the preconditions*, might be marginally there for the case of contemporary China. I therefore substituted these with other *assistants to the preconditions* which are playing a guiding role among Protestants in China (mainly *Millenarianism* and the presence of a *charismatic leader*).

This research again intends to check the validity of my theoretical argument: the impact of the belief on perpetual assurance of salvation (PAS) on self-efficacy, favoring economic success for the case of Chinese Protestant Christianity. I am not directly interested in measuring economic success, but to testify of the presence of the impact of PAS on this cognitive process that, among other determinants, has already been proven to be correlated with economic success. I am not denying the strict social role that many of these elements display (see, for example, *house churches*). From a Weberian methodological perspective however, my main focus remains to investigate the role of a specific belief in building up a subsequent socialized *ethos*. As I've already mentioned several studies lack a clear understanding of Weber's theory on the internalization of a religious belief in someone's life, and how such belief reflects in daily practices and in the formation of a specific economic ethos (Table 5.1).

The city of Milan is a good candidate to investigate this phenomenon in the diaspora. It has a heterogeneous spectrum of small businesses, managed by Chinese hard workers who displayed economic success despite an ongoing economic crisis. Among those Chinese workers, there is also a growing social mobility which took place for the past 30 years

Table 5.1 Dynamics of the relationship between the Chinese Protestant entrepreneurs' beliefs and the economic ethos according to the theoretical argument in its empirical application

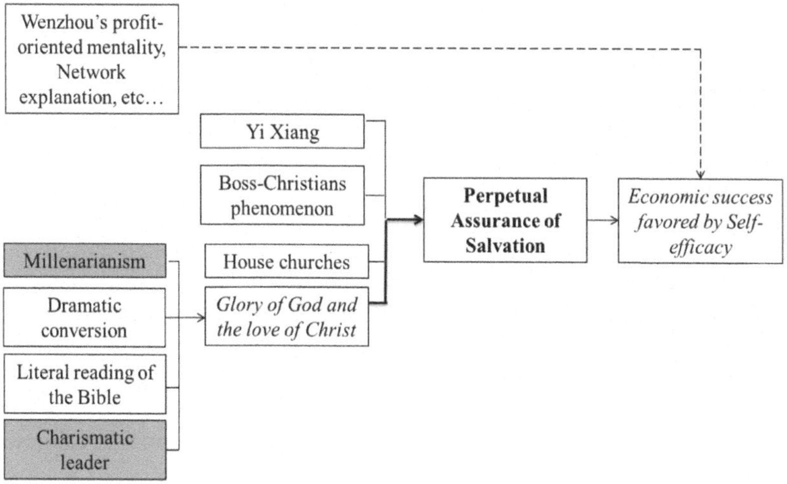

(from workers to multiple business owners, from street vendors to large-scale buyers, from waiters to graduated business accountants, from a machine operator to sales managers). Such a setting provided enough insights to be chosen as an ideal candidate for a fieldwork. That is why I've decided to do a qualitative in-depth study in such context of the diaspora. My target was a group of Chinese Christian entrepreneurs from Wenzhou, involved in small businesses creation and multiplication living in the city of Milan. The majority of Chinese people that live in Italy come from the city of Wenzhou, and the greatest part of them is involved in entrepreneurial activity, running some business while at the same time being part of a Protestant church. Entrepreneurs from Wenzhou have transported to the West a family-based culture of entrepreneurship, self-reliant, ready to assume economic risks as well as keeping long working hours, making low-profit margins and displaying financial capacity through their network. I sought therefore to identify the external influences involved in the migratory process of these 'Jews of China', which are proving to be so important for the rise of Chinese entrepreneurship. Milan, after Prato in Tuscany, is the second-largest community of Chinese immigrants in Italy (IDOS, 2014). These Chinese entrepreneurs played a central role for the spread of the global supply chains in the past decades. Today apart from some key examples, the most common pattern among Chinese entrepreneurs in Italy is to leave those factories to become small business owners. I have chosen the geographic area of Milan because of the availability of the cases and the economic relevance of the area.

Since the 1980s, the economic rise of Wenzhou led many migrants from that region to the West. Some scholars pointed out the interesting evolution of their business activity (AA. VV., 1997a, 1997b). First these entrepreneurs started through informal economy as peddlers or owners of small shops, focused only on unique products, then, expanded and diversified their business through bars, restaurants, wholesale shops, financial activities up until holding almost a monopoly of certain kinds of business, managing entire commercial enterprises. In this gradual opening toward economic activities which impacted public relations, the contribution of the second generation was crucial. During my ethnographic observations and interviews, it was evident that being the son of a Chinese entrepreneur made life easier for the Chinese entrepreneurs of the second generation, since the necessary finances and social capital were already circulating for decades. Interesting fact is that, in today's economy, those

Chinese enterprises represent a parallel and self-sufficient economy. The Chinese tension toward entrepreneurship is unique or at least peculiar, if someone was to compare their entrepreneurial tendencies with other migrant groups present in the same area of Milan (Ceccagno, 2014). Many Italian enterprises today depend on Chinese labor force, whereas vice versa Chinese enterprises are gradually infiltrating in businesses that in the past were only managed by the local labor force (Cologna, 2006). We must ask what is then the element, in their specific set of values that led to such evolution and to the rising of an undeniable Wenzhou's profit-oriented mentality.

My approach was from the theory to the fieldwork. Having previously studied the theoretical argument on the impact of the belief in the perpetual assurance of salvation, I wanted to check the validity of this model through this ethnography of a group of Chinese Protestant entrepreneurs in the city of Milan. The research strategy that I have adopted is a comparative holistic design that focused on the Chinese entrepreneurs attending the evangelical church in Milan, accompanied then with a second group of Chinese non-Christian entrepreneurs in Milan, without any contact or adherence to the Protestant faith. The methodological strategy is then similar to the one of an *extended-case method* (Burawoy, 1991). This specific perspective in qualitative research conceives methodology as a link between technique and theory and is primarily concerned with the relationship between data and theory. In this case, as well as in other qualitative studies, the extended-case method uses participant observation to reconstruct theories of advanced capitalism, which are oriented on a macro level of analysis, despite the particular significance of the social situation under study. In this the extended-case method differs from the ethno-methodology as well as from the grounded theory, or from the participatory action research and the institutional ethnography approach (Babbie, 2015).

Since entrepreneurship and economic success are the elements under my analysis, I focus on the particular external forces that shape it among Chinese entrepreneurs both in their motherland and in their migratory journey to the West. In other words what I observed on a micro dimension is an expression of the macro level. The fieldwork in this methodological perspective is not less theoretical than the primary analysis that generated it. In fact, the field is often seen as an expression of those theoretical questions. My focus was the construction of genetic explanations of particular outcomes (mainly economic success). In his description of the extended-case method, Burawoy mentions Weber's analysis of the motivational component provided by the Protestant ethic as an example of his own approach. Weber tried to point out differences between similar cases in order to point out the connection between the elements under analysis. I looked for the similarities among disparate cases and different social situations such as the Chinese Protestant entrepreneurs and Protestantism during the sixteenth century in Western Europe, in order to evaluate the consistency of the Weberian formal theory (Babbie, 2015). What is significant for me is how this informs me about the world in which this phenomenon is embedded. At the same time, other aspects are significant, such as the societal role of this phenomenon.

The research started with the entrance in the field through a mediator, Delun, who opened the door to the group of entrepreneurs under my investigation. The contact with the community was facilitated by the presence of this informant, a Chinese Protestant who had perfect knowledge of Chinese and Italian and who was already linked with the community of interest. I had a good relationship with my informant for many years before I took with him the role of researcher. The issue of 'first impressions' therefore were almost totally out of the picture. There was no potential hindrance for the successive phases of the investigation. Yet a good amount of diffidence, especially during the first interviews, was present among the informants due to the distortion of information, presence of partial points of view on the matter as well as my lack of knowledge at that time of all the different aspects of the phenomenon. At first my entrance in the field caused a high amount of suspicion. I incurred several times in breaking cultural rules such as sharing pictures of other people, talking to married women prior to having the authorization from their husband, going too ahead in discussion with certain bosses before receiving their complete trust… For this reason, I tried to establish a relationship with the subjects first, beginning with those participants that were more open to my presence, trying to receive their support and cooperation. During the period of my research, my involvement in the social life of the entrepreneurs was very intense. I took part in their religious gatherings, meetings in McDonald's, dinners, travels around the city, visits to family members, activity on social media (WeChat…), excursion to Chinatown and even traveling to China to visit people in Wenzhou connected through family and religious relations. In those circumstances I had to be flexible and adapt myself to long periods where I was simply silent and listened to them speaking in Chinese, discussing about personal matters, faith, work and family life. In almost all of those occasions I was the only non-Chinese person with them. This captured the curiosity of people but generally, given the fact that after a while they knew me, I became somehow part of the group.

At this point the research took two different paths: on the one hand I decided to do in-depth semi-structured interviews and on the other hand I've started to 'job-shadow' several entrepreneurs in their day at work. Job-shadowing consisted in following silently the entrepreneur in his daily work-routine through a kind of observation as invisible as possible, almost 'like a fly in a room'. My data collection strategy was the one of 'being on the job', engaging in their same activities, with an experiential approach (Ocejo, 2013). Together with this, many times those techniques were accompanied by observations and ethnographic surveys. The reason why I decided to introduce job-shadowing in my research was due to the need to observe the behavior of the entrepreneur in his work, not just through his partial interpretation of it expressed in the interview setting. Almost all the important aspects of the social process were observed through 'being there'. At first, I tried to pursue this through a form of participatory observation, working together with them. Since this was not always possible, I then decided to pursue the option of job-shadowing. The challenge in the beginning was big, since it was my first experience of this kind and the entrepreneurs felt somehow uncomfortable with the idea. My request faced several rejections even among the closest informants. After this first wall, I was able to proceed.

In order to avoid the problem of my presence in the field both during the job-shadowing and during the interviews, I tried to be as invisible as possible in the first case and intervene as less as possible in the conversation during the interview once the dialogue was established. During my job-shadowing I always had my notebook to write down any type of action, what I saw and what I thought, with a particular focus on the recording of episodes closer to research interest, together with unexpected events. Not trusting in my limited memory, the transcription of job-shadowing was done almost immediately after a day spent with the entrepreneur, even adding more details that came into my mind and that I did not write on the spot. Non-important details that I wrote down, later on demonstrated to be crucial for my interpretation of the events. My presence in few cases determined a strong rejection as for example with friends and family members of the person I wanted to job-shadow, who were totally opposed to my presence in the store at Chinatown because they thought it to be intrusive. Those and some other rare cases witnessed a negative rejection. In light of them, I was nevertheless able to continue my research and not be excluded nor considered bad by other individuals that I encountered later in the field. At times the job-shadowing was particularly tiring, because of the high expense of energy of certain working activities done by the entrepreneur, certain days full of stress. Also, when I've started the procedure of job-shadowing, following some entrepreneurs during their work-life, my lack of understanding of the Chinese language represented a challenge. Giving the language barrier, the presence on the field of the cultural mediator was crucial as well as the use of backtalk during job-shadowing or ethnographic observations. Together with this informant, I benefited from other Chinese Protestant who speak fluent English.

Despite being perceived as an external member of a different ethnic origin, the access to the community was compensated by the fact that I was already inside a network of evangelicals in the city of Milan and therefore I relied on my credibility as an actor inside their network despite our ethnic difference. The study made no reference to sensible data. I assigned to all the participants a nickname to respect their privacy. I've started my investigation with a wide perspective, doing observations at church, then I've later on begun to focus more on their work activities, doing ethnographic observation and interviews at their workplace. After a first explorative stage which served mainly to encourage the building of trust and familiarity with the culture, I've alternated moments of participatory observation to 30 semi-structured interviews.

The first interviews that I've done were not prepared in advance, then later on, on the basis of my theoretical argument and also in search of the best way to obtain information in a spontaneous setting and interaction I've developed a series of questions. I talked rarely, almost all the time the respondent was dominant. Especially in the beginning of my research, one of the first challenges was their rejection of me as an intrusive foreigner. Therefore, at the moment of being asked questions many were silent or gave me few words. Few times in the beginning I had the respondent answering with only one or two cold sentences, being frustrated for the wall there was between us. My role in the interviews was more the one of a 'miner' rather than a traveler, in the sense that I had enough general information while my goal was to investigate (Babbie, 2015). At times I went around having natural spontaneous conversations with individuals, but this was not the predominant trend in how I collected information for the interviews. Sometimes the interview was preceded by an introductory natural conversation about the life and story of the entrepreneur. Accidentally I had the chance to do one focus group in Wenzhou with less than 12 people, where I submitted in a schematic way the interview chart to the people interviewed at the same time. The participants were not chosen according to any probabilistic method of sampling.

5.2.2 *Methods*

The people that I've interviewed were male and female entrepreneurs between 25 and 55 years old. They were first- or second-generation migrants from Wenzhou, living and active in the trade sector and commerce in Milan. My primary focus were Christian entrepreneurs on high role positions as managers. I also tried to identify the role of religious leaders (pastors, elders) in business. I sought to focus on regular workers, to observe their perception of the workplace and duties. Ethnographic observations as well as interviews from the same family group took place even when inter-generational. Part of the interview also included biographical records in order to analyze their business start-up, their religious background, their status as second-generation (*Cultural explanation*) as well as their perceived identity. It was interesting to notice the variation from one generation to the next. I followed the procedure of thematizing the interview according to purpose and concepts I wanted to observe, projecting the acquisition of information (Babbie, 2015). The majority of the questions were descriptive, with few structural questions (on network). Sometimes, especially in the last part of the research, even 'contrast questions' were added on the spot, not being specified in the original list (Spradley, 1979).

Recollecting the journey of migration among those Chinese entrepreneurs allowed me to identify the key elements that led them to decide to migrate in the first. When their reason was financial, perhaps it was to start a new business or to diversify a business that already existed. Those Protestant workers stressed the importance of sharing their stories of how they became believers. I took advantage of such bridge, especially in my initial stage entering the field. Added to biographical records, these stories allowed me to observe the impact of the perpetual assurance of salvation in their daily life, through the reconstruction of their past professional life, achievements, failures, risks. All this information was collected in a natural way, without forcing the link between the belief

Table 5.2 Scheme of the typical biographical journey of the Protestant believer

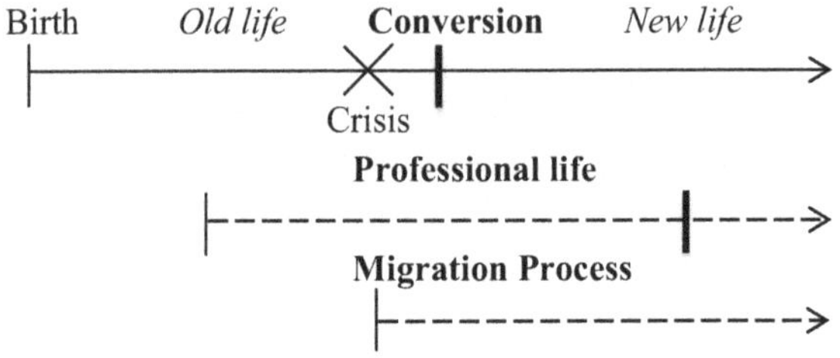

in PAS and self-efficacy. Personal testimonies and biographical records allowed me to identify mainly the person's reaction and behavior in situations of economic risk. In order to observe the impact of religious belief in their daily life, stories were recorded in a non-religious context.

Also, in order to avoid any process of rationalization of their recollection of events afterwards, I placed a strong emphasis on factual verifiable changes, more related to their professional life. This generally did not represent a problem, since I knew them personally well enough to spot any re-interpretation of their story (Table 5.2).

In order to avoid circular reasoning, which in this case involved receiving certain answers just because they were asked to give that exact answer, many of the questions addressed the topic in an indirect way. I submitted the same questions for both groups. The questions of the interview were just a guideline. None of these questions referred directly to their religious practices. They focused mostly on their professional life and business, in order to permit the information to come out spontaneously from the entrepreneur's own words.

After the interview I also asked connections of other Christian entrepreneurs to include in the research. The main goal of the interviews was to investigate the validity of my question on the impact of the belief in the assurance of salvation on work ethic and economic success (see Table 5.3 and *Theoretical Argument*). Since my focus was checking the presence of a certain religious belief and its impact on self-efficacy, the technique of in-depth interviews was insufficient. For this reason, together with interviews I spent long hours with the entrepreneurs in their daily work through job-shadowing, in order to observe how they lived their beliefs practically.

Table 5.3 Interview chart of the beliefs among entrepreneurs

Questions	*Underlying Topic*	*What we expect to observe*	*Elements to compare with non-Christian Entrepreneurs*	*Supplemental techniques*
"*What are your working experiences? How did you accomplish them?*"	Introduction	Have a detailed idea of the kind of work they do, check if they perceive economic status as a result of God's blessings and favor	Involvement in jobs with higher success, more motivation and dynamic attitude, peculiar perception of a link between success and God	Visits at work, biographical records
"*Why work is so important for you?*"	*Assistants to P* Predestination, perseverance of the saints, sovereignty of God, literal reading of the Bible...	Check of lack of moments of doubts (anxiety of salvation), test the presence of the inheritance of the Calvinist doctrines and their influence on economic ethos, see for the cases observed in China the presence of the same elements on a trans-national level	A stronger economic ethos, less traditionalism, self-confidence and self-efficacy, more drastic opinions, frequent search for purpose,	Analysis of his religious literature, attendance to church activities specially sermons
"*In which way do you express your identity at work?*"	*Precondition I.* Boss Christians phenomenon	Notify their dominant role in business, measure the presence of an inner-worldly asceticism, describe how this push them into an economic propensity	An higher involvement at work in top-level positions, higher resistance to stress, an use of beliefs in work, control of conduct, saving tendency, effect on business strategies	Visits at work, shadowing, his/her business literature, biographical records, inter-generational ethnographic observations

(continued)

Table 5.3 (continued)

Questions	*Underlying Topic*	*What we expect to observe*	*Elements to compare with non-Christian Entrepreneurs*	*Supplemental techniques*
"*Why did you came to Italy? How did you find this job?*"	*Precondition II*. Yi Xiang	Check if they perceive work as a calling, notify the characteristics of the Chinese Beruf, moral perception of work	A purpose-driven life, strong meaning of his work, passion, higher dedication and devotion to his job, motivation	Witnesses from other's church members, biographical records
"*Are you part of a network of Chinese business? How it helped your work?*"	*Precondition III*. House church	Role of network in economic success, presence of the house churches in the economic tissue in China and trans-nationally	Recurrence to a certificate of honesty, self-examination, personality, charisma, receive much trust from other people	Church attendance, participation in house gatherings, visits to families, passage of information's
"*What is the main purpose in your work?*"	*Precondition IV*. Glory of God and love of Christ	See their priorities in life, check the inheritance of the Calvinistic belief in the glory of God as the ultimate purpose in life	Higher motivation, higher sense of duty, dedication, clear goals, strive for excellence	Participatory observation, shadowing, church attendance especially sermons
"*Did you had challenges or difficulties at work? How did you react? What helped you?*"	*Research Question* Perpetual assurance of Salvation	Consequence of PAS in feelings and at work, what lead the person to achieve business goals, reaction to situations of risk, stress and difficulties	What makes it different than other people beliefs, how would you live without the belief in PAS	Participatory observation, shadowing, visits at work, church attendance especially sermons

I used several qualitative techniques to check the validity of my theoretical argument, such as the 'trick of metaphorization', in this case seeing the church as an economic enterprise with all its members as entrepreneurs, or the trick of null hypothesis: what would happen if PAS was subtracted. I also utilized several times the 'trick of the unexpressed major premise' (Cardano, 2011; Emerson, 2001; Ricolfi, 1997). The 'unexpressed major premise' refers to cultural convictions implicitly held by people under investigations that couldn't be identified simply by asking questions. For example, I couldn't observe apart from job-shadowing whether an entrepreneur was doing well with his business. In the case of Chinese Protestants, I invited the respondent to submit also a questionnaire (Maurer, 1998) and the General Self-efficacy scale (Sibilia L., Schwarzer R., Jerusalem M., 1995). Since I was seeking to observe a psychological attitude, the scale allowed me to check the presence of self-efficacy among the two groups. In the case of Protestant entrepreneurs, a second section of the scale was utilized to measure the relation between self-efficacy and PAS (Table 5.4).

In the case of the Chinese Christian entrepreneurs, I've spent a lot of time observing their activities at church through participant observation, job-shadowing and other unobtrusive techniques of measuring. This not only involved the religious gatherings but even working routines. I helped three entrepreneurs in their work, observing their different business practices. Being an ethnographer, my task was to describe a specific culture, the way they expressed themselves in different areas of life: religion, family, circle of relationships, as I then focused on their business. The goal of this ethnography was to grasp the entrepreneur's point of view, his perspective on life, his worldview (Spradley, 1979) without any judgment of value. I spent long periods in continuous ethnographic observation (6–7 consecutive months). I investigated the daily life of those Christian entrepreneurs, their conversations, through a reconstruction of their routine, being involved in their free time, inquiring their social environment, their cultural schemes, their perception of the outside world.

In the beginning, I've used a broad strategy of observation (from descriptive to focused and selective observations). I collected in the beginning much information in the field that seemed to be not necessarily linked to my topic of interest ('trick to meet the unexpected'), paying attention to the environment. Borrowing from ethnomethodology, I

Table 5.4 Part of the questionnaire that I submitted to respondents in order to test the presence of self-efficacy. Even having reached a quite satisfactory number of respondents (n = 79), the application of such instrument to my study must be taken with caution and with no intent of giving any ultimate answer to the matter

For the next questions please choose a number 1-4 and write a number in every statement to identify how you agree with the statement.

1	2	3	4
Not at all true	Hardly true	Moderately true	Exactly true

1.	_____	I can always manage to solve difficult problems if I try hard enough.
2.	_____	If someone opposes me, I can find the means and ways to get what I want.
3.	_____	It is easy for me to stick to my aims and accomplish my goals.
4.	_____	I am confident that I could deal efficiently with unexpected events.
5.	_____	Thanks to my resourcefulness, I know how to handle unforeseen situations.
6.	_____	I can solve most problems if I invest the necessary effort.
7.	_____	I can remain calm when facing difficulties because I can rely on my coping abilities.
8.	_____	When I am confronted with a problem, I can usually find several solutions.
9.	_____	If I am in trouble, I can usually think of a solution.
10.	_____	I can usually handle whatever comes my way.

decided, especially in the first stages of my research, to often ask clarifications in order to discover elements that I might have taken for granted (Babbie, 2015). I also focused on Chinese Protestants who were not part of the group of interest, observing their behaviors even if not necessarily linked to my specific focus. The main reason was to intentionally challenge my theoretical convictions, keeping my eyes opened toward unknown research inputs directly from the fieldwork.

After this stage, I then narrowed my focus on the aspects under my interest. Two or three entrepreneurs were followed in their workplace, to observe the relationship between their economic transactions and their religious values. To see how they interpreted their actions according to their beliefs. I then alternated intense periods of observations to moments of departure from the fieldwork, in light of my need to analyze the empirical documentation. Then I came back again to the fieldwork with a different focus. Many of these Chinese entrepreneurs in Milan were also part of several associations. The research included some visits to events organized by those associations. On the field I also contacted local

Italian entrepreneurs who were interacting with the field to observe their perception as 'outsiders'.

My focus remained on the Chinese entrepreneurs. Prolonged observations were made of non-entrepreneurial Chinese Protestants, in order to see if they still displayed any economic ethic. After a first phase, I then started another simultaneous group, interviewing 20 Chinese entrepreneurs with no link with Protestant Christianity who worked in the Chinatown in Milan.

The collection of this second sample was not done through an informant but through a 'snowball strategy', from a contact list. I had in this case the challenge of building trust, facing their suspect, adapting to their busy schedule, postponing meetings. I had several shut doors or negative responses, but after a first phase I was able to proceed.The entrance to this second field was particularly challenging given the lack of integration of Chinese people in the Italian context. I was perceived as an obstacle, a native Italian seeking to take advantage of them. The interviews therefore sometimes suffered, being poor in the amount of information that I was able to gather.

My visit to Wenzhou, China on the other hand, was much more productive. I was able in the second year of my research to do this visit to the motherland. In such circumstance, I was perceived by the entrepreneurs as a western foreigner, warmly welcomed. I received their full attention, curiosity and a solemn response. There information was very easy to be gathered. The visit to the motherland was an additional confirmation of what witnessed in the diaspora. The second sample of non-Christian entrepreneurs in Milan worked for me as a second group of analysis, useful for checking the empirical evidence apart from the belief of the first group.

The main reason I've introduced this second set of interviews was to check any noticeable difference between the two samples of entrepreneurs with different sets of values. The intent was to check the validity of my theoretical argument, through a case–control study. I wanted to make sure that no intervening factor such as social influence, cultural values, network membership or any other element may lead to identify a pre-existing profit-oriented mentality. Many scholars have pointed out, for example, that the impact of the institutional context together with the market context are crucial in shaping people's life toward short- or long-term decisions (North, 1989). I needed to include this component in my explanation. I wanted through this second sample to shed light to

Table 5.5 Different options of outcomes related to the theoretical argument and sample composition for gender, age and religious identification

Total of People Interviewed	61 men 22 women - 2 outsiders

	Economic Success	*Economic Insuccess*
Protestant	i) case study	ii) outcome 2
Non Protestant	iii) case control	iv) outcome 4

	Men	*Women*
Protestant*	25 / 14	9 / 2
Non Protestant	16 / 6	7 / 4

*** Focus Group**	1 female Entrepreneur 27 y.o., 1 male Banker 43 y.o., 1 Pastor 44 y.o., 1 male teacher 28 y.o., 1 male Interpreter 26 y.o.

the dimensions which may impact the relationship between belief and economic success (Table 5.5).

Concerning the selection of the sample, the case-control was organized in four outcomes, comparing the case i) and iii) in this sample. I am not denying the possibility of categories ii) and iv). In fact, in few cases entrepreneurs did not experience success. Among the Christian entrepreneurs for example, I included a flea market, where they were selling sashes or glasses and other low-cost merchandizes. This type of business that was more typical of the first generation of migrants is not a case of economic success. In any case, during my qualitative research I observed a general tendency toward economic success in terms of number of businesses, new investments, number of clients, etc., … for both cases. 90% of the Chinese attending the Protestant church were involved in entrepreneurial activities.

The main sample was selected from an ethnic-based evangelical church, a community that was migrant and auto-referential (Naso, 2014). My observations focused on Chinese believers involved in entrepreneurial activities (bar manager, store manager, merchant, supplier, manufacture export, clothing store manager, enterprise employee, farm clothing employee, web designer…) who showed a certain degree of economic success. The measurement of success was done on the basis of profit, income, age, number of businesses, history of work activities and customer-employee and owner's satisfaction. All these are elements that traditionally are treated as indicators of economic success.

5.2.3 Comparisons

After the first phase, in order for me to have a more objective understanding of entrepreneurship, the second group was introduced. Special attention was given to the selection of this sample of Chinese non-Protestant entrepreneurs, avoiding self-selection (interviewing only those who are willing to be interviewed) and enhancing the homogeneity of the sample. As much as possible interviews were done to non-Protestant entrepreneurs who shared all the characteristics of the first group (region of origin, time of arrival and seniority of migration, gender, composition of family migration and lineage tradition, age, level of education, social and economic status) except their beliefs.

The majority of those Chinese non-Christian entrepreneurs were either atheists or Buddhist. Although it was not a completely representative sample, it nevertheless served successfully for my main theoretical purpose. I included this second group of entrepreneurs in order to check any alternative explanations. The aim was not a general comparison of economic success between two samples. I was concerned with the presence/absence of any other element that could demonstrate the fictitiousness of the religious effect. In particular, I wanted to make sure that none of these categories could play any dominant explanatory role: a general attitude to work (Stakhanovism), the lack of awareness on human rights, working hard only because being under constraint, the role of Chinese mafia, a 'religion of Communism', family values, education, cultural orientation to work, opening toward the outside world after centuries of segregation, success just based on their involvement in migration process, their social network, their duplicating abilities or their economic price competition, etc.

Even taking into account all those elements, trying to consider any intervening factor on the relationship (*Wenzhou's profit-oriented mentality*), it was still difficult to explain where this strong profit-oriented attitude came from. Why Chinese entrepreneurs have a tendency to accept long hours of work, lower payment and still achieve high economic success through their entrepreneurial mindset? My goal here was to check the consistency of such component by the 'trick of Wittgenstein' and 'trick of Lindesmith'. I used the process of subtraction and counterfactual control: what will happen to an event X, namely economic success, if I subtract the quality Y, namely the belief in PAS? (Wittgenstein, 1953; pp. 175–178) Does the work ethic still holds for the case of

Chinese entrepreneurs if I subtract the component of the belief in the PAS? This doesn't mean that I pursued a causal explanation, as if no economic success could be possible among the Chinese entrepreneurs of the second group. Rather, the focus was to check the impact of any association between Protestant beliefs and economic success, pointing out the absence of any economic ethos able to push the individual toward economic success. The questions that I've asked to the entrepreneurs in this second group were intentionally identical to those asked to the interest group. This was done in order to identify or detect the role of other possible explanatory elements such as those listed here in Table 5.6.

Apart from the interviews once again, even for the second sample I added participant observation. For the case of non-Christian entrepreneurs, I tested the validity of the research question through a series of interviews. The application of such strategies depended on their reaction to my research interest, giving the fact that migrant communities often are closed toward outsiders. This resulted to be at times an obstacle, aggravated by the fact that with some exceptions the Chinese community was more unapproachable than other migrant communities. At the same time, I analyzed the empirical documentation and adjusted the questions of the interview as needed. From initial questions about their beliefs and their relation with business, I changed into more neutral questions about work, letting the data emerge by itself. This resulted in an a posteriori re-formulation of the theoretical argument (see Table 9.1). After the interview, I proceeded with the transcription into a condensed account, usually no more than 15 days after, analyzing the material and verifying the reliability of the information. Then I proceeded to the presentation of the material in light of the sociological relevance of it (Babbie, 2015). This strategy went on until the necessary level of theoretical saturation was reached. The analysis of the material from the interviews covered the entire final phase of the research project.

Documentary material on religion and China were also collected at the Center on Religion and Chinese Society of the Purdue University in Indiana (USA), as well as during the sojourn in Wenzhou (China). The visit to Wenzhou was possible through contacts both through the academia and the fieldwork. The trip was also possible through my personal connections entrepreneurs that during my job-shadowing were going back to China for a business trip. My visit to Wenzhou was not void of challenges, given the control from the government over Christian activities in China. Foreigners like me were technically not allowed to be

Table 5.6 Part of the interview chart that refers to the explanations that I want to check among the Chinese non-Christian entrepreneurs

Questions	*Underlying topic*	*What we expect to observe*	*Elements to compare with Christian Entrepreneurs*	*Supplemental techniques*
"*What are your working experiences? How did you accomplish them?*"	*Introduction*	Identify their perception of the reasons of success, if individual (hard work), social (friends, connections) or economic (business strategies), check the results of absence of calling, make sure there's no Stakhanovism	Higher materialism, compromises, lack of purpose, unwillingness to fight for a goal	Visits at work
"*Why work is so important for you?*"	*Communist explanation*	Check the lack of political involvement, make sure the communist ethic doesn't play a dominant role	Absence of the impact of any ethical system (even secular) on their behavior	Analysis of today's Chinese politics
"*In which way do you express your identity at work?*"	*Constriction explanation*	Make sure economic results don't depend on lack of human rights or their willingness to work hard only because under constraint	Lack of motivation, no higher meaning in work apart from the satisfaction of personal needs, lower results, no significant and positive impact of constriction	Witnesses from other's workers
"*Why did you came to Italy? How did you find this job?*"	*Minority explanation*	Make sure success cannot be determinant of their migration process and their status of minority	The fact of being foreigner doesn't explain significantly the relationship	Participatory observation, shadowing, visits at work

(continued)

Table 5.6 (continued)

Questions	*Underlying topic*	*What we expect to observe*	*Elements to compare with Christian Entrepreneurs*	*Supplemental techniques*
"*Are you part of a network of Chinese business? How it helped your work?*"	*Network explanation*	Make sure that economic success may not be related to Chinese lineage, mafia, or a strong involvement in a social network	Network of Chinatown entrepreneurs does not provide the same economic result as in the Christian example	Visits at work, shadowing, passages of information, participation in events
"*What is the main purpose in your work?*"	*Cultural explanation*	Check if the role of family values is predominant, with education, or a general cultural orientation to work	Absence of the values observed in the Christian sample and no significant cultural influence on economic success	Analysis of his/her cultural interests, visits to families, passage of information's
"*Did you had challenges or difficulties at work? How did you react? What helped you?*"	*Economic explanation*	Check if some economic variable explain dominantly, such as price competition, duplicating abilities or an opening towards the outside world after segregation	Economic factors in itself not able to cover all the phenomenon	Analysis of economic dynamics of business, shadowing

in contact with Chinese pastors, church members in the area of Wenzhou. My presence therefore was sometimes felt as intrusive, which became a challenge for the Chinese Protestant believers already at risk of imprisonment because of persecution coming from the communist government. I went to Wenzhou in a critical season for Christian churches in Wenzhou. The fact that the visit lasted only two weeks made it easier, together with the fact that I moved from place to place to detect any interception from the police. This visit and the ethnographic observations that I did there allowed me to compare entrepreneurship in China and in the diaspora. The visit was planned during the summer of the second year of my research, at a moment when the data collected in the diaspora offered a sufficiently clear idea for comparison. I was able to witness the impact of the migration process as opposed to those in the motherlands. In following chapters (see Cp. 6.2) I will further deal with some cases that confirmed what I previously observed in Milan.

Once the collection and analysis of empirical documentation reached the necessary level of theoretical saturation, I then proceeded to harmonize the empirical documentation with the original theory. The research therefore went through three phases. The first phase was characterized by an analysis of data regarding the theme chosen (Max Weber's theory on Protestantism and Capitalism, history of Christianity, aspects of reformed theology, Chinese Christianity, etc.). A second phase involved the collection of information directly in the field through entrepreneurs involved in business activities. Finally, the third phase was a synthesis of what was collected in the field in tune with the sociological theory based upon the initial objective.

When facing drawbacks on the availability of the cases, I proceeded with the use of my personal network of other Chinese churches and entrepreneurs operating in the same area. In some cases, the list of questions was not followed rigidly. This gave room for non-structured and more discursive interviews. The research also had the benefit of giving a better reputation and higher visibility to the communities and entrepreneurs under my analysis. It served also to shed light into a context of analysis overlooked. My description was able to give an account of the complexity and diversity of Chinese entrepreneurship related to values and economic outcomes. My data necessitated the respect of the privacy of the people involved in the study, give the risk involved with the political and ideological control coming from the Communist government.

References

AA. VV., 1997, *Cina a Milano. Famiglie, ambienti e lavori della popolazione cinese a Milano*, Abitare Segesta Cataloghi, Milano.

AA. VV., 1997, *I Ching. Il libro della versatilità*, UTET, Torino.

Babbie, E. (2015). *The Basics of Social Research.* Thomson Wadsworth, New York.

Barbera F., Negri N., 2015, 'Rituals as Mechanisms', in *Paradoxes, Mechanisms, Consequences: Essay in Honor of Mohamed Cherkaoui*, edited by G.L. Manzo, Oxford, Bardwell Press.

Burawoy M. (Eds.), 1991, *Ethnography Unbound. Power and Resistance in the Modern Metropolis*, University of California Press, Berkeley.

Cao N. 'Christian Entrepreneurs and the Post-Mao State: An Ethnographic Account of Church-State Relations in China's Economic Transition', from *Sociology of Religion*, Vol. 68, No. 1, (Spring. 2007), pp. 45–66.

Cardano M., 2011, *La ricerca qualitativa*, Bologna, Il Mulino.

Ceccagno A., 'The Mobile Emplacement: Chinese Migrants in Italian Industrial Districts', in *Journal of Ethnic and Migration Studies* (Oct. 2014), pp. 1–21.

Chicchi F., 2006, *Per un'analisi critica dell'Economia delle convenzioni: alcune brevi riflessioni sul suo statuto teorico e sul suo rapporto con la sociologia del lavoro*, in Franco Angeli, Milano.

Cologna D. 2006, *L'immigrazione Cinese in Italia, una realtà in Rapida Evoluzione*, Aesse-Azione Sociale, n. 8, Codici s. c.

Duneier, M. (1999). *Sidewalk*, New York, Farrar, Strauss and Giroux.

Emerson, R. M. (2001). *Contemporary Field Research. Perspectives and Formulations*, Long Grove, Illinois, Waveland Press.

Hannerz, U. (1980). *Exploring the City. Inquiries Toward an Urban Anthropology*, New York, Columbia University Press.

IDOS, 2014, *Rapporto Immigrazione e Imprenditoria*, Edizioni IDOS, Roma.

Maurer J. T., 'A Comparison of Likert Scale and Traditional Measures of Self-efficacy', in *Journal of Applied Psychology*, (March 1998); Vol. 83, No. 2, pp. 324–329.

Naso P., 2014, *Fratelli e Sorelle di Jerry Masslo. L'immigrazione Evangelica in Italia*, Claudiana, Torino.

North G., 1988, *Puritan Economic Experiments: Puritans and Government Controls*, Institute for Christian Economics.

Ocejo E. R., (Eds.), 2013, *Ethnography and the City. Readings on Doing Urban Fieldwork*, New York, Routledge.

Ricolfi L., 1997, *La Ricerca Qualitativa*, Carocci, Roma.

Spradley, J. P. (1979). *The Ethnographic Interview*. Holt, Rinehart and Winston Inc.

Wittgenstein L., 1953, *Philosophical Investigations*, Basil Blackwell, Oxford, pp. 175–178.

CHAPTER 6

The Case for a Chinese Capitalism

> Today is hard, tomorrow will be worse. But the day after tomorrow will be sunshine.
>
> —Jack Ma

6.1 The Life of Chinese Migrants

6.1.1 Their Economic Presence

This chapter is intended to introduce the reader to the fieldwork under observation. While some of the content might appear to be redundant to some readers, its relevance will become clearer later in the book. Let us begin by looking at Chinese entrepreneurship in the west. By looking to Chinese migration one can rightly define it as a real diaspora. What I will point out regarding the Chinese presence in the city of Milan in Italy can be extended to what is going on in the rest of the West (Benton and Pieke, 1998) and even to other places around the globe where a consistent Chinese presence among migrants is witnessed. Migration from China has reached unprecedented levels of rapid and intense scale, more than any other developing countries. The majority of those migratory flows historically originated from the Cantonese and Zhejiangese provinces. As for the rest of Europe the Chinese communities came mainly from the southern Zhejiang hinterland of the port city of Wenzhou and from the rural area

O. Palombaro, *Christianity and Capitalism in China*,
https://doi.org/10.1007/978-981-97-3549-5_6

around the town of Qingtian. The majority of them came to Europe with the intention to find a better life, to start a business and to work. A final wave of Chinese migrants recently came to Milan as well as to other major European metropolis with a very different background from the previous Wenzhounese flow. Today those Wenzhounese migrants are already second or third generation migrants. The more recent wave is composed by well-educated city dwellers from the north part of China.

The substantial difference among those two branches (Wenzhouren entrepreneurs and Northern intellectuals) is in the economic ties, that in the first case are much more developed, as to represent an ethnic niche in the diaspora economy. This geographical split results in a lack of cohesion and interaction between those two branches. The Wenzhouren migrant sees other Chinese migrants as different. This is accompanied by competition and conflicts. An example of this animosity was the conflict that existed between the many Chinese associations and social groups that I came into contact with during my study. Any effort to promote cultural or social activities not beneficial for the community as a whole were seen with suspiciousness. Like in other European urban metropolis, the Chinese community of Milan traditionally located in a Chinatown spread its ties into other parts of the city. This is centered on different businesses and typologies that I will later on classify: restaurant, bar, clothing store, hair shop, phone store, supermarket and traditional food stores, massage center, travel agencies, tailoring, Chinese bank, Tobacco and betting establishment.... Each of them usually is linked with suppliers of Chinese factories sometimes located in the West sometimes in China. Those different categories are repeated and coined in series and customized through an imitation process.

Even though the Chinatown of Milan has some correspondence with the idea of ghetto, it is also different. Chinese workers do not live there and do not necessarily even buy things there. That's why it is more proper to consider it as an 'imaginary ghetto', a core place for certain social, economic and cultural functions that are connecting the migrant to his Chinese homeland. The Chinese workers in the Chinatown of Milan experiences sometimes peaks of hostility and ethnic exclusion. One example of this came when in April 2007, due to tensions with the government of Milan and continuous sanctions on their business, more than 300 Chinese entrepreneurs violently protested in the Chinatown. Another example, for example, came on December 2013 when in the city of Prato, a Chinese textile factory was burnt causing the death of 7

Chinese workers. Many stereotypes related to events like these caused the spread of a negative and unbalanced way of seeing the Chinese presence.

In this vacuum of legitimation many associations and social groups were created (associations made of people coming from the same region, Chinese chambers of commerce, etc., ...). Many of them work as informal networks where resources are concentrated in the hands of few people that allocate access to these resources. The Chinese community and its networks are very closed toward the outside culture and sometimes even toward other Chinese externals. Being from a different Chinese town or from a different migratory time caused individuals to be excluded from the network. Even though internally integrated, the Chinese community of Milan is not integrated into the society largely because of linguistic difficulties. But even in the case of the second generation of migrants, the pressure and constraint to remain inside the traditional network is larger than any desire to be assimilated into the local society.

After the major economic crisis of 2008, those Chinese communities that focused on business had to work in a hard context. Milan experienced almost 8 consecutive years of downfall in business, where many entrepreneurs were forced to close or sell their activities. This was due to the high taxation or the lack of finances to keep going. Entire zones near the center of Milan were, and are still, forced to shut down. Yet, under this tragic and dramatic spiral of failures and economic crisis the Chinese migrant community of entrepreneurs, above any other migrant community, saw their golden opportunity. Instead of failing or decreasing their economic benefit, the Chinese business flourished at the point of almost replacing many segments of the local economy. This negatively affects the perception from the public opinion and mass media permeated of jealousy and antagonism. The Chinese community is seen as 'stealing jobs' from the native people and doesn't follow the legal parameters of work. Giving the already critical condition of the economy and the competition over few resources, this tension often exasperated. If someone might ask why Chinese entrepreneurs are witnessing this business success despite the surrounding economic crisis, it is crucial to consider several factors. First of all, the links of obligation in the Chinese society added to the quest for moral superiority and other modes of behavior that are distinctly Chinese (paternalism, nepotism, family ownership) indicate the presence of a certain 'spirit of Chinese capitalism'.

One of the strengths of the Chinese migrants in Milan that immediately stood out in my research was the direct link between business enterprises and family. This was particularly crucial in the first initial stages of their settlement as it was pointed out by the entrepreneurs during the biographical records. Being attached to their traditional values, those migrants were often benefitting from the capital of family savings and loans involving also future generations. Just to give an example, Ning, one of the entrepreneurs that I have interviewed, almost immediately pointed out how he related his success to some sort of 'moral obligation' toward the family:

> I worked making money, working hard, in order to ask not [finances] to the parents, for my-self, to grow. [...] I want to make money by myself, to be independent. I am a positive person, I want to be a better man, even if I don't succeed I try hard. First, apart from the family that tells me to study hard, I think on what I want to do, to have the strength and realize my dreams. (Ning, Jilin, Milan, 20/01/2016)

> Hard work is from culture, since childhood, our parents come after us with a gun on our back [*laughing*]. My parents own a publishing company. Family pushes a lot to work, there are many people, in order to find a job you need something special. (Jing, Chong Ching, Milan, 22/01/2016)

Businesses oftentimes are based on a family nucleus. As time went on the Chinese ethnic niche of certain typologies of business was a protective mean in order to rashly achieve economic affirmation. The push for migration comes from deeply introspected cultural patterns, where the individual looks for an opportunity to become quickly rich as he aspires to start an entrepreneurial activity on his own. The aspiration to entrepreneurship and self-employment was so strong that capitals and energies inside the family, communities and social networks, were quickly mobilized. Powerful ethnic networks favored immediate employment of Chinese migrants at the arrival in Italy, missing among other migrant communities. And even among Chinese migrants those coming from Wenzhou and Qingtian benefited from the social networks on an international scale more than Chinese migrants coming from other areas.

One of the first features of Chinese small businesses, when compared with the Italian context, is their flexibility, the fact of being able to guarantee a faster production and reduced times of delivery. This competitive factor is able to guarantee the survival and even the good profit in situations of crisis. On the other hand, longer working hours, lower payment, tax avoidance, undeclared work, lack of security were all recurrent problematics among Chinese entrepreneurs in Milan. Because of personal debts or social pressures from the family, the Chinese worker tends to work in extreme conditions. The individual in this circumstance is forced to conform himself to the migratory career of the group, working as much as possible and learning the first elements of the Italian language. An example of this came during my frequent conversations with Minzhe and it was interesting to hear what she had to say:

> Many Chinese work in factories, they spend time only working. They have false passports, they are obligated to come here just to work. The students can go anywhere but the Chinese don't go anywhere, they are forced to work, if they work hard they can make more money. Since they don't have documents they must work in order to buy their documents. Some Chinese have Japanese [fake] documents. In Prato I met a woman that stays in the factory and doesn't talk anymore 'cause her son died inside the factory! She is alone now and doesn't want to come back, her heart broke... [*sight*] The boss makes pressure but also the workers want to work, they are the same, the majority works in clothing. (Minzhe, Shuzhou, Milan, 20/01/2016)

The outcome of such a frugal lifestyle, cutting all the possible expenses to the minimal, is what gives them the ability to reach the status of entrepreneur. People from Wenzhou see dependent work as a cage, a condition of weakness that goes against their aspirations of becoming self-employed (AA. VV., 1997, p. 135). Once the worker becomes the owner of a store it is like a 'passage of status' in front of the rest of the community. As business grows he can then consider the possibility of multiplying his business activities. Sometimes the workers were active even on the weekend and at night, at times working 30 hours of work alternated by brief naps. For this reasons the social life of the Chinese workers tends to be radically compressed, sometimes even forcedly removed as something that can obstacle the production. Marital life, parenthood and family life are all subordinated to the affirmation of work. In this sense someone may properly consider the social life of an entrepreneur as work itself where every sphere of life revolves around it.

6.2 Profiles of Chinese Entrepreneurs

6.2.1 Ideal-Types

I now begin to outline the observations from several key ideal-types to my study first from the Chinese Protestant entrepreneurs. In this section, I will examine the results from the job-shadowing conducted among Chinese entrepreneurs in the city of Milan. The aim of this section will be to give a description of their job, regardless of any reference to religious values or ethics, which will be treated in another section of the book. From the data of the Chamber of Commerce of Italy and the Italo-Chinese chamber of commerce, it emerges that there are approximately 20.000 Chinese resident in the province of Milan (5.9% of the total population of foreigners). Half of them is composed by women (9.600 47.7% of the total). At the third semester of the year 2008, the number of individual Chinese enterprises registered in Milan was 3.131, 9.8% of the total Italian number of Chinese enterprises and 68% of which are active in the city area of Milan (Source: Italian Chamber of Commerce, 2009). The number is much higher because many of those enterprises and small businesses are not necessarily registered at the Italian chamber of commerce. After the Egyptian community, the Chinese is the second non-European migrant community involved with entrepreneurship in Milan and its province. The entrepreneurship rate inside this community is high, 1 out of 8 Chinese is an entrepreneur in the city of Milan.

Imprese cinesi a Milano attive al III trimestre 2008

settore	tot cinesi III trim 2008 Milano	TOTALE extracomunitari Milano	tot cinesi III trimestre 2007 Milano	tot cinesi Italia 2008	variazione cinesi 08-07	peso settori 2008	peso cinesi tu tot extracomunitari	Cinesi MI/cinesi Italia
Attivita' manifatturiere	972	2.176	922	13.731	5,4%	31,0%	44,7%	7,1%
Costruzioni	44	6.149	41	248	7,3%	1,4%	0,7%	17,7%
Comm.ingr.e dett.-rip.beni pers.e per la casa	1.316	6.158	1.292	15.176	1,9%	42,0%	21,4%	8,7%
Alberghi e ristoranti	576	927	425	1.873	35,5%	18,4%	62,1%	30,8%
Trasporti,magazzinaggio e comunicaz.	35	1.936	38	160	-7,9%	1,1%	1,8%	21,9%
Intermediaz.monetaria e finanziaria	8	121	9	18	-11,1%	0,3%	6,6%	44,4%
Attiv.immob.,noleggio,informat.,ricerca (servizi alle imprese)	48	2209	36	282	33,3%	1,5%	2,2%	17,0%
Altri servizi pubblici,sociali e personali	90	491	33	162	172,7%	2,9%	18,3%	55,6%
Altre imprese	42	424	41	162	2,4%	1,3%	9,9%	25,9%
TOTALE	3.131	20.591	2.837	31.812	10,4%	100,0%	15,2%	9,8%

Elaborazione Camera di commercio di Milano su dati registro imprese al III trimestre 2008

[1]

[1] *Source* Italian Chamber of Commerce, 'In Arrivo l'Anno del Toro', in *Camera di Commercio di Milano*, (Jan. 2009), Milan, pp. 1–2.

I've already pointed out how Chinese entrepreneurship from the area of Wenzhou represents a significant economic portion for the case of Italy. In fact, as I've already mentioned 80–90% of Chinese immigrants living in Italy comes from the city of Wenzhou and 70% of them are involved in businesses. Many of them own restaurants and bars whereas 20% of them are involved in commercial activities. Lombardy, and its regional capital Milan, is very significant for Chinese business. It is second only to Tuscany in number of enterprises (18% of the total number of enterprises in the area) and right after Prato and Florence in terms of Chinese presence (15.5% of the total migrant community). In 2008 the Chinese was the second migrant community living in Milan, and it gave the highest economic turnover: 46 million € with an average of 63.000 € for business (Bressan, 2013; Fatiguso, 2011; AA. VV., 2002).

Classifica nazionalità titolari stranieri di imprese individuali attive a Milano al III trimestre 2008

posizione	nazionalità	Comune di MILANO	nazionalità	Stato di nascita	TOTALE prov Milano
1	EGITTO	3257	1	EGITTO	4932
2	**CINA**	**2085**	**2**	**CINA**	**3131**
3	MAROCCO	809	3	MAROCCO	2032
4	PERU'	697	4	ALBANIA	1302
5	BANGLADESH	669	5	PERU'	1074

Elaborazione Camera di commercio di Milano su dati registro imprese al III trimestre 2008

Residenti cinesi a Milano - anno 2007

	Maschi	Femmine	Totale	peso donne
residenti cinesi prov. Mi 2007	10.565	9.629	**20.194**	47,7%
residenti cinesi prov. Mi 2006	10.044	9.084	**19.128**	47,5%
variazione 2007-06	5,2%	6,0%	**5,6%**	
tot stranieri prov. Mi 2007	175.344	169.023	**344.367**	49,1%
peso cinesi su tot stranieri prov. Milano	6,0%	5,7%	**5,9%**	
residenti cinesi comune di Milano 2007	7.739	6.984	**14.723**	47,4%
residenti cinesi comune di Milano 2006	7.392	6.631	**14.023**	47,3%
variazione 2007-06	4,7%	5,3%	**5,0%**	
tot stranieri Mi	88.770	87.227	**175.997**	49,6%
peso cinesi su tot stranieri comune diMilano	8,7%	8,0%	**8,4%**	

Elaborazione della Camera di commercio di Milano su dati Istat 2007

Tasso di imprenditorialità dei residenti a Milano nel 2007

Residenti	Tasso imprenditorialità	Rapporto imprese/residenti
cinesi prov. Mi 2007	0,14	1 su 7
cinesi comune di Milano 2007	0,13	1 su 8
italiani prov. Mi 2007	0,04	1 su 27
Totale residenti prov. Mi	0,09	1 su 11

Elaborazione Camera di commercio di Milano su dati registro imprese e dati Istat 2007

2

More precise statistics show that the Chinese enterprises in Milan and its province at the third semester of 2008 focused mainly in three sectors: trade (1.316 enterprises, 42% of the total), manufacturing (972, 31% of the total), restaurants and hotels (576, 18.4% of the total). Compared to other non-European migrant communities, the Chinese entrepreneurs in Milan are more focused on restaurants and hotels (62.1% of the total of enterprises with non-European holder) and in manufacturing (44.7%). Overall, the Chinese enterprises in the Milan province at the third semester of 2008 were growing of the 10.4% if compared to the same period of 2007 (Source: Italian Chamber of Commerce, 2009). The biggest growth can be observed in public social and personal services passing from 33 to 90 enterprises, hotels and restaurants (+35.5%) and services to enterprises (+33.3%). From 2008 to the more recent years, those numbers are estimated to be exceedingly growing and expanding.

This huge involvement in business of the Chinese community did not happen over night. Since their first migratory flows in the 1800 the Chinese people from Wenzhou started to be involved in very low payed jobs as hawkers, street vending, domestic workers, construction work, loading or unloading in central markets, etc., … with few specialized skills, without a stable income and living very disintegrated from their European counterpart. Their first consistent involvement in migration started in France after the Second World War. Soldiers enrolled from China decided to remain in Europe after the war, spreading their connections in other countries like Germany or Belgium (Chee-Beng et al., 2007). In Italy the first presence started from the 1930s, as one of the earliest immigrant communities. Their arrival grew more consistently from 1950s where they started to occupy the sector of restaurants, although having a very low economic impact at the time. The first settlement was precisely Milan, followed by Bologna, Florence and Rome (Benton and Pieke, 1998). But their presence in the native Italian society was hardly visible until the mid-1970s. As China became the 'factory of the world' many of those Chinese people started to make connections with their motherland in order to start exporting their merchandises.

[2] *Source* Italian Chamber of Commerce, 'In Arrivo l'Anno del Toro', in *Camera di Commercio di Milano*, (Jan. 2009), Milan, pp. 1–2.

From 1984 Wenzhou benefited of her position as an international harbor for export. The city started to bring trade in Italy during the 1980s, first in the food and leather sectors, later on in the textile sector. At first, they worked for Italian retail companies then with the capital accumulation and exportation of it in China they started their own enterprises. As time went on those initial migrant workers experienced a progressive upward mobility and economic thrive in jobs that required more skills (from worker to multiple boss owners, from street vendors to large-scale buyers, from waiter to graduated business accountants, from machine operator to sales managers). This was also due to the introduction of the legal right of family re-union. The request for a residence permit was since then usually driven by the desire to become business owners. Differently from other migrant communities, Chinese workers can benefit from opportunities to work in sectors of the labor market formed by businesses owned and managed by co-nationals. Many of those migrants arrived or are currently in a condition of 'irregulars' having been involved in 'migrant smuggling' organized by groups specialized in this trade (Ceccagno and Rastrelli, 2008). Once arrived in Italy the migrant then finds contact with his relatives or family members for housing and work in order to raise the necessary resources to pay back the smugglers.

In thirty years, the Chinese presence in the economy of Italy has grown very high and the level of integration into specific sectors of businesses thrived (Zhang and Zhang, 2016). Through family and social networks in the motherland, starting from small productions, those Chinese entrepreneurs began to be involved in trades of large scale. Wenzhou counts thousands of factories, mainly family-owned, focused on high production and characterized by long working hours (7 AM-10 PM). Even though under the pressure of heavy industrialization, much of the family business in Wenzhou has transformed itself into a managerial form of capitalism. This is still not the prevalent case in Italy, where small business has been growing and flourishing. The stress on those types of investments is very high to the point that every company tries at best to survive with no external help. Many of those Italo-Chinese businesses in fact have a factory in motherland China that provides the products (whether clothing, appliances or food) and receives those products from an intermediary company charged for the shipping of those low-cost products.

Today what is traditionally known as the 'blue chips' (large-cap companies) left room to what is commonly known as 'red chips' (enterprises more exposed to the Chinese market). The economic sectors more impacted by this 'Chinesization' of the traditional business are those of luxury (e.g., Minzhe), cars and durable goods. In particular the world of luxury reaches important levels of revenues so that the revenues of the main European fashion houses depend largely on the trend of the Chinese economic market. But what are the features of their businesses and what kind of peculiarity they bring in the context of Milan?

First of all, I was able to identify four major categories of different entrepreneurs that I observed in the field: (i) *property-based business* this is often the case all over Italy of Chinese entrepreneurs that work in the clothing sector owning a store, restaurants, one or several coffee bars (like the case of Delun, Heng, Shaiming, Enlai, etc., ...). This first case is the most common among the Chinese entrepreneurs from Wenzhou living in Milan and represents the majority of their business activity. The people from Wenzhou have this peculiar view passed on from generation to generation that, even when compared with being the employee of a powerful organization gaining a consistent amount of money, it is still better to own a small business created and maintained with their own personal energy and efforts. In the public imagery this finds its classical example almost everywhere in the typical Chinese restaurant, owned by a family migrated from Wenzhou of whom the father or the mother is the entrepreneur and boss. More recently for the Italian case this has developed into new frontiers where those Chinese entrepreneurs decide to invest their profits coming from other businesses in new types of activities such as Japanese (or other Asian) restaurants, Coffee bars, Italian restaurants, etc., ...

Side by side with this involvement in catering services, another crucial sector in which this category is flourishing is the clothing industry. Starting from the factories decades ago, first in the motherland then exported to Italy, many Chinese entrepreneurs are involved in an intensive mass production of clothes that spread almost everywhere. With the economic growth from those investments, many entrepreneurs passed from owning a factory to selling directly the products to the customers without the help of intermediaries. This is how therefore clothing stores or stores specialized in the wholesale of household products spread like wildfire almost everywhere. In several cases due to the big amount of revenue or due to the desire of entering into business partnership, many entrepreneurs were able to develop chain stores. A common trend of this mainline Chinese entrepreneurship is the emphasis on low and competitive price in the market despite the losses in quality. Although representing the larger section of Chinese entrepreneurship, in the next future such form of entrepreneurship under the pressure of increased costs of life in China will inevitably change its shape.

Then there is the: (ii) *intermediary business*, which is the case of firms or group of associations which role is to connect different Chinese enterprises that come in Italy to start an activity and that need partnership (like the case of Boqin, Peng, Yi, etc., …). A classical example are state agents, office accountants or associations for the civic society owned by Chinese and specifically designed to help other Chinese entrepreneurs in their business.

The third category can be defined as iii) *self-employed business* where on his own the entrepreneur starts a personal business as buyer or freelance and then in due time, he grows big enough to open his own firm (like the case of Minzhe). This category differs from the previous because it lacks its intermediary purpose among different businesses. Here the Chinese entrepreneur basically works on 'solo' many times even without any specific legal recognition. This category, being the same for many other migrant communities, was the most common type of business during the first migratory cycles. Starting low as mere hawkers many of those Chinese entrepreneurs in few decades were able to grow and discover different and better ways to do business. This can find a correspondent today in the role of Chinese buyers.

Finally, there is the: (iv) *managerial business*, which is the most traditional way of doing business. Only through the second generation of Chinese entrepreneurs (like the case of Ya or Biming) this type of business is starting to involve consistent transactions. This includes, for example, the Chinese shareholders involved in international investments or banking. Such classification drawn from some of the literature (Collino et al., 2014; Miranda, 2014; AA. VV., 2008, 2012) and from my empirical investigations for the area of Milan, serves only for the purpose of simplification, and it does not intend to be exhaustive of all the different cases of Chinese entrepreneurship today active in Italy or elsewhere.

The typical day of an entrepreneur, category (i) being the most common, involves mainly a man and leader of a nuclear family. I will consider here an entrepreneur typically working at the Chinatown of Milan. His day starts early in the morning, leaving his home to go to his workplace usually located far from where he lives (the suburbs or

Table 6.1 Evaluation chart for the first three Chinese entrepreneurs under shadowing. The extension of the dark circle signifies the low/high presence of several key factors of economic success as I observed the entrepreneurs during the job-shadowing

	Confidence in his/her skills	reaction to challenges	expression of values	Hard work	relationship with the customer	Integration with other Christians
Delun	◕	◕	◐	◕	◕	◐
Minzhe	◐	◐	◐	◕	◐	◕
Heng	◕	◕	◕	◕	◐	●

other villages around the city of Milan). Whether in Chinatown or in other parts of Milan, each entrepreneur is owner of one or more businesses and starts the day taking the merchandise that arrived the day before early in the morning (6–7 AM). Usually his business is not isolated but is strongly connected with other Chinese firms, so each entrepreneur spends time talking, giving and receiving help in everyday incumbencies. The activities are spent between calls, moving the merchandises, receiving clients and talking to friends and neighbors. Then during lunch breaks the entrepreneurs gather all together to eat Chinese food, sharing their thoughts in close friendship. During the rest of the day, he receives more visits from clients and he spends time presenting the merchandise to the potential clients almost always available on wholesale instead of retail.

The entrepreneur receives almost everyday visits from his Chinese suppliers that bring the new merchandise in the warehouse of every store. Some of the stores stay open until late hours and follow a non-stop schedule of work. This raises the question of what could the source of such hard working attitude be. The working hours last frequently until 9–10 PM for seven days a week. This rough schedule however changes according to the specific job that the entrepreneur does. For the cases under job-shadowing of entrepreneurs, I observed some relevant variations that I will describe in the following pages (Table 6.1).

6.2.2 *Investors*

Delun belongs to the (i) case of property-based business, the most common among Chinese entrepreneurs from Wenzhou living in Italy.

Delun is part of a family that was already active in business of cafes before him. He first worked with the cafe of his parents 8 years earlier in San Giuliano Milanese, in the suburbs of Milan. After six years then, having collected the savings he decided to open his own new café. He first started by working 16 hours a day from 5.30 AM to 10 PM at night for one year and a half. Even his brother had a different business of cafes and his aunt was co-partner with Delun's fast food. During my job-shadowing with Delun that lasted for several continuous periods alternating from 6 to 10 months, I had the chance to observe him passing from owning two businesses in the beginning of our contacts, then back to one business at the end of the first year and opening a new fast-food chain and SUSHI bar the third year.

Delun opened then his fourth business and during all the period he was involved in several tenders for the management of several businesses already existing. As I've started my research Delun recalled to me how he got involved in business and entrepreneurship:

> *Me*: Now, coming to your job, what type of work are you doing?
>
> *Delun*: I am a barman, I manage a bar.
>
> *Me:* Tell me the trajectory, did you always managed a bar? What type of jobs have you done before?
>
> *Delun*: when I finished the school I decided right away to jump in business. At the time, six years ago, because, before managing a bar of my own, I worked already together side by side with my dad, since we already had a bar.
>
> *Me*: your father owned the bar?
>
> *Delun*: he had a bar correct, for this reason I already knew this job and I started to do this.
>
> *Me*: then you open another bar or you owned the same bar of your father?
>
> *Delun*: another bar, that, you know... I manage on my own.
>
> *Me:* and then you also expanded I remember that you had your own bar...
>
> *Delun*: Then after a couple of years I wanted to buy another bar, ok, it was very stressful.
>
> *Me*: In short, a lot of work. To what do you attribute this success in your work? That is, you started with business right away, you've joined your father then began your own bar, then you have opened another one... Why do you think you had this success?
>
> *Delun*: We had this big success because we want to give this contribution, because we are Chinese who have a very strong entrepreneurial will.
>
> *Me*: ok, and what do you think is the first reason for the success?

Delun: eh .. working hard, the Chinese culture, especially the Chinese culture that encourages us to always run the risk in trade. (Delun, Wenzhou, Milan, 06/08/2014)

Delun mainly started with a café then he hired several Chinese workers for it as he usually spent the day going on errands for the different businesses he owned. When I've observed those workers, I clearly saw the absence of any social skills and the lack of warmness that I saw in Delun. This is perhaps one of the most challenging aspects in Chinese entrepreneurship in Italy in general. The Italian culture displays a level of warmth that Chinese workers lack, especially those first-generation migrants. Competitive price and quick service were often not accompanied by customer service. In those cases, even regular attenders to the cafe complained about it. Chinese workers at the cafe didn't necessarily follow a strict working-hour schedule. They were flexible depending on circumstances. Delun was frequently late to appointments, due to his busy schedule. Yet, Chinese workers were still willing to work extra hours without any complaints. This is another unique aspect of Chinese workers, compared to the local counterpart. This caused Delun to experience several cultural misunderstandings on the relationship between boss and worker, when he hired local workers in his business. In the morning Delun made several calls to the suppliers, then he went by car to pick up orders in several districts of Milan. The merchandises were bought wholesale, while some products were brought directly at the café. Other supplies required more bureaucratic work. Even during his time at the café Delun received several calls both from his mobile and landline, mainly to stay in contact and keep the other store under control. I spent long hours listening to his phone conversations about a product to buy, problems in clauses of contracts. As he arrived to the café, in clear contrast with the workers, Delun brought happiness, warmth, easy talk and an attitude of service.

Delun usually had several typologies of clients: regulars, occasional and visitors. Regulars were usually those that standing at the counter bought coffee or some drinks, as well as those sitting down at the slot machines. Occasional clients were those who bought bus tickets or lottery tickets, and those sitting down at the tables taking beverages or food. Visitors were clients that didn't live in the area and that probably were just passing by the bar (whether tourists or people from a totally different neighborhood or city). Delun recognized those categories almost immediately and applied a different treatment for every single typology. His relationship with the regulars, for instance, was totally different than the relationship with visitors, or even with occasional clients. Delun sometimes had to learn how confidentially he could talk with clients. This required Delun to have a strong memory of faces, conversations, names and voices of the people and in cases where this was missing, friendship or trust from the customer was at stake. At the bar he had a special section where he collected receipts and credit cards. During the last part of the day, Delun spent time at the counter with a calculator, to close the day. The Chinese employees usually were at the bar as he was out buying and transporting some merchandises or meeting some business partners.

Daily, Delun moved between the fast food and his café. He usually waked up at 9:00 AM. At 10:00 AM he came out of his house and had a list of things to do during the day. He did 3 or 4 calls from the house to the bar fixing appointments during the day. In-between those things, Delun had to do many bureaucratic errands. For example, he had to make economic declarations, visit trade unions, visit the Chinese and Taiwanese embassies for obtaining the VISA for migrant workers, visit the office to hire new workers, visit insurance offices and the lawyer, etc., ... Delun was very busy because of those many administrative tasks and he felt uncomfortable with all the bureaucracy of the local government required to manage his multiple businesses. By 12 o'clock or 2 PM depending on the day, he went to the phone store and controlled the progress of the store there. Sometimes his schedule was so tied up that he arrived at the phone store after 8 PM when it was already closed. There were times when Delun received more than 100 calls in a single day, especially when he was hiring new workers for the new businesses. In order to be able to control the progress of his work, Delun had a system of cameras on his computer, so he could supervise the workers at the other workplace and check the amount of clients entering in the store. He usually checked the back of his café, where he also had a refrigerator and a microwave to warm sandwiches and foods that the clients needed. Then in the afternoon (around 4.40–5 PM) Delun, and sometimes even his wife, came to his café to open the slot machines, check the counter, the cash (counting the revenue of the day), giving directions to his Chinese employees, always in a warm and kind way. Sometimes only one or two Chinese employees were working at the café. The workers left the bar around 8:15 PM and then Delun was spending time there, speaking with regular clients until 9:30–10:00 PM, before closing the bar. At this point,

Delun came back home and after having dinner with his family he calculated a general account of the expenses, planning what he would schedule for the next day.

In some of my job-shadowings at his work, I had the chance to observe Delun's wife at work. She generally worked there in the morning or during the early afternoon. The same that I've observed concerning Delun was generally valid for his wife. She was professional, fast in her job, kind but differently from Delun she was less extrovert and she did not speak the local language very well. As Delun she was always at the counter, receiving money from clients, serving coffee or washing the dishes, often speaking with the Chinese workers (2–3 women, one at the counter another cleaning the place, windows, machines…). Delun's wife had a good relationship with the Chinese workers that her husband hired, and the environment was always friendly between them. Several times the baby-sitter of Delun came to the café in order to visit him. Especially during the last part of the day, Delun was busy washing dishes. A machine to change coins for the slot was always crowded with the same people from 5 PM to the closure of the store and when they won, they went to the counter to collect the money.

Sometimes there were some arguments at the slots among people, but Delun was always firm in re-establishing the balance. Delun provided for them also drinks and beverages according to their regular taste and he passed from table to table collecting the used items as he quickly threw them in the trash. The café also provided lottery tickets. During my period of observations, 1.000 € were won at the café through lottery. Delun came usually at that time also to exchange place, because one of the Chinese women left the bar and there was a need to have always at least two people working.

I've observed the same dynamic for the case of the fast food of Delun where however the amount of employee was greater (7–2). The employees were usually well treated by Delun, which did not pressure or threat them. Delun treated people always with respect and understanding. Differently from many other Chinese entrepreneurs, Delun was committed to pay the salary to his workers at the end of every month without any delay, even if that would have represented a risk for his business. In one sense Delun didn't want to lose authority but he also was concerned to follow good principles of treatment toward his workers. Also, in both cases, Delun was the boss but during the day at the store he was always surrounded by a group of employees and they worked as a team. The employees were usually warm and kind in an environment of friendship. This however didn't mean that in the workplace employees under the leadership of Delun were not diligent or not working hard.

Both places were crossroads of a lot of Chinese as well as local visitors and Delun succeeded in having many clients (5–6 each 10 minutes). Depending on the day, sometimes there were a lot of clients sometimes less. When there were a lot of clients Delun demonstrated to be multitasking, being able to serve 4 or 5 clients simultaneously. Delun's view of the client was very high, clients had the priority over everything. For example, if I was speaking with Delun and a client came into the store, then he stopped speaking to me and focused all his attention on the client. I witnessed the presence of many regular Chinese clients that were coming regularly at the café but also local regular clients, both being in warm and friendly relationship toward Delun. Sometimes the warmness of Delun was invasive with shy clients. Out of three clients at least one knew Delun's name. Delun demonstrated to know about their private life and, vice versa, some clients knew about his trips to China. At times there was a witty environment, as some of the clients did not even pay when they took something, because, as regular clients, they had an open account. Many were the regular clients that came in Delun's stores.

Sometimes regular clients were coming and going for two or three times to the store. They had a friendship with Delun, they were well treated, but they also received from Delun some friendly nicknames like 'uncle', 'aunt', 'doctor', 'mister!', 'friend?', 'Sir!' and 'children'. In his gestures and words, Delun always had confidence, for example in unplugging the receipt or closing the counter. He wanted to give a good impression on clients. Sometimes it was common to see Delun joking with his clients. Delun's strategy with his clients was to be very friendly, always greeting, gentle, smiling, knowing all their names and their tastes, laughing, being ironic, seeking respect and empathy, often showing his generosity offering food free of charge, promoting a very warm relation with them. Very often Delun postponed the payment of the merchandise of regular clients in order to help them and facilitate their day. Even if clients didn't pay back his kindness, he didn't let this bother him but kept working. At the same time Delun treated the client like a prince, he tried to be fast and efficient in answering their needs, giving them fresh beverages or well-prepared food. He was fast and kind at the same time.

When preparing coffee Delun was very fast, in a fraction of seconds he already served the drink. Delun was very extrovert and started often conversations with the customers about several topics such as the quality of a certain plate, or wine, the situation at their work, giving details about their personal jobs, the weather, some purchases done (e.g., phones or articles of the house) in a friendly climate that was lacking when Delun, the boss, was away from the workplace. This unique environment often left the clients surprised, glad, feeling invited to come back. Everybody knew Delun in the surrounding area of his business and he was highly esteemed. They appreciated to come in his café or fast food, even if there were stores that offered the same type of service around. Sometimes it was common to hear some clients at the counter say 'you are good people' referring to Delun and his family members. Some clients in their conversations were marveled about the absence of any Chinese accent in Delun, and were considering him at this point as a local because of his experience and ability to relate to the local culture. Many times, the clients referred to what they ordered adding statements like 'as you know how to do' or 'I take the usual'. Such environment of hospitality and warmness reflected also among the clients themselves that felt like being at home as they were acting like a family. The café usually stayed open until 9 PM, Delun warned the players at the slots that the time was out. He then closed the freezer and the machine of coins for the day and counted the money in the cash. Several clients were marveled to know that his café stayed open until such a late hour. Sometimes Delun had the last minute client before he closed the cash, shutting down the lights and closing the door.

In the café Delun selled coffee, drinks, food, etc., ...while in the fast food Delun selled lunches, trying to introduce a new style of food in the area which was quite innovative and still original if compared with other local big chains. After 10 years of working and saving investments working in his café, Delun created 'Dutch Chips', a fast food producing fried food, vegetables, chickens, sandwiches, burgers... The fast food had several workers (one from Philippines, one Brazilian, some Italians) and one chook. They were organized in two shifts: one in the morning and one in the afternoon, changing turns at 5.30–6.00 PM. It was hard in the beginning for all the workers to get accustomed working with a Chinese boss, so 3 workers during my period of job-shadowing were changed while 2 others had to be fired. Usually, the fast food had more clients on Saturday while on Monday it was almost empty. The first months of the business were hard because the workers were not necessarily equipped, as Delun was working with them for the initial periods for about 12–14 hours.

Close to the fast food the aunt of Delun had a café, so she was responsible for the training of the workers at the fast food, since she was already in direct contact with the food industry. As Delun's café, his aunt had a café in front of the entrance of the underground. Considering together all the family members and distant relatives, Delun was part of a network of 30 cafés. Delun's aunt was very rigid, demanding and controlling. As time went on, Delun was more responsible for the administrative aspects while his aunt was managing the place. During my job-shadowing the fast food was in disadvantage because of the summer heat. People preferred to eat ice creams instead of fries. Even as the winter came, the fast food had less movement despite its strategic position in an area of town with the headquarters of large companies attended by rich people. The clients in fact were completely different from the bar or the High-Tech store. Delun had decided to open this new activity after he went to China for a business visit. He went to Shanghai because he had invested into an activity there and he met a business partner over dinner. Delun in fact like many Chinese entrepreneurs, apart from the businesses running in Italy, had invested 2 years in a pharmaceutical company in China. The company was implementing special treatments in the Zhejiang province near Wenzhou and from there into all of China. As Delun was having his dinner with his business partner, he expressed how bad the economic situation was in Italy at that time. The youth unemployment and the concern he had for the situation. His friend's advice was to use his values and hire those people in difficulty. At first Delun's reaction was negative, since working with Chinese people is the norm for the Chinese Boss wherever he goes, as it is easier to manage them. This is true because they are more ready to make sacrifices, work extra hours… So, as an entrepreneur Delun was thinking about the economic interest, but he also thought of how to resolve this issue. He wanted to overcome the partiality and ethnical exclusivism that other Chinese entrepreneurs were displaying in not helping the local people in the diaspora.

After the trip, Delun had to choose between four business opportunities: to open a fast food, to be a financial broker, to be a retailer of luxury goods or to be a representative for merchandises in the cosmetic sector. Only the first option involved other people and could provide a salary for people. So, Delun decided to pursue this option in order to give a solution to the problem of local youth unemployment. It was quite unusual for a Chinese entrepreneur to hire non-Chinese local workers, because the expenses were high, the willingness to work on hard schedules was lower, and the economic risk was big. Even if it was not necessarily convenient or attractive economically, Delun took this decision anyway. The fast food in fact had at times seven local workers. Delun followed principles of correct concurrence without corrupting anybody, pursuing an honest earn, respecting fully the rights of the workers according to the law and never abusing them.

Another example of Delun's interest in establishing business partnerships of social significance was his project to start a new business with Bingwen. Delun started the traditional Chinese café as many other Chinese entrepreneurs of second-generation migration. Then he broke with this traditional way of doing business exclusively with Chinese people, first through the transitioning phase of the fast food then changing totally the sector through this business focused on Hi-Tech and other more modern sectors. After working in the engineering sector, Bingwen decided to start working in the business sector as a salesman in a fashion company in Milan. Since profits were not expanding for Bingwen, his friend Delun came with the idea to open a new store in business partnership with Bingwen, a store for phones and new technologies. Delun realized that everybody needed a cell phone in order to be in contact with people, and this need was not going to change in the short period. I knew both of them before the start of this cooperation and I was surprised in the change of relationship between the two. Since Delun now was his boss, Bingwen was worried about giving him a good impression, especially during the first months of their relationship. Even though Delun knew that Bingwen did not had skills on the field, he decided to hire him as a business partner for this activity. He wanted to entrust it to somebody he could rely on since he was already very busy with other things. Bingwen recalled how Delun got the idea to start a new business together:

> [...] Delun had an idea because there is a market, everyone has a cell phone and will keep having one, if the business is for something that lasts only for ten years is not good. At first [he] tried with two other people but they didn't want to do it, then he though about Bingwen that is available, is connected to what I know, on electronics, we had a dinner together then we said yes, and after two weeks I started to work for the training in Hangzhou. (Bingwen, Tonglu, Milan, 18/11/2015)

Bingwen then went to China for one month to start a training on new technologies, in order to learn the basics notions and start to work in the store that he and Bingwen rented in Milan. There were several training schools in China, in Guangdong province. Bingwen decided to leave Italy for one month and likewise to go. Together with Bingwen there were many other Chinese people taking the course and even a second-generation Chinese migrant that had the same idea.

This other person at the young age of 21 years old was already first working as a barman then into a factory and now he was involved in training to learn competences in Information Technology as well as other ideas (opening Italian restaurants in China). During the training they taught Bingwen to fix phones and technological items, to study composition, circuit and parts. Essentially, Bingwen and all the other Chinese workers had to take broken phones and change the screen. If the phone was damaged by water, they had to find a solution to fix it. The training was an investment for Bingwen (700 €) but he decided to do that only for one month and go back to Italy to start the business. This was increasing the challenge for him and Delun since it was a very complex work. At first Bingwen did not have any particular interest on the type of activity nor did he have any confidence. After the first challenges, he was able to develop his skills. Bingwen was available to Delun, who on the other hand knew could trust Bingwen. Delun encouraged Bingwen and the other Chinese workers to do their best, to assume their responsibility and to work hard.

I followed the initial steps of establishing this new business during my job-shadowing. The store was located in an area of Milan, full of foreigners and with plenty of stores that were already doing the same type of business of cell phones and high technology (I-Phones, Samsung, etc., ...). The clients at the store were of different ethnicities, since the area was full of foreigners. Many Chinese friends of Delun were regular customers, especially during the first stage of his business. On the video monitor Delun regularly displayed pictures of phones but also of the whole group of Chinese Protestant entrepreneurs during the inauguration of the store. People heard of his new store and came presenting their problems with phones and were involved in Delun's work if he needed help of any sort. The neighborhood of the store was surrounded by similar stores that repaired cell phones, supermarkets, hairdressers. Some of them were Chinese, others were Arabic. People were coming to the store of Delun despite the saturated market of the competitors due to the good customer service provided in Delun's store.

Even if other stores could have been more professional in repairing and had more technical experience with suppliers, the store of Delun, with his good customer service represented an added value to the transaction from the side of the client. The design and furniture were modern and more unique if compared with the surrounding stores. Furthermore, Delun and Bingwen showed a strong entrepreneurial spirit in their ability to learn to manage their business. This was due to their commitment. Their dedication led them to always being busy, never giving up if they couldn't find a solution to problems. This difference was clear when comparing them to the other workers in the store. Sometimes clients came to fix their phones, change their SIM card, ask about a specific type of model (3 G, 4 G, etc., ...), place a new phone cover, sell or to buy. Sometimes they stayed for a long time discussing what decision to take on their purchases: whether to give the phone and repair it or not, due to the price.

As phones were given to Bingwen, Delun or the other Chinese workers quickly tried to determine what was the problem and approximate costs. Sometimes fixing required only few minutes, other times days or weeks, with an average of one phone repaired each day. Sometimes the customers just came to ask prices and test the waters without buying anything. Then the customer was asked if he wanted to leave the phone, and if after the repairs he wants to sell it. At times the store was empty and workers were watching their phones or talking with one another. Delun usually tried to motivate workers, always in team with them almost like a coach. The same pattern that was present at the Dutch Chips was repeated in this environment. Sometimes Delun did also delivery and technical support in the homes. Customers had problems of Wi-Fi or other technical issues. It was not always easy to proceed in price evaluation because mistakes were common. The Italian worker, Giulio, was always at the counter as front office with the clients due to his proficiency in the Italian language. In fact, many Italian clients were sometimes suspicious of Chinese people so as soon as they saw an Italian worker, they felt more willing to stop in and buy. Gulio was also responsible of managing the bureaucratic staff. He was an Italian guy that worked first for 5 months at Delun's Dutch Chips and then transferred to the Best-Tech store. As I was doing my job-shadowing at Delun's new Best-Tech store, I had many chances to hear his interesting point of view:

> Since the beginning I worked always for Chinese people, a bar buffet in the Loreto area, the owner was Chinese, the chef was Italian. It is hard to work with Chinese, their view of work, a life based only on work, many hours, the rest doesn't exists. In one sense is hard for the rhythms but they teach you well the job, they can't think outside the lines. They give you a lot of orders, piercing eyes, mr. know it all, no matter what I do is wrong, they like to have the situation under control. Delun compared with my ex-boss is more ready and able to help, it's been a long time since he arrived in Italy. [the previous work] It was hard, the Boss and his mother, it wasn't going good. (Giulio, Milan, Milan, 16/01//2016)

Giulio was not necessarily always in agreement with all the procedures followed by Delun but he obeyed nevertheless. After the transaction was over Delun and his workers went back speaking in Chinese with one another. The counter had at least two people together as the others were downstairs repairing phones. Usually they tried not to leave any unfinished work from the night before, but they sought to immediately find the technical solution to the problem.

The choice of suppliers and prices as well as the way the workers had to proceed were very important. There were delicate aspects in this business compared to previous professional experiences that Delun had. In this new store, Delun had to hire 2 workers at the front office and 2 technicians. His choice in this case, differently from Dutch Chips, was to hire Chinese workers since he recognized that they were more efficient and fast on their job. A Chinese worker, according to Delun, 'is able to do in 30 minutes the same work that an Italian does in a day'. Italian stores around were taking a long time in fixing phones, doing less effort but still having high prices. The Chinese store of Delun, on the other hand, followed a different strategy: fixing the phone as fast as possible, even under the eyes of the client, with a 'paying and going' approach. The most important task was to be able to fix and repair cell phones of clients in the quickest way. The prices were in accordance with the amount of hours required to fix the problem, trying not to be dishonest. Delun and Bingwen from the beginning were therefore to be directors of the business, sharing 40% of the investment on the side of Bingwen and 60% of the investment on the side of Delun. Delun took the majority since the idea was his and he wanted to take control of the company. This was done in order to avoid conflicts involved in business leadership in cases where the setting was 50–50% (see Chun).

Since the beginning of the business Delun was coming every day to the new store because his presence was indispensable and he actually enjoyed being there. Even if he was always busy, he had more interest, he liked innovation. Usually Delun did not hire a person that he knew personally since as a Boss Delun needed to be direct in giving suggestions and critics. With a friend this was risky because there was a fear of losing a friend. In fact, Delun recalled when that happened as he hired a Chinese woman that was his friend and as soon as he made a critic she was offended and left the job. But with Bingwen the case was different, the two knew each other very well and were in mutual trust through their common Christian beliefs. They shared common values, which really enhanced their common vision for business. Bingwen and Delun were considered the directors in the store, the others as workers. Often Delun was sharing and discussing with Bingwen administrative stuff, asking him his advice. Delun knew that there were a lot of people involved in the market of phones, so he started to contact his first potential clients. Delun during this period spent 18 hours of work each day between those three businesses.

The new tech store opened at 09.30 A.M. every day. Friday and Saturday were considered as the peak days with 20–30 clients. Some other days the store only had 5 customers. The store closed always around 08:00 P.M. and there were shifts among the different workers. Delun usually came to the new store around 11:00 in the morning. He arrived always after the workers and Bingwen already started his job. Workers were busy in putting the phones in the window, waiting the clients to come, cleaning the place and starting the works of repair left unfinished the previous day, like broken cell phones that needed to be fixed. There was no specific timetable during the day at the store. It depended on the number of clients. Some were just coming in to ask opinion on a phone they already had: if it was a fake or an original phone and how to sell it. Other clients were coming to fix their phone, for example to change the screen or to buy used phones as well as new ones with a cheaper price or just to receive information about making an ID with I-clouds. The neighborhood was not the best and often some of those clients were not honest in their deal. At first many clients were just coming to check the prices of repair. As they came in Delun asked questions on how the work was going in an environment that was warm and friendly. He usually stood at the front office, the place that he preferred because of his good relationship skills. He also occasionally came downstairs to fix phones, change screens, batteries and cameras. Even if he enjoyed fixing phones in the calm environment of downstairs, his primary place was at the front office. This somehow was perceived by Bingwen as 'his territory'. Delun stayed at the store usually at least for 5 hours a day, but sometimes if the workers had any inconvenience he would remain at the store for 9–10 hours. The store also had a roster to sign entry and leave of the workers for Delun to know their schedule. In the initial stages of any of those businesses Delun always had many workers and apprentices but as time went on, he selected only few among them to work for him on a regular basis.

As the client entered the store Delun asked them if they wanted to sell or buy. Two of the Chinese workers were responsible of repairing the phones in the room downstairs. Bingwen usually repaired easy-to-repair damages leaving the more hard repairs to the two Chinese experts, while he was trying to learn from them. Those two Chinese workers were experts because they already worked as apprentices in other stores. Bingwen and Delun needed also to control the workers and to make sure that they were doing what they were supposed to do. In their economic transactions sometimes people brought things that were stolen. In those circumstances, Delun tried to maintain the law. Those situations were easy to discover because the price required by the customer was blatantly lower than its real value. Delun wanted to make profit but not to use wrong strategies to achieve it. For this reason, he refused to take merchandises under unethical circumstances.

To fix a phone it was a delicate operation. Sometimes the damage required an obvious action while other times it was a problem due to chips, the motherboard of the phone, etc., … First Delun, Bingwen or the other Chinese workers needed to define what was the problem, then they had to come up with a solution. This process required experience, knowledge and skills. Some cell phones required only 10 minutes to be repaired, in other cases it was something impossible to fix. In this case some irremediable mistakes were done. This was causing a loss of profit. For example, often a phone was sold for 1.000 € but then the workers discovered that the real cost was 1.200 € with the addition of taxes, ending up then losing profit. Another difficult task, especially in the first months, was to find suppliers for new phones and parts of the cell phones, machines, computers… Italian suppliers (mainly from Rome or Lecco) were slow in shipping the parts needed to repair. Sometimes even wrong pieces were sent instead of repair. This slowness was resulting in the client coming repeatedly to the store, even if the merchandise was not ready, waiting for a long time. Almost every Monday Bingwen was receiving at the store deliveries from the suppliers, paying them for the products. Those products were usually spare parts or new phones, cheaper than what he could buy online or in other stores. The Italian worker, on the other hand, was hired because he spoke the language. He was also helpful to get all the paperwork, the corrections on the information to publish in the website or at the sign. He also knew how the software of cell phones worked. According to Delun, he was not the typical Italian, arrived in time to the appointments, open with Chinese people and easy to talk with. Delun knew him as he worked for two years at the Dutch Chips before passing to the new business.

As Delun started this new activity slowly the leadership and management of the fast food was given by him to an entrusted worker as he progressively focused his attention to new business. His role then became just the one of owner and overall director of the previous business. This decision required an ability to delegate, trust and not holding on to past successes but constantly aiming for the unknown future developments of businesses. Sometimes the Italian worker that managed for Delun his fast-food came to visit him at the café to give a report of how the business was going: taxes to pay, behavior of workers, use of bricklayers for the new building. With him Delun was trying to establish a business partnership still in the framework of a boss-worker relationship but somehow more friendly and based on trust and accountability. This Italian worker trusted Leo's leadership, he was friendly and satisfied with their relationship, sharing the commitment of Leo.

Sometimes Delun had to face situations of risk, especially with his business at the fast food. Some breakdown in the machines to be repaired (fridge, cash desk…), tablets that stopped working or disconnected cables that were blocking the line of clients at the counter, were all sources of challenge. I witnessed how even at his café, when clients were having bad reactions, taking advantage of his generosity, Delun was always kind and confident. For example, sometimes regular attenders to the slots were disappointed because they had lost a lot of money at a particular machine. Yet Delun tried always to answer to their occasional complaints with the friendly attitude of a pacificator and proposing them to change machine if necessary. Sometimes because of the slow bureaucratic process of Italy in receiving a specific documentation Delun had to block the whole work at a store which caused a lot of challenges. Several conversations at the phone with the suppliers were about those problems, sometimes leading Delun to withdraw from the contract.

Despite those multiple problems connected to the lack of professionality of some suppliers, Delun was always confident and focused on his goal. Delun's big challenge during my job-shadowing was related to his new fast-food chain, Dutch Chips. He had trouble finding some business partners that could join the company. He also had to deal with cases of plagiarism from other fast foods around the city of Milan copying similar brand (like 'Amsterdam Chips'). When Delun started this new fast-food he had a lot of revenue, the place was full of clients up until 12.00 AM at night, whereas, later on, the place became almost empty. The problem again was due to the fact that many people just copied the brand and started a similar business stealing his clients. As the business grew Delun had to fire 3 workers because of taxes and bureaucracy. The reason was for the many expenses, the suppliers, the rent and salaries. The fries and vegetables came directly from special suppliers, so their price was more expensive. Delun had to make many efforts in order to pay the workers. Their work was done in a very narrow timeframe and he was not making any profit. This element of risk caused Delun to be bitter, at times because of the Italian system that was full of privileges and protections. Even if in the beginning the store was full of people, after a while because of the competition with the rival store, the number of customers was decreasing. The problem with this type of business was that it was badly oriented. It would have been more suitable in other areas of town. For this reason, during my period of job-shadowing Delun decided to remodel the Dutch Chips and change it into a Sushi bar (Sushi express) with the business partnership and help from his cousin's husband. Seeing that the business of Dutch Chips was not growing Delun decided to change and innovate again restructuring the whole store. Delun's philosophy was that if a business was not growing, he had the option to either close it, sell the activity at a low price or like in this case transform the activity in a more strategic way. Sushi was a type of food easy to manage by Chinese entrepreneurs. During the time of preparation for this new business, Delun was very busy collecting the ideas all by himself, the Japanese recipes for food, the bills and facilities. Delun felt that his role was the one of 'the living soul' of the firm. Anytime he was trying something new in business with all of its challenges he saw it as a training experience.

Another challenge came when Delun had to manage three businesses because of the new store of high technology. During that period Delun at the same time had the possibility to participate successfully to a tender and indirectly manage a chain of 18 stores in the undergrounds of Milan.

Among them, 8 or 9 of those stores were stores to fix phones, but there was a lack of specialized personnel. In the area of his business, there was high competition from more than 19 stores. The unique strategy of Delun in this context was to focus on trust, good image, professionality and efficiency. In those periods Delun was over-loaded with responsibilities. He appeared to be 'death tired', challenged by the many worries in a situation of high economic risk. To open always a new business causes many bureaucratic problems, it is a season full of tension and stress. It was hard and difficult for anybody to manage the stress involved in those circumstances, yet nevertheless Delun was surprisingly calm. Even though sometimes he was tired, nervous, he was generally optimistic, peaceful and confident, smiling, without tension, trying to maintain the patience in front of the client and other employees.

Even Bingwen said during our conversations during job-shadowing that Delun was a model for him because he was able to work the whole day but still was able to be happy in front of the client, adapting to any situation. His determination despite his tiredness in those circumstances was remarkable. Another source of risk in the new business was when the phone of the client was accidentally broken by the workers. In those cases when the worker personally had to share expenses and to compensate the losses to the client. To accept the assignment of fixing a phone was therefore always a challenge. Sometimes Delun or Bingwen had to spend the whole day trying to resolve the problem without being able to find any solution. It was a frustrating experience, but they did it anyway, searching online or through the personal trainer in China explaining him the problem, trying to find a solution. Again in those circumstances Delun was determined even though he lacked specific experiences and was discovering an unknown and risky territory.

6.2.3 Buyers

Minzhe belongs to the (iii) type of business, she is self-employed and works as a buyer in the surrounding area of Milan. The role of buyer in the field of fashion is becoming very common among Chinese entrepreneurs in the area. She started doing this type of job at first only to help a friend. Then, for the past twenty years, she was involved in selling and buying products of high fashion from Italy to China. She started just talking with some of her old friends through the Chinese social network WeChat. They noticed how luxury goods had different prices in different nations and therefore she decided to make a business out of it, first opening a market in Malaysia then later expanding it to China. I observed Minzhe in her work as she was very focused, and tried to pursue this work with the best of her capabilities.

The target of products for Minzhe was usually luxury goods, high-quality clothes, that usually in China may cost a fortune but that are more convenient to be purchased through a buyer directly from Italy. That's why Minzhe chose to buy expensive clothes in order to make more profit. During my job-shadowing observations, the Chinese buyers around Minzhe were choosing less expensive merchandises. A big problem was the amount of taxes that the buyer had to pay for the expedition. Many times the company tried to come in help of the buyer offering a tax-free transportation in China, passing through Hong Kong. Like for many Chinese entrepreneurs her strategy was not to buy a certain fixed quantity, but to buy on demand. First, she went to the store and took pictures of the products, then she immediately sent them to the website publishing the price declared. This was done in order to see if there was anybody interested in purchasing it and on the basis of the demand she bought the product. Sometimes the feedback from the client took 3–4 days so Minzhe came back to the same boutique to buy the product she selected before.

The e-commerce represents today a great portion of the business in China and Minzhe was not an exception to that. The Chinese government was not so happy of the spread of this commerce online because of the tax-free market that internet provides. Minzhe started to work as a buyer long time ago and when she first started, she initiated a business with Malaysian clients through a Facebook page. Then she decided to start to sell in China through a Chinese friend, using a Chinese social network (Weibo, the Chinese version of Twitter), then later on she also began to use the Chinese social network WeChat where she posted pictures of the products and received notice of interest from clients. For the payment however she used other more trustworthy websites where it was more safe for the payment.

She used frequently websites like E-bay and Alibaba, a popular Chinese website for selling and buying. Particularly Taubau, a sub-group of Alibaba, is dedicated to buyers that sell products and became extremely popular among younger people in China who wanted to buy from online platforms. The founder of this website, Jack Ma from Hangzhou, a city close to Wenzhou, started the company with a budget of only 200.000 €.

Jack Ma is today one of the wealthiest persons in China, with 14 billion of dollars in profits. Yet to have a personal page in Taubau was not as easy for Minzhe. Sometimes it was a 24 hours work to upload pictures of products, design, describing every detail for every single picture. Through the chat, people asked questions on the store page that required an immediate response, unless the client decided to go to another store and buy there. The same difficulties were present among other Chinese entrepreneurs focused on e-commerce like Lei and his Chinese version of Groupon website (Guua):

> What I would like to do is to connect stores and restaurants and put them online. [...] 30–40 years ago China was poor, the basic things of business were not mature, now the e-commerce takes and make you rich, people can spend more money. (Lei, Milan, Wenzhou, 21/01/2016)

Lei had to work sometimes up until 4 AM in order to keep in contact with customers in China and update his website. Yet he found inspiration and strength through imitating famous business figures like Jack Ma or Elon Musk.

Taubau also solves the problems involved with e-commerce of possible fraud through a payment system monitored by the company. The seller sends the product and the company is involved in the transaction to guarantee that none of the parts is fraud. The buyer then receives his payment that can be payed to the seller even if the client commits any type of fraud. In order to avoid suspicion and to have trust from the clients in China, Minzhe had to go to the different boutiques in Milan and take pictures of herself with the merchandises to demonstrate that she was personally involved in the purchase. She was known by her clients to be an expert on fashion and had a strong desire to please the desires of the client. Buying merchandise in stock was very expensive and Minzhe preferred to buy only when the customer in China already expressed his interest in the product and deposited the money on the bank. Usually the product was not sent in China by itself, but only after a certain amount of orders from different clients was reached, then orders were sent to China to lower costs of transportation. The merchandise was not sent to China until it reached a total accumulated value enough to make some significant money out of it.

During my job-shadowing, I was able to follow Minzhe to her visits in the stores of Milan. Usually she went to famous Italian brands of wholesale stores, as a frequent customer. Her primary providers were 8–9 stores in Italy, especially Milan, where she was a regular buyer. Among her first choices she went to the Rinascente in the center of Milan. She went there every 2–3 days, depending on new arrivals and orders or to other stores in small towns close to Milan like Tod's. Each brand she chose gave her revenue of 15% extra on the Chinese market. She also went to another store in the surrounding area of Magenta (usually every Tuesday), Serravalle (usually every Monday). Other boutiques around the center of Milan that Minzhe visited were in Via Montenapoleone (Chanel, Pisa Watch…) or in other stores at Rinascente (Miu Miu, Bottega Veneta, Bovary, Chloé, Celine…). She usually went there once a week because there were a lot of stores. Another place sometimes Minzhe went, was an outlet close to Florence (The More) because she knew a Chinese worker in Prato that introduced her to the products of that store. She usually was focused on buying and selling bags, fashion shirts, shoes, wallets, belts and clothes of expensive brands (Gucci, Prada, etc., …). As she arrived to the usual store she was introduced by the owner that knew her very well. She went to the warehouse to see the new arrivals of products together with other Chinese buyers. At Serravalle they sold the same type of products as the other stores but more updated, especially for what concerned the new seasonal samples. The best moments of the year for her business were after the Christmas season and the Chinese New Year (December-January) or other holidays when it was time for discounts and there were pre-sales in every store.

When she went to the Rinascente in Milan she usually started with the store of Gucci where she was known to be a regular client. The people at Rinascente usually spoke English, since there were a lot of Chinese people that didn't speak Italian. Sometimes I witnessed how Italian workers had trouble understanding the needs of the clients, so it was necessary almost every moment to have a Chinese salesman there. Even for Italian salesmen it was at times required to speak Chinese, and some stores had people speaking up to five languages. Another ethnicity that was very active in the business of buyers at Rinascente were Russians. Minzhe waited for the regular saleswoman that stayed in contact through social networks and gave her all the details about new arrivals. As she waited for the saleswoman at Rinascente or in other stores of Milan her most important duty was to choose among the different products exhibited in the warehouse, checking the prices and the quality of the different brands. In stores like Gucci at Rinascente or other boutiques around the city,

I observed the same process of taking pictures with bag after bag in front of the mirror. At Rinascente not only there were a lot of Chinese buyers going around but even the saleswomen and salesmen were mainly Chinese. Minzhe told me that at least every store at Rinascente had one Chinese salesman, some of them were second-generation migrants and the majority of them were from Wenzhou. Sometimes Minzhe had trouble speaking Chinese with them because their Wenzhounese dialect was not easy to understand. Some stores were so crowded (e.g., Louis Vuitton) that it was hard for her to enter and to find what she was looking for.

Minzhe like other buyers started to take a lot of pictures of the merchandise that she selected to post in the website. The process of taking pictures was very detailed, at least she took two or three pictures for each merchandise, internal and external pictures of the bags or of the clothes, evaluating how many pockets or belts the bag had. Usually she chose the best sample on the basis of what was most trendy in the sector, what was currently in fashion, a specific color (pink, red…). Then she took pictures of the merchandises. Minzhe had precise criteria of selection, as she looked at the details of the product, the practicality, the use and tastes, which required special ability and an eye for purchasing. During my job-shadowing it was frequent to see Minzhe surrounded by three or four Chinese people, sometimes even entire families. At times they were small 'family buyers' like a mother and a daughter and they were doing the same type of job. Sometimes they were steering at Minzhe, a witness to the high competition involved in this kind of job. When I was doing job-shadowing at the Rinascente close to the center of Milan at least one out of three clients was a Chinese buyer like Minzhe, going around to visit different stores, taking pictures and doing calls to check the interest for a product from the clients. Many of them were the same age of Minzhe and one out of two clients was Chinese.

Minzhe went to the store at Rinascente usually to pick up new arrivals. When she came there she generally chose specific fashion brands. Her choice was based on the need, names that were popular, which Chinese people loved, depending on the season and the popularity in China. For example, one time at Gucci store Minzhe was informed ahead of time of an arrival, so she went to pick up the order. Before the period of sales (January and July) Minzhe together with 10 buyers received pre-sales discounts at Rinascente, since she was a faithful client there and bought a lot of merchandises. Because of her privileged position, Minzhe received pictures of the products and was notified of every new arrival. Minzhe told me about a time that together with those 10 buyers she bought more than 1.000 products at the store of Gucci in the Rinascente. More than 100 products was already a huge quantity for a client in stores of that level of costs. When January came, Minzhe sold many bags from Gucci and since people kept asking for them, she stayed there the whole day. Like Gucci every store at Rinascente did pre-sales. This particular company allowed to buy only a limited number of samples at their store so several Chinese buyers asked after Minzhe to take her ratio if she could use her name to allow other buyers to buy more.

Among the many Chinese buyers at Rinascente, usually many were students that started to get involved as buyers first for purchases to their families and friends then through broader clients. This was a symptom of the competition in selling which buyers had to face together with the high demands for specific new products. Yet Minzhe was notified ahead of time by the Chinese saleswoman. They shared their contact on WeChat and the merchandise for Minzhe was set aside due to their friendship.

Another time she went to look for a new brand of shoes in a special store at the Rinascente which she knew was tax exempted. The store was full of Chinese buyers and Minzhe was not always able to find the sample she was interested in. Those stores allowed only selling few samples of the same brand, in order to block people from taking advantage in re-selling. Minzhe controlled the merchandises, took out a sample and quickly took a picture of it to post it in her website, selling them as soon as possible, being worried for merchandises in stock that she was not able to sell. Sometimes she sold them in few days, other times weeks or months. Every boutique had a manager responsible to help the buyers in their selections and purchases. He usually led the buyers to the warehouse and checked the list of prices for the new arrivals. When Minzhe was at Rinascente she was primarily focused on bags, but she also took belts, wallets, scarfs or shoes. Minzhe had a phone with more than 10.000 pictures of products, every day she made from 100 to 300 pictures, 5–7 pictures for each sample. Only 30% of all merchandises was sold, depending if clients appreciated the product. Sometimes she was going from store to store and came to a final decision.

The manager of the buyers as well as other workers in the company knew Minzhe very well and the manager talked with her often. After buying a product, for example a brand shirt, she also added money and sold it to the customers in China. The competitors around Minzhe did the same kind of activity, they often watched one another, seeing what type of product the other persons was choosing to publish on their websites. As Minzhe was, for example, choosing a brand at Rinascente, another Chinese buyer was choosing the same afterward, or simply watching to see which sample Minzhe was taking. This environment of competition was particularly felt in the center of Milan, in big stores such as the Rinascente or other boutiques. Even if they did the same kind of job, the buyers usually didn't speak with one another and tended to be unfriendly instead. For this reason, Minzhe tried often to opt for unknown boutiques, in order to receive discounts, better deals and maintain secrecy from other competitors. Minzhe was at times surprised and disappointed to see many buyers coming at some of her favorite stores.

In my job-shadowing I was able to witness how in few minutes many products were sold online, so Minzhe arrived too late to buy a certain brand. Several times Minzhe, after having evaluated the products, was immediately at the phone waiting for some quick responses and make a purchase in order to anticipate competitors. Her relationship with the clients or with the seller during the transaction was straight to the point. The results generally were very positive compared with other competitors, Minzhe was able to sell the product almost immediately. Many times competitors were standing around where Minzhe was looking to different products, in order to check which merchandises she would choose. The indecision of competitors contrasted with the confidence that Minzhe was able to display during the job-shadowing was remarkable, given the constant race to succeed in selling as much as they could. As soon Minzhe she took a picture of one product she was already having her eye on the next one.

Furthermore, her reaction to situations of risks was very significant. Sometimes we had to stay in warehouses with hot temperature and uncomfortable settings, yet she never losed her focus selecting, evaluating, comparing prices… Under the strong pressure of competition, Minzhe always demonstrated to be confident in herself and able to handle difficulties. Other times, when there was some inconvenience, like when the owner loosed his patience, or a worker did some mistakes, not knowing how to determine prices, or could not identify what was the right color for the merchandise, Minzhe was always displaying strong confidence. Also, Minzhe often felt this in a situation of crisis:

> I feel tired, I go to work at 10 AM and I come back at 6 PM. Even if I make money it does not satisfy me, I feel like is empty, I don't have time to think on what I am doing. [...] After two years I feel tired, I am not helping people. Use my time is fundamental, in my job I lose time. Sometimes we are lost but then we find the way, even if I'm sad. (Minzhe, Shuzhou, Milan, 19/01/2016)

Minzhe sometimes felt a situation was difficult. She, for example, wanted to have other people working with her but it was not easy to find them. Even in her business partnership with Enlai and Fai, she felt it was complicated because they were not living in the same environment (Enlai and Fai were in China at that time). Fai, for example, was already busy with his 5 online stores and managing the factory. Enlai, on the other hand, after he started a business partnership with Minzhe was not reliable, didn't finish the task he promised to do to Minzhe. This led her to be particularly frustrated because it was also difficult to find committed clients. In this kind of job, it was crucial to have the right clients. In this situation of high competition, Minzhe decided to start a cooperation with Enlai in China in order to find a 'customer niche' to survive situations economic risk. Enlai tried to find more clients in China, through several websites, and, when he caught their interest, he went to visit them, presented the different categories of products that Minzhe could buy for them, in order to give supplementary tools to what the e-commerce, so common in China today's business, was not able to provide.

During his visit in Italy, I had the opportunity to follow Enlai and Minzhe during their beginning of a business partnership. Enlai's wife was the owner of a Jewelry store in China but because of the downfall of business and shutting down of some factories, he decided to start this international business partnership with Minzhe. He tried to make some appointments in order to understand if there were discounts for the merchandise, and tried to speak with managers in order to find a better price of transportation, given the taxes involved. Several times Enlai asked me to translate his e-mails to managers of stores in Italy, doing some screening of the different websites of companies and make some visits at their boutiques. The surrounding environment of Minzhe and Enlai was of high fashion and yet I observed sobriety in them which contrasted their surroundings. After the period Enlai visited Italy for business reasons, Fai was also called by Minzhe and another Chinese entrepreneur in China to start a joint effort to expand sales. Fai was entrusted to do the biggest part of the online business for Minzhe, since he owned 5 online shops. Fai took pictures from the website of Minzhe and shared them in his online shops. After Minzhe collected the pictures, Fai was delegated to collect the pictures and Enlai took all the information about the product and gave them back to Fai who therefore posted them on the commercial websites. Apart from these things, Minzhe also had another business partner in Shanghai to whom she sent pictures.

Usually Minzhe shared her revenues with them, approximately 10% to Enlai, 10% to Fai and 40% to this last Chinese business partner from Shanghai while she kept 40% of the revenue for herself. The visits at stores usually ended with several purchases in accordance with all the requests received by the clients. At the Rinascente Minzhe went around several stores collecting booked merchandises that arrived. Very often there were at this point discussions about exemption from taxes and expeditions. The total of the purchases varied. Minzhe checked the merchandises once again, making sure that she took the right sample. Then since Minzhe was a regular and trustworthy client the manager gave her a big discount on the merchandises. The reason for the low charge was due to the high competition. If Minzhe raised the price, the client went to another buyer, as there were many competitors.

The transaction didn't conclude that day since Minzhe usually went back some days afterward to do further purchases on the basis of feedback received from clients. Sometimes Minzhe had moments of risk at work, especially in the past 2 years since the business was not so high like in the past. Chinese people, she said, didn't have a lot of money to spend like years earlier. Some of them kept buying but the amount of turnover was going down. In the past clients were buying a lot of merchandises without thinking about details, now they bought more selectively and they were more careful with their budget. This required a much higher effort in selling from the side of Minzhe. As a consequence, Minzhe had to reduce the amount of stores she was able to reach. Years earlier she was used to go to other boutiques in Switzerland, she had another buyer helping her, doing a lot of work on her behalf. Now on the other hand because of the fall on the demand she had to do it on her own. Minzhe in this sense represents a type of what I observed in other buyers.

6.2.4 Boutiques

Heng like Delun belongs to the (i) most common category among Chinese entrepreneurs in Milan, property-based businesses. Differently from Delun however Heng is more focused on the clothing sector. I had the chance to observe Heng managing a clothing store during my visits of the Chinese wholesale shopping center and after the opening of his new business in Via Paolo Sarpi, the Chinatown of Milan. In his workplace, Heng worked together side by side with his wife Nuo and his sister-in-law (Meixiu), since the first business was inherited from his wife's parents. In this, Heng was part of a typical Wenzhouren family business, being in partnership with his in-laws. Heng started working for them in order to send or receive merchandises from China and to control invoices, numbers of orders, contracts and bills. In terms electricity, like many Chinese businesses in Chinatown, his store was not affiliated with local electric companies but with Chinese electric companies among Chinese circles. The founder of China Power was friend of Heng, a second-generation migrant that graduated at one of the best Universities of Milan, studied the electric sector for several years and then decided to open a company for Chinese entrepreneurs living in Milan and in the surrounding areas. Added to this, Heng also had a Chinese worker charged with the control, unpacking and moving of the merchandises while Heng was working at the computer making orders. Heng with his wife Nuo was more focused on the new business of jewelry, although he already had some experiences in the same field at his first store. His jewelry store in Chinatown compared to other stores was more modern-looking and clean. Being a second-generation worker helped him to have a more innovative perspective. Sometimes Heng had to exchange place with his sister-in-law Meixiu (Nuo's sister), going to the store at Girasole while she stayed in the Jewelry due to the absence of her parents, often traveling to China for business and family visits.

During my job-shadowing at Heng's Jewelry and at his first clothing store, I had the chance to observe the same kinds of products wholesale. As soon as the client entered the door of the store, Heng or Nuo asked always if it was 'wholesale'. In case the client was not interested in wholesale but in retail he left. It was important for Heng to do only wholesale in order to have good quantities of sales and make profit. Heng, differently from many Chinese entrepreneurs in the same area of Chinatown, understood that profit on wholesale did not depend on numbers but on the quality of products. The funds necessary to open both stores came through the economic support of his mother and father-in-law, both entrepreneurs and first-generation migrants from Wenzhou. Heng did both e-commerce and sold directly at his stores, then he spent a lot of time checking the website of his business, taking pictures of the jewels with his professional camera to put online. In other occasions Meixiu, Nuo's sister, was responsible to take pictures of the products to post online. Heng used websites like Taubau to buy merchandises from China, but unlike Minzhe he didn't sell merchandises in China since it was not convenient for his kind of merchandises. On the other hand, Heng spent a lot of time organizing and storing merchandises. His daily working activity started from 9:00 AM to 7:30 PM while at his other store, as he opened the new one, he kept several salesmen. Wing, one of them, took care of the clients. Despite his hard work, Heng took also breaks for a snack during the day.

Both stores always had a lot of new arrivals, so Heng spent a lot of time packing and unpacking merchandises. The store also had 5–6 cameras to detect stealing. Very frequently Heng, after booking from websites certain merchandises, received calls, answered e-mails or visited the 'managing products recalls' to take the merchandises. Heng had several suppliers and more or less they were the same for both stores. The person delivering the merchandises to the store was usually Chinese. It was an image often seen in Chinatown: Chinese workers from one shop to the next with their car or bicycle, taking or delivering merchandises. Lately, because of the improvement in the working conditions of Chinese small businesses, this type of task passed on to other migrant communities. The boxes were opened, Heng checked its nature, the reference code. Then some of the products that he was able to sell were put together in groups, ready to be shipped to their destination. Every box had a specific code that corresponded to a catalog were all the jewels were inserted. Rings and necklaces were put inside specific containers in order to be shown in the window.

His wife Nuo almost always worked together with him. During the period of my job-shadowing, Nuo had a baby and in order to keep running the business, Heng hired a Chinese worker to organize all the merchandises in the store. Some merchandises were lifted with metal rods and hanged on the wall. Rarely the same merchandise was left hanging for a long period of time, in order to give the idea to the client of newness. Part of the time was spent doing calls to providers or receiving calls from potential clients, both in Chinese or in the local language, in order to coordinate times of delivery or describe the details and prices of certain products. The majority of calls were from Chinese business people or friends to whom Heng passed contacts of local businesses, gave suggestions or proposed partnership for specific events. Sometimes Heng received voicemails from great distribution clients from Milan interested in buying their products, having noticed the pictures in their online shop. Also, Heng received calls from clients asking for a delivery of merchandise in several parts of Milan. In those cases, Heng asked the Chinese worker to bring it to destination by car and usually tried to be as fast as possible. Usually Heng had regular customers with specific requests. Those regulars knew Heng's private life and spent a lot of time talking about the merchandises, coming to withdraw new packages. Among them the main clients were other store managers that brought Chinese products to their warehouses from Heng. Sometimes they came at his store during the week, asking for new arrivals, details on products of gold and silver, bracelets, new colored merchandises made of zircon, necklaces, their measures.

January was usually a favorable time of the year for his business because of the change in seasonal products (different colors, bright or dark jewels). In this time of the year, Heng was particularly busy adjusting new arrivals. The new arrivals were put inside specific coded closets according to the type of jewels and their prices. The amount of merchandises to put in those closets was regularly very consistent. First the merchandise just arrived was unpacked from the boxes and put inside shelves, specific wardrobes in the case of very precious jewels. Other merchandises were packed and sent to some client that bought them, especially through e-commerce and the website.

Several websites were the target of Heng, of selling or of providers. Heng had a specific brand for every type of product of jewelry in his store. Often there was bureaucratic stuff to organize so Heng spent a lot of time looking at the website of the national tax office, controlling receipts and bills. Compared to the clients face-to-face Heng gained much of his profit through clients online from all over Europe. For example, he had clients from Germany that decided to buy from him, since the prices were too high in Germany. Sometimes he received sudden visits from Dutch clients from Netherlands. The majority of his clients though came from Milan or from north Italy. The market was good according to Heng because people were willing to come there even from far away. This was because the products were of a better quality and Heng didn't sell the same kind of products that any European customer could find in other places. This kind of market was the guarantee of a good profit. Usually, clients found his store through his website or through Google Maps, or just going around stores in the Chinatown of Milan. There were other jewelry stores in Via Sarpi yet Heng had a modern-looking store and high-quality products that helped him to attract more clients. Yet an outgoing relationship with clients was somehow missing in Heng.

Beyond this, Heng always gave me the impression of being organized and rigid, trying to keep everything in order. The work was done in couple with his wife Nuo, as she made some calls or fixed the prices as he was packing and unpacking the merchandises. The client entered into the store and started to observe the different merchandises hanging (necklaces, bracelets…). Sometimes clients came to ask for a specific type of jewelry that was missing. In those cases, Heng invited the client to look around to other Chinese stores or to accept to order them in advance. Heng explained the qualities of the products under attention (crystal, silver…), and gave the exact price for each product (usually very cheap). The store was a warehouse and many samples of a single merchandise were usually bought by one client. Usually, the client tried to low the price which was already fixed and Heng maintained the price as it was, although he applied some discount on the final price. Then after choosing the merchandises, Heng packed all the products and gave them to the client with the checkout payment.

Heng tried to be efficient, fast in his transactions, kind and thankful to the client. Heng usually had some regular clients that came to buy at his place because he gave a good discount to them. Right after the conclusion of a transaction with the client Heng was quickly back to work, opening more boxes, controlling more packages, checking the materials and cataloging them. The jewelry store also had an upper floor were the merchandise in excess was preserved. On the back of the store, Heng had a warehouse where he kept the ordered merchandises. Heng usually moved with a basket to collect special ordered merchandises unpacked and set apart. Usually a time of the day was spent by Heng, Nuo, Meixiu or the saleswoman to use the calculator and the ticket machine to check the revenues of the day or to use the price machine to fix the prices that needed to be applied to the products. In both stores the time was characterized by the sound of envelopes moved from one place to the other.

During specific periods of the year, Heng took part to public fairs and exhibitions of his merchandises in the city of Milan. During my job-shadowing I had the chance to observe him working four days at a two weeks public exhibition in the suburbs of Milan. This exhibition was repeated twice a year and gave Heng the opportunity to increase his profit, added to the two stores he already managed. During this period Heng came at the exhibition to work all day long with very little time for a break. It was very tiring for him to assemble and disassemble the merchandises at the exhibition. Decorating was very crucial for this type of job in order to attract clients. Because of the high degree of competition, Heng was challenged in taking entrepreneurial risk through even participating to those events. Often as he worked Heng had a peaceful attitude, he worked with confidence in spite of all the tasks ahead of him. Since the environment in this case was a family business.

After this first phase of observations through job-shadowing among Chinese entrepreneurs in Milan, I then started a second group of observations among others Chinese entrepreneurs from another sample. This second group of entrepreneurs under job-shadowing was composed by entrepreneurs that did not had any contact or affiliation with the Protestant faith. This process of selection was done simultaneously with the interviews of my case control, through specific contacts in the list of entrepreneurs that after having done the interview showed an interest and willingness to be observed in their workplace. The observations of this second group were done after the end of my first year of research and lasted for several consecutive periods for a timeframe from 6 to 10 months, alternated by a period of analysis of the empirical documentation. In the beginning this process of selection of a group of entrepreneurs with no contact at all with the Protestant faith was very difficult, as it went through several rejections or impossible circumstances due to the context of work that did not allow a job-shadowing strategy. For example, in offices with co-workers or superiors my presence was considered intrusive. This was particularly clear in the case of Biming that openly refused to be involved in this practice. For what concerns the second group of entrepreneurs I was able to do job-shadowing with the following Chinese entrepreneurs in a more consistent way (Table 6.2).

Table 6.2 Evaluation chart for the second group of Chinese entrepreneurs under shadowing. The extension of the dark circle signifies the low/high presence of several key factors of economic success as I observed the entrepreneurs during the job-shadowing

	Confidence in his/her skills	reaction to challenges	expression of values	Hard work	relationship with the customer	Integration with other People
Ho	◐	◔	◔	●	◕	◔
Chun	◕	◐	●	◕	◔	◕
Guozhi	◕	◐	◔	●	◕	◐

6.2.5 Salesmen

Even here we have several ideal-types, the first one of a Salesman. Ho arrived in Italy as a student and was son of an already successful entrepreneur living in China. Ho compared with many other Chinese immigrants spoke the local language quite good. During my time of interview with him and in the following months Ho started to work as a salesman in a chain of a multi-national company (a company that realizes 20% of its revenue in China), a job that he was able to find through a work agency. The period of job-shadowing was composed of 6 months of observations during the international annual event of EXPO that took place in the city of Milan in the year 2015. Although his ambition was to become an entrepreneur like his father, Ho did not start his career as an entrepreneur. Compared to Chun there was a clear difference in Ho's younger age and in his different migratory trajectory as a student than as a worker. Ho therefore did not have at the time his own business and he was not a self-made entrepreneur already. Nevertheless during my research it was interesting to see his successive evolution as a marketing developer for a widely known Chinese company and boss of his own brand of fashion design. For this reason, it was significant to insert him in the investigation and see his trajectory from being a worker to being able to invest his money to realize his own entrepreneurial project. His father in China was boss of an important business in the field of construction in the city of Nanjing and he had a past history of strong involvement in business activities of all kinds: automobile shop, rice production company and several intermediary businesses. After graduating in Fashion Design in Milan, Ho decided also to start his own company of fashion clothing together with a colleague living in China. They started their own brand created by Ho, then his Chinese colleague was responsible to look for suppliers and potential clients in China. Differently than many Chinese companies of clothing Ho wanted to find a creative and new way of doing this business which didn't look like a typical Chinese 'copy and paste' company. His brand was a brand for high fashion clothing import–export. But within this new project Ho was mainly working as a sales assistant.

At his workplace Ho operated inside a team with other colleagues (at least 4–5 and the store manager for a total of 13 workers). Some of them were Italian, others Chinese. The team always had a store manager among the more mature that had worked in this shop for a longer period of time. Among them one was a very diligent and hardworking Chinese saleswoman that, although being less outgoing compared with the store manager, was much more organized and systematic in her work. The store manager often went around and controlled that the salesmen worked efficiently, whether in engaging with clients, explaining the product or using properly the checkout.

Another important role of the store manager was to encourage the salesmen in moments of challenge, especially when a transition with the client didn't reach the intended conclusion. With new salesmen the store manager had to train them in the use of the store and on how to resolve problems. Ho usually had a good relationship with his store manager. He was not too rigid but friendly with him and talking often about several topics. The store manager was satisfied with the work of Ho with clients. Compared with other Chinese colleagues Ho was much more effective although being less outgoing than the colleagues. During a typical working day, it was frequent to see the salesmen exchanging place with one another, coming and going, changing shifts. As Ho approached the checkout with a client, he talked with him about the product. Many of the people that came inside the store simply went around the store without buying anything.

His turns at work were varying from time to time (10 AM–1 PM, 1 PM–6 PM, 4 PM–11 PM). The store was almost an open place, rounded and at the center there was a column with a small warehouse where the watches were kept together. On the wall of the door, there was a table with the working hours and shifts. Working together with Ho, were other Chinese salesmen and saleswomen. Ho often was busy going around the platform of the store, from one side to the other, stopping every person with a smile, introducing himself, asking if they needed instructions on the products, showing specific models of watches. Once the client displayed interest in the watches, Ho went to the counter and took a copy of the sample from the warehouse. Many times, after the choice, Ho asked the client if he wanted to see other products before the checkout. The purchasing went on very smoothly, a lot of people took and bought things without much thought. In this case Ho went to the counter, printed the receipt, gave a signature and quickly stamped the invoice with the warranty. Ho was usually very fast in serving the client and right after he finished the transaction with one client he was back at work, going non-stop around and seeking new potential clients.

What created stress, was the fact that clients were potentially interested but after minutes of conversations decided to leave. This had a negative impact in Ho who was unsatisfied and stressed, moving his arms or scratching his head and chasing the clients under pressure, receiving little response to his offer to give help. In the real life Ho was a very nice person but under the pressure of work tended to have a lot of tension. Sometimes this was due even to the fact that some people did not like to engage in conversations with Chinese foreigners. Other times the stress in Ho was caused by the high degree of competition among the sellers around him. In several occasions they were fighting over talking to the same client, or sometimes if somebody was introducing the client, the other worker was at the counter stealing the client from his colleague. When the store was crowded Ho went slowly and spoke with groups of people, trying to be friendly. Ho had to smile, asked if they were interested in anything in particular and made statements like: 'Good morning!' 'welcome!' 'are you together?' 'how can I help you?' 'do you need help?' 'did you visited the Chinese Pavilion here at EXPO?' 'are you interested?' 'are you looking for something in particular?' 'which one do you like?'. When finally somebody showed interest, Ho became then very excited. As he presented the product (sometimes more than ten different types of watches), its prices, its qualities and features (color, type of material, etc., ...) he showed them his own watch, praising the qualities of it in order to engage the client in buying it. Ho followed the client around the store, gave details after details, answering their doubts and questions with no assurance that the client was finally intent at buying something.

This lack of assurance was creating tension in the side of Ho. If the client had a friend, Ho tried to involve him too in the conversation, trying to be warm, joking, but also presenting the product with determination. Compared with other Italian salesmen Ho was much more incisive. Sometimes people asked specific questions such as 'can I find the same product elsewhere?' or 'how much period of warranty there is?'. To those questions Ho needed to be prepared to answer quickly, he tried to answer in the most convincing ways. However, when a client was asking many questions, it didn't necessarily mean that the customer was really interested in buying. Ho in those occasions was frustrated and annoyed by their indecision. In other occasions those same people that left then came back again after 20–30 minutes and decided to buy from Ho, at his own surprise. Very often Chinese clients, both young couples and old people, entered the store, since the store was located in front of the Chinese Pavilion at EXPO. This was a strength factor for Ho, since he started to speak Chinese with them. Ho knew their culture, he was able to relate with them and engage them in the purchase. Ho told me that the Chinese clients from Wenzhou were particularly impolite. Ho came from Nanjing and, like many people from other parts of China, had a low view of people from Wenzhou, considering them as uneducated and focused only on money. Even though he had his suspicion, Ho was always in contact with those Chinese people coming out of the Chinese Pavilion. It is for this very reason that Ho and other Chinese people were hired for this specific position.

During those occasions Ho was very anxious, stressed, nervous. His look was impatient as he tried to approach clients. He was trying to be able to stop somebody among the people passing by. Ho was stressed because he was trying to conclude a deal, to have some client that will stop and buy. Like him also the Italian workers displayed the same stress as sellers. Differently from them though, Ho was much more diligent, without having any break (except for drinking water), without ever checking his phone, spending all of his time trying to engage clients. The Italian sellers on the other hand, although being more outgoing, were chatting with each other, making jokes. Several times I noticed that as all the other sellers were talking with the boss and laughing with irony, or in a state of laziness and low professionalism, Ho was the only one that kept on working. He did not associate with them but kept on reaching more clients, trying to do more even during idle times. It was interesting to notice that Ho's hard work disposition was not dependent on the control of the boss. Secondly Ho didn't have any direct economic benefit or commissions for selling to more clients, he could had just done what was enough, but he wasn't satisfied with it, but he felt it as his duty to work hard anyway even apart from any direct advantage.

During my period of job-shadowing with Ho, he was promoted together with another salesman as 'the best seller of the month'. In few cases there was an exception to this, when some Italian saleswomen were better able because of language proficiency, catching the attention of the client, smiling and being kind, even doing a better job than Ho. Some of his colleagues, for example, were in few occasions much more engaging than Ho, going even outside of the store to talk with the potential clients and inviting them to come inside and take a look at some watches. In an interesting occasion, I had the chance to witness how some clients were interested in the merchandises but none of the team of sellers noticed it, although they were all looking forward to talk with customers. This lost opportunity was very significant and lasted for several minutes until the store manager noticed it. Many times Ho had to stay at the counter repairing some watches that were damaged and needed to be adjusted, cleaned or replaced. In those occasions he often used a hammer, scissors, pliers or screwdrivers. In less than a minute Ho was able to resolve the problem. Sometimes he had to repair several watches at the same time. During this time, he showed to be expert and precise in moving the different parts. As he was working in this specific task, Ho smiled at the client, had conversations with them, explained the problem and tried to find a quick solution. This attracted the people that stood by the way. It was interesting to notice that among all the salesmen Ho was responsible for this type of task much more frequently. Many times Ho had to serve several clients at the same time.

The store was often crowded, even during regular days of the week and not just during the weekend. People were coming at intervals of 40–50 people, since they were coming out of the Chinese Pavilion in different waves. For this reason, the store had a big turnover and Ho talked with people of all kinds. In reality through the day there were also slower times. In this situation of continuous change, from too many to too few, it was not always easy for Ho to establish balance. Sometimes I witnessed days when Ho was working until the closure time (11 PM). In this occasion, Ho was attending the closure of the counter, in frequent tension with the supervising boss. He had to count the cash and receipts to estimate the sales of the day and then do the counting of watches in the warehouse. The economic turnover of this type of business was very high for the company. Sometimes there were situations of difficulty at work, when the counter and tablets were not functioning properly.

After this experience Ho started his own company business in fashion design. The goal of this new brand was to open an import–export company of high fashion in Milan with a Chinese target. Also Ho started to work as a marketing developer, trying to grow his skills in order to become one day a business owner. Ho once again was a special case for his young age, yet, even if not totally matured, his entrepreneurial spirit was very visible.

6.2.6 Food Industry

Chun instead is a first-generation migrant that came in Italy from Wenzhou to find a job. From 1998 to 2006 he lived together with his cousin. Then they decided to start working together. His cousin before opening the business was a waiter. Chun's wife was the business owner of a clothing store in Wenzhou with her brother. With the advent of e-commerce however, Chun's wife had to change her business strategy and started to use e-commerce. The value of stores in Wenzhou was dropping, exporting from China became too common, importing from the west was no more convenient, since students or migrants of the younger generation bought those same products but without taxes. Because of the advent of e-commerce Minzhe's mom constructions factory, as well as Chun's wife store, had to shut down and other businesses were barely surviving like Bingwen's parents' factory. As I've already pointed out, Minzhe perceived this change and was able to adapt her business strategy to the impact of web. There were stories of success even in the second group of entrepreneurs, mainly among the youngest generation like Chun, who was able to see the signs of the times and took action for seeking a change. Another example of this passage to e-commerce was the group of Chinese entrepreneurs revolving around Lei and Ning who invented a Chinese version of Groupon to help Chinese people find restaurants, goods, deals, through an App created by them:

> I like creating websites since I was young, I then studied in Turin [city in north Italy near Milan] in a Chinese company to create and maintain websites. I arrived in Milan in order to expand my business and I created

> the Chinese Groupon named Guua. I want to connect stores and restaurants online. O2O (online 2 online) is already developed in China [...] and it will change business. (Lei, Wenzhou, Milan, 21/01/2016)

Lei played a key role opening the market for business investors as a starting point for Chinese investments in Milan. Yet it required hard work for many hours (sometimes until 4 AM). This was done in order to communicate with clients and technical supporters in China or to respect the deadlines for certain parts of the websites. Even Guiying as an entrepreneur and photographer had to adjust to those changes, so he started to work for an e-commerce agency that sponsored several Italian brands (Casa Day, Geox, etc., ...). He found the job because he had a Chinese friend that worked in the e-commerce company. When she needed a team for design she immediately thought of Guiying and his Chinese friends. Guiying had also to take pictures for famous people and a newsletter during the 'fashion week' in Milan for both Chinese and Italian media, collect posters, shoes, sweaters, etc., ... Guiying also developed a website that with an online platform tried to connect different Chinese people who wanted to sell products. This type of work was however particularly tiring for Guiying because he had to take pictures for more than 50 clothing outfits in one day using Photoshop. Despite the fact that Guiying works together with other 7 Chinese workers, it was still very challenging to do this as a photographer, while the traditional business of food and beverages with his restaurant was much more doable. In this case, like Chun, Guiying was the owner of a food and beverage store, a Chinese restaurant, making typical Chinese food.

Chun like many other Chinese entrepreneurs started a traditional business. He was just an observer of those changes and he was forced to move in step with those changes in order to survive. In this situation of difficulty Chun then started his partnership with his cousin and an Italian businessman. In partnership with Luca, an Italian outsider of the second group of entrepreneurs, Chun opened his own café and tobacco shop where he was co-boss and where he worked every day. Both of them gained from this business partnership, since the Tobacco shop was property of Luca while the rest of the resources were given by Chun. In fact, Chun still had to pay back debts to his family members and to his close friends that lend him money. Luca embraced Chun as a friend and business partner, although they were of a different ethnicity and became managers together in their business despite the cultural challenges. The reality was however that Luca was taking advantage of the fact that Chun was willing to work long hours under any circumstances.

Chun's daily routine at work started at 07.30 AM when he left home to go and do some commissions, to buy products for the bar in the morning. He went to the bank, at the post office and in other public offices, with his business consultant, in order to resolve the bureaucratic matters and to pay the suppliers. His cousin usually did the morning shift while Luca, the Italian co-boss, stayed in the early afternoon shifts until 5.30 PM. Apart from those family ties, Chun didn't have an elaborate network of friends around him, so his daily routine basically rotated around the café. Then from 4 PM Chun went to the bar and started to work there until 09.30 PM (10–11 hours a day, sometimes 14 hours). Chun had specific suppliers for the products he sold at the store. He was putting a lot of emphasis on the right management of it. Sometimes people were coming at the café to make their proposals as suppliers of certain products and Chun needed to evaluate expenses. Mainly Chun worked at the counter of the bar, then sometimes he worked directly at the machines making coffee when his workers needed to take a break for lunch. Compared to Chun Italian workers were slower at the counter. Together with Chun, his Chinese cousin worked every day at the counter. Chun also has 3 workers that always stayed at the café while Chun covered them in case of an emergency or illness. There was a conspicuous change in manpower. In the past Chun had 4 workers but he had to fire one of them due to the economic crisis. Chun often gave instructions to those workers as a boss together with his Italian business partner. The fact that the business owners were both Italian and Chinese increased trust for Chun. Even the old people, that usually didn't talk a lot with foreigners, were very friendly with Chun.

The store was organized in the structure of a corner. It was a big store, clean and inviting. One side had the cabinet for lottery while the other side was the café and tobacco shop. The space of the lottery had 3 different monitors to display the results of every interaction. The store also had two other rooms, one for clients to sit on tables and another for slot machines. Chun added also a section with homemade ice creams, although he decided to cut on the number of slot machines. This reduction of the number of slot machines to one-third of the original quantity was due to the fact that many people were using online shops or playrooms open twenty-four hours a day. Together with the lottery, the café, the tobacco shop, the ice cream and the slot machines, Chun also offered happy hours and food services at tables. As he worked at the lottery, Chun was very fast in giving tickets. Especially when results from the lottery came the café was packed, otherwise it was less crowded. Chun also had to charge people for the monthly and yearly pass of public transportation. For this reason, at the beginning of the year or at the beginning of the month he had a large crowd of people to serve. For the lottery Chun had a lot to do, keeping receipts, dividing between tickets and sending them to the general quarters. If a mistake took place Chun had to pay a fine. For this reason, the task required a lot of attention. He had a lot of people and needed to rush through his tasks, yet he needed to write down the exact amount for each client, making sure that the word he heard was correct.

The philosophy of Chun's business was that the better services he was able to offer, the more people were coming to buy. In order to please the clients Chun examined often his merchandises, making sure that he had everything needed, every type of cigarettes and detailed kinds of coffee. He however also had to face the limits of labor costs. Chun at work went around often with whole packs of cigarettes or with a paper list of merchandises that he needed to check. The people that bought cigarettes were often Italian, in few cases foreigners, while the lottery was mostly chosen by foreigners rather than Italians. When Chun was at work at the counter, he lingered in talking with the clients that came. Sometimes Chun gave advice to his clients, offered favors, helped and gave directions. In some occasions and at certain hours of the day packages of merchandises came, for example cigarettes, fruits, drinks or other packages of products (10 or more boxes for each delivery). Chun then took all the merchandises and placed them in specific containers and closets. Chun chose the suppliers on the basis of who offered the lowest price. Although being a foreigner Chun had a personal relationship with clients, a loud voice, very talkative with the regular customers. He knew their names and tried to put himself at their same level, imitating the dialect of Milan. Some regular customer stayed at the counter speaking with him for a long period of time. The clients at his bar were people from around the neighborhood that knew each other already and that came at the café as a social place of gathering.

Chun was usually kind with them, people knew him and did not just spent few words with him but had entire dialogues about their lives. Sometimes he had conversations with them about working hours, expenses at the supermarket, discounts or taxes. He or his cousin changed turns frequently, depending on the number of people in line at the counter or at the betting shop. Chun never left the counter, since there were so many clients every day. For this reason, few were the breaks for Chun at work. In fact, Chun's role was of working at the counter on a stable basis, giving his best to save time for people and treat well the customer. As he was always at the counter, he was very fast to serve the customers that came to him. He used the tablet for the lottery in one hand, then the counter for the café on the other since his activity moved daily from the betting shop to the counter. He was often busy giving the receipts of the betting shop, working in pairs with his cousin even though Chun was the most talkative. When no client was in line at the counter, Chun spent time at the phone, reading the newspaper or going to the betting store discussing with the people there and shouting out loud the numbers that recently came out at the lottery, counting the lottery tickets. The atmosphere was of loud volume, exchange of ideas.

During the day I noticed how sometimes repeatedly the store was full of clients in line at the counter and then almost desert for a while. It was common to see Chun totally forgetting his clients in line, especially when he was busy at the betting shop. Sometimes there were more than 5 or 6 clients in line while Chun was absent from the counter. Other times the line grew up to 10–15 people especially on Thursday, since the day of the lottery was drawing near. In those situations, Chun tended to be more stressed, as he tried to satisfy them. He needed to go straight to the point with the requests from clients, in order to save time for attending the customers behind. As he finished serving one client Chun moved his feet in sign of impatience waiting for the next order. The clients usually were old people both men and women, sometimes families with kids or single young individuals from the neighborhood, living around the bar, or retired. It was difficult in this area to find new clients. Some people came for the lottery, others came to take a coffee at the bar section.

Chun likewise had to face several situations of economic risk. The first example was when he and Luca took over the café several years ago. Luca had to do a mortgage on his house while Chun had a lot of difficulties in understanding all the bureaucracy. In the beginning they had to transfer the shop from one side of the street to the other and had to face a lot of extra expenses. During my period of observations, they were paying the rent but they could not effort the loan due to costs. Chun had to adjust to the local culture, even in the way he was doing business, because of some of his initial reactions to clients, his lack of friendliness with the customers. In particular Chun, like many other Chinese workers, was often very cold in his relationship with clients. Staying at the counter he didn't even say hello to the people that were coming in. Among the Chinese entrepreneurs like Chun, there was a lack of proactiveness, building relationship with the client, describing the characteristics of the products and giving alternatives. Even if Chun improved from being a silent worker he still had some trouble adapting. Because of this, clients, not feeling welcomed, became angry since they did not receive greetings. This was a big problem also because clients were unstable in their requests: some wanted to be greeted, others did not. Chun unfortunately was often impulsive in his reaction to those situations.

Chun's cousin was even worse, almost a social with customers. He wasn't able to create that necessary bridge with the clients. The lack of smiles and 'thank you', which for the worker meant a lot, the result was the loss of clients. When Chun was explaining products, he was going straight to the point instead of engaging in explanations and social interactions. Luca was lamenting the lack of hard work in Chun at times, his negligence in cleaning up its consequences on the revenue of the café. Hard choices needed to be taken, especially when having to fire a worker, low periods of turnover. Chun lamented the consequences of the economic crisis during the job-shadowing. Particularly he blamed it on the turnover, contributions, salary while he, as a boss, needed to pay high taxes.

Chun pointed out how a boss in China simply managed a restaurant or a café without having to work directly, while in the west the Chinese boss needed to work together with the workers and at times even more than the workers. Chun was expressing his struggle with me: payment of taxes for the business and workers. All of this was precluding any chance to make profit. Other situations of risk and difficulties for Chun came when difficult clients were around, either dunked or hard to talk with. For example, sometimes clients were upset for a statement, so the circumstance required Chun to be firm. Many clients did not speak the language well and this was causing many misunderstandings. Chun was particularly nervous in those circumstances, turning his face away, losing his patience. Even if he was trying to interact with them he appeared still visibly anxious. Several times there were situations of complaining from the side of the clients saying that they didn't receive respect or needed attention. Chun usually didn't take part in the discussion, since he did not want to take responsibility for what happened. He experienced tension and was afraid to be blamed for any misunderstanding.

6.2.7 *Boss*

Guozhi in many ways resembles Chun or Delun, by the fact of being a café and tobacco store owner of a second-generation Chinese migrants from the area of Wenzhou. Guozhi came to Italy when he was only 10 years old. Guozhi's father was employee in a bar. Then after accumulating the necessary funds, he bought his own café. Before, his father, like many Chinese entrepreneurs, owned for 25 years a clothing store wholesale at Via Sarpi. Guozhi was working there together with his parents. In this Guozhi was more similar to Heng. A peculiar element in the café and tobacco store of Guozhi was that, after bying the business from Italian entrepreneurs, Guozhi and his father kept the whole amount of Italian workers. Many Chinese small businesses owners were following this strategy, by simply absorbing local businesses in debt but keeping the whole structure as it was:

> For me to work good you need the right people, not just saving, to work better you must invest, foreigners or not to have quality you need personnel of quality. The previous owner has selected, we kept them, we added then [a new worker]. Before I was working in the tobacco shop of my ex- girlfriend, for my parents, and as an interpreter during exhibitions, then I opened an Italian restaurant in Shanghai but then I gave up and came back here, I sold. Also the clothing store of my parents at Via Sarpi working was different, more free hours, more quiet but it was a differend period, with the crisis everything changed. (Guozhi, Zhejiang, Milan, 31/05/2016)

Guozhi left his investment in Shanghai and came back to Italy because there was too much concurrence in his motherland. To have a business investment in Shanghai was very hard, trade was at times brutal and it was necessary to be already part of a cycle of acquaintances. To survive in the business of Shanghai it was fundamental to have a joint stock company or a limited company. The market was very different and Guozhi knew that there was no middle way: either he would had failed or won with a new brand but in due time, with the necessary money and connections. This would had meant trying to survive for at least five years of business then being able to flourish and multiply. Yet Guozhi decided to come back to Italy and invest with his father in a new business. The work on the tobacco store of his girlfriend was for Guozhi boring, being located in a little small town and attended mainly by older people.

Nevertheless, Guozhi tried to connect this professional opportunity with his family, trying to convince them to start this same type of business elsewhere. Because of the economic crisis in Italy Guozhi and his parents decided to sell their clothing store at Via Sarpi and started a business in a new field: food and beverages. Having obtained his Italian citizenship Guozhi could have authorization to manage a tobacco and a betting shop. Guozhi started his working day around 6:00–6:30 AM to open the café and bar store. Then around 12.00 he went back home to eat, rest and then after 4 hours, he came back to the store for the closing hours. At 8:30 PM he closed the store. On Sunday Guozhi only worked half a day. The bar and tobacco shop was located in a very strategic crossroad of two streets in a wealthy neighborhood of Milan. The adobe and furniture of the place were very Italian. Usually Italian workers were at the counter for coffee or at the tobacco area taking turns with Guozhi while Guozhi's father was at the betting shop. The Italian workers were on average very young in their age, at times they were undisciplined and noisy. Sometimes Guozhi's wife was at the counter with him looking at her phone and just killing time. Guozhi had a very good Italian pronunciation, better than many other Chinese workers. Guozhi was very open with clients even though he was just going through the first months of his business. People already knew him and made friendship with him.

The tobacco and café store was just bought by Guozhi and his parents so the business, inherited by others, was already in place in its initial stages. In order to start his business Guozhi had to take loan and experience a great challenge afterward, just surviving in order to pay the debts. As the store had many workers, the season was very challenging for Guozhi. He had to learn to know his workers, how to cooperate with one another despite their different cultures, how to share advices to them and know the customers. Guozhi's store had to offer a good service, always seeking to improve it. Guozhi knew that if clients noticed any loss in quality due to the change of ownership, it would have meant the loss of many clients. For this reason, Guozhi always sought to offer better services to his customers.

Another challenge for Guozhi's business materialized in connection with some renovation works that were taking place right in front of the café for the construction of a new stop for the underground. Those works were going on for many months and stores like his were losing clients because of that. The street was blocked and clients could not find a parking spot nearby, so they did not attend the café regularly anymore.

Guozhi had to go to a public re-union of traders from the area to signal this problem. He was lamenting how he received very little help from the government despite all the expenses he had to bear for acquiring new products. Under those circumstances, Guozhi was forced to fire some of his workers.

To strengthen himself Guozhi recalled that the previous generation of his father from Wenzhou was the first of Chinese entrepreneurs, which had to make even harder efforts. Between the city of Wenzhou and the diaspora everybody in the circles of Guozhi knew each other, whether through family links or friendships. If, for example, somebody worked well in the family, Guozhi brought alongside others that from their part invited others to follow the same business idea. In less than a decade the whole neighborhood of Guozhi in Wenzhou was involved in a network of traders engaged in all sort of small businesses. From there this Wenzhouren model of business reached the rest of the world, as many, like Guozhi's family, decided to emigrate in the west. Guozhi was part of a large family of entrepreneurs: 4 uncles and 2 aunts working in different parts of Italy, some in Bologna others in Rome. Some of them were small business owner of tobacco and cafes like Guozhi, but others had clothing stores. This role of Guozhi's family leads me now to introduce the last point in the analysis of the job-shadowing, concerning the financial aid that these Chinese enlarged families, as well as other forms of network, are capable to give among Chinese entrepreneurs. Whether during difficult times or special occasions, like marriage, family plays an important financial role for Chinese entrepreneurs.

6.2.8 Financial Network

How is business commonly created among Chinese entrepreneurs? Why is it possible to observe such rapid and exponential growth in many parts of the west? In order to answer these questions, I spent these periods of Job-shadowing among Chinese businesses in the area of Milan. During my ethnographic observations at Via Sarpi, the Chinatown of Milan, Ah Cy pointed out how the enterprises of the area followed a common path in the creation of business. First of all three or more entrepreneurs who already had a relation of friendship, or belonged to a similar network decide to incorporate themselves into a joint venture. Among those, one plays the role of a *founder* (A in Table 6.3) who manages the firm, provides the initial investment and is followed by other's support. The financial resources that the entrepreneurs put together through loans from family members in China are useful to avoid loans from banks which make things harder. Usually somebody sells his business in China in order to guarantee his relatives in the diaspora to open a new firm. This was said by Giulio, an Italian worker collaborating with Delun, to be the strength factor of Chinese entrepreneurship in spite of the eventuality of failure:

> Their power is that they are many and they cooperate between the family, they give help to one another, they will never fail, it is hard that a Chinese is in loss [economically], they know how to manage the investments. Delun thinks always things in big, he never stops. (Giulio, Ibidem)

Such reciprocity based on faith among Protestants is also enforced by a traditional Chinese cultural pattern of social relationships (*Guanxi*). I will later discuss further the implications of the Guanxi principle, when I will analyze the *Network explanation* in the second case-control group. This structure was basically interchangeable in the sense that sometimes the family lineage was used to accomplish a similar purpose like in the case of Jiahao, Yan and many others:

> Relatives and friends help us a lot, from the weeding we had many gifts from family and friends, many were invited, we received large amounts from relatives and friends. Letters of wedding where high, 500–1000 euros with all the people we invited, we had a great capital, if I didn't invest had to give back to the next wedding. [...] I've found the workers through word of mouth, in the market we are like a family, among friends and family we present people to each other, and the workers themselves help me to find new workers when needed. (Jiahao, Milan, Wenzhou, 9/05/2016)

> I had a debt, I had to pay my relatives therefore I was working a lot. We continue to grow new businesses, the Italian goes through failure but we work 16–17 hours and we succeed. As the business reaches his autonomy we delegate, we change mentality. (Yan, Milan, Wenzhou, 25/01/2016)

Yan in fact is the boss of two businesses. Like many other entrepreneurs, when her small business reached a level of autonomy, she decided to turn it over to other Chinese workers as she started a new one. People are united on the basis of favors and obligations reciprocally exchanged which often take the form of monetary loans (Ceccagno and Rastrelli, 2008).

Table 6.3 Illustration of the role of network in business among Chinese entrepreneurs under job- shadowing. In red the family, green the house church and blue external connections. Lastly the typical financial circuit behind business multiplication through network in the Chinatown according to Ah Cy

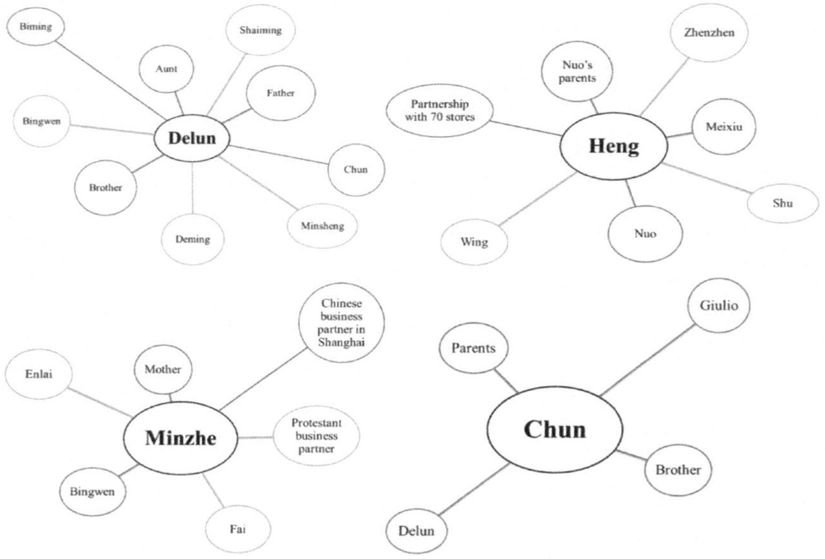

(continued)

Table 6.3 (continued)

		Label	Motivation and Mission	Degree of Contribution to Business	Economic Services Offered	Number of Nodes Generated	Inside/outside Dynamic
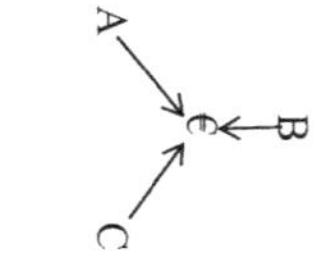	*House Churches*	Religious Network	Based on the commonality of Faith to expand the message	High	Business ticket, Charisma, Partnership, Jobs, Information	> 100, mainly on a local level	Exclusive orientation, once part of the circle there is plain access to all the services
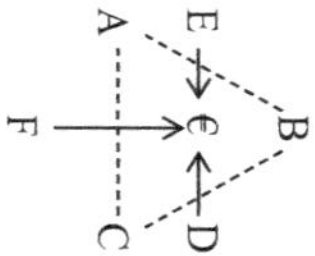	*Family and Lineage*	Family Network	Based on blood and marital lines to help those part of them in life	High	Financial help for initial stages and times of emergency, jobs,	< 5, mainly local but also transnational because of migratory flux	Exclusive orientation based on genetic and marital status
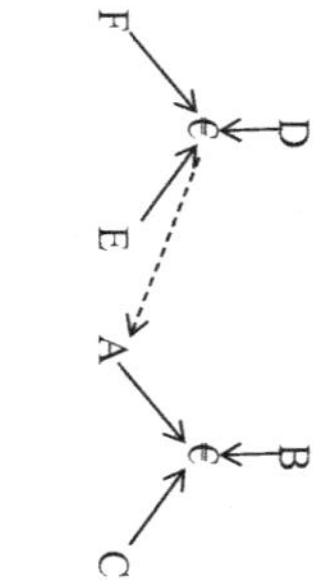	*Associations*	Organizational Network	Groups of civic society focused on a variety of social issues, including business.	Medium / Low (costs and constraints, not always effective)	Partnership, Connections for jobs, Information	> 100 both local and transnational	Exclusive / Inclusive orientation vary based on the specific nature
	Circle of Friends & Personal Connections	Informal Networks	Friendship and acquaintance to build informal type of relationships.	Low (sporadic cases of success)	Connections for jobs, partnership	< 5 based on few scattered connections	Inclusive orientation based on the share of common experiences

After a certain degree of development, the boss together with those *founders* who helped him in the initial stages decides to open a new business finding *cooperators* that as substitutes will take over the initial business (especially in the case of members of the second generation of migrants connected through a network) as they plant a new business. This strategy is very important for the first stages of a property-based business of the first type, which is the most common form of business among Chinese entrepreneurs in the area of Milan. One of the many examples of this was pursued by Heng when he left his clothing store outside of Milan in the hands of Wing and decided to open a jewelry in Via Sarpi, leaning on the financial resources from his initial business for the expenses of construction, rent, taxes and lack of clients in the initial phase of the jewelry. It is in fact very hard to make any kind of revenue from a business for the first 5–6 years of activity due to construction expenses, taxes and building up the portfolio of clients. For this reason, every 4–5 years a new business is opened, leaning on the profits of the previous business guaranteeing the sustainability in the first years of losses, in times of crisis and, most importantly, guaranteeing a state of continual multiplication of businesses which ideally leads to economic success. The greatest example of this is Ning's store, part of 11 other restaurants in the area of Milan, owned by Jiahao, ran through Chinese workers in each of them:

> To have a strong working team is crucial power and stability. In every restaurant I have people that I trust, I don't have to carrying it on by myself, I go according to the need, not everyone is new, then the others keep going by themselves. [...] I don't need to contact the suppliers anymore, every restaurant has his own entrusted person, that takes care of it in my place, I just have to manage it in the background, rarely I go visit my restaurants unless it is in the initial stages, but once they can sustain themselves I'm ok. Now the businesses can sustain themselves, I just need to manage them. (Jiahao, Milan, Wenzhou, 9/05/2016)

As Jiahao started her business from family savings, every time one business was able to stand on its own she moved on opening a new one as she entrusted somebody to manage the previous restaurant in her place. Despite the lack of knowledge of the Italian language and other issues, those networks of Wenzhouren workers, with their flexibility and adaptation, working every day and sleeping only 4 hours each night, are able to guarantee an easy multiplication. They are more capable to face challenges and avoid failures. Yet Ning also wanted to clarify a change in the times where such quick road to success may be no longer possible:

> Since the Laoban [Boss] came early twenty years ago, at the time there weren't as many Chinese as today, it was easy to grow, today is not that easy, everybody is selling and replicating. (Ning, Ibidem)

Ning and her network of 11 businesses is not an exception but it clearly comes from investments that started long time ago and that today may be harder to implement because of the market saturation in Chinese entrepreneurship. After the passing of those critical initial stages however, if the business results to be fruitful the Boss and *founders* of the business come back to their initial business and take over the business as Boss employing the *cooperators* (D, E and F in Table 6.3) for starting a new business. This is a strategy often used by Chinese entrepreneurs. The number of people involved and the timeframe may change but the model is still the same and it is what ultimately helped Chinese entrepreneurship to develop and thrive in the long term in the diaspora. Such results are partially confirmed by the literature on social networks and economic success (Egbert, 2009; Kristiansen, 2004). Particularly this goes in line with the theories on 'relational embeddedness' where one cohort of successful companies invests in successive generations providing the financial, human and social capital to start new ventures through a system of cooperation, spatial proximity and transmission of technical and managerial know-how (Thornton, 1999, p. 32). Such process also is able to function only through the family. Members of a family have a propensity to create small productive structures. Once established these structures tend to generate new units on the basis of the development of a new family nucleus. On a geographical level then those groups tend to aggregate closest to the location of the firms (Carchedi F., Ferri M., in Benton and Pieke, 1998, p. 275).

This leads me to define here an important cultural principle underlying those economic transactions, which is the one of *Guanxi*. Guanxi is a basic dynamic in personalized networks of influence among Chinese people and it can be best described as the relationship individuals cultivate with others in terms of reciprocity (Wong, 2007). What I was able to witness in Jiahao, Peng, Delun, Yan, Yi, Na's parents, up to other examples on a macro-level such as AUMAI is this principle in action. Behind those financial circles and roles lies a driving principle which is able to hold together different people, allowing for a fast and successful multiplication. Guanxi is the basis for such success in many of the entrepreneurial circles I observed, whether based on family relationships or on associations. The person inside the network feels a compelling reason to reciprocate and therefore allows the circulation of financial resources and other forms of business investments among Chinese entrepreneurs.

Guanxi is also significant when it comes to establishing its function as producer of social capital. This doesn't actually mean that Guanxi somehow substitutes in all its forms social capital but most of the times it definitely becomes a producer of important relational social capital. There are similarities and differences between those two concepts, but it must be carefully noticed how the Chinese Guanxi differs from Western preconceptions about social networking (Huang and Wang, 2011). Both of them involve social relations but Guanxi does not relate exclusively to social capital, it has more to do with interpersonal relationships that are particularly crucial when, like in this case, the focus is small business multiplication. Guanxi has to do with the relationship between two or more people, direct particularistic ties where relationships are seen as an end in themselves and people are divided into categories, being treated accordingly. It is brought to life by gift-giving and then it becomes a long-term relationship, pervasive in every aspect of life, including business. Guanxi-based business practices are able to produce strong effective networks (Huang and Wang, 2011). Within corporate environments this concept is often lost and leaves the space to what commonly is defined as social capital (see also: Egbert, 2009; Kristiansen, 2004; Loscocco and Leicht, 1993; Thornton, 1999, p. 32; Carchedi F., Ferri M., in Benton & Pieke, 1998, p. 275).

If we were to sum up the impact of network in economic success, instead of just dealing with types of networks, what seems more effective is this underlying principle. Regardless of the type of network, if a Chinese entrepreneur is member of an Association, a House Church, common lineage or circles of friends, the study confirms that what is crucial for the achievement of economic success is the presence of such guiding principle of Guanxi. Business multiplication and the activation of an effective network for business purposes is usually not possible, without the proper activation of this sociologically relevant specific component. That is why, as it is visible from Table 6.3, the contribution to business tends to be higher in types of networks where relationships are already consolidated from a long time and not necessarily just because of specifics of a case. However, the concept of Guanxi carries its issues since it is mainly based on indirect forms of reciprocity that are often unstable and it operates in a context often self-interested, such as business and carry with them other clear problems when connected with destructive circles such as the Chinese mafia. Beyond this broad description, it is time therefore to move to analyze the place of values in this picture.

References

AA. VV., 1997, *Cina a Milano. Famiglie, ambienti e lavori della popolazione cinese a Milano*, Milano, Abitare Segesta Cataloghi.

AA. VV., 'Imprenditori Cinesi a Milano: Quasi tremila, 560 Milioni di Fatturato, il 40% è donna', (Febbraio 2008), Camera di Commercio, Milano.

AA. VV., 'Milano, ogni giorno nascono due imprese cinesi', su *Il Giorno*, (Dicembre 2012), Camera di Commercio, Milano

Benton G., Pieke F. N., 1998, *The Chinese in Europe*, London, Macmillan Press.

Bressan N., 2013, *L'Imprenditoria Cinese in Italia. Due Casi Studio: la Ristorazione Cinese a Milano e il Distretto del Porfido a Trento*, Università degli Studi di Trento.

Ceccagno A., Rastrelli R., 2008, *Ombre Cinesi? Dinamiche Migratorie della Diaspora Cinese in Italia*, Roma, Carocci.

Chee-Beng T., Storey C., Zimmerman J., (Eds.), 2007, *Chinese Overseas. Migration, Research and Documentation*, Hong Kong, Chinese University Press.

Collino A., Biggeri M., Murgia L., 2014, *Processi Industriali e Parti Sociali. Una Riflessione sulle Imprese Italiane in Cina (Jangsu) e sulle imprese Cinesi in Italia (Prato)*, Firenze, Firenze University Press.

Cologna D., 2004a, (a cura di), *Asia a Milano. Famiglie ambienti e lavori delle popolazioni asiatiche a Milano*, Milano, Abitare Segesta.

Cologna D., 2004b, 'La Comunità Cinese a Milano', su *Mondo Cinese*, (Maggio-Agosto 2004), Milano, n. 117.

Egbert H., 'Business Success Through Social Networks? A Comment on Social Networks and Business Success', in *The American Journal of Economics and Sociology*, Vol. 68, No. 3 (Jul., 2009), pp. 665–678.

Huang K., Wang K. Y., 'How Guanxi Relates to Social Capital? A Psychological Perspective', in *Journal of Social Sciences*, No. 7–2 (2011), pp. 120–126.

Kristiansen S., 'Social Networks and Business Success: The Role of Subcultures in an African Context', in *The American Journal of Economics and Sociology*, Vol. 63, No. 5 (Nov., 2004), pp. 1149–1171.

Miranda R., 'La presenza Cinese in Italia. Numeri, sfide e prospettive', su *Formiche*, (Giugno 2014).
Thornton P. H., 'The Sociology of Entrepreneurship', in *Annual Review of Sociology*, Vol. 25 (1999), pp. 19-46
Wong M.. 'Guanxi and Its Role in Business', in *Chinese Management Studies*, Print, no. 1–4 (2007), pp. 257–276.
Zhang Y., Zhang M., 'Can Overseas Migrants Develop Sustained Entrepreneurship? Multiple Case Studies of Wenzhou Migrants in Italy', in *The Journal of Chinese Sociology*, Vol. 3 (2016), p. 4.

CHAPTER 7

The Protestant Dimension of Chinese Capitalism

I will call them 'my people' who are not my people.

—Romans 9, 25

7.1 The Chinese Version of the Protestant Ethic

7.1.1 Introduction

During my period of ethnographic observations and job-shadowing, there was an important element that needed to be taken into consideration: the fundamental centrality of the religious belief among Chinese Protestants in the business practices. Those Chinese entrepreneurs in Milan, beyond their ethnic origin, shared something else in common that was in my view playing a predominant role in their daily work ethic: they identities as Protestants. In the previous chapter, I pointed out how among the several entrepreneurs under job-shadowing there were some significant differences on the way the business was pursued. The way they reacted to situations of economic risk as well as the way they worked was different also on this basis. Those differences cannot simply be due to the application of different business strategies, accidental circumstances or mere coincidences.

To better understand how this works, it is now necessary to consider the personal and private sphere of those entrepreneurs, in particular their

O. Palombaro, *Christianity and Capitalism in China*,
https://doi.org/10.1007/978-981-97-3549-5_7

social identification with a system of beliefs, whether Protestantism in the case of the first three entrepreneurs under job-shadowing or other types of cultural, social and economic backgrounds like in the case of the second group of entrepreneurs under job-shadowing. At first, it might sound strange to introduce such religious component in a scientific investigation, especially in the mind of skeptics, since economic activity operates according to its own laws rather than being affected by something such as religious belief. Because of the primary role of beliefs in the work-life of those entrepreneurs and because of their deep connections with the business outcome it is crucial to consider it anyway, even if as much as possible done from an impartial perspective. As it will be clear from the next pages, the field tells us of the centrality of such argument, even if it must be considered in light of other explanatory dimensions.

This research started with a theoretical argumentation that dates back to the roots of sociology and went through major adjustments in the past decades. The question of the validity of my book in the contemporary realm requires therefore, the necessity of investigating things with the proper method, the proper field, with the right information. So many times, reality is very far from expected theoretical principles, and it may require a change in the premises. For what concerns the results on the evaluation of my research questions, after preliminary observations and the empirical context, here's a list of the Christian entrepreneurs interviewed each assigned a nickname to protect their privacy (Table 7.1).

Now I proceed examining whether it is possible to trace the presence or absence of the set of beliefs that I previously described in the model and if the identification of economic success is due to that same *ethos* described by Weber or to some other element in the field. What will be presented in the following section is a detailed definition of religious dynamics in order to check the presence of any significant intervening element for the case of the Chinese entrepreneurs under my investigation in the diaspora. In other words: if the Protestant belief has some observable effect on the conduct of the individual, what is the degree of such effect for the case of Chinese entrepreneurs? My main expected result from the research was to see a positive effect. After having checked the empirical evidence of the main theoretical argument I noticed that PAS (perpetual assurance of salvation) is able to impact significantly self-efficacy and favor indirectly economic success. From my analysis of the interview materials for Wenzhou's entrepreneurs, I was able to move in part toward the direction of giving a positive answer.

Table 7.1 List of the Christian entrepreneurs under investigation. The ones with the gray line were part of the job-shadowing activity, Mario and Giulio are the Italian outsiders

Nickname	Work Sector	City/Region of Origin	Age/gender	Date of the Interview
Minzhe	Buyer	Shuzhou	28 F	12/09/2014
Bingwen	Engineer	Hangzhou	28 M	12/09/2014
Hop	Architect	Shanghai	28 M	15/11/2014
Heng	Store Manager in clothing and jewelry	Wenzhou	28 M	08/11/2014
Huizhong	Store Manager in clothing	Wenzhou	26 M	14/05/2015
Jun	Travel Agency	Wenzhou	30 M	08/11/2014
Kong	Shopkeeper in clothing	Wenzhou	26 M	14/05/2015
Minsheng	Business employee	Wenzhou	25 M	20/12/2014
Shaiming	Cashier in clothing	Wenzhou	23 M	29/11/2014
Shing	Boss of lamp business	Wenzhou	45 M	30/01/2015
Shu	Store manager for multiple stores in clothing	Wenzhou	45 M	30/01/2015
Wing	Administrative for multiple businesses	Wenzhou	23 M	06/12/2014
Bo	Shopkeeper at Swatch	Wenzhou	27 M	22/11/2014

(continued)

Table 7.1 (continued)

Nickname	Work Sector	City/Region of Origin	Age/gender	Date of the Interview
Delun	Store Manager for multiple bars and cafe	Wenzhou	24 M	08/06/2014
Nuo	Shopkeeper in clothing	Wenzhou	37 F	30/01/2015
Deming	Factory packaging in clothing	Wenzhou	27 M	08/11/2014
Yongnian	Store manager in clothing	Wenzhou	34 M	14/05/2015
Meixiu	Shopkeeper in clothing	Wenzhou	23 F	30/01/2015
Zhenzhen	Store manager for multiple stores in clothing	Wenzhou	40 M	30/01/2015
Zixin	Shopkeeper in jewelry	Wenzhou	28 M	14/05/2015
Enlai	Store manager of multiple stores in clothing	Chong Qing	28 M	15/11/2014
Fai	Factory packaging in clothing and export	Yun nan	26 M	22/11/2014
Ah Cy	Store manager in clothing	Wenzhou	26 M	22/11/2014
Ting-Ting	Shopkeeper in clothing	Wenzhou	31 F	14/05/2015

(continued)

Table 7.1 (continued)

Nickname	Work Sector	City/Region of Origin	Age/gender	Date of the Interview
Ah Lam	Trader	Wenzhou	37 M	29/11/2014
Guang	Shopkeeper in clothing	Wenzhou	23 M	18/07/2015
Ling	Neuro-physician	Baoding	30 F	29/05/2015
Mario	Relator	Milano	45 M	30/01/2015
Xiu	Boss of a factory of LED	Pan Qsiao	34 M	28/08/2015
Yi	Store manager of 9 pharmaceutic stores	Wenzhou	45 M	23/08/2015
Zhong	Director of English School	Pan Qsiao	28 F	28/08/2015
Tai	Boss manager of 3 kindergarten	Tangxia	47 F	26/08/2015
Min	Commercial designer in a factory of furnishing	Wenzhou	27 F	23/08/2015
Da	Boss in a factory of printing and packing	Wenzhou	36 F	25/08/2015
Bai	Boss of multiple businesses	Wenzhou	28 M	20/08/2015
Chao	Saleswoman in a supermarket	Geu Xi	32 F	26/08/2015
Nai	Boss of two factories of materials for hospitals	Wenzhou	41 M	24/08/2015

(continued)

Table 7.1 (continued)

Nickname	Work Sector	City/Region of Origin	Age/gender	Date of the Interview
Qiang	Manager of a bar/library	Wenzhou	46 M	26/08/2015
Xun	Manager of clothing store and President of WCMUA	Wenzhou	46 M	22/08/2015
Ning	Boss of 'Thien Hai' foundation	Wenzhou	47 M	24/08/2015
Ya	Banker	Wenzhou	43 M	23/08/2015
Kun	Teacher	Wenzhou	28 M	23/08/2015
Zhi	Pastor	Wenzhou	44 M	23/08/2015
Hung	Pastor	Pingshan	26 M	26/08/2015
Yong	Pastor	Rui An	45 M	27/08/2015
Niu	Pastor	Qing Tian	46 M	13/09/2015
Na	Worker at a Clothing Store	Wenzhou	20 M	14/12/2015
Yan	President of Association and Bar Owner	Wenzhou	45 F	25/01/2016
Fang	President of Association and Pastor	Wenzhou	50 M	25/01/2016
Giulio	Chook and Store Manager	Milan	25 M	16/01/2016

7.1.2 *Clarifying Factors*

Those first findings reveal that Christian entrepreneurs belonging to evangelical churches (see group b of Table 4.2) hold the auxiliaries to the *preconditions* that I've defined in the model for the Chinese case. I was able to see the continual presence and emphasis on a dramatic conversion for any member of the church. This corresponds to the role of precondition on the Perseverance of the Saints typical of Calvinism. Also, a literal reading of the Bible with all of its implications in their daily conduct was present which confirms the role of Sacred Scriptures according to the model for the case of Calvinism. One of the common explanations given by entrepreneurs is the application of principles of wisdom from the Bible to their business:

> From the Bible, the Word of Jesus, it helped me specially in life, first we need to be immersed in the Word of God, it gives you the meaning, because when you don't work you can rest and find directions. (Zhenzhen, Ibidem)

During my shadowing and ethnographic observations, I was able to see many cases where the entrepreneur takes the time during breaks or when there are not a lot of customers, to read the Bible, listen to Christian radio, sermons, devotional books for practical application or, in the case of deacons and leaders, to do sermon preparation. Delun, for example, always had Christian Chinese music playing at his café as a way to witness through his business. Also, Delun during my job-shadowing of his new business spent 4 hours from 11 PM to 3 AM reading the Scriptures. Bingwen in the same way spent his hours of travel from his house to work listening to the Bible on his phone. All of those activities are ways in which they express indirectly their faith during business activity, something that gives them a meaning and purpose as they accomplish their daily tasks. During my job-shadowing of Heng I witnessed how he passed a lot of time using social media for sharing his faith, inviting people to church events, preparing and posting Bible verses and questions for the weekly Chinese Bible study, listening Christian music at his workplace. Another of the preconditions that I was able to observe during the ethnographic observations is the belief in the doctrine of the perseverance of the saints. As I mentioned already, this belief proper of Calvinism survives today in large portions of evangelicalism. Such belief gives the entrepreneur an emphasis on discipline, accomplishment of tasks and hard work, not as a way to control their state of salvation but out of a desire to grow in their faith. During the ethnographic observations I've observed this in their stress on striving for the fulfillment of their salvation with fear and trembling. Concerning conversion, a dramatic experience is always stressed by the entrepreneurs as a common trend. Of special significance is the identification of the migratory process, with all of its challenges, as a crucial element in re-enforcing the faith or causing the individual to embrace the faith in the first place:

> I arrived here in 2009 since six years and I've got baptized here in Milan, now I know very well, before [in China] I believed a little bit but never so deep like it is now, I understand and I believe a lot. (Zixin, Ibidem)

Many studies have been done in Sociology and Cultural Anthropology on how the migratory process intervenes in the practice of conversion. Specifically, for the case of migration and conversion to Protestantism among Chinese communities, a study has been conducted for the case of Paris and France (Vendassi, 2014) confirming such influence. But what I mainly want to underline here is how the dramatic conversion, that starts for Protestants with the acquisition of PAS, relates to the realm of work and, according to their biographical reconstructions, brings a radical change in the way they do business after such event. The entrepreneur sees a clear difference between his past life before acquiring the belief in PAS and his present life, also in the realm of work:

> I saw changes at work since I became a Christian, those are things that you can't see but the more you feel them at work and in life, you feel that somebody is protecting you. (Kong, Ibidem)

This dramatic conversion permeates every area of life and is perceived as a prerequisite to belong to the community. In other words, if a Chinese entrepreneur attends the community but doesn't have such testimony of a dramatic conversion he can be considered still as an outsider to the social group, regardless of his involvement or family background. All this emphasis pushes then the individual to activate a process of self-examination that I saw in action even in the realm of work. The entrepreneurs under shadowing, Delun or Heng, were particularly concerned about the impression that their business life may have in front of the Christian community. They emphasized their struggles and how their belief in PAS helped them, they frequently shared their testimony of salvation and they were making a strong emphasis on business primarily as a God's blessings on their lives. In order to conform to other members of the church, the entrepreneurs wanted to give an impression of successful business in the eyes of the community. Nevertheless, I witnessed also some exceptions to this element in the field, also according to previous studies done in Wenzhou on the same topic. The *Assistants* to the preconditions for the case of Calvinism that I've mentioned before (sovereignty of God and anti-superstition) were present in the field as well. For example, Xun or Yi held them, but this precondition didn't seem to play such strong role as the one of the belief in Millenarianism (emphasis on the return of Christ to rule one thousand years in Jerusalem) and especially the presence and role of a charismatic leader such as Shu or Zhenzhen. Their role of leadership in the church and involvement in business is nevertheless still included in the *role of sects* theorized by Weber. Also, from several ethnographic observations and interviews I can identify the role of the belief in predestination only as peripheral, which however was so crucial in Weber's interpretation:

> [...] Many people think that we are predestined I don't think so. We are all sinners and with Jesus we are saved with His blood. I can change the future with the Christian faith. (Delun, Wenzhou, Milan, 06/08/2014)

This doesn't mean that this evangelical church doesn't believe in predestination or election, since in my ethnographic explorations I've witnessed the presence of such belief. It only implies the peripheral role of such belief in the daily life of many individuals and disconnect between this belief and a supposed state of perpetual anxiety as Weber thought. In fact, concerning the potential effect of the belief in predestination, generally speaking in my ethnographic observations I've noticed a sense of predilection, a clear distinction between the believers and the so-called pagans, unbelievers, even when relating to other Chinese immigrants, instead of a state of anxiety and frustration. This leads the individual under job-shadowing to feel special, different from the others, better, even when he is challenged by other Chinese people. This therefore reveals the presence of a state of being confident through the belief in predestination, a directly inverse finding from the one theorized by Weber, if not at least very far from the anxiety he described.

7.1.3 'Calling' to Work

Coming to the main preconditions of the model, through my interviews the presence of the *Yi Xiang*, the Chinese Christian version of Weber's *Beruf* emerged clearly:

> [...] If I have to choose a job all things are allowed but not everything is lawful. If you go in difficult places there is God but there are consequences, it is better to do a good work for you and God. To me being a businessmen in trade is lawful and you can obey God. (Bingwen, Hangzhou, Milan, 12/09/2014)

> To find a job the evidence is that I served in the church always up until today. In the beginning I served teaching students or other services then I felt that I wanted to be a pastor, I took a calling, if I open the bar it will benefit more people, if God opens this bar it is an opportunity to do the Gospel, God guided my steps. (Bai, Ibidem)

In the words of Bai it is possible to see the progress of such calling in the life of the entrepreneur. First Bai thought to serve in the church but later, as he was multiplying his businesses, he felt the calling to open a new café, a place where he was able to respond to God's calling through the accomplishment of such job. This belief is even sometimes unconsciously related to the realm of work and leads Bingwen to the search to find a job that will fit his spiritual drive. The believer, as Bingwen in this case, looks for a job that is in tune with his beliefs and all that he has to do is to discover where God wants him to work. Then the believer is supposed to display God's plan through accomplishing such work. The job is perceived by those Protestant entrepreneurs as God's calling, it is something in their view already arranged by God. The duty of the believer therefore is to discover which is his particular calling in the wide spectrum of worldly professions. During my visit in Wenzhou, for example, I had the chance to interview Yi, a successful boss and also a pastor in a house church. Yi talked about this sense of calling that was fulfilled little by little through the expansion of his business:

> I was often in church, I thought I was called to full-time ministry. In 2003 I thought I would spend all the time at church because there was a need for workers for the harvest that would reach out new believers, then I

> decided to transform my business into a multiple company with the help of some brothers from the church [...]. (Yi, Ibidem)

> [...] Little by little faith help us to know the kind of work to do, the kind of trade to open [...]. (Delun, Ibidem)

> [...] I'm not saying that I know for sure the purpose of my life, I'm still looking, God will prepare the best for us. (Minzhe, Shuzhou, Milan, 12/09/2014)

> [...] I thank God because He found the job for me. [...] when I start anything I pray and think about those things [...] where I work right now is exactly what I was looking for, an international company, a door opened by God. (Hop, Tsinghua, Milan, 15/11/2014)

> [...] Something has happened and God prepared the things for Him that He wants me to do. (Jun, Wenzhou, Milan, 08/11/2014)

> [...] Before I had the job I prayed always God to tell if choosing that job. (Deming, Wenzhou, Milan, 08/11/2014)

> Our life depends on God and what He sends me [...] I hear of people, you can't do too many things, our lives are special, they say ' I want to do this', but at the present how can you know? I've understood that God brings us into existence so that we manage, even at work, He wants that we manage. (Zhenzhen, *Ibidem*)

> Since I have the faith I work very hard, God let people have many jobs, some do business but God let me study working in the education and I work very hard for God not for myself. (Tai, Ibidem)

How can such a list of statements merely metaphysical relate at all with their profession as entrepreneurs? What really interests me here is not necessarily the factual reconstruction of the event or the validity of their view but their interpretation of it. Delun and Minzhe who were under my job-shadowing, both viewed their job as something to be discover with the help of faith, something already divinely prepared before them. Moreover, Hop, Jun, or Deming sensed that their job was a response to a divine calling, part of a higher plan of which they felt part of that, something that can be discovered only trying to understand what profession, what specific environment and what detailed tasks cold be a clue to discover it. There's no room for casualty, similarly to the deterministic interpretations of events typical of Calvinism.

There is also no room for feeling forced to do a job out of chance, as in the surrounding non-Christian environment of entrepreneurs. Even when the job is hard or not ideal, I never heard them complaining about things or feeling in the wrong place. This belief, contrary to the case of the non-Christian entrepreneurs, gives a purpose to their job and, in sociological terms, provides a sense of purpose and freedom from alienation. The entrepreneur through the *Yi Xiang* must not remain a passive victim of circumstances, but he needs to choose concretely a profession, discovering the plan of his life ordained from above. The entrepreneur, as in the case of Enlai, is in a 'training process', in a continuous effort for an excellent accomplishment of his duty, in order to be in 'God's schedule' as in the words of Fai:

> […] To sell and boutique was my target that I choose. Then I found the job. God took me as in training. I thank God to let me go in that difficulty. (Enlai, Chong Qing, Milan, 15/11/2014)

> […] Right now I would like to be a businessman, to open a factory […] I'm very happy that I am in the right way toward my schedule, answering to what God asked me to do. (Fai, Yun Nan, Milan, 22/11/2014)

> […] In this job I try to serve God […] we have to grow and feel God how He directs us to what to do. (Ah Lam, Wenzhou, Milan, 29/11/2014)

> At work I don't worry if there is or not a job because I know that God will give it to me and set before me according to his purpose. (Shaiming, Ibidem)

> When we do something we always first pray asking direction to God, if everything goes well we do that work, if some bad sign comes then we don't do that. I was in the retail sector and we prayed then decided to do that job […] when I have challenges, if I have to choose a product or other things is God that send the client to me, God helps me to choose the right deal. (Yongnian, Wenzhou, Milan, 14/05/2015)

Notice how words, such as 'schedule', 'target', 'direction', 'purpose', 'choice', are stressed in their responses to a neutral question such as 'how did you find this job?'. Those words speak of the detailed planning strategy behind their business which is so important in order to achieve economic success. Only later on, this planning strategy and sense of calling in work is loaded with all its spiritual and supernatural interpretations. This belief, which is by definition metaphysical, achieves its factual role in directing the behavior of those entrepreneurs toward a reasoned and rational strategy so important for their business. Every choice in the case of Yongnian or Shaiming is under complete divine control and nothing in business as well as in daily life is perceived as fruit of just chance. Also, I must mention the intensity of such belief, demonstrating the fluid interpretation of its role in their long-term economic activity. Particularly, in the process of trying to understand his calling the entrepreneur demonstrates to be never totally satisfied until he finds and responds to his particular calling as in the case expressed by Wing:

> I've found a job first I was a waiter at the bar as service, when I came back to Italy I didn't want to do it then I prayed to Jesus that He could give me another kind of job and I've found it [...] as I came there I didn't know the boss was Christian. (Wing, Wenzhou, Milan, 06/12/2014)

As it will be possible to see in the next pages very often the entrepreneur senses a progressive development of his business from bottom-up, as was the case of the Puritan self-made man. Yet the origin of the tension toward success here is not just within some cultural trait or external circumstances, but it is connected with this spiritual interpretation. Wing strived to find a better job, believing in his mind that it was already out there, ordained from on high for his future. His duty was to believe and to go forward in his search for it. This element proper of the *Yi Xiang* is of great motivation, able to push the entrepreneur to think big about his professional life at whatever level he may find himself at the moment.

7.1.4 Boss-Christian

Another result of this belief is the constant presence of a vision for someone's life that many entrepreneurs displayed, mainly the *Boss-Christian phenomenon* (老板—Lǎobǎn). This element connects the theoretical model with the inner-worldly asceticism of Weber. Delun is a good example of this, throughout my job-shadowings I followed him in the process of opening his third and fourth businesses. Delun can be considered a 'man of vision'. He often told me of his vision both for the Christian community in China and for the local church in the west. He was working and serving in order to find a building for the church, Bibles, making financial donations for religious purposes. But also, Delun's strong vision for his business was tied strongly with his faith, it was seen as an expression of his faith. At the same time, Delun saw his proliferation of business activities as a direct consequence of his answer to a call from above. During our trips, he listened to Chinese Christian music and showed me Gospel tracks that he shared with the people he came into contact with. All the logos that he chose for his businesses had a Christian underlying message.

I had long conversations with Delun about famous Protestant Chinese preachers, like Stephen Tong, a famous Chinese Calvinist preacher that was responsible for large part of the current Christian revival in Asia. Delun admired him a lot. During his work, early in the morning or late at night, Delun often had a headphone, and as he was working he listened to sermons for more than ten hours. This was said by Delun to give him strength to work harder. Sometimes at work it was common to see Delun praying or reading Scriptures. When asked by clients if he was open on Sunday, Delun answered saying that Sunday was a holy day, so he closed the store as a sign of his Christian identity. This not only gave him strength and motivation during his job, but it was most importantly a sign of his Calvinistic work ethic. An example from my job-shadowing with Delun of the role of Calvinist ethics in his business came when Delun had to choose between several business activities. He prayed for a long time. He did not know what to do at first. Then he recalled the three questions that Stephen Tong, this famous Chinese Calvinist preacher that he admires, shared once in a sermon about making wise decisions: (i) Does it glorify God? (ii) Does it contribute to others? (iii) Is it under the power of sin? For example, Delun and Bingwen in their economic transactions at their new business sometimes had to face situations where people brought things that were stolen. In those circumstances, Delun tried to maintain his ethical standard and to oppose taking advantage of stolen items. Delun wanted to make profit, but not at the expense of integrity, so he decided to follow the Biblical standard, refusing to make business at someone's else expenses. The workers even in the store, compared to

Delun and Bingwen, were very different. For example, after trying to fix a phone, if the action failed, workers were immediately concerned with individual losses, refused to do risky jobs for fear of failure. Delun and Bingwen instead were willing to assume their own responsibilities, and took risk, overcoming fear of failure. Even if they failed in a job, they kept pressing on.

Delun followed Calvinistic principles and discovered that many people instead made business damaging others, placing unfair prices, through financial fraud or unfulfilled payments. In this case Delun decided to open his new business with the fast food which from the outside appeared to be a regular store, but that within follows still a Christian agenda. Delun must not be considered as the average example of a Christian Chinese entrepreneur, since I was able to observe a wide range of differences both in terms of economic success and involvement in religious activities among Christian entrepreneurs. Nevertheless, I had the chance to notice that his identity as a 'man of vision', with a plan for his business activity, can be legitimately related to his religious identity, if not even consistently being stimulated by it. This attitude can be observed among many other entrepreneurs, where religious faith is by no means perceived in contradiction with work. In this particular form of inner-worldly asceticism the entrepreneur, having first identified his calling, pursues an accomplishment of this calling, not through just religious practices, but through his professional life, a component that for the case of Wenzhou is well known in literature as the Boss-Christians phenomenon:

> Faith can help the business to progress. [...] The [Communist] government feel threatened by the West. An example of this is Christianity but the principles of the Bible can resolve the economic imbalances. After the economic opening the number of Christians multiplied, at Wenzhou there's a lot of Christians and Laoban [Bosses]. With the help of faith it contributes the business, it gives positive energy to people. [...] Wenzhouren go where other Wenzhouren are, they bring business and the Gospel. They are called Jews because they are good in making business. (Niu, Milan, Qing Tian, 13/09/2015)

> The clients that are regulars, my old customers, I keep them through friendship, sometimes they come and we speak about religion. (Zhenzhen, Ibidem)

> Sometimes I express my faith especially with clients who wants to talk but among our clients we have some that trust me and some that don't. (Zixin, Wenzhou, Milan, 14/05/2015)

From what it is possible to see in those words from entrepreneurs such as Zhenzhen or Zixin work is seen also as a platform to express their religious identity. For example, during my job-shadowing of Delun and his wife, I witnessed how Chinese workers hired by Delun, although not being Christians, were surprised by the kindness, better treatment and better quality of work that Delun was pursuing. Something was different in Delun, if compared with a regular Chinese boss, which was attractive to workers and that attractiveness involved his religious belief. To some, there may be nothing special or different from a Buddhist or a member of another religion who may share his personal convictions during his working activities. Yet what is behind this assessment is interesting for the sociological that lies behind it. What is interesting for me is the profound connection that this expression of faith has with something profane such as business, that usually by mainline religions is considered in complete contrast with religion. The interpretation that Ling, Guang or Wing give of their religious identity goes in the direction of an inner-worldly asceticism that is able to see accomplishments in their professional life as a fulfillment of the will of God:

> I have a boss who is Christian [...] some share the Gospel, help the workers and bring them to Christ. God convinced me about my ethic at work [...] God didn't want me to go out of the world but to stay in the world to know and seek people that are not Christians. (Ling, Ibidem)

> I work as a warehouseman and I think at work faith is a part, faith.. work is like God says you are in the world but it doesn't mean you don't have to work, it can't be missing. (Guang, Ibidem)

> I work in a firm and the "grandmother boss" is a Christian. [...] I work for Jesus surely I do my job but I work for Jesus [...] I talk and if there's the opportunity I share. (Wing, Ibidem)

> [...] therefore the two serve one another, to be a manager is very important in order to be a preacher [...] How to reconcile faith and money? Money can support the church, establish a biblical culture in the company different from companies around me. [...] We help missionaries that are

> dedicated to churches and foundations. I want that the company has values, I think it is very important to have this mission that very often many don't have. [...] it is an important resource of values, then I share this with other entrepreneurs. The Gospel and my company are balanced, I studied theology, business administration and I don't ask myself which is over or under, I want to meditate the two, some companies don't know the management, I suggest to learn it, I preached this morning about knowing the social, newspapers, web, to understand things. (Yi, Wenzhou, Wenzhou, 23/08/2015)

> I opened this bar-library [...] the government supported us even if they knew we were Christians. The Christians have big numbers therefore do business. [...] Many Christians don't understand, we want to create a bridge between church and society, influence the world around us. [...] When people enter into our bar-library we share our vision for this library with them, many people are interested to know us. Make it possible that they hear the Gospel is our responsibility. If they accept it or not God knows, we do our best this is our purpose to have this library. [...] Since we do so many social activities even the local TV and the newspapers gave a good report of us, therefore we have a good and big influence. We try to do our best to witness the love of God in a concrete way. (Qiang, Wenzhou, Wenzhou, 26/08/2015)

Both Qiang and Yi, for example, apart from their business are also pastors in their churches. Their strong dedication to their business and the success they have must be framed by necessity within their personal religious convictions. The café-library of Qiang had a customer service that many times surprised the customers, offering beverages for free and books with a Christian content. This peculiar interpretation of their religious identity at work can have therefore its effect in encouraging the involvement in business among Protestant circles. I was able in fact to witness that among church members, the majority, if not the totality of them, both from the first and second generation of migrants, were involved in some sort of entrepreneurial activity. Another effect of this Boss-Christian phenomenon among those entrepreneurs which is important to notice and that is connected with the next precondition of the *house churches* is the reinforcement of their conduct, tension toward honesty and the imagine of a respectable entrepreneur, all such important aspects to create trust, respect and a potential portfolio of faithful customers as it is expressed in the words of Minsheng:

> Compared to other colleagues my words are different, the things that they do I don't do them, in difficulties I pray, they don't pray. And my colleagues then know that I'm a Christian and they respect me, they are happy to know me. (Minsheng, Ibidem)

> God helps you at work but if there are righteous people then there is an intelligent hand, we must work for God, we help the church, the needs, the Gospel the spread of His Word [...] God changed my life even others can know we must share the Gospel for the unbelievers. (Shu, Ibidem)

Again it is possible to see this almost 'maniacal' propensity in seeing the accomplishment of worldly duties as a response to a personal mission that differentiates those entrepreneurs from other common Chinese entrepreneurs which was in fact what Weber alluded to in his sociological interpretation. Another important aspect, perhaps the one that involves this book the most, can be traced in the strive for economic success, efficiency and accomplishment of objectives, so important for the good result of a business activity and observable in the words of entrepreneurs such as Shaiming or Fai:

> The reason for success in business is to have a good relationship with the clients, and in this my faith helps me a lot. (Shaiming, Wenzhou, Milan, 29/11/2014)

> The strong faith helps me in the job to work efficiently, I have to finish the job and do more. With faith and duty I can have success and passion and accomplishment of the purpose. Especially for Christians they have to set an example for others. [...] I would like to produce and share with them my faith, threat them well, grow together and let them know faith and love in the factory as example. (Fai, Ibidem)

Since some arguments may be brought forth for a gender distinction of such peculiar economic propensity that may explain why those Chinese entrepreneurs are so much involved in business it is therefore important to notice that a quite similar behavior can be observed for the case of women:

> At work I try to be honest with the client, smiling, I offer coffee, the others notice that I'm kind and I do what I can. [...] first I was working dependent on others but now I came to Milan and decide to do this

> entrepreneurial investment. This because we weren't satisfied with our salary [...] Work brings life ahead, you are not a Christian and you don't work, people then think that we are lazy, we work hard but not with deception, even in order to differentiate from other non believers. (Nuo, Wenzhou, Milan, 30/01/2015)

> Christians [...] don't work on Sunday, they educate more the children through Sunday schools [...] we work as Christians for five days others six days [...] we put our faith in work, if the boss let us work on Sunday we say no, we obey the Bible to work. (Chao, Ibidem)

> In the past work faith made me honest, righteous with the client, the prices were raising up and going down but I was buying and somebody was having debts but not me, so I acquired the trust from clients. In the past doing business I bought materials and the price was low, the others saw this and they said that they were buying but then they didn't, however if we make a contract as Christians we must fulfill it, we don't act this way. After some years of purchases the prices raised up and we gained a lot of money. Therefore if a Christian does well his work he can gain a lot of money. My company dedicates 10% to the church, some shareholder are Christians and there is a good environment, the nonbelievers want to join us and then they become Christians [...]. There is a relationship between Christianity and business of Wenzhou, there are many Christian enterprises in Wenzhou [...] while the unbelievers [entrepreneurs] don't pay taxes. (Da, Wenzhou, Wenzhou, 25/08/2015)

> This I believe that only God can bring success, not me. If God wants then I can have success. (Minzhe, Ibidem)

> I try to be more sincere with clients, more honest with the people that come into our business, first I was working in a factory then in a high technology factory and then we opened this store to become autonomous. My grandparents were Christians already so we are all Christians we all went to church and live out our faith. (Meixiu, Wenzhou, Milan, 30/01/2015)

The behavior of those Chinese women entrepreneurs can be considered to be very unique in their context. Another important element to bear in mind is the secondary role of women in the traditional Chinese view of business, whereas here I see their direct involvement in business at the same level as men as for the case of Minzhe under job-shadowing.

Another interesting fact to notice as a confirmation of this strong inner-worldly asceticism is how often the entrepreneurs that were not very involved in church activities, indistinctly saw their faith in contradiction with their work. On the other hand, those entrepreneurs that were strongly involved in church activities even in position of leadership, as is the case of Zhenzhen or Shu, did not see any contradiction between their faith and their business. Not only that, but generally they demonstrated to have better results at work, less difficulties and experienced more economic success in terms of number of business opened, income or number of clients. Delun gave me a good example of the *ethos* that this Boss-Christian phenomenon was able to build through the Christian association of entrepreneurs from Wenzhou of which he was member. The rules of the association required every Christian trade member to follow four 'golden rules':

a. never delay the pay-check of the employees. Usually, many Chinese entrepreneurs decide to delay the pay-check for three or four months, to have the money necessary to re-invest, forcing the employee to be unable to thrive. In this way the entrepreneur is enslaving the people.
b. Pay the taxes fairly. Many Chinese businesses usually avoid paying taxes especially in the name of the economic crisis, but the Christian entrepreneurs decide to avoid such disrespect toward the institutions.
c. Produce merchandise with equity. Many Chinese businesses produce merchandise at a very low cost, so the quality and health of the products are often in jeopardy. The Christian entrepreneurs decided to avoid products that damage health or the environment, trying to safeguard the origin of the product (against labor exploitation).
d. Not engaging in extra-marital relations. Very often, especially among the richest Chinese entrepreneurs, the pressure for extra-marital relations is high, almost as a badge of being in step with the times. The consequence is a high rate of divorces and double lives. But the Christian entrepreneurs decided to condemn such behavior.

Those entrepreneurial practices are an example of good strategies to manage businesses and to hold the distinctive identity of the Boss-Christians accountable. In fact, before any worker left a job, whether because fired or due to some argument, Delun always gave them a Bible, sharing his personal testimony of how God saved his life, inviting them to read it. Those were moments where he needed to make hard decisions, yet Delun always wanted to treat them with dignity. In one sense he was ready to rebuke the workers with impartiality when needed, but he also did everything in the context of treating people with dignity. This process was particularly challenging since he had to transform several times his business. Also, in his time under my job-shadowing Delun never delayed the payment of the salary, even if the business was not necessarily doing good, because he respected the rights of the worker. Many Chinese entrepreneurs in this context of economic crisis, on the other hand, were delaying payments and even making threats to the workers.

However, before jumping in a too much romantic and optimistic view of this process, it is important to consider the fact that the findings among the Protestant entrepreneurs were at times contrasting. For example, Bingwen in opening his new store with Delun came back from China with machines that however needed to be declared at customs. They almost got fined for this infraction of international law. Cases like this were even worse during my visit in Wenzhou. I had the chance to do a focus group with some entrepreneurs that belonged to the house church and I asked the opinion of the pastor, in his regular counseling of the people he knew:

> I saw negative things often among entrepreneurs, I don't notice any difference between believers and unbelievers. They leave the creditors, they hide their profit before they go bankrupt or they transfer it into other bank accounts. Many have illegal businesses, they practice usury, they are not sensitive to the nature of business. Since the economy goes down, they take advantage of it. (Zhi, Focus group,Wenzhou, Wenzhou, 23/08/2015)

The picture that Zhi gives of the phenomenon is far from being optimistic. Even during my job-shadowing at times this contrasting feature came out. For example, Minzhe lamented with me that sometimes she had to lie at work in order to make more profit. If she wanted to receive the same merchandises, she had to lie on her real name because of limits on the amount of merchandise the same person could take. It must nevertheless be considered that together with those bad examples, Zhi still recognizes a positive impact:

> Some other however are honest they prefer losses and clean the debts, even if they suffer a lot. They think about being righteous even if the local officials try to take advantage of them [...] Then there is a third type that do their job, gain trust and resist. [...] there are cases of Christians that live the faith and are strong in business. (Zhi, Ibidem)

Together with these examples, also the ethnographic observations during my visits at work show a similar emphasis on the conduct to hold outside the church, how to fulfill a spiritual purpose through different tasks at work. Their spheres of life: worship, prayer and work were put all on the same level, in order to be a 'living testimony', in front of the outside world. Many of the conversations and interactions that I listened to stressed the idea that there is a divine power working in each person, that all success must not be for themselves but for a higher purpose. It is this divine power that, according to their interpretation, does things through them and therefore they give 'glory to God' through their job. I was also able to witness a strong emphasis on the right use of time, against laziness. Those are all elements that I already described before in the Puritan ethic that finds their ultimate origin in the Bible.

This modern version of the inner-worldly asceticism involves therefore a constant self-examination that, as I shall explain later, is also connected to the next precondition of the *house churches*. Such process of self-examination and control of the conduct among the house churches are not separate but in addition to the social network. It is able to generate trust, respect, honorability among those that buy products from those entrepreneurs, their suppliers. This generates a fertile ground for business transactions:

> [...] faith helps me to become more fair, to become a right person in trade, more just [...] the Christian faith compels us to be loyal always correct [...] in Italian trade is not easy because everybody cheat [...] in the beginning I may lose something [...] but after a while you feel more happy inside [...]. (Delun, Ibidem)

> The people that I work with know that I am a Christian, I don't go directly to share the Gospel, but reacting with my acts and mentality they see it. (Heng, Ibidem)

In my behavior and words I try to say to every business company that I am a Christian, my tone is more hearty, this helps me. Directly I share my faith. (Xiu, Ibidem)

All my students appreciate my classes, some of them don't believe in God and I take the opportunity to share the Gospel with them. [...] I do my best, if I am efficient in the little things the parents will choose us [...] if a parent choose us he must trust me he must be there. (Zhong, Ibidem)

I tried very hard and I wanted to be an example at work to demonstrate the love of God, it was a way of work that was different from others, I didn't curse anybody I didn't do anything nasty, I respected and honored people, I didn't complain. [...] The reason of success at work is God, the power of God, because when I was weak He was strong. For example He gave me wisdom to manage the relationships with colleagues, how to treat people, honor my supervisor and clients, how to succeed with colleagues. (Enlai, Ibidem)

I wanted to build education and connect it with the church we express our faith with the kids, the principles are based on the Bible, we teach them to follow the Bible, and the small kids come and we try to build good men [..] the reason for this business [success] is that God blesses as God blessed the Jews [...] in the kindergarten I can show Christ's culture [...] some people come to the kindergarten and they are not Christians but then they believe, even among the teachers, the families, the kids, we invite them to church I say to everyone that I am Christian [...] if I work hard the people will pass the word in the city. (Tai, Ibidem)

In moments when I was doing other jobs there were dishonest clients and I thought this, unfortunately we have this sense of revenge from the devil, you receive something evil and you try to react in a bad and frustrating way [...] but at the end it doesn't happen like the Bible says you forgive the other and somebody will forgive you for the evil you have done. (Kong, Ibidem)

For example, during my job-shadowing, Heng has several suppliers from China for the merchandises he sold in his two stores in the west. Some of Heng's friends came from the area of the trade city of Yu and Guangzhou. Those partners in trans-continental business with Heng find suppliers of products and are also involved in a house church made by hundreds of migrants from Wenzhou. Their commonality of faith becomes a factor of involvement in business partnership. Once again it is possible to see also the impact of house churches on the quality and professionalism with which work is accomplished, which ultimately favors economic success in entrepreneurial activity:

> [...] Success at work is given by the fact that work is acknowledged in its quality. Faith is for every job you do, if you do it for Christ you have success. [...] I don't work for myself, you see many people do less than I do, but I do it with all of my strength because I know that I work for God [...] I do things that my colleagues don't do and I'm different in a positive sense I don't follow the mass. (Bo, Ibidem)

> Success is related to honesty, if you cheat with a client he knows and don't come back, at Paolo Sarpi there are 300 shops, if he doesn't come to you he goes to another one. (Ah Cy, Ibidem)

> You need to have courage to open a new business, faith then gave us that courage. [...] you don't have to lose that trust, for us trust is crucial, we can lose money but we can't lose trust. We believe in God if we lose faith then the non Christian think bad: 'those Christians lose faith'. (Yongnian, Ibidem)

Part of this inner-worldly asceticism features also a saving mentality that was the real key element for the spirit of capitalism as outlined by Weber's[1] as opposed to a mere love of money common to all mankind. Those studies showed that some of the beliefs proper of Protestantism push the individual toward the necessity of embracing a saving mentality so important for the advent of modern capitalism. The love of money in and of itself or the desire to be rich could not generate this by themselves. This will be clearer as I will examine the results for the case of the second group. This saving mentality proper of Protestant Chinese people stands out even when described by surrounding Chinese people. A good example that I was able to find is from the side of non-Christian Chinese

[1] See Weber M. (1930 [1905]) for his analysis of it regarding Methodism or Benjamin Franklin and Wisman, J. D. and Davis, M. E. (2013) on the more recent declines of such saving mentality in the American case. Also it is useful to compare it with Burkett L. (1990) works as an example of a contemporary application of those principles of Protestantism into business.

people such as Chu Hua that recalling her perception of Protestant people in China, mentioned this saving mentality:

> I know some Christians in China, they are different, they always work, they don't work just to have fun like all of us, they don't work to buy a new car, they don't work to buy fancy clothes, in this the Christians in China are different than us. (Chu Hua, Heilongjiang, Milan, 28/03/2015)

Chu Hua makes here a very interesting point on the perception of Christians in China as economizers, savers, with their sober way of living and consistent work-centered life, which finds its origin in the inner-worldly asceticism that I've described. Significantly, such statement was made by a Chinese interviewed from the second group. It is also true that this is perceived as also part of the Chinese mentality, not so much as a conscious result of their faith, like for Kong:

> We Chinese come from a land that is very realistic concerning money, there it is a land difficult based on money, we come to Italy because we have this mentality, if you move and you don't work, you don't make money, if you want to do less just stay in China. In Italy you find very often racism and we are here for our job, if someone tries to do less, he loses a lot of money [...]. (Kong, Ibidem)

> Around Wenzhou there's mountains and the ocean, we don't have natural resources, we are not a big city like Shanghai, we must do business if we want to survive. (Min, Ibidem)

Among the factors orienting toward profit, the geographical position of Wenzhou played a decisive role. Like Chu Hua, many Chinese students that came from China to study at the university are not from Wenzhou and are useful for giving an outsider perspective on this Wenzhou's business-oriented mentality, regardless of their religious identification. A very interesting case during my observations in Milan was when I attended Bible meetings of students in their houses where Chinese students from different parts of China expressed their concern in being able to integrate with the Chinese people living in the diaspora. In their mind the people of Wenzhou had a different way of thinking, more oriented to business, and it was difficult to relate with them for a Chinese person from another area:

> The Wenzhouren are rich, traders, more ahead than us, they have basis to do business. Many in quantity. Before they were doing import–export now they do mainly food, and family is very important for them. [...] To me the Wenzhouren are more closed it is easier to enter in their group, I thought they came from another world, the dialect, they are very closed with students. [...] Hard work comes from culture, since I was a child, behind us our parents very insisting. They have a publishing house. Family pushes hard to work there are many people, to find a job you need to have something special. (Jing, Milan, Chong Ching, 22/01/2016)

People from Wenzhou in Milan were part of the first migratory flow, already consolidated in their networks. The new more recent migratory flow of Chinese students coming from north China like Jie found it very hard to integrate with them and followed a different business strategy:

> We don't have a network, we are students, we come after the Wenzhouren, they have a different dialect and mentality, how things work, the culture, they are particular. The worker that works with me goes through a lot of misunderstandings, he doesn't responds, he doesn't understand the question. With other people is easier. (Jie, Milan, Hebei, 28/01/2016)

The same was mentioned by Ho during my job-shadowing referring to cultural associations owned by Wenzhouren. They were organizing meetings of Chinese entrepreneurs to which Ho was participating. During those meetings Ho felt like a fish out of water and noticed how despite his being a Chinese entrepreneur he was not considered one of them by the already established elite of Wenzhouren networks. This points to the possibility of a *Wenzhou Profit-oriented mentality* where economic propensity can be explained through a pre-existent economic propensity due elements that subsist in both Christian and non-Christian entrepreneurs.

7.1.5 House Churches

Another precondition that can be found among those Christian entrepreneurs is the *House church*, particularly in its influence designed by Weber as the role of sects. The house church is framed in the bipartition of Protestantism in China between the official church (TSPM) and the unofficial churches (house-family churches). Although in the context of the diaspora with relative religious freedom the emphasis tends to be blend, its role in shaping the conduct and social relationships it is still a thing. Those entrepreneurs belong to an evangelical church that is basically a house church, simply trans-planted in the European context. Their members during my ethnographic observations tended to always emphasize their detachment from the official church of China, perceived as an 'apostate' church, weak in its doctrine and unable to assure the presence of true converts. This bipartition, very close to Weber's distinction between the official church and sects, is the center of many diatribes from the Chinese communist government because the house church is difficult to control and is spreading everywhere. During my visit in China I had the chance to visit and interview people belonging both house churches and TSPM. Hung is a pastor of a house church and he travels between several churches in an environment of persecution and threats from the government. He also points out how the Boss-Christians help substantially the finances of the church:

> if some businessmen wants to support us we are more than happy, we let them build the church, more people come to church and more people can know God. The building is high and the cross visible, therefore they want to tear it down. [...] I was there when they wanted to destroy the church. They took the car licenses plates and interrogate the Christians [...] every time the government says something different and contradictory. The people are put to jail and beat. [...] They come late at night or early in the morning like thieves to steal the cross. (Hung, Pingshan, Wenzhou, 26/08/2015)

> The people from the house churches don't speak with us from the TSPM even if now the situation is getting better and we try to defend ourselves. The TSPM church must obey to the rules of government, what you preach must be in harmony with the social dimension. [...] The government wants to do something bad, they will remove crosses by force, they will order to obey to the government, they will make pressures on Christians, if you have a business they will threat you to be fired. [...] Before they were saying that it was a problem of spaces now they destroy everything even if you abide the rules. We have no security, we don't know when the government will come. (Yong, Rui An, Wenzhou, 27/08/2015)

Yong, on the other hand, is a pastor of a TSPM church but he suffers the same type of persecution from the government. His church has received threats to remove the cross and he has personally been several times in jail even during the time of my investigation. Therefore, a climate of persecution was on the background of our conversations. Many Christian bosses are helping financially the church, but this creates a potential threat for the Communist government that decides to fire those workers or damage their businesses. Because of the silence of the media and the long time of separation from their motherland, the Christian entrepreneurs from Wenzhou living in the diaspora have only a vague idea of the seriousness of the situation. Delun during my job-shadowing recalled how in China many churches have the intention to promote the involvement of Christian bosses in financing building, organizing meetings of commercial fellowship and share business opportunities with its members:

> For the Chinese government the Christian church now is a threat, I always have experienced intimidations and even persecutions but the Christian faith even though the Chinese government does not allow us... doesn't want that we grow, we grow anyway incredibly [...] in China there are two kinds of churches, the one recognized from government and the one who's not [...] the one recognized must declare to be independent from foreign associations, they must love the homeland [...] that they don't have any contact with western people and then there are those not recognized from the Chinese government, they call them house churches that are private organizations [...]. (Delun, Ibidem)

> [...] In Shanghai the same church there are 12 ramifications, it was an house church, family church, 50-70 people, not state church, in a private house. And maybe every six months the believers of all churches will get together, 500-1000 people, a wonderful moment [...] I shared my work experiences, we will pray to God and ask God. [...] when I went to church they motivated me shared their experiences, I was encouraged and I came back home that I wanted to grow. (Fai, Ibidem)

This last element from Fai about 'motivation' introduces us to the reason why the house church model is significant in sociological terms and not just for religious or political reasons. Those small-group communities function in many ways exactly as the *role of sects* that Weber formulated. Apart from the encouragement that Fai received through the adherence to such social groups, he was more specifically led to 'grow' in his spirituality as well as in his conduct in life and business. The house churches, as the sects at the times of Weber, are crucial because they uniquely are able to foster a control of the conduct, 'being the right person', enhancing a process of auto-affirmation, a strive for quality and charisma, in order to receive good reputation (being 'trustworthy') and rewards (such as 'working together'). As it will be clear in the comparison of this social group with other cases, the house church has among its functions the one of a social network but it is not limited to networking. What I intend to emphasize here is that this process starts with an internal quest in the individual that belongs to this specific type of communities that influence economic success much more than granting networking. It is possible to identify the details of this internal process in dynamics such as self-examination before becoming a member, the support of a common goal, the self-examination of the individual in order to be the 'right person' but more importantly here it is often brought in their professional life, projecting the same qualities in the realm of work:

> The church at work helped me to remain calm without anxiety because anxiety can't resolve all the problems. I've always prayed to have Jesus near me. I would like to get baptized but I think I didn't learn enough. When somebody get baptized must understand all the rules and someday I do some mistakes. (Shaiming, Ibidem)

> Christians really helped me, they come to greet me or they pray for me, when I have some questions they answer me and help me if I don't know how to do something at work. (Huizhong, Wenzhou, Milan, 14/05/2015)

> Christians helped me at work and in life, in difficulties, we talked with each other, we will get together and I've received counsel from them for major decisions. (Zixin, Ibidem)

> I have received no direct help from other Christians but in daily life yes, even just a greeting, will encourage me, it makes me understand that we are multiplying as believers. (Kong, Ibidem)

> The community of faith [...] in the end helped me a lot to be a right person, to be a just person, the other people understand you when you are trustworthy, that they can work with you, then when they see that you don't want to take advantage of them, that you want to be loyal, you want to be just, for you is a lasting feeling, because you gained their trust, people trust you, then there is a greater approach that push you to start a

> business with other people that trust you and this help me, because if you say you are a Christian this helps you [...] the people say that they would like to work in business with Christian individuals, nevertheless they will not take advantage of me, they are sincere, they are sincere people [...]. (Delun, Ibidem)

Together with this positive influence on the behavior, Delun introduces us to another role that the house church also plays. Its role is very important in giving a useful identity mark for the outside world, especially in the realm of business. Belonging to a house church results to be like a 'business card' for the entrepreneur, guaranteeing the building of a climate of trust and respectability that is very useful for business. It is in this that can be found a clear corroboration of the Weberian role of sects from the entrepreneur's own words, enhancing the business of Zhenzhen and Shu:

> The clients that comes I speak about Bible and religion [...] this helps me at work because they see that is not just the relationship of business but also the friendship, this is my future, is very important, the customer that comes I'm not anxious to sell or earn money. (Zhenzhen, Ibidem)

> Religion gives you respect, you believe in God and in Jesus Christ then it means you help others in anyway. When I had God helping me I've success, you help others and you live His plan. (Shu, Ibidem)

Lastly but not in terms of importance, the house church inevitably plays a role in the creation and use of an internal social network, made of strong and weak ties that are very important in the business world. A consistent current of thought already pointed out the absolute centrality of social networks in order to build trust and exchange of information. But if the commonality of faith among those individuals is so often associated with economic interactions someone may say that it is precisely because of the already existing economic interest and motivation to profit that a person decides to instrumentally join the church and embrace those network resources that are able to bring economic success. We must understand whether an entrepreneurial person creates a successful business or a successful business creates an entrepreneurial person. Following this line of thinking, it is precisely because of the economic interest that someone might embrace the religious belief with a 'justification logic'. As we know in the theory of justification propositions and beliefs are understood to certify certain actions by providing a reason for them. According to this view, the religious belief has the purpose to merely justify, not generate, a behavior that is already in place. The reality of the matter however the relation between economic interest and religious affiliation is a much more complex relation across time and space given also the role of external structural influences. Embracing a rather deterministic view that sees the identification with this religious network as only instrumental to profit is something we should discourage. It is true that in the diaspora, new waves of immigrants from Asia tend to struggle to improve their economic status by adopting a religiously legitimated work ethic. Religious groups involved in migration patterns with a distinctive ethnic and regional origin, as the Protestant Chinese entrepreneurs from Wenzhou, often occupy different niches in the labor market and at that point it becomes difficult to distinguish between the religious motivation and the motivation for profit.

Be that as it may, in the Chinese context the case can be made for the Protestant faith to be in a certain sense a mean of 'rationalization', a source of motivation to economic success, that neither the traditional cultural values nor communism were ever able to foster. The fact is that the results from the field and existing literature on the subject disagree. First of all, social networks, do not bring in themselves economic success, on the contrary sometimes they can even hinder economic success. Social networks, whether with or without religious connotations, are able to favor the 'survival' of a business but not necessarily the economic success of it. For this specific function individual strategies and personal sources of motivation seem to play a more decisive role. And that's the unique added value of the house church compared to any other generic social network. Secondly, it is not always the case that a person joins this type of network just for the economic benefits that he can get out of it. I've already pointed out how generally those that identify with this type of network do so despite the risks of persecution and sanctions from the communist government. The entrepreneur that joins the Christian church may as well lose its business because the Communist government could decide to confiscate it or shut it down. The identification with the house church network therefore goes far beyond a mere calculation of costs and benefits.

Nevertheless, it is true that the social network of the church sometimes may be just an instrumental mean for the flow of business activities. The house church provides several crucial additional resources that need to be kept in mind. The network of the church is crucial in the first stages of someone's professional life or to start a new business. Bo testified about members of the church that had the intention to open together a new business, or in other cases one member of the church hired the other and decided to work together with him. This last case has been observed especially concerning the relationship between the first and the second generation of migrants. The house church works then as a social organization made by experts that are able to give advices to entrepreneurs, providing contacts with other Christian entrepreneurs to whom people can talk, meeting other companies managed by Christians that help people living still in Wenzhou.

Another important role of the network provided by the church involves the stage of development of the business. It is possible to see this in the description of Deming about an association of Christian entrepreneurs of which he was part of and that connects together people that are doing different businesses, grafting new people arriving from China and desiring to start a business. Another important case for the role of house churches as a network for business was witnessed during the job-shadowing of Minzhe. Minzhe works as a buyer in Italy of expensive fashion products to sell in China. During our timeframe of observation she decided to connect with Enlai in order to establish a partnership. Enlai, living in China, was able to provide and manage the clients needed by Minzhe in Italy. Minzhe, on the other hand, had to provide the products from different stores in Italy. Enlai came to Italy for a visit. I often had to translate messages and e-mails that Enlai had to send to different managers here in Italy, asking to meet them, see new merchandise, finding a good deal, with the eventual possibility to be tax-free passing through Hong Kong for the transportation of the goods, etc., ...

All this trust (*xinyong*) between the two was possible because of their connection with the same house church. Furthermore, during their visits to different stores in Italy, they decided to go to Tuscany for a business exploration with another businessman from the Chinese church. Here too the commonality of faith given by the house churches was an important element in guaranteeing a bridge useful for their business. This third Christian entrepreneur was a common friend for Minzhe and Enlai and all three persons involved were sharing different contacts with other Chinese stores and local stores without which it would have been difficult to grow their business. After their several visits to different suppliers during their daily tours, Minzhe and Enlai were having a regular planning meeting in order to structure their business strategies for the future once Enlai would had gone back to China.

After the visit of Enlai Minzhe also contacted Fai, that at that time was living and working in China. Minzhe decided to involve Fai in his business as well in order to develop a bigger portfolio of clients in China. Together with Fai and Enlai, another Christian entrepreneur was contacted by Minzhe for this reason. The commonality of faith provided by the identification with the house church in the case of Enlai, Fai and this other Christian entrepreneur was for Minzhe the element of trustable to establish her personal network of business partners in China. They all started their business activities through a common conversation in social media, meditating Sacred Scriptures, often praying that their business will be able to follow the spiritual directions of their common faith. The religious identification, as at the time of Weber, is still a 'business ticket' among those Chinese Protestants, a source of trust and a flow of information.

Also, from the ethnographic observations with Ah Cy that I introduced before (see Table 6.3) it is very important to mention here that the type of structural strategy oriented to the multiplication of businesses is here very similar, if not identical, to the religious strategy proper of the house church model (as opposed to the traditional building-oriented form of church planting). The house church is oriented toward a multiplication of small groups of faith, and goes sometimes hand in hand with entrepreneurial transactions, as members of this network are connected through religious interactions. The house church then promotes a circle of information about work vacancies and opportunities, in tension toward multiplication as it becomes an instrument for the establishment of business partnerships, something very important for the achievement of economic success:

> [...] together with other brothers and sisters we created a website for Christians and work. The shareholders of my enterprise are my relatives, 600 workers all Christians, if somebody introduces a Christian he is welcome into my company [...] The Christian enterprises establish social enterprises, they are sensitive to profit but also how to help others. There are many foundations to whom the company is entrusted. (Yi, Ibidem)
>
> Many customers are Christians and when they are Christians they come to me and they speak because we have the same language [...] as Christians

let's say that they helped me they prefer to buy from other Christians. (Yongnian, Ibidem)

The work that I'm doing right now is for a brother of the church, I worked because we got together and agreed with a brother to work together for that person [...] it helps me to be more confident, we are friends other than colleagues. (Bo, Ibidem)

I came in Italy to work, I've found it because in Italy there was a lot of Chinese [Christians] (200) my sister has a store and I worked as a saleswoman. The husband of my sister was the first that came to Italy, in Florence, they let them work in a factory then he searched by himself and he found in Trieste, a lot of Chinese, many Chinese arrive there [Prato, Florence] then they go somewhere else. The family helped me to find a job, the church introduces too the job, if somebody is a boss takes and assume workers in church. (Chao, Ibidem)

My father is the owner of this business. My parents started 10 years ago here [Chinatown] this year at Cernusco [suburbs of Milan] they opened a new store. [...] The church helps in the first years I arrived and they helped me [...]. Before 2005 we opened factories, difficulties were not on the salary... the church provided help. (Na, Milan, Wenzhou, 14/12/2015)

I started this activity ten years ago with several Christian [business] partners [...] three Christians in particular helped me to build three kindergarten, we work together since six-teen years. In the beginning was difficult but we work well together because we grew, we are very united. The most important thing is that we are Christians and this connects us. (Tai, Tangxia, Wenzhou, 26/08/2015)

There is a circle of connections between Christian entrepreneurs, we have the laoban [bosses] fellowship, and our church was doing a fellowship of laoban, connected one with the other. (Da, Ibidem)

I'm the president of Thien Hai ('love from heaven') [...] we encounter many people that do business [...] it is time to have integration among different organizations so that Christian can impact society. The mission is to know and collect talents, a social energy to resolve social problems. [...] Many Christian entrepreneurs support our foundations, we as Christian entrepreneurs founded this association, that connects socially several entrepreneurs [...] here in Wenzhou we are very active, we express the Christian culture to the public and to the government, like in a mission. (Ning, Wenzhou, Wenzhou, 24/08/2015)

For what concern business and faith there is a group of 40-50 people and a teacher from China that came 40 years ago, he was very rich, now he is very rich spiritually of love to give to the people. We have an office in Milan to help and serve the brothers who are foreigners in Italy. (Deming, Ibidem)

The last case of Yongnian reminds the impartial reader of the instrumental role of the house church for business despite its religious connotations. The commonality of faith becomes a guarantee for the availability of a portfolio of customers and suppliers that are already in the network and therefore can be quickly used for business reasons. As it will be clearer through other examples from my visit in Wenzhou like Xun, this overlapping is not just driven by an instrumental reason that pushes the entrepreneurs toward this identification with the house church. Yongnian, as Delun, is member of the 'East & West International Cultural Exchange Association' whose purpose is not only to promote Chinese culture through social and charitable activities funded by entrepreneurs but also to connect entrepreneurs and evangelize. During my research, I had the chance to speak with the president of this association, Yan. As a woman entrepreneur with two clothing stores, one in the Chinatown of Milan and the other in the city of Alessandria, and as the boss of the association, Yan had a high position in the Protestant Chinese community. Her association in fact unites together Protestant entrepreneurs from the different Chinese churches in Milan (the main Protestant Chinese church, the Taiwanese church and the Pentecostal Chinese church). The goal of this association was to integrate the entrepreneurs in the European culture mainly in terms of security, environment and other gaps:

With the Chinese of Milan we don't speak only of money we motivate them to link the business in China or to be more responsible here in Italy in their way of working. In the exchanges we help a lot the local italo-Chinese businesses, for example a member does twinning between Italian and Chinese cities. We try to create a school for unemployed foreigners, how to hire them in Chinese stores, we do this type of job. [...] We have good relationships with the laoban (Chinese word for boss) among 500 businesses, many are Christians. We have meeting places with them

> to dialogue and they take to heart what the association does. (Yan, Milan, Wenzhou, 25/01/2016)

The association also helps Chinese entrepreneurs in their motherland. They do that by providing useful information about business or contacts of people interested in making business. 90% of the members of the association are Christians. Through the association they come into contact with one another and with people of high standing. During conferences they meet managers, public officials, discussing official matters but also sharing their faith at the table. The association also helps Chinese missionaries or Chinese students that need financial help to pay their rent. On the other hand, Da told me how in Wenzhou almost every house church has a meeting group of Christian bosses and entrepreneurs connected with one another in business through their commonality of faith. Those 'commerce fellowships' are involved in events and meetings intended to promote their economic success on the basis of Biblical and Christian principles. Another example of this came during the job-shadowing of Heng. Heng's store sometimes was visited by other Chinese people bringing advertizing for entrepreneurs of the Chinatown: a business consultant or help with bureaucratic administration. Yet talking with Heng I discovered he already had a business consultant, a 'Christian brother' from the church that started a partnership with a local business consultant to assist Chinese Christian entrepreneurs in Chinatown with the governmental bureaucracy. Furthermore, the level of personal help through the commonality of faith reached also the area of finding a job among family members. Heng's younger brother works today for this Chinese Christian business consultancy.

In several of those businesses, it is then already possible to see the presence and role of the church as a network, which impacts positively on business. However, in Weberian terms, it must be remembered that the *role of sect* played by the house church is more than simply being part of a network. As from the words of Shaiming, he still feels a lot of pressure and control over his conduct to become a member of the church. Shaiming together with his father also works in a big Chinese store that sells all sorts of products, a kind of store very common among Chinese entrepreneurs today. He has a lot of clients, speaks the local language perfectly. Because of these skills, he could not leave the store for any reason, and during my visits at his work he was always kind and serene, but also very diligent and professional. These were qualities that he developed through his acquaintance with other Christian Chinese businessmen. This element shows that the simple connection with this network in and of itself, despite providing a strong help for the business activity, does not necessarily substitute all the other possible explanations. To be connected with the network in and of itself does not create any *ethos*. It is still necessary to be an active part of the house church to enhance the self-examination, the stress on Charisma, the identity-trust that according to Weber's model are able to push toward economic success. This element, as I've recalled before, is the most important element.

It is also true that the family plays a role in the dynamic for many of those entrepreneurs over their house church network. Especially in the case of the second generation, the entrepreneurs inherit sometimes their business from their parents or they found their job because some member of their extended family hired them. There is therefore a frequent inter-generational component in those family businesses of Chinese entrepreneurs that needs to be taken into consideration for the business potential added by the presence and accumulation of inherited financial resources. This, for example, was clear during my job-shadowing of Heng. The business where Heng was working was inherited by his wife and the financial involvement of her family in the opening of Heng's new business was crucial in guaranteeing his growth especially in the initial steps. Engagement celebrations and marriages were also very important in the community. Nuo's sister Meixiu was getting engaged during my job-shadowing with another Christian Boss in Chinatown. For those reasons, it is not hard to imagine why it was common to mix business and lineage.

This leads us toward recognizing the role of networks and especially in the specific case of Chinese culture the role of the network through family clan and lineage (*Network explanation*). It is undeniable that the house church as well as other social networks are an exploitable channel, sometimes even apart from religious reasons, to guarantee the faster passage of trust and information. Yet, it has to be remembered that social networks give no guarantee for economic success and the aspects of the church network able to foster success are those that influence the conduct of the individual, not the network in itself. In networks such as the family or the membership to a certain association this key element is absent. This argument will become clearer as I will compare those findings with the case of the second group. In any case, among the many entrepreneurs I was able to observe, although there is an influence of the family, it is still the larger church network that seems to produce its role in business especially through the provision of job opportunities to its members as it can be seen behind the polite words of Nuo:

> Faith helped me, if you are alone is hard to resist, instead with the church you can accomplish more, initially I resist, but then I lose heart, is better to have the church help you. Everybody is seeking for business opportunities here so we talked with one another. (Nuo, Ibidem)

> My uncle is the owner of the store here in Milan with him we first opened a store at Lake Maggiore [...] we are all believers in our family and the experiences with my uncle. My uncle does the job and I learn from him. (Guang, Wenzhou, Milan, 18/07/2015)

Guang is just one of the many examples of a person that belonging to the house church can profit from membership in a business that is based on the commonality of both faith and family. His uncle is the owner of a store in a very strategic and central part of the Chinatown of Milan. His family arrived in Milan in 1989 after the events of the Tiananmen square, he is third-generation Christian. Before arriving in Milan his family had factories of different merchandises to sell in Italy, then they were able to open their first store in 2005, and finally after 15 years, they opened a new store in the suburban area of Milan. It is in fact a common experience among many members of the church to be hired by a boss who is a Christian or whose wife is a Christian. The house church then works as a link for their search for a job. Some examples of this came into the surface during my job-shadowing activity with Delun and Minzhe, as I was involved in the creation of business activity through their network of Christians. Enlai, Fai and another member of the house church are an example of this network. Also Minzhe and Bingwen in the case of Delun were significant links. In other words, the commonality of faith led Delun to start a business with Bingwen as his Christian business partner and co-Boss:

> [...] inside this dynamic I was a brother, that trusts not in himself but in God, we can talk, we have the same basis, secondly I didn't had a job and I was available, and it was right for me, skills linked with my background. (Bingwen, Ibidem)

To manage a business with a commonality of faith was said by Bingwen to be an encouragement which positively influenced his personal growth. Sometimes during my job-shadowing of Delun it was also common to see business interactions with other members of the house church. One time a brother from the church came at the café of Delun to discuss the installation of cameras at the new store. Another brother from the church (Deming) was responsible to help Delun for the fixing of lights and so on. Every single member of the church had a specific skill and used it in reciprocity (*bao*) to help the other members of the community of faith in their business. This type of network is particularly strong because it is based on a common ethnic, religious and relational background, based on their friendship, their commonality of purpose, their mutual 'brotherhood'. All this enables the work to be a hundred times easier because of the trust already in place between them. When such a spirit of comrade is present, problems and difficulties are never too big. Conversations about business are alternated very easily with daily life exchanges of experiences. If I look back to the first generation of Christians however, something slightly different happened which is very significant for this book. Many of those first-generation migrants such as Shing, Zhenzhen or Shu decided to join their enterprises together with some other Boss-Christian members of the church, regardless of their family background. This was done with the specific purpose of strengthening their partnership and vision for business on the basis of their common faith (acting as weak ties). In those cases, they started their business bottom-up. They describe a gradual progress in their professional experience where the help of the house church or of the family, which in the case of Zhenzhen corresponds with the church, represents somewhat the positive turning point of their business growth:

> Before I was working in the business of shoes, then clothing, then in a store of the brothers from the church, then I've started my own business, from some months I manage this store selling lamps for companies. (Shing, Wenzhou, Milan, 30/01/2015)

> First I was working into a Chinese restaurant, for two years, I couldn't speak Italian, I was washing dishes, cleaning, then little by little I was helping the cook, then I became the cook, then several other works in the kitchen, then little by little I was helping Chinese students at University, I was preparing learning Italian, I was buying Italian books, then they could study them at home. Then I've changed job into an Italian restaurant,

> then I became a barman for three years, I was managing the bill and in 1999 I started my own business in clothing, I just tried everything. (Shu, Wenzhou, Milan, 30/01/2015)

> Before I was working in a restaurant as an employee with others, I've opened my own restaurant then since five years I work in the clothing business. I can see a growth and God helps me, I don't look for greatness, the things he gives me I'm happy, but God leads me on, this job is to support those of my religion that Jesus tells me. Life is not just for work is working for the faith, as I work we must prepare sermons [...] I started little by little under others, then in a little shop, then I created a pizza place, then a restaurant, the money was growing, and my family helped me and our work prosper more and more as I grow bigger. (Zhenzhen, Wenzhou, Milan, 30/01/2015)

As it will be clearer when I will compare those results with the second group of entrepreneurs with no link with the Protestant faith, the house church in this case works just as a functional substitute to what the family lineage, identification with the same ethnic group or membership into an associations are for the second case: network generators. Secondly Shing, Zhenzhen or Shu are also what I can call the perfect example of a 'boss Christian' from Wenzhou.

They are all first generation of Chinese immigrants, very successful in their business but also very involved in leadership roles inside their church. Particularly in those cases the element of lineage (strong ties) seems to play a secondary role compared with their image of a 'self made man'. Only in later parts of their life those entrepreneurs started to use the network of the church inside business. It must be also noticed that their belonging to the first generation of migrants meant the absence of economic support from both church and family in their primordial stages of business life when they arrived in Italy. From ethnographic observations I was also able to see that not only Shing is very involved in business, he has a vision for leading business and start always new activities, but he is also very involved in the church, being a core member, a deacon, always very active in all the religious activities.

The case of Shu is even more interesting for this matter, as he perceived and described his professional life in terms of a continuous process of growth toward success, from low-paid jobs into independent business ownership, being very visionary toward his economic future. Like Shing and Zhenzhen, his brother Shu is very involved in business, helping other

Christians to succeed, having also a role of key leadership in the church as a deacon, seen and treated as a role model for younger members and being leader both in church and in business. Sometimes this positive influence comes out of the boundaries of the house church and involves even the non-Christian entrepreneurs. One example of this came through interviewing and job-shadowing Chun, a non-Christian entrepreneur, in his relationship with Delun, a Boss-Christian. Chun is a first-generation migrant and at first he had a lot of difficulties integrating in the Italian society. It was at this point that the connection and help received from Delun really represented a turning point for Chun. This is unusual even among Chinese entrepreneurs:

> When there's some problem other entrepreneurs [looking at Delun] will help me. There are few people like Delun, kind that will help you. A lot of people think always about themselves, it is difficult to receive help, before I left to go to Italy I've met Delun. (Chun, Ibidem)

It must be noticed that a specific Chinese cultural structure of the church is very far from the historic division between pastors (also called elders or teachers as leaders) and deacons. This cultural structure of the Chinese church tends to be very elaborate and must be taken into consideration in order to understand the role of leadership. The function of the pastor in many of the evangelical churches of Wenzhou seems to take second place due to the frequent cases of persecutions so that the role of deacon as the one of Shu or Zhenzhen becomes the actual leadership inside the church (Table 7.2).

Because of the frequent persecution coming from the Communist government, many pastors were imprisoned or killed. For this reason, the church in Wenzhou developed a specific type of leadership that is present still today. The evangelist (*Chuandao*) takes the place of the pastor in situations of leadership vacuum caused by persecution. But in this particular situation, in the long term the Tong Gong is the real decision-maker and leader of the church (see, for instance, Zhenzhen, Shu or Shing for the case under my analysis). This complex organizational scheme that allows the church to act as a surrogate of the Chinese lineage might re-direct my original theoretical considerations on the different church models of leadership (see Table 4.2). We must take into account their further evolution in light of the cultural context of China. This is especially true for the influence of lineage and indigenous forms of government in Wenzhou.

Table 7.2 Peculiar organizational structure of the Chinese evangelical church under my ethnographic investigation

Mushi (pastors, teachers)
Chuandao (evangelists)

Tong Gong (co-workers, committed disciples, managers)

Regular **church members**

China follows the 'descriptive' kinship system of classification, also called 'Sudanese kinship system'. Such system is among the most complex and, particularly in the region of Wenzhou where ancestors' worship was very important, it results in the centrality of the enlarged family in every aspect of life. For this reason, lineage needs to be taken into consideration as a central aspect into the religious practices even of Chinese Protestantism and for its application to the structure of leadership inside the Chinese church, as well as many other aspects of their daily life, even their business.

Such structural shape of church organization in China was also due, for example, to the influence of famous Chinese Christian leaders such as Watchman Nee or John Sung who developed a new type of church leadership (the idea of 'older brother' instead of pastors or deacons) which finds no correspondence in the West. What is interesting to notice here is the profound influence of lineage and family clan not just on the social structures but also on the economic structure of relations and strategies of those Chinese entrepreneurs. Lineage in other words tends to shape those elements during the migratory process and engagement in business activities. The strong involvement of Wenzhou in the migration process all over the world is in fact also due to the strong role of family networks and lineage. It works like a chain, starting from a single migrant up to entire villages or larger social groups. For example, Shu is the first person of his family that came to Italy, and then all the other members of his extended family decided to move and start a business in the diaspora. This shows the ramifications of businesses all over the world that allows them to survive in times of economic crisis because of the extended lineage. However, the role of lineage for the case of the Protestant entrepreneurs seems to work inside an already influential context. The people that can be directly involved in the network in the house church is broader and deeper. Furthermore, as many studies in economic sociology have shown (AA. VV., 1990, p. 482), during the migratory experience lineage, as well as any form of traditional authority in the family, tend to go through moments of breakdown that weaken its potential role.

Zhenzhen, Shu's younger brother, is also a very successful businessman, a typical boss-Christian. He is very visionary in his job and purpose-driven. He works very hard and at the same time is also involved in a position of leadership as a deacon in the church. This element goes together with the network, in which the sphere of influence tends to be larger than lineage. From ethnographical observations on Zhenzhen, I saw his professionalism in action, his trustworthiness with the clients, his working hard and at the same time his busy schedule in ministry, serving the Chinese church. Zhenzhen goes every weekend to a different Chinese church around Italy (Florence, Venice, Genoa…) to preach sermons and build believers. This complex network of evangelical churches, as it has been notified by Zhenzhen (more than 44 churches all over Italy, plus other contacts with Pentecostal churches which raise the number to over 100), provides also the ground for business transactions, through contacts, word of mouth and mutual economic support as well as itinerary ministry in preaching. His desire to become a Tong Gong and later a Mushi (a full-time minister) is shared also by Delun who started to preach in several Chinese churches in Milan receiving the favor of other church members, in tune with being a successful entrepreneur. This success was supposed to show character qualities that are essential in order to be accepted in the church and that are also used in business (courage, dedication, humility, sacrifice, setting high goals…).

Another important example of how this house church network works on the job is what I had the possibility to observe in the group of Christian entrepreneurs linked together in business among the larger group of Chinese businesses. Zhenzhen and Shu are a leading part of this network and they often organize a group of entrepreneurs to go around the different shops of the pavilion one by one to build the relationships, encouraging people, having spiritual conversations with them and inviting them to come to religious meetings. This is a good example of how those entrepreneurs, already engaged in a network through the house churches, expand their influence in the context of business through friendly engagement based on their religious identity. It is important again to see that it is not just a form of network that is at play here but also we have an expression of their inner-worldly asceticism through it, which helps them to portray an image and identity in the face of the surrounding social context, without any contradiction between their religious beliefs and their job.

7.1.6 Framing Success

Economic success as God's blessing, which I have described before and that has been identified in the area of Wenzhou, is subordinate to a major supreme objective which represents another precondition: the *Glory of God*. Among the different descriptions of the purpose of their work, in their own reconstruction, this particular precondition stands out as predominant. When asked about the main purpose of their work, those entrepreneurs regularly referred to a metaphysical idea of 'bringing glory to God' in everything they did. When compared with the non-Christian Chinese entrepreneurs who only focused on support for the family, living a decent life, I received a quite different response from them. But what exactly does it mean and why is it interesting for my argument to speak of such emphasis on bringing glory to God through work? From what I was able to observe on the field, this specific belief strictly connected with the other preconditions, such as the inner-worldly asceticism, sees every single activity, especially work, as having an ultimate higher purpose, no matter how low or humbling it may be. It must be recalled how low-level jobs in ancient Asian cultures, as well as in the Greek classical era, were considered bad and in opposition to the pure benefit of intellectual investigation. Here instead, behind the religious interpretation, it is possible to see the exaltation of work at any level, even the lowest, as a way to accomplish their goal both spiritually and professionally. This is a conviction that results in creating duty, meaning and purpose for business. Every activity, therefore, even the most repetitive or challenging finds a greater meaning and higher purpose:

> [...] God will prepare the best for us, whatever I will do the most important thing is to bring glory to God. [...] If I wasn't a believer I would be doing business only for myself but now I do this asking myself if I'm bringing glory to God. (Minzhe, Ibidem)

Life must be offered to bring glory to God [...] work with all of your strength to give glory not just to myself. Any work you are doing this has to bring glory to God. [...] The main purpose in life is to bring glory to God. (Bo, Ibidem)

To have a sense of mission helps you [...]. Some churches gather the laoban [bosses] and ask them to dedicate themselves for the church, some don't do that, they don't focus in the company, we have instead to grow the company so that it will glorify God. (Yi, Ibidem)

The purpose [of work] is maybe to make money but if you want to make money you must follow the rules of the Bible and glorify God, you must gain money but money is controlled by God. (Da, Ibidem)

I worked to change my life, to give to my family a good life but since I became a Christian it is not just the money my goal, I must manage the money for God, work together with colleagues, bring them to the faith, make God happy, for the glory of God. (Nai, Ibidem)

I investigated many stores and decided to rent them and I thought to find something to glorify God, sometimes very important for me, therefore I opened the foundation. (Ning, Ibidem)

For me the purpose [of work] was make money and support the family, now if work can express my faith it is good. Working is for God, but sometimes is hard, we have to work hard and make money, if it can grow for God I will be blessed. (Xiu, Ibidem)

Accomplish goals is important but put always God at the first place and don't ever forget Him. (Hop, Ibidem)

To obey is important, Jesus wants me to obey, the true life of the persons is important, the goal remains the kingdom of God. (Jun, Ibidem)

The purpose of my life is to be always with the Lord the other things that the Lord puts ahead of me I live them according to this principle. (Minsheng, Ibidem)

I have to discover daily what is the purpose of working, now many live just for the sake of living, but the most important reason is Jesus who gave it to me. (Zixin, Ibidem)

The interesting element here is how Zixin, Minzhe, Bo or Hop apart from their religious fervency, common to other forms of religiosity, hold to an unusual strict connection between this belief and the way they do and interpret socially their work. During my visit in Wenzhou, I had the chance to see through the interviews of Yi or Xiu how the degree of connection and personal interiorization between these two elements was far higher. Also, from ethnographic observations and job-shadowing at their workplace, a strong emphasis from the participants emerged on the importance to 'glorify God' even in the worse of situations, and that each individual must do it in as many ways as possible. This helps also the entrepreneur to find the strength necessary to face difficult tasks and at the same time to 'think big' about any business action. Once again, apart from judgment of values on the particular content of the belief, such precondition seems to enhance a sense of self-efficacy. Work and business find a different special source of motivation that brings them to have a good relation with the clients, colleagues, suppliers and anybody else they come into contact with. Pushed by this belief, the entrepreneur feels an obligation to share such conviction. Even economic transitions can become the opportunity for 'sharing the Gospel', not just being focused then on the material aspect of it. This gives them the motivation, purpose as well as the trust toward the good success of the economic transaction:

> As a seller I want to give to customers the love of God [...] the purpose of course is the kingdom of God, to bring salvation to the souls. (Deming, Ibidem)

> [...] I have this faith I have to give the news of the Gospel share and let them see God. [...] I have to help the people to find purpose, meaning. [...] if I do something I worship God, is not me. (Fai, Ibidem)

> [...] the Gospel is an opportunity to glorify God through work, how can you share otherwise, to work is to glorify God the only motivation that I can work hard. (Ling, Ibidem)

In this situation Ling, Fai and Deming see themselves as mere executors of a higher plan. Ling found a purpose that led her to working hard. They all search for a unique ingredient that can give motivation and effectiveness to their work. From the micro-level of this social phenomenon to the macro-level, it can still be possible to see the major role of this belief. Some of those entrepreneurs are particularly encouraged by what is happening in China today, through the Protestant revival. This revival is seen by Delun or Xun as something that will lead the whole world to benefit from China turning into a Christian nation. These new economic contributions and benefits that China is experiencing today are seen by him as a direct consequence of China's acceptance of the Gospel. In light of such perceived climate of spiritual and economic revival, Delun thinks that he too has to do his part through business, to make things happen:

> […] Many of us think that in 15 years if we reach 30% of Chinese population then China will become a Christian country is this that we want to believe in China, when China will become a Christian nation, it will be a contribution and a benefit for the whole planet […]. (Delun, Ibidem)

> Relationships were focused on business, me as a pastor I thought we don't have to stay just for money, but exchange culture, thoughts, ideas, the most important thing is faith in all the exchanges is easier. […] Our roots of faith we want to bring them in society, religion doesn't just refers to the four walls of the church but we are the salt and light of the world, we reveal what we have from the Bible, we have the duty to witness, we show what we do in research, technology and mass media that speak about us. […] we have to move in the social (arena) and this the government likes it. (Fang, Milan, Wenzhou, 25/01/2016)

> The Christians in the future will be very important, they will be the center of support in China, without any doubts. We see a nation that want to rise up, the heart of this energy comes from God. (Xun, Ibidem)

Because of the implications on the macro-level and the pervasiveness of this view in every aspect of life, this precondition ends up having priority over the others. This set of preconditions can be conceptualized in progress: from choosing the job (*Yi Xiang*), to the way they work (*Boss-Christian*), with what kind of social resources (*house churches*) for what ultimate goal (*glory of God*). To these elements, some significant premises must be added (the presence of a *dramatic conversion*, a necessity of high standards, a stress on *charisma* and a clear view of the future). All those aspects seem to have a common denominator in pushing the individual to work hard through a meaningful set of values. It is clear however that in and of itself a propensity to work hard is not the ultimate guarantee for economic success in business. There must be an internal state of being able to direct such propensity toward a functional economic action. In the field a sense of self-confidence emerged that seemed to contradict with the Weberian idea of anxiety about salvation.

7.1.7 Assurance of Salvation

In the realm of salvation (central aspect to the Protestant faith), what I was able to notice through ethnographic observations, job-shadowing and interviews was something slightly different if not totally opposite to the central aspect theorized by Weber. Like for the case of Calvinism those Christian entrepreneurs hold the belief in PAS, that consists in believing without doubt in the *perpetual assurance of salvation* (Que ju, 确据) as a result not of works (*total depravity of men*), but of God's divine work through Christ's sacrifice at the cross. Having received by grace through faith (xinyang de endian 信仰的恩典) in Jesus the total forgiveness of all their present, past and future sins, those individuals experience a perpetual assurance of salvation. This means that the individual who holds such belief knows that when he dies he will surely go to heaven, not because of his good works, since he perceives to be a depraved sinner, but because of Christ's ultimate sacrifice for his sins at the cross. But the question may rise: What does such strictly metaphysical element has to do with work and economic success? If what concerns the realm of salvation among those Chinese entrepreneurs is true, as it will be showed through interviews excerpts and job-shadowings, then, in accordance with the historical sources on Calvinism, it will prove to be a confirmation of the reality of a reversal of Weber's thesis. It will become evident that the Weberian connection between belief and economic success was going in the right direction but with the wrong conclusions. Before passing on to analyze the validity of any alternative explanation let's define first the details of such belief from Delun's own words:

> [...] Because of the faith that I received [...] all of us are condemned to death, we are all sinners but with Jesus Christ we are saved in His blood, then we can change the future trusting in this Christian faith. (Delun, Ibidem)

> I believe I'm saved, Jesus said when I will come back I will bring you into heaven, the eternal life, when Jesus will come. [...] Life then is very

> peaceful and when something bad happens I know Jesus will help me. (Huizhong, Ibidem)

> [...] You can have salvation if you believe, you will receive love and you will have peace in every difficulty, it will give you joy, hope in your life [...] I'm totally changed, now I have eternal life. (Minzhe, Ibidem)

> Jesus say I care about you. It was the most peaceful night I ever had, I didn't had fears, I slept like a child [...] I went through many difficulties but I was following Jesus and the Bible that helped me to overcome difficulties. (Enlai, Ibidem)

Enlai in this line is reconstructing the details of his dramatic conversion and how in that moment of salvation he felt freedom from anxiety. The same thing is possible to see in Huizhong: a sense of peace and assurance that has an impact on future events, leaving the individual in a perpetual state of assurance about his eternal destiny, in a sort of 'self-fulfilling prophecy'. In trying to understand how such belief can influence the achievement of economic success, it is important to make two considerations: (i) this belief generates a feeling of confidence and peace, (ii) such feeling is said to be very important in bad circumstances and moments of difficulties. The centrality of such belief becomes evident by answering the question: 'did you encounter challenges or difficulties at work? How did you react? What helped you?' The answers were almost uniformly related to PAS. Also, a sense of peace and confidence is the direct output of this belief, and I will explain later why it is so important to emphasize it. Not only through interviews but also through ethnographic observations I have witnessed during several social meetings how the entrepreneurs had to answer to several questions and among those addressed these were some of them: 'when you obtain salvation, how do you live? What does salvation brings in you?' or 'when you are weak do you think God loves you? In which situation you didn't received what you expected?'. Listening to their spontaneous answers I saw repeatedly a reference to a sense of peace, a condition of comfort in challenges and an ability to overcome difficulties. Referring to difficulties at work one of the participants to the meeting mentioned his testimony of how the business at his shop was not going good and how 'knowing to be saved' helped him to overcome the challenge through calmness.

Not only that, but both from the interviews and the job-shadowing, the belief in PAS emerged repeatedly as the guiding element of their life, particularly in times of struggle. If someone was to subtract, by using the trick of Wittgenstein, this belief from their religious experience, the entire structure of their system of values that guides them in business, looses its meaning and relevance. Without this belief, according to their own estimation, it is better to stay atheist or Buddhist, life loses all its meaning and purpose, there's simply no ultimate support, all the castle of preconditions falls down. Those entrepreneurs relate directly to this belief in every aspect of their daily life, especially work. The belief in PAS generates in them a state of 'confidence' that has everything to share with what I've described as the main characteristic of self-efficacy, a trait that in the field of psychology of work has already been proven to be related with economic success. This perpetual state described by Minsheng, Bingwen or Hop as 'efficiency', 'confidence', 'peace in the heart', 'joy', 'God's continuous presence' is able to lead them to overcome difficulties, particularly in trade and work:

> Faith in God helps me to stay calm, I work more efficiently with less inconvenience, I used to feel a big hole in me, now God gives me peace and I'm always calm and everything goes well, I overcome problems at work and in life all because of God. [...] It changed me a lot, I'm not like the others, somebody who doesn't believe in this religion, when he puts his trust in him everything changes. (Minsheng, Wenzhou, Milan, 20/12/2014)

> Sometimes is difficult to have peace in your heart in difficulties, you will have fears, you will be nervous, evil thoughts but [...] to God it matters [...] He will helps you to overcome them, therefore you will have peace and joy in every situation. Salvation is based on faith [...] I know that if I believe I have eternal life, and I know that God cares about me, when I have difficulties, I will pray and God will be with me, it's easier to overcome difficulties, I know that God is with me and I will not be nervous. (Bingwen, Ibidem)

> Before I didn't believe in God and today I don't have anxiety anymore, in difficulties that God helps me. Even if I had success without God my heart will be empty, I have a hope for the future [...]. I don't cry in front of difficulties, nothing depends on my efforts but on the hand of God. (Hop, Ibidem)

> Whenever I was weak, poor, it happens something terrible, this doesn't scare me, I have a spiritual eternal life, I know that when I will die I will go to heaven. (Jun, Ibidem)

> Jesus already saved me I feel I'm more calm that with Jesus near me nothing bad will happen to me. At work I pass every day without worrying about how much money I gain, Jesus is enough, the things we obtain are the things He gives us. Even if you want more you don't obtain it, if He gives you that part then is enough you don't have to worry. (Shaiming, Ibidem)

Once again, behind their religious interpretation what really interests me here is the strict connection with the realm of work, and the psychological and sociological considerations that it is possible to make from that. Economic success as it is known from the literature has various explanations and among those, there is the necessity of a strong belief in someone's abilities to reach his goals. In a strictly formal way, that's exactly what it is possible to see in Jun and Shaiming. Not only that, but even from their own perception of how success in business is achieved Delun goes beyond his own skills or competences and talks about a source of strength and confidence derived directly from his belief. For example, Delun and Bingwen during the first stages of their shared business of high technology were particularly challenged by the newness of what they were trying to do but also by the lack of any certainty of success. Sometimes one of them was particularly discouraged by circumstances but having a 'brother' as a business partner was a good influence. When some of them had to face a problem, both were able to find a way out together. Bingwen and Delun in this case had confidence and assurance in the fact that the necessary clients would have been provided for them. In direct response to the risk and challenges, Delun showed confidence, not in himself but in a supernatural force. When he faced a problem there was an ultimate solution. Bingwen was giving an example of this related to his task of printing phone covers at the Hi-Tech store. When they found a spot in the picture, risking to lose a client, they tried in a matter of weeks to resolve the problem. Wisdom and confidence were necessary in those situations where it is hard to work every day without any certainty that the problem can be fixed. Their faith helped Delun and Bingwen to be calm and to find a solution to resolve the problem.

But the reason for economic success goes also further than static definitions of it. The belief in PAS and self-efficacy can show their dynamic role only when analyzed in moments of true economic risk. For example, Shaiming reveals the significance of this when he shared with me his difficulties at work. Shaiming lamented the fact that 4 years earlier the business was going very well. Yet this was not anymore the case because of the competition coming from bigger chains of Chinese stores providing the same type of products. He was referring to AUMAI, the Chinese chain of franchising born from the idea of three Chinese brothers in 2004 that later on spread all over North Italy. Those stores are 10 times bigger than Shaiming's store and only in the area of Milan there are 50 of them. In reconstructing his past experience before and after having believed in PAS, the entrepreneur acknowledges a drastic change in his life, especially in his management of economic risk:

> [...] I think that success in business is due to God's blessings [...] in the beginning I thought that was destiny, skills, because I'm smart, but as time went on I understood that wasn't the case [...] in difficulties then there is a reason beyond that, a God that blesses you [...]. (Delun, Ibidem)

> Faith helps us all at work [...] so, it is that in times of difficulties through our faith we are able to go ahead. (Guang, Ibidem)

The belief in PAS, instead of creating anxiety, gives Hop and Heng the important resources to manage the anxiety derived from the 'competitiveness' of their job at any level:

> [...] When I'm doing a competitive job it doesn't matter how hard it will be, I know that God will help me [...] I don't get worried, I'm not mad anymore, God healed me. Emotionally I have an ability to overcome the difficulties and to be at peace. (Hop, Ibidem)

> In my experience I had shopkeepers clients that are difficult to communicate, I had pain speaking with them, in prayer Jesus helped me to love also people who are difficult to love. (Heng, Ibidem)

Even when under pressure, the entrepreneur has that peace that comes from faith, he is able to lead his company within the strength of this higher power. During hard moments, whether because of economic crisis, difficulties with clients, during hard managerial decisions or facing debts… what really motivates the entrepreneur is focusing on a higher reason that will help him to stay focused and avoid becoming a 'slave of his bad circumstances'. This is provided again by the belief in PAS, a belief especially beneficial in the case of Zixin or Fai, which helps them interpret their challenges as opportunities. Economic risks, failures and defeats are as much important as economic success for Bo, Enlai and Zhenzhen. They must be faced, accepted and they bring to a response that will favor a lasting success or that at least will remove confusion. In order for that to happen the emphasis switches often to an higher unshakable source of assurance which is able to help in managing inconveniences and provides the necessary perseverance to go ahead 'facing the challenge, going right through it':

> There are difficult moments at work, but I'm joyful, I believe that Jesus helps me always and I'm not afraid of things of this life. Sometimes it's hard, when I came here I didn't had anything, I had difficulties and God helped me. It wasn't easy, at that time I thought: why this is happening to me? My life doesn't have to be always straight, some problem must occur so that I will become stronger, succeed in overcoming fear and become a better man. (Zixin, Ibidem)

> When I have stress at work and pressure, I have this, I believe I can pray read the Bible ask in church to other believers the meaning, if I wasn't a Christian I would had acted in a bad mode drinking alcohol seeking a way to release the stress and difficulties that is not good, now I have a way to release my stress I have peace. (Fai, Ibidem)

> If something difficult happens at work is good to go on knowing that God is always with me. (Deming, Ibidem)

> In moments of difficulties you don't know what happen tomorrow but you have a landmark the goal you reach not as a mere earthly success but toward eternity you already have everything. In risk you trust that you will have your bread it gives you confidence in what you do. (Bo, Ibidem)

> I was confused and anxious about future, I read the Proverbs and I've found directions on where to go. When I am down and sad I know that God is with me and comforts me whatever may happen. God is creator […] the fear in difficult and unknown situations the people that I'm not able to deal with it is exceeded by God […] I have Jesus and God I have

> the Spirit and I have confidence with any person not because I'm smart but because my treasure is in heaven and He prepared the best for me. (Enlai, Ibidem)

> We have to set what's important, the important thing is life after [death] I work in light of the things that after we will have to do as we enter into eternity with the rewards from the things we are doing now. (Zhenzhen, Wenzhou, Milan, 30/01/2015)

The fact that the entrepreneur believes in the afterlife is not really exceptional to this religion neither in and of itself brings him to economic success. But given the connection between the belief in an assurance and the preconditions providing a constant, unchangeable confidence and self-efficacy, the entrepreneur is strengthened in times of economic crisis. Wing especially in his beginning stages of business needed strength and patience in order to be able to 'never give up' even in the most difficult situation, and that came from his awareness of being saved:

> When there's every difficulty what I have in my heart I can't say to my friends but I say to Jesus. At work when I'm mad I pray the name of Jesus to give me patience [...] I prayed and I'm not mad anymore [...]. The first job that I was doing as a dishwasher was very hard, the first day I started to cry in my heart, tears were falling and I thought why is this so hard and then I thought where in the Gospel is written: Jesus suffered for our sins at the cross and then God abandoned Him. So I thought I remembered in the Bible this and that I am saved, I don't think how is difficult or I'm alone Jesus suffered for me I just suffer a little bit. (Wing, Ibidem)

> I sent 200 flyers and only one student came, I kept pressing on [...] I never worried of numbers, God provides. God takes care of me he provides good scores and success. [...] The reason of my strength is that I go to church, I pray and I read the Bible, if I didn't believe in God I would have given up but I never gave up, I do it, the Bible speaks to me, up until now I have no anxiety [...] People ask me why I don't get worried, but I don't do it, but God will do it. (Zhong, Ibidem)

Zhong while working at the Kindergarten faced challenging moments, and through those situations of risk she felt the strength to persevere and 'never give up' because of her religious convictions. Another element connected to PAS and that might need to be added to the model is the practice of prayer at work. This was a recurrent phenomenon in their business activity. In the eyes of the entrepreneur praying in situations of difficulties at work really helps him to overcome challenges, to find his peace and the necessary confidence. Once again, I'm not advocating that prayer somehow helps the business, since prayer can be found in many other religions and from an outside point of view it doesn't have any factual result. For some, to introduce prayer as a practice in itself inside a model about economic success may be a critical step to take. Nevertheless, it must be taken into account especially in light of their personal interpretation.

If I consider such religious practice outwardly there is no factual difference between a Buddhist meditating, a Catholic praying the rosary or a Protestant praying at work. The difference with other religions, however, is that prayer here, as well as other beliefs, is more connected with their material needs, their business life and their daily difficulties at work. Also, the confidence and strength in their abilities generated by PAS are the unique container of such practice that therefore becomes important for my argument. This practice for Huizhong, Kong or Zhenzhen turns into a mean able to transform situations of economic risk into a chance to grow their business. A difficulty at work turns into an opportunity to work better. It is not something therefore that must be avoided but it needs to be faced and embraced. Prayer stimulates the believer's confidence:

> [...] I've passed through many difficulties at work and God helped me through prayer, I've asked Jesus to help me and he helped me. I've many stories that I can share, being here in Italy, when I did an accident for example I prayed Jesus and I pass through it because Jesus helped me, people don't understand when I tell them, you know that is Jesus because when it happens he helps you. (Huizhong, Ibidem)

> If we have difficulties at work we pray to God to resolve the problem [...] we all believe in God therefore this gives us the strength. (Chao, Ibidem)

> The situations of difficulty... I had them in my business. First we prayed together as shareholders we have not blamed each other, we find the confidence even if somebody did something wrong, we unite together to win the difficulties. When some investment failed, I felt sadness, I prayed to God, prayer gives peace, joy, hope and confidence, the promises from God make me feel even better. (Da, Ibidem)

> The things you ask God he gives them to you. I've asked to God things for this business, He gave them to me and He strengthened my beliefs in God. [...] When I was working somewhere else I had few customers but I was serene because I knew that there is God with me, maybe he gave me this path to become more honest and stronger, there are tragedies but they are good, I've prayed and surely they are moments that God allowed you to have so that you improve. There's a lot of Chinese Christians that pass through those moments allowed by God to bring fruits in your life. (Kong, Ibidem)

> In difficulties that I need to face the first important thing is to pray, to trust in the salvation of God. (Yi, Ibidem)

> First I pray when I am in difficulties, about what to do. But the major things I ask to God, the smallest I do them by myself because I think I can do them by myself. (Xiu, Ibidem)

> Whatever difficulties comes it is God giving us an assignment to learn those things here, when there is difficulty, this piece I must learn. [...] When you don't understand why there is this problem it is Jesus that explain to you all those problems and gives you a solution. (Zhenzhen, Ibidem)

> We all have difficulties, I often pray to God, it is very important in order to have the peace and the faith that gives you peace, I bring my burdens to God and I feel relaxed. [...] In difficulties the faith helps me in the company to be righteous, to take guided and focused decisions, it helps me to raise up and face the difficulties to overcome them, it gives me the daily help, if I'm in difficulty I pray, I read, I ask for help. (Nai, Wenzhou, Wenzhou, 24/08/2015)

Everything has its purpose and from every circumstance in business there is a lesson to learn. Beyond their explanation in spiritual terms, what really counts is that economic risk and difficulties are the factual elements and the reason for the difference in the reaction to those challenges. This is what interests me the most here. In fact, another cause of anxiety and risk on a large scale is the peculiar situation of economic crisis that those entrepreneurs went through. The financial crisis of 2008 had touched many entrepreneurs like Shu and many businesses in the surrounding environment failed as a result of it. During my observations a current topic was the financial fall of the stock market of Shanghai. During my ethnographic observations at Via Sarpi, the Chinatown of Milan, Ah Cy shared with me his feelings on that critical situation he was dealing with. Ah Cy sensed that the level of inflation in China caused an increase in costs and a need of higher salaries so that many companies in China were in trouble. The only thing that helped Ah Cy, from his own words, was the network of Christian entrepreneurs he was part of. This gave him hope for the future even in the midst of difficulties. This consolation came from his religious beliefs and by imitating the example of other Christian entrepreneurs around him. The stress caused by bad behaviors, debts… finds its solution in Delun's use of prayer as a social act, uniting different entrepreneurs facing the same obstacle or in Shu's perception of it as a source of strength:

> I had to go trough many moments of difficulties at work, there was the economic crisis and also since 2008 is very hard but always prayer to God helps me. My heart then is peaceful, all that I lose, debts, failed clients that cheat on me and I lose a lot of money but I'm here, I'm not scared they want to cheat me but I'm a believer. Up until now people own me 300.000 euro's but I don't go there with a gun, what should I do? Faith in God helped me, God never fails me, I've listened and I've heard, always he helps me, the things that I lack I don't want to push, not everyone has bad behaviors, but when I meet them I must pray, Jesus has done this. (Shu, Ibidem)

> […] when somebody finds difficulties, feels exhausted and desperate, it happens sometimes in the trade, because not always things go right, it happens sometimes, for example with the financial crisis that impacted us heavily, then we started to pray, then prayer helps us […]. (Delun, Ibidem)

Again prayer must be considered here more as a formal mean. What really must be taken into account is its sociological and psychological implications. In other words, in absence of such interpretation the business would have lost part of its revenue or it would have become bankrupt, like for many of the surrounding businesses operating in the same field. A very interesting case came out from the description of Yongnian about how in a circumstance of economic crisis and depression prayer and an interpretation of business as centered around a higher purpose intervened to actually bring him out of that economic crisis:

> God always give us courage to work, when we do things we always pray, we thank God for everything. When I've started the business I prayed to God and He sent me many clients and many people. But then I forgot about God, and I finished all the merchandise, I've stolen from God blessings, I thought it was because of my abilities to sell, then the second season I've bought a lot of merchandise that was blocked in the store, it was hard to get the bill going, then I went to God, I've prayed confessing my sin and little by little I've finished selling all that was blocked in the store. (Yongnian, Ibidem)

Yongnian cannot explain in purely mathematical terms why his business was able to survive to a concrete threat of failure. Coming out of an economic crisis for him and many other entrepreneurs meant the putting in practice of those beliefs which were the necessary source of strength and meaning. Another great example of this came from the interview with Xun that while reconstructing his experience of conversion he pointed out how his experience of salvation helped him to overcome his difficulties:

> For three years I had debts and I didn't know it was because of God, I didn't want to listen to the warnings, God was correcting me. I tried with any system, I gave away money, I asked to the police, people around me but it didn't work. My mother called me, she asked me what I was doing, I said that I'd found the money I needed but my mother was praying for me. At that moment I gave up and I've accepted that she pray for me, half hour late the shareholder of the company that did not acted honestly gave me back the money. It was a miracle. (Xun, Ibidem)

Xun here is telling the story of his conversion. From being in a moment of crisis, both for his business and for his personal life, he decided to 'give up…and accept', to give his life to God embracing the Christian faith. This experience led Xun to embrace Christianity and led him to a drastic change in his life. He started to share his beliefs, to follow honest principles of business in an environment of corruption and economic crisis:

> In the beginning and for several years the deficit of the company was high but I insisted, I insisted and God was taking care, I followed the biblical Christian values, it wasn't easy but I overcame it. God gives faith and confidence, I had a courageous heart to resolve the things in a managerial way. […] When we lose riches we feel anyway peace and grace and we can face the problems. (Xun, Ibidem)

Up to this point I was able to show the presence in the field of the theoretical model, with some contextual adjustments and some additions to the preconditions. It shouldn't be surprising to find the presence of this set of beliefs among today's Protestant Chinese entrepreneurs, in the same way any social structure reproduces itself in a different historical context out of the same cultural origin. This does not happen without a certain degree of syncretism, like for the case that I mentioned of the Chinese organizational model of the church. So far considering these results, the belief in PAS seems to have its effect on how an entrepreneur works. If someone wants to consider without bias the business practices of those Chinese entrepreneurs he must consider the role of this irreplaceable set of beliefs. Evaluating whether or not such explanation is the only one valid will be the object of the following section.

7.1.8 Closing Remarks

Before I turn into the analysis of the results concerning the second group of entrepreneurs with no link at all with Protestantism, I must report some statements of Protestant entrepreneurs that may lead the reader to consider the possibility of the intervening influence of a *Wenzhou's profit-oriented mentality* beyond the Protestant ethic. I've considered this category as an all-encompassing factor that for a number of reasons (cultural, economic, social…) may lead to the same conclusion about economic success without necessarily bringing in the religious beliefs. Since my very first interview with Delun the possibility for such explanation came to the surface:

> […] we had this success also because we are Chinese and we have a very strong entrepreneurial willpower. […] to be an hard-worker… the Chinese culture, mainly the Chinese culture that encourage us to take the risk in trade […]. (Delun, Ibidem)

> The business is strong in Wenzhou, they pay low taxes, there is more money therefore they accumulate more. […] In Wenzhou the business is strong because they work hard […] the people of Wenzhou travel a lot, we are like the Jews of China, in all Europe we are known for this. Since ancient times we are of a stronger thought, also the other cities consider us this way. (Chao, Geu Xi, Wenzhou, 26/08/2015)

> The Chinese people are known to be hard workers everywhere. It also depends by which part of China they come from, the people from the south work harder, you give them opportunities, they make money then they work harder because they see the profit very clearly. (Ling, Baoding, Milan, 29/05/2015)

> In the mind of Wenzhounese the money is very important, it come first, they think that if you have a lot of money you can speak louder, you can have a strong voice, it doesn't matter if you are a good person. (Xiu, Ibidem)

> In the beginning Wenzhou was poor, you had to work very hard, many [now] do business and are successful, if you live here you want to learn from those that have success, is the environment. (Tai, Ibidem)

The case for a Wenzhou's profit-oriented mentality can be made both on the basis of results from this sample and findings about Wenzhou's contribution to business compared to other areas of China in the diaspora (Vendassi, 2014; Cao, 2013). Ling introduces here what will be identified as a cultural propensity toward business already present in the area of Wenzhou. In several cases I saw the entrepreneurs identifying their entrepreneurial uniqueness primarily on the basis of their Wenzhouren's identity, even when compared to other cities and regions in China (as it is evident from the words of Zixin). Among the Christian entrepreneurs, there is another important element that came out from their own description and that may interfere with the interpretation of the model. Such element concerns the absence of awareness on human rights, according to their own words which results in Stakhanovism: a behavior characterized by hard work not as a consequence of a set of values but as a result of mere constriction (what will be described as *Constriction explanation* for the second group). When Kong is asked about 'why work is so important for him' he did not give any interpretation based on belief or values but he confessed to be 'forced that way'. Shaiming even criticizes his countrymen, especially the first generation of immigrants arrived in the west during the 1980s from the surrounding country side of Wenzhou.

The first generation came out of poverty and saw work as a necessity, they were led to work hard just to escape from poverty. Yet it is because of this first generation of migrants that such economic boom has happened. During my visit in Wenzhou for example I had the chance to hear the story of how the parents of Bingwen were able to grow in few decades from being a poor family of farmers in the village to become the owners of a textile company in the city, exporting all over China and abroad:

> If somebody tries to work less he loses a lot, the other person is forced to proceed and take his place, some tried to work less but you can't accomplish anything, in some sense we are forced that way. (Kong, Ibidem)

> [...] the world is very beautiful but many of us Chinese we don't look at it we only know how to work. Chinese people have will, a will that for me comes from poverty, when the people is poor. It also comes from following the others, if you have a job, I see that you work and the same will to do the same work comes on me. You are rich and the other person spontaneously wants to become rich, they copy each others after all. (Shaiming, Ibidem)

> I work hard because those that come from China here to look for a job and improve their economic condition. (Guang, Ibidem)

> Many people come from mainland China and the economy wasn't good, things weren't easy, when policy and freedom came then it changed their lives, because they were not able to do that in China, to make money was hard in mainland China. (Ling, Ibidem)

Guang and Ling, although being Protestants, tend here to give a quite more materialistic interpretation of hard work, based on the mere desire to make money. Ah Cy during my ethnographic observations at Via Sarpi, confessed with me that beyond the 'romantic' view of work the tension toward profit was only due to the love of money among Chinese people, regardless of their religious beliefs. Ah Cy lamented how Chinese businessmen in Via Sarpi thought always about money. He gave me a clear social interpretation of the role of money among those workers. 'If you don't make money', he said, 'you are not respected. You may be a person full of qualities and good values but if you don't have money, you are nobody for them', both in the eyes of Christian and not Christian entrepreneurs. This points out another important element involved in this constriction explanation, what I call 'the law of imitation'. It is very common among Chinese people, and particularly among entrepreneurs to just do what others are doing. If the other people around you become rich, then you want to have the same things. Many times if somebody among friends or relatives decided to open a clothing store, the other people around him decided to open the same type of business. During my visit in China, I interviewed Mei, an entrepreneur that stated the influence of such process of imitation in Chinese business:

> Another reason is that people are competitive and jealous, if your neighbor has more you want more, if you are poor they don't respect you, if rich they respect you. It doesn't concerns things but the culture, it comes from the culture, they search respect so they want to come out of poverty. (Mei, Ibidem)

The same goes for Christian entrepreneurs. For example, during the interview with Nai, it came out that the business environment of Wenzhou pushed him to decide to be involved in business. And this process of imitation led them to use their surroundings also as a personal network. During my visit in China, I've witnessed how among the family members of Bingwen his parents started first a business, then one aunt decided to do the same business with the same system of fabrication but with modern machines. Then another uncle was appointed to pack the material and send it to a trading center where the majority of products that many foreign companies buy are shipped and sent all over the world. Likewise, at Via Sarpi, if a store opened during the holiday, then all the other stores remained opened. In fact, Chinese entrepreneurs bring the same exact pattern of business, the same type of products in the diaspora from their motherland in Wenzhou. Ah Cy sees also a difference between the first and second generation of Chinese immigrants. Young people are more integrated with the local culture in the diaspora. They have less propensity toward money whereas the old generation is more oriented to become rich at all costs. It must be noted that even among Christians there were cases of ruthless actions, taking advantage of others for the cause of money. This witness from Ah Cy may then lead us to consider how critical it is to establish a multifaceted view of the role of beliefs in business.

In order to understand the real role of the religious belief, it was very important to adopt an ethnographic strategy based on asking the perspective of the 'outsider'.

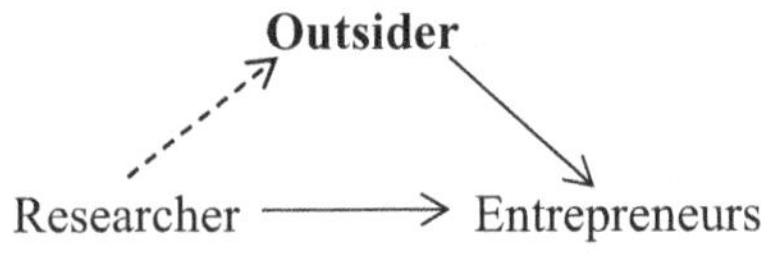

The outsider in the case of the interest group was an Italian entrepreneur. I will call them here Mario, Luca and Giulio. During my ethnographic observations, I had the chance to interview several outsiders. Mario with his business was always in strict relation with the network of Christian entrepreneurs that were part of my investigation. I've asked him particularly if he noticed any difference between the Chinese Christian entrepreneurs and the rest of Chinese entrepreneurs that he encountered on a daily basis. His answer gave me some interesting insight on how difficult it is for an outsider to do business with Chinese entrepreneurs and how the Christian Chinese entrepreneurs helped him get started, especially in the case of Heng:

> When I first came here it was hard because there was suspicion, to whom could I talk to? The only one who gave me trust was Heng [...] he helped me because there was a wall with everybody else [...] I thought the problem was that I was Italian but then I understood they were afraid if what I proposed was legal, why this suspicion with business? [...] now the benefits came when there was mutual trust in the job concerning merchandise, payments [...] they don't let me enter the circle because they thought I wasn't trustworthy. (Mario, Milan, Milan, 30/01/2015)

Mario started working with Chinese entrepreneurs after his own Italian business of furniture failed. He initially experienced a cultural shock. Nobody was willing to cooperate with him among the Chinese businessmen until Heng, a Chinese Christian entrepreneur, decided to give him a chance. Later on, Mario, because of his knowledge of the local language, became the administrator of the whole storehouse of Chinese stores for the administrative things. The Christian Chinese entrepreneur that acts inside a context of Chinese entrepreneurship worked in this case as a bridge and offered what was missing in the surrounding Chinese entrepreneurship context: trust. Added to this Mario expresses his external view of the Christian entrepreneurs in a context of other Chinese businesses. When I interviewed Mario, he did not necessarily know that those Chinese entrepreneurs were Christians, but what appear to be just a uniform environment had some fundamental differences in the business approach. Even if Mario did not know that they were Christians, he noticed from the beginning something different in their behavior that those entrepreneurs had in common and that was crucial to build trust, to guarantee the flow of economic transactions and make for better interactions:

> I didn't noticed this immediately among Christians, now I see it better in Heng, Bo or Zhenzhen [...] recently I understood, is not just friendship but something more that they have in common, I appreciate it although I don't belong to it, there is a better dialogue, I give value to their behavior in business. (Mario, Ibidem)

There is a substantial difference in the way those entrepreneurs do business depending even on their religious identification. More interestingly, during my job-shadowing with Chun, I had the chance to witness the presence of another outsider who was working in partnership, Luca. During our interview, Chun described how after working for a long time with Luca they decided to open a new business together. It must be noticed that it is very unusual for a Chinese entrepreneur to get into a business partnership with outsiders. Chun underlined how this partnership helped him to start his own business (*Network explanation*):

> Then with an Italian associate we decided to start, for one year and a half, two years, he is my friend. We work together and there is a good relationship between us. (Chun, Milan, Wenzhou, 06/10/2015)

This inter-ethnical unusual business partnership represented a huge potential for the range of economic actions that Chun was able to activate. The Italian law prohibits strangers to own a tobacco shop, unless they obtain Italian citizenship. Working with a local helped Chun to open a bar and also a Tobacco shop, increasing his business potential in an environment of mutual trust and friendship. Luca, on the other hand, found it easier to work together with a Chinese colleague because of the notorious Chinese flexibility on the job. What came out from Luca, the outsider in the case of the second group, may lead to the acknowledgment of the possibility of trust and multi-ethnic network creation regardless of the religious factor. During my interview with Luca, it was interesting to see his perspective on the Chinese people he was working with (Chun and his cousin), their mentality, and the differences in the way they do business compared to the Christian Chinese entrepreneurs:

> Chinese people have a way of thinking, an ideology, they are too much framed. We often argue because we have different ideas of working [...] Chun is framed in his theories, I don't understand much his way of doing. Compared to what I see in China I see that Chun is immersed in work but is more Westernized. [...] Between Italian and Chinese is difficult to work together, the way to express themselves, the ideologies, it is the most critical part. The positive part is that they are more malleable, willing, which can be a positive thing but also negative since people take advantage of it. [...] I don't see all this hard work in Chun, his cousin also does not reason properly. In China they are rigid, I wish they were rigid here too. I don't see it here anymore today. (Luca, Milan, 14/10/2015)

Luca points out here the challenges of working together with a Chinese entrepreneur running the same business as a co-boss. Particularly, according to Luca's perspective, there is an emphasis on work among entrepreneurs of Wenzhou, but after coming to Europe they lose such emphasis. Also, apparently in the eyes of Luca, Chun is not particularly different from other workers in his hard work, although he is more flexible and willing to work long hours (*Stakhanovism*). However, according to Luca, many Chinese entrepreneurs who come to Italy lose their hard work propensity. Apart from this element, and contrary to what I mentioned about Mario for the first group, there is no real significant difference then in terms of the external perception of their business. Another clear evidence of this came when I interviewed Guiying. Guiying had to decide who to hire for his new restaurant and he gave me an interesting reason for choosing Chinese workers instead of locals:

> Chinese guys work faster, work is work, we must do it. Even with strangers [non Chinese] but is slower, they come late. It is not easy for a Chinese to find a job, the level is high in Italy and still low in China, we must grow. The restaurant is always full of Chinese people. Working hard is normal in China, before us [in this company] there was an Italian group with twenty products but we were forced to do more, even Friday I finished but the Italians want that we do Photoshop. We are forced. They don't work as us, they are lazy. (Guiying, Beijing, Milan, 22/01/2016)

Furthermore, after submitting the questionnaire on the measurement of the General Self-efficacy Scale to both the first and second group of entrepreneurs, there were interesting results. Results seem to confirm, with necessary caveat, the presence of self-efficacy for both groups. Self-efficacy seems to be more strongly present in the case of the Protestants. Exception must be made however for items two and three, since they contradict their ethical values. If I go to the second group of questions based on the Self-efficacy Scale through PAS, the level of agreement with the items tends to be more than double. Those findings confirm the presence of self-efficacy, that, although not uniform in the sample, is not accidental and remains in line with my original theoretical argument (Table 7.3).

The results, with some exceptions, show therefore the presence of the preconditions and the presence of self-efficacy. It was also possible to isolate the crucial effect of the belief in PAS on self-efficacy. In this way the impact of PAS on the economic success was measured indirectly, especially considering their exposure to situations of economic risk and crisis through job-shadowing and reconstructions done in the interviews. The next step now will be to see if this argument can still be valid by considering the findings from the second group of Chinese entrepreneurs with no relation with Protestantism. Another critical aspect that may affect my final analysis so far is the difficulty in verifying the borders between the different categories of the model for the system of belief. In other words, even if the Protestant belief should be playing a determinant role, it remains still a challenge to define the degree of such role.

7.2 Further Evidence from Wenzhou

7.2.1 Same on a Larger Scale

As I've examined the economic interactions of those entrepreneurs involved often a strict relation with their Chinese motherland. The migration process in fact was not a hindrance for the networks of relations of those Chinese entrepreneurs living overseas. In order to investigate more in depth and to have a clearer idea of the phenomenon under my analysis went straight to the origin of this profit-oriented mentality as I visited the city of Wenzhou. My access to the field there was possible both because of personal contacts through the entrepreneurs living in Milan and also through support from Academic circles. Through my personal connection with some professors at the Beijing University, I was able to enter into contact with an informant in the city of Wenzhou that as a researcher in the same field, already interviewed many people in the area and was

Table 7.3 Results from the questionnaire on the presence of self-efficacy for both first and second groups. It is possible to see a higher presence of self-efficacy among the first group particularly from the area of Wenzhou. It becomes more than double considering the belief in PAS. Regardless of the belief however self-efficacy tends to be prominent among young male small business owners

n = (48 C + 31 NC) = 79

self-efficacy > 3

m AGE = 30

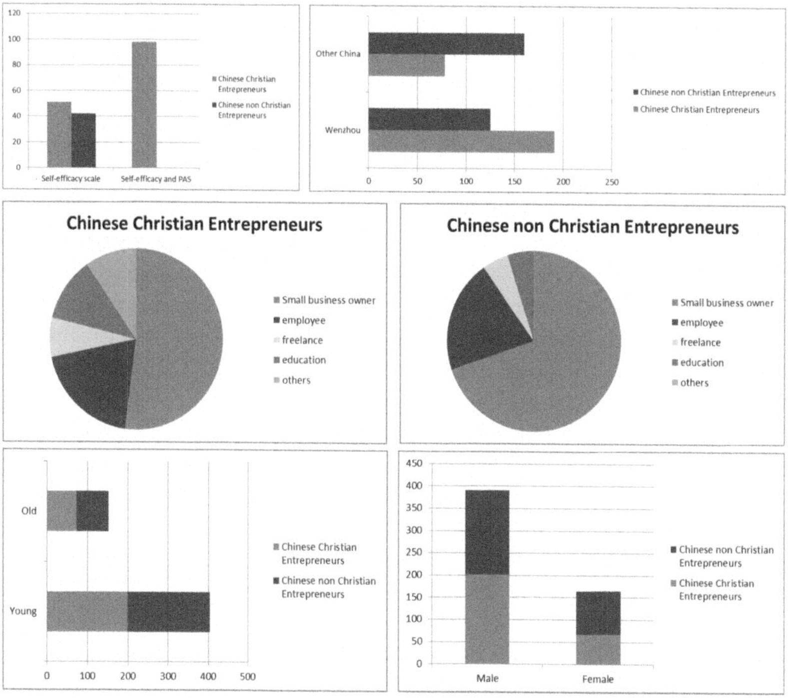

willing to pass contacts along. In Wenzhou I had the chance to interview a consistent amount of entrepreneurs and to visit their workplaces. The visit also helped me to expand my framework and understand better all the background of the reality of Chinese entrepreneurship, its Wenzhouren model and the impact of Protestant Christianity. Many of the elements that I've observed and found in my fieldwork in Milan were confirmed in the motherland and sometimes on a much larger scale than what I was able to observe in the diaspora. One example that almost immediately captured my attention was the large-scale presence of the Boss-Christian phenomenon:

> I share topics of faith during work [...] doing these activities can help to share the Gospel, I put my faith in my job and I can work for God as I share through the job the Gospel. My job is to build a platform to share thoughts not just among Christians, they come to the table to share 15 people only 5 are Christians. In the beginning the brothers could not understand, it is not common, if you serve you serve in the church but this is a bridge, some came to help in the beginning we were few, by the time it attracts more clients. (Bai, Wenzhou, Wenzhou, 20/08/2015)

Bai is a good example of what a Boss-Christian really is. During my visit in Wenzhou, I had the chance to interview him and to witness his strong work ethic mixed with a huge involvement in church activities. Bai first worked in the logistics, then from 2005 he started his own business for hardware accessories. In 2012 he opened a Photoshop store for weddings and in 2014 he started a café and center for social activities. Apart from his strong entrepreneurial spirit, Bai used his funds to support students to study theology in seminaries. He supports Chinese missionaries to Southeast Asia and he directs a fellowship of Laoban (Christian Bosses) in Wenzhou. During my visit I had the chance to attend such fellowship of Laoban and I had the privilege to interview Xun, a visionary businessman and president of that same association. As I interviewed him, he told me how important it was for him to find and promote a religious-based identity for his business:

> One year later the 'commerce fellowship' changed into a traditional church, I thought however that was important to maintain that emphasis on business, so that I created my new fellowship of commerce. [...] In the new fellowship I changed the target and became World Chinese Association not in the form of a church but as a voluntary association based on biblical values that can contribute the nation and give thoughts rooted in the Bible and in the thought of Christ with the purpose of having an economic growth. (Xun, Ibidem)

Xun is a great example of successful Boss-Christian in Wenzhou. He is also director of the fellowship of Laoban (Christian bosses). His association has a leading role in promoting the expression of religious values through the accomplishment of business success. Even when he had the chance to go back to a more traditional type of religious activities, he could not imagine to disconnect himself from his managerial activity and business. This led him to the decision of creating a new business fellowship which had a strong impact in the community of Wenzhou, especially among young boss-Christians. Cases like Yi or Qiang are very significant examples of Bosses (Laoban) also permeated by a vision for their business that goes beyond the mere working activity.

During my visit in Wenzhou, I also had the opportunity to attend a meeting of more than 30 Christian Bosses called 'commerce fellowship'. The meeting consisted of a lecture from professors both from Hong Kong and Wenzhou on how to be able to succeed in a financial crisis. The meeting started with a time of worship then several professors participating to the meeting spoke about business, trying to understand how to glorify God in the situation of economic crisis, how to become strategic with new forms of management, utilizing the web and other sources of information, adopting a new 'community economy'. This type of meetings promoted by the World Chinese Merchants Union Association encouraged the Boss-Christians to enter into a social network for business in order to achieve greater results with the change brought by the advent of e-commerce in China. Every business strategy however in this case found its origin in the principles of the Bible.

The case of Xun or Bai was not an isolated one. Those strongly involved in church leadership were also Christian bosses of multiple businesses. Yi during my interview gave his interpretation on the source of motivation for his business:

> I opened the first store and I was teacher on Sunday school. After graduating in 1993 I worked for ten years at the store but I was also part-time preacher [...] In the past there were a lot of part-time preachers, then I thought innovatively that the church is structured to enlarge itself, for this reason I changed the store into a multiple business, this is my reason [...] some companies don't know the management, I suggest to learn it [...] the other companies don't know how to plan, they only think about money and perhaps they even obtain them illegally. (Yi, Ibidem)

Yi found the motivation to increase his business in the application of a religious principle of multiplication. The success that came out of this strategy was evident: Yi managed directly 9 pharmaceutical stores all over the Zhejiang province. His company is objective-oriented and he was able last year to open 100 new stores in the Wenzhou area.

Another element confirmed by my visit in Wenzhou is the one of gender. Men and women alike were strongly involved in business creation and success. At the same time the religious interpretation seemed to remain the same in their personal interpretation of being a Boss-Christian woman:

> [...] we don't cheat people we give the ordered products, with reasonable prices, we don't invent false growth of sells, my sell is true we don't cheat. We give trust even if others cheat us. We don't share our faith with everybody but we [mostly] talk of production. (Min, Wenzhou, Wenzhou, 23/08/2015)

In Wenzhou after interviewing Min, I also visited the factory owned by her and Ju, two sisters that perhaps best represent the important role of women in business creation and economic success. Min and Ju are designers that together created and are currently running a factory for export of furnitures in Wenzhou. They also have an online store with Taubau and are very involved in export overseas, specially Europe. Min frequently travels to Europe to do business. Her company produces high-quality furniture and cabinets for big chains of shopping stores. Contrary to almost every factory in China, Min and Ju decided to change recently their production strategy and transform into a customer made production. They had the visionary strategy to change the image of 'made in China' from low-cost and low-quality products to good quality and reasonable prices. Min expresses her faith as a Boss-Christian woman in the way she manages her company and the workers. They have in the factory an area of rest for workers. She tries to treat the workers well and with respect, differently than most of the businesses around her in China.

During my visit in Wenzhou, I had the chance to interview also Du, a Boss-Christian woman that does business with chemical products for printing and packing, and a clothing store. Moreover, she is also a pastor in a huge house church at the last floor of a skyscraper in the financial area of Wenzhou. Chao is also another interesting case for what concerns the migratory process. She is a woman entrepreneur that I had the chance to interview in Wenzhou and that lived in Italy for thirteen years. Like many Chinese entrepreneurs, she was divided between their children living in China and relatives working in the diaspora. Chao was also able to integrate herself in the foreign context through a big Chinese church with more than 200 members. What is important to take into consideration behind the words of those women entrepreneurs like Min, is also that trust is a very rare element in today's Chinese society and is rarely displayed outside the circle of family.

Another element confirming the findings that I have witnessed in the diaspora concerns the role of the house church. Xiu, who I had the opportunity to interview during my visit in Wenzhou, is a Christian entrepreneur that owns a factory of LED lamps and exports them in the west through the contacts he has with believers of the Chinese churches in Italy. Mainly Bo, Deming and Shing, three Christian business partners, were selling those same type of LED lamps in Italy, produced by Xiu in his factory in China. Even in Wenzhou Xiu has many clients from the house church:

> I provide LED at church when it was built I provided the lamps with a cheap price, if you buy them in the regular market is expensive. Another church knows that I make LED lamps, some people introduce me and they let me build the lamps. […] We have many Christians, many people ask but ask because the prices are high. (Xiu, Pan Qsiao, Wenzhou, 28/08/2015)

Another element confirmed and deepened by the visit in Wenzhou was the assistant to the preconditions of my model on the *role of Sacred Scriptures* in business. During my visit in Wenzhou, when I attended the meeting of Boss-Christians called 'commerce fellowship', a group of visits to several Christian companies was publicized, in order to teach the participants how to use the Bible in order to do business, how to manage an enterprise, how to advance the values of a company and how to do effective advertising:

> I also follow lessons in Shanghai about Bible and management, then in Taiwan I follow the 'Joshua management' to follow and rule the business. The brothers helps me if I have difficulty, we talk and they help me with advices. This year for example I had great difficulties and the brothers gave me advice about what to do, which decision to take, it was very good. (Nai, Ibidem)

During my visit in Wenzhou, I also had the opportunity to interview Nai, a Boss-Christian who was also very involved in his house church, connected with a network of Christian fellowships for Bosses (Laoban). Nai is a manager of two factories of materials for hospitals in United States. Through connections with other Boss-Christians and applying principles of management from the Bible Nai wondered how to manage his company the best way, deciding to enlarge his factory, expanding his portfolio of clients, having a better communication according to international standards. Such emphasis on the Sacred Scriptures (*Literal reading of the Bible*) involved teaching and training focused on the application of biblical principles to business strategies such as 'being an agent of change', 'believing in the impossible', 'living with a purpose', 'having high expectations', 'living according to high moral standards', 'striving for excellence', etc.,....

But the greater and exhaustive example of the network role of house churches during my visit in Wenzhou came when, after participating in a 'Laoban fellowship', I had the privilege to interview Xun, an excellent case of Boss-Christian, president of the World Chinese Merchants Union Association and member of honor of the Chinese Chamber of Commerce. Xun worked in the clothing sector with his own brand and as a successful entrepreneur was involved in training younger Bosses like Bai. When Xun was telling me the story of his dramatic conversion to Christianity, he recounted how the real turning point of his life was when he met a 'commerce fellowship' of Boss-Christians, a place where Christians of all sorts, some Bosses, some party members, some University professors, met together to talk about business, something that let his faith to a drastic growth:

> In the commerce fellowship they were talking about business, it was a new world for me, my eyes were wide open. In this job life and business can go together, it was an important place for me a new earth. [...] Belonging to this association [Laoban fellowship] helps people to build relationships, it is like a part of the whole, a line inside a bigger composition that combines many contacts and every part is important, and the influence is big, from Wenzhou to Guangzhou or Shanghai. Our association has its points between the lines and its circles, some of them are interesting, all based on business. The impact is also on the development of personal talent, this is what we seek, the services of the Association help the industrial élite or other sectors. If we introduce the Gospel inside those points and lines and circles of relationship they will impact more areas of China, more businesses of what we by ourselves can do, it is very important. We have 200 areas combined, exhibitions, people that convert

[to Christianity], constant communications, we are all together somehow connected and we express the values that have their impact on business. (Xun, Wenzhou, Wenzhou, 22/08/2015)

The spiritual conversion of Xun occurred when he finally found the possibility to connect his business with his personal faith. As it is clear from his personal biographic reconstruction such choice to belong to the house church had its instrumental reasons, but it was not limited to them. Xun therefore felt like he was an 'helper', a support, a business consultant and a network promoter at work. He used his resources especially to help the young members of the Association. He shared his business wisdom with them and did a pioneering activity, asking experts to train young members of the Association to establish partnerships and share resources.

The visit in Wenzhou also helped me to look beyond the romantic representation of the phenomenon and to realize also the downfalls in the theoretical background. For example, during a focus group in Wenzhou Ya pointed out that, although Wenzhou still remains the capital of private economy in China, the city was facing a financial crisis at that moment. Many traditional businesses were failing, the government had a huge public debt and many companies were not able to face the crisis. Ya worked in a bank and gave a lot of loans to Christian entrepreneurs that were facing situations of economic debt, which caused discouragement and depression. Yet they remained confident and had hope that in the future the economy may grow back again. Economic risks, challenges and difficulties usually tended to cause stress, frustration and hypertension in any entrepreneurial activity and, if not addressed, they led to failure and substantial losses.

When it comes to facing economic risk, the visit to Wenzhou also helped me to see the consistency of the impact of the belief in PAS in the life of those entrepreneurs. When I was in Wenzhou I participated to meetings of Laoban with more than 30 Boss-Christians, a speaker talked about the importance to 'relax' and 'rest in God's salvation' as a legacy in front of the financial crisis that is taking place in China today. The same reaction was present in the entrepreneurs that I have interviewed, even though it was not possible to apply more prolonged techniques of observation due to limits of time.

Another interesting dimension that seems to confirm what I have observed in Italy was observed in Mainland China as well among entrepreneurs with no relationship at all with the Protestant faith. It has to do with being a minority in the diaspora. Can the fact of being a Chinese migrant in a condition of minority in and of itself lead to economic success? During my visit in China, I had the chance to interview Cheng, a Taiwanese migrant living and doing her business in China:

> In the beginning I had difficulties to get settled in China, the language was a problem, even if for me not so much since I'm from Taiwan, I'm strong and I was able to face the difficulty. (Cheng, Ibidem)

Cheng was an important exception to the study, the norm was to see Chinese people constantly migrating overseas not the other way around. The economic market in Taiwan during the past years was not doing so good, therefore Cheng decided to establish her own factory in China where labor costs were cheaper and there was the possibility to achieve higher profits in Wenzhou. However, with the rise of labor costs even in China she had to face challenges and economic risk. While in the other cases under my analysis, the migrants were coming out of China to the west, she was a migrant from Taiwan to China and expressed the same type of challenges, the same lack of network for support, added to the lack of cooperation from workers, who were just copying her design and re-selling it to other companies. Yet she was able to overcome those difficulties without any significant consequence on her work ethic. Therefore, Chinese migrants, when becoming a minority in the diaspora, usually are more oriented to pursue business. The reason why such minority-effect is not equally valid for other ethnic minorities will be analyzed in the following chapter where I move to non-Protestant entrepreneurs.

References

AA VV., 1990, *Economy and Society: Overviews in Economic Sociology*, London, Sage.

Burkett L., 1990, *Business by the Book. The Complete Guide of Biblical Principles for Business Men and Women*, Nashville, Thomas Nelson.

Cao N., 'Renegotiating Locality and Morality in a Chinese Religious Diaspora: Wenzhou Christian Merchants in Paris, France', in *Asia Pacific Journal of Anthropology*, Vol. 14 (Feb., 2013), pp. 85–101.

Vendassi P., 'Religious Change as Migration Chinese Converts to Christianity in Shanghai and in France', at Palacky University, Paper presentation (Nov. 2014).

Weber M., 1930, *The Protestant Ethic and the Spirit of Capitalism*, London, Unwin Hyman [ed. orig. 1905, *Die protestantische Ethik und der Geist des Kapitalismus*].

Wisman J. D., Davis M. E., 'Degraded Work, Declining Community, Rising Inequality, and the Transformation of the Protestant Ethic in America: 1870–1930', in *The American Journal of Economics and Sociology*, Vol. 72 (Nov., 2013), p. 1075.

CHAPTER 8

The Native Dimension of Chinese Capitalism

If you work hard enough at it, you can grind even an iron rod down to a needle.

—Chinese Proverb

8.1 A Purely Chinese Capitalism

8.1.1 Materialism

I come now to present the results of my investigation from the second group, made of Chinese entrepreneurs in Milan with no contact with the Protestant faith. The information collected from interviewing and job-shadowing Protestant entrepreneurs is then here compared with the second group of Chinese entrepreneurs with no link with the Protestant faith, in order to check the presence of other possible sociological explanations (Table 8.1).

This second sample of interviews points out the potential influence of several factors that may play some role in enhancing hard work and in contributing to economic success. This section may be an interesting test to understand the dynamic of economic success from a neutral perspective and see if the theory on the belief can still hold its value. The purpose of

O. Palombaro, *Christianity and Capitalism in China*,
https://doi.org/10.1007/978-981-97-3549-5_8

Table 8.1 List of the non-Christian entrepreneurs under investigation. The ones with the grey line were part of the job-shadowing activity and Luca is the Italian outsider

Nickname	Work Sector	City/Region of Origin	Age / gender	Date of the Interview
Shilin	Tailoring	Wenzhou	40 M	30/03/2015
Ruomei	Manager of Restaurant	Wenzhou	32 F	30/03/2015
Quan	Marketing	Zhejiang	26 M	23/04/2015
Quianfan	Store Manager in a café	Wenzhou	32 M	30/03/2015
Boqin	Boss of a corporation of entreprises	Zhejiang	45 M	26/03/2015
Ho	Shopkeeper in watches	Nanjing	26 M	30/03/2015
Chu Hua	Psycologist	Heilongjiang	19 F	28/03/2015
Fuhua	Customer Assistant in fashion	Laoning	28 F	20/06/2015
Chun	Bar and Tobacco shop Manager	Wenzhou	25 M	06/10/2015
Bao	Store manager in a restaurant	Wenzhou	24 F	30/03/2015
Mu	Store manager in a restaurant	Wenzhou	44 M	14/07/2015
Peng	Business advisor	Zhejiang	26 M	06/07/2015
Sheng	Store manager in a restaurant and business advisor	Wenzhou	23 M	08/07/2015
Ting	Food Consultant	Wenzhou	46 F	13/07/2015
Zan	Store Manager in clothing	Wenzhou	47 M	06/07/2015
Jiao-long	Store Manager in a restaurant	Wenzhou	51 M	30/01/2015
Cheng	Manager of a clothing factory	Tonglu	45 F	20/08/2015
Ju	Boss manager of a factory for furnishing	Wenzhou	29 F	24/08/2015
Mei	Boss of a clothing store for children	Tonglu	43 F	20/08/2015
Qi	Boss of a clothing factory	Tonglu	44 F	20/08/2015
Ping	Boss of a clothing factory	Tonglu	47 M	20/08/2015
Biming	Banker	Taizhou	26 F	22/09/2015
Luca	Bar and Tobaccco shop Manager	Milan	36 M	14/10/2015
Jing	Art Dealer	Chong Ching	34 M	22/01/2016
Lei	Founder of Sales website	Wenzhou	25 M	21/01/2016

(continued)

Table 8.1 (continued)

Jie	Restaurant and Bed & Breakfast Owner	Hebei	28 M	28/01/2016
Guiying	Photographer and Restaurant Owner	Beijing	27 M	21/01/2016
Ning	Waiter and Web Manager	Jilin	20 M	20/01/2016
Tao	Bar Owner	Wenzhou	31 M	30/01/2016
Chang	Restaurant Owner	Beijing	29 M	02/02/2016
Jian	Project Manager of a Travel Agency	Henan	28 M	15/02/2016
Jiahao	Multiple Restaurants Owner	Wenzhou	38 F	09/05/2016
Guozhi	Tobacco shop and bar Owner	Zheijian	34 M	31/05/2016

adding the second group was to check the presence of a *Wenzhou profit-oriented mentality* beyond any religious identity. More importantly, in the case of the second group this idea was in fact brought up by Fuhua:

> [hard work] depends on the area, in the Zhejiang province they work a lot, we from Beijing we want to work but we also want to enjoy life, so we understand better when is time to work, if there is free time I want to do what I like, for example knowing the culture, music, passing time with friends. (Fuhua, Ibidem)

> Wenzhouren are rich, traders, more ahead of us [rest of China], they have the basis to do business. A lot in quantity. At first they were doing export-import now they do food, and family is very important for them. [...] for me Wenzhouren are more narrow-minded, it is easier to enter if you are part of their group, they think we come from another planet [rest of China] the dialect, they are very closed with [Chinese] students. (Jing, Chong Ching, Milan, 22/01/2016)

> In Wenzhou the people are different, for them is not important to study, more important for them is money and work, since their grand-parents they don't focus on studies but on business [...] the culture of Wenzhou is different from north China [...] also there is more religion and superstition in Wenzhou [...] in that region they have a greater propensity toward the outside world. (Chu Hua, Ibidem)

Chu Hua goes even beyond the surface description of the phenomenon and tries to provide a cultural reason for such propensity for money and work in the area of Wenzhou. Before I go on explaining such possibility, I will orderly examine all the possible explanations that may potentially invalidate the model. First, I can easily reject the validity of any self-evident explanation which leans on the impact of the communist ideology (*Communist explanation*). Once again, Chu Hua, although growing up learning about the ideology as many of her colleagues, belongs to a second generation of migrants. Like many other Chinese people, she directly denies the reality of such ideology as a guide or source of identification. Very few people in China today, apart from the governmental elite, believe in Communism. After the economic reforms of 1979, Ting senses a radical change in Chinese society toward capitalism. The economic reforms re-directed the purpose of the people from a socialist project that in its nature was against entrepreneurship and private property, into an open effort to transform China into a capitalistic country:

> I've heard of Marx in class growing up [...] thirty years ago they believed in communism but when I was a child they didn't tell me anything, my parents work for the government but there is no identity in it, like government here in Italy, is not communism, nobody thing that anymore. (Chu Hua, Ibidem)

> [...] also the culture before the reform we always worked but now no more for Communism but for money. Chinese people think to be Communist but they are not! (Ting, Ibidem)

> In the case of Chinese people living outside of China we perceive communism in ideological and symbolic terms but inside China you don't feel this way, compared to the past now there is future, before there was the Chinese empire, then the civil war, finally freedom, we passed through the bad times of cultural revolution that damaged our culture, but after the political opening we are close to the western society, we study the market system economy, the market economy, the project economy. We also had many influences from the Soviet Union, we learned from them, they failed because they didn't used a capitalistic system like the one of United States. Thirty years ago China had already abandoned the ideology of communism, today the Chinese don't talk anymore of communism or defend the ideology. (Quan, Wenzhou, Milan, 23/04/2015)

Quan holds what I consider a more polite view of the Communist ideology. She acknowledges the benefits that Communism may had played for her country, and she is reluctant to address governmental control. In any case, Quan acknowledges that nobody among the common people in China believes anymore in Communism and in its ideology. The only indirect role that Communism might have played in the economic realm was its ability to uniform the country and bring it to a necessary level of cohesion. This became important in the following economic development of China. The fact that the Communist ideology has lost its priority in the lives of most people in China today however does not mean that communism does not exert a central role anymore. In fact, many are the examples still possible to notice today in China of a strong control over the mind and the social views of people. For example, the system of education in China is still today controlled by the government, permeated by a Marxist ideology that indirectly exalts the value of work on a macro-level. The Communist explanation can nevertheless be dismissed as having any guiding economic role other than a negative one toward capitalism.

Also, in the biographical records of the older generation, a sense of exploitation by the government emerged, all the way from the cultural revolution. This was hindering any form of economic development. From 1979, with the end of 'real communism' on the other hand, Chinese workers were finally left free to trade, and quickly China was transformed by the hard work of its people. I can see in several cases the signals the presence of a form of Stakhanovism, a willingness to work under constraint due to the lack of human rights. For example, Minzhe was recalling the fact that many Chinese people come in the diaspora with false documents and work in a factory spending their whole time trying to pay off their debts:

> In Prato I've met a woman in the factory that didn't speak, her son died in the factory, she stayed and doesn't want to go back to China, her heart broke. The bosses do pressure but also workers want to work they are the same, the majority in clothing sector. (Minzhe, Ibidem)

This leads us to consider the possibility of the *Constriction explanation*. From the descriptions of Boqin, Fuhua or Mu it is possible to identify the struggles of the first generation of migrants, coming from the surrounding countryside of the province of Wenzhou, who started their business with no background or education. The peculiarity of those people was simply a strong desire to escape poverty:

> [...] among farmers [first generation immigrants] where everybody knows that to survive in China the population has always been numerous then everybody knows that in order to survive they need to work, the land. (Sheng, Ibidem)

> First of all in their generation the condition of life in China thirty years ago was that everybody was poor, they suffered, they are afraid of poverty, then they transmit also to the next generation those bad memories, and [desire to escape] bad life. (Boqin, Ibidem)

> In the Zhejiang province they work harder because they are very poor, they come from the countryside [...] they didn't come as regular immigrants, how they managed to arrive in Italy? Many died. Therefore surely when they arrived they tried to work and gain money. (Fuhua, Ibidem)

> From the beginning my parents worked very hard, the money wasn't there, the food was missing, I saw my parents working hard and I wanted to have the same thing. (Mu, Ibidem)

> We Chinese guys work faster, work is work, we must do it. Even with foreigners but is slower, they come in late [...]. To work hard is normal in China, before us an Italian group had twenty products but we are forced to do more. Friday I finished working but the Italians want that we work on the Photoshop. We are forced. Work not as much as us, they are lazy. (Guiying, Milan, Beijing, 21/01/2016)

> Among all my friends I arrived that we didn't have anything, we sweated and worked hard, giving up a lot, there was no holiday and no Sunday. My first holiday was when my son was 4 years old, for decades I didn't have any holiday. And to us not to do any holiday or Sunday rest, for us is normal, if there is work to do you work, if you have this lifestyle you don't have that need, you don't even think about it. (Jiahao, Milan, Wenzhou, 09/05/2016)

> We work hard in order to work and have more money, I work so much until three in the morning to live a better life, to make more money. (Qi, Ibidem)

During my visit in China, I had the chance to visit the factory owned by Qi. The machines were working twenty-four hours a day with turns of sixty years old women. Such type of factory, so common in China is a witness of the reality of Stakhanovism due to the lack of human rights and a desire to escape from poverty. The direct consequence of this evasion from poverty is therefore a willingness to work hard, to the point of having no personal will of their own, no desire to change their condition of being exploited as it is the case of Shilin or as indirectly described by Sheng:

> I come from Wenzhou and in China I've worked as a tailor and working here it has been painful, it was a painful experience, all that I do is the tailor as it was in China so here. (Shilin, Wenzhou, Milan, 30/03/2015)

> [...] The economic crisis led me to open the restaurant in the middle of the crisis and I must say we opened the restaurant during the crisis and we didn't feel it, you feel it if you have a comparison with the previous years. (Sheng, Ibidem)

> Yes I work hard because there is competitiveness, if you want to have a career but you don't work for it others will substitute you. We Chinese are more willing to sacrifice, is culture, since the state was never free or democratic, we are not like you [Italians] that pretend. (Biming, Ibidem)

> The Chinese people work hard, before they were poor, having the possibilities now we do a lot of efforts. The lifestyle is different, we are interested in the next generation. For me work is to have money good life and wealth for the kids. (Ping, Tonglu, Tonglu, 20/08/2015)

During my visit in China, I had the chance to see the factory of Ping whose produce is exported outside of China through the help of a trading company. Ping pointed out during the interview how the realm of rights at work in China is finally changing. Workers require a higher salary since the costs of life and inflation in China are rising. Many of those wholesale factories have dislocated to south-east Asia, where the labor cost is cheaper. Ping points out then an important consideration concerning the limit of this potential impact represented by the constriction explanation. This shows how drastic and important was the change that took place in the 1990s with the advent of the second cycle of migration, mainly from the urban part of Wenzhou to the west. Consequently, we saw the rise in the role of the second generation of immigrants in the economy of the diaspora. Such transformation that Jiao-long, Ting and Quan describe, reveals the centrality of these recent interesting developments. The constriction and lack of human rights today are under challenge. This will change the way work is understood in China, beyond the idea of cheap labor common in the public opinion:

> When we arrived here we wanted a better future from the 1990's we arrived in many, the food safety was hard in China. I worked first as a dishwasher, then at the restaurant, then as a cook assistant lifting the level. (Jiao-long, Ibidem)

> At first the Chinese worked in a factory but since the 90's it starts the import-export, the power of investment, the possibility to invest [...] the Chinese gain few [money]? He saves money, he works four-teen hours, twenty hours... he works and always like to work the Chinese, also the culture before the reform always worked. (Ting, Ibidem)

> After the 90's life, everything has changed, in the 30's everybody was trying to survive, find a job, help their family [...] those who are born in the 90's didn't have any difficulties, China has changed, people didn't work with difficulties anymore, but the past generation passed this tradition [of working hard], the new generation search freedom, to travel, to have a good life. (Quan, Ibidem)

> The question is it is a class of different people, first all those Chinese from the country came, especially from Zhejiang, they don't understand what is the great power that is developing China and they remained at the mentality of those years. The last generation is growing as soon as they enter diverse sectors and places. (Peng, Ibidem)

The turning point represented by the 1990s and the advent of a new social class shows how a constriction explanation is no longer valid today and it will not be valid for the upcoming future in China. Furthermore, although such explanation frequently emerged from the data in both groups, especially in the case of first-generation migrants, it is still unclear how such constraint can lead to accomplish economic success. If someone were to compare this social group with many other cases of constriction, for example, the exploitation of children in Africa, it doesn't necessary brings to same output and the same propensity to work hard. On the contrary, those cases under constriction in the long term are a limit to economic success. They block the power of action in the individual and all his potentials. Constriction is indeed still a reality among Chinese migrants, as results from job-shadowing demonstrated, but constriction does not act as a catalyst for economic success.

In light of such challenges, and the alienation caused by work, it is clear how the Christian entrepreneur tries to find an elaborate system of beliefs to instead give meaning and purpose to his economic activity, even by pushing himself to achieve economic success. The question may rise on how do Chinese entrepreneurs with no relationship with Protestantism react to this challenge. What pushes them toward the accomplishment of economic success? Frustration and lack of meaning in the job is often evident among those entrepreneurs and there is no substitute to this system of belief. On the contrary, there is no corresponding long-term purpose for their working activity. In the case of Fuhua or Shilin, purpose leaves room to a materialistic enjoyment of commodities, a love of money that is common to all history:

> […] I want to gain money, I want to find meaning in life, that I'm important, I wanted to be important, to serve others, I want to learn to know other people at work, trying to improve myself. (Fuhua, Ibidem)

> In China work is very important, I want a house, gold, I want to live, to have a car and live in a better world and I work more for this reason. I don't have dreams I just wish my life can be more comfortable […] I just would like to live better in the future. (Shilin, Ibidem)

> My dream is to have an happy life despite work, I do a job to gain and have a better life, to travel, to have money therefore working hard. (Jie, Hebei, 28/01/2016)

> Like everybody want to have success, Chinese people are ambitious, they always want to go higher, I've worked here, if there is no channel to go up then maybe I need to change and work in another place, the best enterprise realize my dream. (Quan, Ibidem)

It is true that also for the first group of entrepreneurs, the love of money sometimes was linked to the desire of receiving social acceptance. In this case, money became an instrumental motivation for the achievement of other goals which change from person to person. But in this circumstances, money and prosperity is just a desire that has no link with any practical step to achieve it, nor is it connected to any sort of higher purpose able to enhance motivation in the individual. Quan nevertheless shows a strive for success, but the source of such success is not the same type. Many entrepreneurs like him have a desire to grow their business simply because they enjoy money and they want to get rich. There is nothing new again here similar to the spirit of capitalism. The absence of values does not seem to make any substantial difference, whether it is atheism or agnosticism and even in the case of other forms of religiosity such as Buddhism. Many of those non-Protestant entrepreneurs identify themselves as Buddhists, in few cases as Confucians or Daoists. These religions hold to a radically different set of beliefs compared with Protestantism and their degree of identification with these religious is very unstable. I will treat Confucianism in a separate section on the *Cultural explanation* more, yet what we can say here is that the religious practice is perceived by Ruomei as totally separated from his business, a completely different dimension of life with no influence whatsoever on work:

> I'm Buddhist, I don't know if Buddha helped me in difficulties because I can't see paradise, I cannot touch it. (Ruomei, Ibidem)

There seems to be so far then no clear and strong source of purpose and meaning for the job of an entrepreneur, whether in trying to orient his view of work, to have a vision for his business or in stimulating the emotional background necessary to face difficulties. Work, therefore, by many of those entrepreneurs, is often perceived just as a necessity, an obligation that becomes even a burden being migrants (*Minority explanation*). Ruomei, Boqin, Quianfan and Quan expressed openly their personal struggle to integrate themselves in the context of the diaspora. Among many migratory groups, Chinese people, while strongly involved in work, still live in heavy isolation from society. They are a very tight group, difficult to access from outsiders, and also hardly welcomed by the hosting country in the diaspora because of fear of competition. A consequence of this unhappy state of things is a necessity to work hard, even above the legal levels allowed (even above 48 working hours each week) without having any legal contract, not the ideal realm of success:

> For the Chinese work is important because family needs to eat not as the other Italians, we have children, we need to bring them to school. (Ruomei, Wenzhou, Milan, 30/03/2015)

> We work hard because life is hard, we are in a foreign land, if I don't work is difficult [...] we have worked so hard as Chinese here then we go back to China at sixty years old, but we need to work hard in order to accumulate cash. (Boqin, Ibidem)

> We work to live, for example you Italians go to school without paying, when you are sick you go to the hospital without paying, in China school and hospital you need to pay, so we work harder for the future, in order to have more money. For us Chinese when we will be old there will be no money to live, so the Chinese works double the time, we work 16–17 hours for kids, for expenses, all has a cost. (Quianfan, Wenzhou, Milan, 30/03/2015)

> Our process is a hard process of socialization, in the same way Italians in the past were immigrants in other countries so for us in China we are passing through this phase now [...] the previous generation of Chinese and us, we are divided in two, one part is studying [in italian schools] so is easier to enter in the Italian society, the other part is undecided and out of the Italian society, they live among themselves. (Quan, Ibidem)

Those migrants from Wenzhou identify their social condition of minority as a cause of their working hard. The question however must be formulated this way: is it because of their position as an ethnic migrant minority that those entrepreneurs work hard? If someone was to compare different migrant communities living in the west (sub-Saharan, South American, etc.,) with the Chinese it is undoubtedly evident that, even if they share the status of minority, they do not all reach the same outcome in the realm of work. In fact, although they live in an even more minoritarian condition than Chinese migrants, all often perform opposite outcomes. Many migrants show no intention at all toward hard work. Being a minority, although at times still being innovative, migrants act as a bridge between two cultures. Yet their status does not necessarily cause them to work hard nor it necessarily lead them to achieve economic success.

8.1.2 Chinese Networks

Coming to the major aspect that seems to play an important role and that may be a potential explanatory factor beyond the Protestant model, especially among Wenzhou Chinese entrepreneurs, is the lineage, strong family ties. In both of my samples, I have observed how often building and acting within networks with Chinese people in a foreign context suddenly became a crucial component. This was especially true for beginning, progressing and accomplishing business transactions. All of the sudden, when a Chinese migrant joined the diaspora, he became part of the 'big family' of all Chinese migrants, regardless of cultural differences between local regions, differences that were no longer crucial in the new context (*Network explanation*). This does not mean that those differences disappear or that local or family networks cease to bear their effect. It reveals however that in situations of major challenges, such as migrating to another country, those differences are suddenly replaced instrumentally by a more general Chinese 'national pride'.

As I have already alluded for the case of Christian entrepreneurs, networks do have a place, depending on their different levels and complex interrelations (whether family, associations, mafia, circle of friends). It is therefore crucial to define more clearly what kind of network operates successfully in the realm of business. The first major role of the network can be found in the weak ties provided by adhering to a Chinese association. This refers to cases of associations for Chinese businesses like Boqin, Mu, Ting and Zan or to other social groups like the case of Peng and Sheng. Sometimes the network provided by association, helped the individual to find a job, like in the case of Ting. Jian during my interview explained how Peng helped him in the realm of his business:

> I've met Peng the owner of the agency, he placed me as a project manager. [...] Peng thinks I am good as a project manager, now I calculate the prices and I look for co-workers among businesses. [...] Peng is the director of both Chinese agencies. Peng and many other entrepreneurs are among those that start a business then they bring it to completion and open a new one. (Jian, Milan, Henan, 15/02/2016)

Jian points out here what I mentioned in previous chapters on the role of networks in business creation and multiplication. Basically, Jian took charge of the business started by Peng, while Peng moved along with a new one. In other cases, it is the circle of friends that plays this role, like for Biming, who was introduced to her job because of her friend who already worked there. Tao, on the other hand, due to the key location of his business in Chinatown and his wide range of influence in the Chinese context, experienced success in his business from a variety of network links: from his circle of friends to the associations, his family, all the way to mass media:

> I started this business with my parents they put finances and mental support. Friends then loaned money, them too young, cleaning, counseling, working together, we've known each other since we grew up together. I subscribed to UNIIC of the second generation of entrepreneurs, the other associations are less used for culture. We grew up here and we help each other culturally for language and bureaucracy, passing information. Each of us does his own business. (Tao, Milan, Wenzhou, 30/01/2016)

More commonly, however, associations connect Chinese businesses, that already exist, together with the purpose of sharing skills and ideas and getting financial help. Such support is crucial in a foreign context, already challenging without the knowledge of the local language. Therefore, this kind of network is useful in the first stages of a business, in order to make connections with entrepreneurs that otherwise, in the words of Mu, 'will not be able to survive situations of economic crisis'. Networks here, like for the case of house churches, provide financial and social support through the flow of information and financial credit. In many cases this network instead of creating business is important for the further development of business, through the passing of information mentioned by Peng. Just as house churches, networks of associations provide also the necessary trust from clients, as Sheng points out. This becomes a sign of identity for many of those entrepreneurs, like Mu.

In their business card I saw how many of those businessmen tend to emphasize their being a president or their being members of Chinese associations, as an element of identity and a distinguishing mark among the other Chinese migrants. All this may confirm the idea that associations can play a similar role to the house church. It must be remembered, however, that networking was only one of the functions displayed by house churches. The main aspect that Weber pointed out about house churches was its fostering individual propensity to business through a control of the conduct among its members. This element is missing here. Surely through associations there is a flow of money, workforce and mutual financial help based on relations of friendship. Operating like weak ties therefore the associations do play a crucial role in the beginning phase of business:

> We have many partners more than ten, many members, a big entrepreneurial network that has competences and personal nodes, mainly somebody may have technical or economic skills in order to help others without them, sharing their channel of knowledge. (Boqin, Ibidem)

> The associations that I'm part of are non profit, the money is based on donations, the purpose is to help the Chinese companies here, if somebody wants to open a business we give some opinions and help, the members open a new job, we give the communications that circulate about offers, another aspect of China is that if there are groups they give economical aid or direction. To be enrolled and boss of an association is also an element of identity, we serve the people, we are connected with the Italian government for events, we organize dinners where we invite the major, then the second generation of Chinese in Italy is also involved. The financial crisis of 2008 has touched but hard work and mutual collaboration can resolve the problems. (Mu, Wenzhou, Milan, 14/07/2015)

> I do business consultancy [...] for many Chinese and Italian enterprises [...] contacts, the passing of word that we do, we occupy several sectors, design, eco-marketing, accountancy, business consultancy. Often a passing of word of the Chinese associations through many events and parties between communities, receiving friends, we engage a lot in community but bringing the members of the associations to do the most useful things for our business [...] in the difficult times that are common when you enter into the work realm I am lucky to have my Chinese friends that helped me both economically and psychologically. The office of consultancy in the beginning was hard, nobody wants to help you. The help we received from friends and we started to do the job. (Peng, Zejiang, Milan, 06/07/2015)

> Concerning the associations [...] we are active for the entrepreneurs of the first generation, UNIIC we are the first of the second generation then ASSOCINA [...] our purpose is to integrate better and enhance synergy with the Italian associations and institutions. Since we are identified as Chinese entrepreneurs they give us a connotation then we make this thing

fruitful [...] among the restaurants we are the most affirmed, the associations they know us, in the beginning there was suspicion, they weren't used to a Chinese opening an Italian store, if Chinese we demonstrated that it is not so, it was sufficient to demonstrate first that we are also Italians because we grew up here and the entrepreneur is independent from the ethnicity and is enough to be and use adequate professionals. (Sheng, Ibidem)

I'm the vice-president of the Association of entrepreneurs from Wenzhou [...] the associations of entrepreneurs [...] and the Association of the Chinese women of whom I'm part of we had a project to help the hospital [...] then this helped me to find a job, among Chinese we help each other for business, we loan money, we create corporations, huge activities. (Ting, Ibidem)

I am president of the Association of Chinese Enterprises in Italy, Chinese enterprises overseas [...]. In my activity in the beginning I received help from friends and family members [...] the association that I manage first of all there are clear information between the organization and the members, they, among the information if there are difficulties of the entrepreneur give help then among each other they have a budget on prices and value so that the economy will not ruin. Perhaps somebody in the economy of crisis undersell and they do things that were out of their own individual possibilities. (Zan, Ibidem)

Sometimes those weak ties provided by associations go even beyond the national borders and connect together in a macro-level several migrant communities. The large and broad expansion of networks is very important again in moments of widespread economic crisis. Since cooperation involves several countries and a wide spectrum of businesses, it is almost impossible for people like Jiao-long to be cut off from the market. Leaning on the reciprocal support, the friendship that Ruomei and other entrepreneurs build up during the years always results to pay back its benefits:

I am friend with the owner of the restaurant here at Sarpi avenue. With him we are in common with the Chinese association in Milan of which I am the president [...]. Opening the restaurant I had a debt in four countries, from Spain, from China, from Spain, from Holland... and they helped me, we help together, if a friend is in difficulty I help him therefore is mutual. We were already friends before, we were part of the same association, we

> helped one another. I had a family member here then in the 1990's and I came here, then my kids and little by little all Chinese people are like that we start with someone selling and then followed by the family. In the economic crisis I have been influenced a lot, the restaurant diminished especially this year. The expenses diminish but we will see how to do it. For the most part I trust my friends if I have problems, work diminished but there is always somebody that is not touched, we keep on resisting, if we have problems friends will help us. (Jiao-long, Wenzhou, Milan, 17/07/2015)

> Sometimes we needed a lot of money to let the business go on, then we asked money to our [Chinese] friends that live here. (Ruomei, Ibidem)

Concerning the main idea of this book then, social networks between Chinese entrepreneurs seem to play its role, especially in situations of economic risk and crisis, regardless of the presence of a belief in PAS. I did not indeed consider the religious as the possible explanation. If the network is considered as the main final explanation for economic success, however, then every typology of network in business should bring economic success.

Before jumping to a way too optimistic conclusion about the role of networks in business, we must therefore take into consideration that many of those network are managed by Chinese mafia. When I've interviewed Ting, she mentioned the role of Chinese mafia which in many of those circles of businesses is predominant and unhealthy. It exploits the network structure. Ting was surprised that I did not asked her about the role of mafia. Although she found herself to be reluctant in giving me more details about this aspect, she made it clear that Chinese mafia was very pervasive inside those business networks. Even if not as a prevalent form of business, Chinese crime in Milan as in other parts of Europe played some role. From the first arrival of the migrant in the diaspora often the Chinese worker who is already in debt is forced to stay under the constraint of a boss that is compromised through illegal traffic and crime-related networks. Sometimes those activities involve prostitution, drugs, technology counterfeit, money laundry, gambling, false documentation, etc. All those illegal activities often undermine the business that goes on the surface. Those activities are often taking place through many forms of violence and despotism. Sometimes those hidden activities sadly touch also associations and social groups recognized on a public level (Ceccagno and Rastrelli 2008). In this case networks become then a negative social structure, based on corrupt relations which end damaging the very nature of business success.

Someone may more rightly say then that network sometimes is an instrument to business success even if it is not always used in an efficient way among Chinese entrepreneurs. If that were the case then networks, regardless of their specific nature and content are a guarantee for a financial support. Secondly, and more importantly, the social network provided here by the Chinese associations or circles of friends, was intended, when functioning properly, to give help in situations of economic risk, to guarantee the *survival* of a certain business, not its economic success. The case of the belief in PAS on the other hand directly pushed toward economic success. Furthermore, I witnessed many cases where instead, belonging to an association made no difference at all for business, especially because of internal divisions and antagonism in the network. Network in both samples provided important resources in several stages of the business trajectory without becoming a sure way to success.

A case for the role of network explanation for economic success is made fully for *house churches*[1] but not for networks in general. There is a substantial difference on the way a house church network operates compared with general social networks. Chinese groups of migrants in the diaspora in general can be considered as families in kinship relation, particular associations that generally are not very supportive of one another. It involves individuals with distinct interests, who are only occasionally united with boundaries of reciprocal unity. Even while belonging to a specific network, they still see each other more as competitors. Their relationship is always subordinate to their individual interests connected with their business (Ceccagno and Rastelli 2008). The house church on the other hand works as an all-encompassing form of social network that unites under a committed identity an otherwise fragmented complex group of business resources.

[1] Apart from providing a network of connections the house churches have the supplemental role of motivating their members to the achievement of economic success. When it comes to economic success the house church surpass any other form of network explanation. But even among the house churches this is just partially valid, only in what concerns the emphasis on performance and control of the conduct, not the network in its generic nature.

Some of the points made by Quianfan, Jiao-long and Zan introduce here what can be considered as a sub-section of the network explanation on the role of lineage and family. Lineage is culturally very strong in China, especially in this area of Wenzhou. Business in fact for the majority of the cases under my investigation was almost never just based on one individual. The extended family was investing as a whole into a specific business. The extended family becomes therefore the first place where the economic network starts and develops. Lineage and extended family helped Quianfan or Mu and many others to find a job. The family helped Quianfan also to initiate the business through their financial support necessary for a new activity. I had the chance to witness this many times during my research. The financial support from the family, which is possible because of the trust present in the family, helps Ting and many others to avoid the request of loans from the bank. Similar role is the one of Qi's family in giving advice, provide clients and offer maintenance of machines, something so crucial at the starting point of a factory. The role of family in Qi's business reveals the importance of the lineage network through granting necessary resources. These sources are needed in order to do successful business, have customers and get advice and skills otherwise hard to find. In the case of Ting the family helped reducing transaction costs too:

> I've found this job when I was still in China, the boss is a relative of my wife then we bought this business[...] my father is a little bit rich and I want a little bit of strength to work for my children. Also, my parents helped me to buy and start the business. (Quianfan, Ibidem)

> The Chinese families help their sons, the brothers, or the parents. Among Chinese is easier to loan money, it is a common custom, not like in Italy, Chinese people do everything by giving their word. (Ting, Ibidem)

> First my uncle wanted to rent a restaurant but then they closed and then the mother of Bingwen advice me to start a business like that. [...] The family helped, how to repair a machine then I improve in the purchases, I started the business, if there's no business the mother of Bingwen will give me some orders that she had. (Qi, Tonglu, Tonglu, 20/08/2015)

> I worked for seven years and then I became the boss of the restaurant. My sister was the boss of the restaurant, she needed a cook so they let me work thanks to the family. (Mu, Ibidem)

> When the parents need help searching to open their own restaurant we help one another […] When I came here I arrived with my parents in the restaurant of my parents. (Peng, Ibidem)

> My parents wanted that I will do business to make more money […] my parents wanted that I marry a businessman and that I may be rich with him. (Zhong, Pan Qsiao, Wenzhou, 28/08/2015)

This last point made by Zhong shows how lineage and the family in the cultural context of Wenzhou enhance the propensity to do business. Zhong felt a lot of social pressure from parents to start a business and be successful in it. In the surrounding environment of Wenzhou every family had at least somebody in the family involved in entrepreneurial activity. The role of family and lineage, therefore, specifically in the area of Wenzhou, goes beyond a mere financial factor. It has its cultural implications, as it is able to shape the propensity to work hard and start new businesses. Ho talked about a circular relationship between parents and sons, a strong view of family relationships, in part rooted in ancestor worship. According to this belief one generation invests in the next and the next generation must pay back what was received. The financial help received must therefore be paid back and all this cultural emphasis on family ends up pushing the individual toward business early in his life. In fact, compared with other ethnicities entrance in work-life among those entrepreneurs from Wenzhou starts very early:

> The parent teach his son to work, is in the culture. Is the family, in part also school, that promote this. (Boqin, Ibidem)

> At first I worked to survive then for the kids of the second generation. Because of the Chinese thinking we must earn something to pass it to the next generation. We Chinese if you gain 1.000 then you spend 200 whereas you Italians if you gain 1.000 you spend 1.000. (Mei, Tonglu, Tonglu, 20/08/2015)

> There is a dream and an objective in me, then the family for which I have to provide specially for children, that they may have a good education. (Cheng, Taiwan, Tonglu, 20/08/2015)

> I work hard, and the reason is to help the family. Parents helped to work and to invest to start this restaurant, investing. […] the family wanted me

> to come here, the family wants that I'm here [...] my family is the one that have built this business. (Bao, Wenzhou, Milan, 30/05/2015)

> The purpose of work is to gain money, first of all, when you have four parents and three children you must pay a lot then you need to gain money [...] then family is important because is a passage from a father to a son the family enterprise. We Chinese work for the children when the daughter is well it is easier. (Chao, Ibidem)

> We work to have a better life compared to others then for the family and for the next generation. [...] The people from Wenzhou is seen by us as work hard and an heart for business. (Qi, Ibidem)

> I believe for every Chinese work is done for the children, it is like a circle between parents and children, you expect an economic return from your children upon whom you have invested [...] the purpose is always to have a good life, our culture you see is different. We don't have holidays, we want that our children live in a good situation we want to have a good life and more money give you a better life, working hard, you are more busy but then you gain more money, the people that come here wants to make money. (Ho, Nanjing, Milan, 30/03/2015)

> I helped my parents in their business of manufacture [...] save money, and then this to maintain the parents, the Chinese families tended to be very numerous, many kids were maintaining better the parents. [...] The family helps because there is the Italian family enterprise that has difficulties but it has always been the stronghold. It is important with more eyes the owner gets the horses to be fat. We do a communion. Then the family favors you with loans there is also an use of patronage and revenue. (Sheng, Wenzhou, Milan, 08/07/2015)

Lineage and family, however, compared with the more wide and all-encompassing influence of associations and circle of friends, have a more limited economic influence in space and time. In other words, if asked about the benefits of all the economic contributions received through this heterogeneous forms of networks, lineage and family play a more marginal role. Without other sources of help, it would not be possible for them to continue their business.

8.1.3 Cultural Value of Work

I said earlier that in the second group of entrepreneurs I witnessed the absence of any correspondent to the system of beliefs of Protestant entrepreneurs. Nothing that could give a purpose or meaning beyond the mere acquisition of money common to all mankind. This can be seen for example in the answer of Ruomei to the question in the interview on 'what is the main purpose in your work'? Every component, such as targeting a job, having a higher purpose or a sense of calling seems to be absent:

> I don't have a target, I have no purpose, I just want to live here and live a decent life (Ruomei, Ibidem)

> I never thought about the purpose of work, not like my sister, for me is just part of life. (Ju, Wenzhou, Wenzhou, 24/08/2015)

Ju is an interesting case, because she is the sister of Min and, together with her, she established a factory for furnishing on an international scale. Differently from her sister, however, Ju is not a Christian and therefore does not see any specific purpose behind her work. In reality Ju was still able to display a strong hard work mindset. Since she was not able to find a company, she decided together with her sister to build one. So, in Ju there may be the presence of a profit-oriented mentality yet it is only partial. Since this potential explanation has no all-encompassing religious system of beliefs to match what seen among Protestant entrepreneurs, the main focus must be re-directed toward a more ***cultural explanation***:

> Wenzhou does not have raw material, therefore we do business. It is a tradition in Wenzhou, we pay attention to the financial business, from parents, compared with other cities we have a financial education since childhood. (Ju, Ibidem)

> The Chinese mentality in the last 30 years is changed, now the important thing is money. The economic reform changed the desires of the people [...]. For the Chinese somebody that works has success, it doesn't matter if the cat is black or white, says a Chinese proverb, what matters is if he catches the mouse. Life is based on money. (Ting, Wenzhou, Milan, 13/07/2015)

Even while Ting tends to justify the presence of hard work among Chinese people because of the institutional changes in China after the economic reforms and 'open door' policies of 1979, she still adds other cultural elements. It is in this case that according to Fuhua the area of Wenzhou finds its geographical, historical and cultural uniqueness, compared to other areas of China. Wenzhou fostered an entrepreneurial spirit. Just as other cities in the west, played a central role in trade impacting cultural traits of those cities all the way to today so it is with Wenzhou. Wenzhou has an entrepreneurial spirit as a cultural trait. In fact, Mu, Zan or Ho describe the details of such Wenzhou's entrepreneurial culture when they point out the common desire of every true citizen to open a new business, becoming the owner of a small-medium business:

> Like us we want to become important but they [the people from Wenzhou] want to have a bar, a restaurant, something that they can decide despise the fact that they don't have a lot of skills, but they work a lot [...]. Like the Italian people come from the south to the north, is different it depends from the culture, the social environment. Like in Genoa people are more stingy in the same way Wenzhou's province, many years ago I saw their boss of the restaurant is thirty or forty years old, they are the first generation that came in Italy [...] I saw a lot of people becoming very rich. (Fuhua, Ibidem)

> People from Wenzhou are very smart, they know how to gain money. We people from the north have the head, we think and we do, they are more practical, they find many ways to live and gain money, they came early [in Italy]. We from the north don't have a lot of will, 100 euros are enough, a travel... they [from Wenzhou] spend a lot of hours for living and working. (Chang, Beijing, 02/02/2016)

> [...] Wenzhou I don't know why they are like that, they want to be on their own, to make money, in my opinion is a cultural thing, is like the Jews, they want to do things for themselves. (Biming, Milan, Taizhou, 22/09/2015)

> Wenzhou, we that come from there we work a lot from generation to generation we passed on this thing, we have the culture of working hard. We have the common desire to reach our own propriety, to open and manage our own personal business, the desire to not depend from others

[…] I don't want to make money but however I want to be the boss of this activity. (Mu, Ibidem)

This is a Chinese trait that the more you work, the more you get reward then the majority of China are all that want to work they need to have a business then by the time the business went well and there is improvement. There is a little bit of difference, the area of Wenzhou the majority of people has interest on work. As the president of China says we from Wenzhou are there, are able to be the boss but also to be dependent and sleep in the pavement, they have a different heart, they are able to endure different situations. Is a provenance from the ancestors, fathers, grandfathers, so then this culture is inherited. (Zan, Wenzhou, Milan, 06/07/2015)

[…] it's a way to contribute to society, to have your own company, personal, if you do it you feel honored, you've succeed in working hard, you help the family, the society, people esteem you, they respect you and they clap at you because you are ambitious. (Ho, Ibidem)

From the Chinese culture we work a lot, when we were kids the parents were teaching us to be workers and educated with the people, to be educated you go to work, you keep the things to do and wealth comes for your family […] if you are employee is easy because you take a salary and you continue life, my job [entrepreneur] has the value of discover the rest of the world, and interesting things to see, to have more dignity […] I believe we have a future to make I don't know which but I seek to do the right thing to do. (Peng, Ibidem)

Our Chinese tradition push us to work in this way, we Chinese have in mind money: he who has more money is respected, we try to be better. (Jiao-long, Ibidem)

Peng and Jiao-long pointed out how important it is to promote the social model of the successful independent entrepreneur able to achieve things with his own hands. Enlai during my ethnographic observations pointed out how people from Wenzhou, due to this cultural trait, would feel more satisfied in owning their own business rather than being the CEO of a rich multi-national company. Among the non-Christian entrepreneurs it is interesting what Chun says concerning this matter:

> I think that our mentality of Wenzhou, people like to do things on their own [concerning business] first starting with others then with others then finding their own [business], it is in our blood, different from north China, without any help from government we built our own entrepreneurship in a free market. (Chun, Ibidem)

It is this desire to work independently that becomes the basis of the Wenzhou's entrepreneurial spirit. But what can be the cultural trait able to account for such entrepreneurial spirit which could go hand in hand, or even work as a substitute, for the Protestant ethic? When a certain sociological factor (*Yi Xiang* and others) plays a definite role on the formation of an *ethos* useful in the realm of business, if an alternative factor it is said to intervene, or even to replace its effect, it must be similar in kind. The role of such cultural explanation becomes therefore clearer when understood in religious terms, involving a specific set of beliefs. I have already shown how Daoism and Buddhism, two main systems of belief part of Chinese culture, are substantially incompatible and opposed to the beliefs of the theoretical model for Protestant entrepreneurs. From the interviews of this second group, a stronger emphasis instead was given on teachings and principles derived from Confucius. This points out the necessity to consider the cultural inheritance of Confucianism. Particularly how its values and principles are applied, even at times unconsciously, by Sheng or Boqin in the realm of business. According to those results, the influence of Confucianism may therefore represent the heart of this alternative interpretation (*Cultural explanation*):

> Hard work in China comes from the mentality, from the Confucian mentality [...]. There is this mentality to work hard and save money for years of famine of bad harvest. It has been shaped for centuries also due to natural disasters, rooted in centuries, the Confucian mentality to make order. Wenzhou is a little bit like the Brianza, each family has an entrepreneur. (Sheng, Ibidem)

> For us Chinese and the Chinese culture there is a thought of prevision of the risk, if there is some inconvenient I must go on [...] there is a way of saying in Chinese that say 'richness don't stand after two generations' so, you must work always, if not where will you be? [...] like Confucius and the moral theories that we derived from Confucius. 'Even if you don't reach your goal don't do any arm to others'. This is the old culture that has in the heart how to treat others. (Boqin, Zhejian, Milan, 23/03/2015)

Working hard, a saving mentality, the importance of order, predicting risk and having goals in mind all are elements said by Sheng and Boqin to be derived from Confucianism. Many of them actually do overlap with some beliefs of Protestantism. Some may wonder how this is even possible. This finding however is in tune with recent studies on work ethic in Asia (Leong et al. 2013) which have shown how both the Protestant work ethic, together with Eastern Confucian values, can influence the attitude and behavior of workers. Both of those systems of values are said to influence today's economic development in Asia. More importantly, some of the values of those two different systems of belief were found to be overlapping. The scholars mention in particular two principles proper of the Confucian philosophy that are said to influence entrepreneurial activity: diligence, education and perseverance (Leong et al. 2013, p. 4). Other scholars (Redding 1992) pointed out how both Confucian ethic and family attitudes significantly relate with the entrepreneurial behavior among Chinese entrepreneurs in the diaspora (Table 8.2).

From those empirical findings, mainly diligence and education, Confucianism therefore does have some principles overlapping with the Protestant ethic, potentially able to influence economic attitudes and behaviors. Those overlapping values could in part act as a substitute to the Protestant ethic and be responsible for the emphasis placed on hard work in Chinese culture. However, the presence of some commonalities between those two sets of beliefs should not bring us to underestimate the role of the preconditions still absent in Confucianism. Confucianism does not have a substitute for the *role of sects*. Although the role of sects can find other ways through associations, circle of friends, family and lineage, in this second group it still lacks elements such as the control of one's conduct, emphasis on Charisma which had the priority in Weber's explanation. The universal and inclusive philosophical stand of Confucianism is incompatible with the Protestant exclusive and Calvinistic view. The set of beliefs which are not present in Confucianism (glory of God, role of sect, sovereignty of God, anti-superstition, etc.) are therefore equally important. A proper understanding on the effect of Confucianism must be achieved prior to concluding one way or the other. In other words, it is legitimate to say that Confucianism contributes in part toward an economic ethos, but Confucianism in and of itself is not able to provide a clear and widespread alternative able to bring economic success.

Those similarities between Protestantism and part of Confucianism are not mutually exclusive. Some parts are shared but other key parts find no

Table 8.2 Comparison between the list of religious values corresponding to Confucianism and Protestantism. In grey are the areas of overlapping between the two systems of beliefs. The list has no intention to be exhaustive but it points out the connections between the two sets of beliefs and business according to the main features of the model

Confucian Values	*Overlapping Principles*	*Protestant Ethic*
Living according to a moral law as ultimate purpose		**Glory of God** as ultimate purpose
	Diligence, personal achievement through hard work and perseverance / **Beruf**, **Inner-worldly asceticism** and Perseverance of the Saints	
Harmony, submission of individuality to maintain harmonious relationships in all social organizations		Minority, tense search for freedom, **role of sects** as primary form of social relationships above other social organizations
	Importance of Universal **Education** / Importance of **Sacred Scriptures** for literacy, bookkeeping, science…	
Necessity of doing good regardless of Divine help		Impossibility of doing good (total depravity of men) and **Perpetual Assurance of Salvation** as only solution

correspondence. In fact, assurance and salvation are completely absent in Confucianism. Confucianism is a system of thought that, like most religions, provides no consistent eschatological solution for the salvation of the soul apart from good works and the pursuit of education, as Catholicism was to Protestantism for Weber. Confucianism actually does not even consider the afterlife as a reality. Although Confucianism provides some ethical guidelines which may impact the work ethic, it is unable to push toward the achievement of economic success in and of itself. An interesting cultural alternative to PAS came out during my interview and job-shadowing with Chun. This belief generates a degree of confidence that can only remotely relate with PAS is the 'I Ching'. This is known as the 'Classic of Changes' or 'Book of Changes'. It is an ancient text, one of the oldest Chinese classics in fact. When asked about difficulties at work and how to overcome them, Chun replied by referring to the principles contained in I Ching:

> When I have difficulties at work I like to read the book of I Ching. All our culture is based on this book that the first emperor wrote. He found a turtle says the story, and from this story come the principles for living. This helps me because all the projects when you develop them there is always a moment of growth but also of decline, and when there is the moment of crisis it is not forever, you must therefore be prepared for all things. (Chun, Ibidem)

Chun's personal interpretation is the closest example to what I can call 'alternative explanation' to the belief in PAS. In front of situations of economic risk, the non-Christian entrepreneur may find his strength to overcome and achieve economic success through the application of principles from the I Ching. I Ching was a text revered since the times of Confucius, foundational to Chinese culture. The book of I Ching invites the reader many times to walk the earth with confidence in the 'One Power and Cause' in order to win and triumph along all lines (Murphy 1999). Through the cultural application of this tradition, I Ching becomes an aid among Chinese entrepreneurs facing situations of risk and economic crisis. In situations of danger, it is said that the person through I Ching can receive symbolic messages able to guide him, both morally and psychologically. The result of this is a state of harmony and confidence. Asking directions through the I Ching is particularly crucial when making business investments of money.

What is interesting for my comparison is that I Ching has been analyzed by famous psychiatrists such as Carl Jung due to its psychological implications (Murphy 1999). Very much like self-efficacy, I Ching provides confidence. The only critical point in this comparison in my view is the fact that the case of Chun was a rather unique one. His view cannot be considered as a widespread phenomenon among non-Christian entrepreneurs. Protestantism instead provided a systematic source for the belief in PAS among every Christian entrepreneur. Furthermore, I Ching is far more mystic and superstitious, often used to cast lots and foresee things. Void of any rational systematic framework for all areas of life, being closer to superstitious practices, I Ching cannot possibly replace what I have described about the Protestant system of beliefs. Yet the determination and perseverance that this concept upholds may exercise some cultural influence on the common people. Yet in the way risk and challenges are managed at work, I Ching does not necessarily allows the individual to overcome these issues:

> I was working in the restaurant, to order another plate is not easy... wrath...relationships problems, when they are too many... I apologize and I try to move on. [...] When I have to write new things for new selling's, I write and I realize I did a mistake, it is not perfect, I write and delete, I lose strength and confidence but I try again. (Ning, Ibidem).

Other than a probable influence, the Book of Changes provides little guidance on how to do business in moments of crisis, how to react and behave in order to maintain patience and confidence in moments of risk. Offering random oracles applying in any circumstance is not enough to guarantee a support strong enough against failure and challenges. Even if determination as a cultural value can be considered as a common value for Chinese entrepreneurs as a whole, the confidence and strength that were present with the PAS are here absent. Ning therefore failed to resist the pressures from challenges and risks. Concerning the last element of my main theorem (*Economic explanation*), only few cases pointed out the possibility for this explanation. Economics tends to exclude sociological or psychological interpretations, seeing economic success just as a result of external factors in the economy. Even considering the theoretical reflection on the matter, it has been the contention of this book to deny the idea that economic success only relates to outward factors.

I Ching was just an isolated case. Not only the majority of the entrepreneurs of this second group do not make the case for any metaphysical explanation, but they even neglect cultural, social or even personal traits as the reason for their economic success. When found under situations of difficulties and economic risk, Fuhua does not appeal to any personal or social dimension but speaks of an effectiveness in business that can be due only to economic and tangible reasons:

> We work hard because we own our own bars, restaurants, if you want to save more or gain more money you must work harder, there's no other way. (Fuhua, Laoning, Milan, 30/05/2015)

> It does not depend on how you manage it for the business we need to pay money, now the problem is only capitalistic we cannot say that there is other reasons. (Chu Hua, Ibidem)

According to Chu Hua then, the only explanation for economic success is still an economic one. 'Save money, make some gain' is surely the heart of capitalism, but why somebody may be led to embrace such strategy as a lifestyle is not part of this interpretation. Beyond the economic transaction and the application of business principles, there must be another kind of reason which is leading China today toward embracing Capitalism. This change happened due to the advent of a capitalistic spirit, which was absent in the communist materialistic past and that changed Chinese society. A deterministic explanation of economic success as a result uniquely of economic factors can be easily dismissed.

Chu Hua is also important because she points our analysis back to the role of Protestantism in the economy of contemporary China. While not being a Protestant herself, Chu Hua had many contacts with Chinese Protestant entrepreneurs while she was in China and, through her role as an outsider, she gives here an interesting external perception of the lifestyle of those entrepreneurs and their role in today's Chinese economy. Such perception is quite different if compared with Chinese entrepreneurs with no religious identification. Her thoughts from an external perspective may confirm the presence of an inner-worldly asceticism, a saving mentality and a control of the conduct that, while partially present in Confucianism, are still able to generate a capitalistic spirit in a degree that is much higher than any other set of values:

> I know some Christians in China, they are different, they always work, they don't work just to have fun as all of us, they don't work to buy a new car, they don't work to buy rich clothes, in this Christians in China are different than us. (Chu Hua, Ibidem)

This last point on the social perception of Protestants in China and their peculiar view of work may reveal that the Protestant *ethos* in business is much higher than any other competing *ethos*, even while taking Confucian values into account.

8.2 The Chinese Factor

8.2.1 Between Causality and Pretext

Whether someone may tend toward acknowledging the role of Protestant beliefs in business or still frame them into a broader set of values, it remains important to give room to a turning point that took place in my theoretical understanding at this final stage of the book. I started my approach to the field with a theoretical background that was more akin to causality, even though I referred to correlation instead of direct causality. Yet my intention was to find the psychological consequences of a belief (mainly the relation between PAS and self-efficacy, and only by implication economic success).

Yet, the reality of this dynamic observed in my qualitative field suggests a far more complex outcome. During my prolonged period of job-shadowing with Delun, for example, I observed the use of a certain Christian vocabulary in order to receive recognition from the community. Also, after a period of observations I realized how he was portraying the role of the Christian entrepreneur in an artificial sense. We must be honest in admitting that this was also an idea recognized among his Protestant circle of friends intended to also foster recognition. The same could be said about Minzhe who started her job for personal interests then began to fill her role as a buyer with a Christian vocabulary in order to give meaning to her activity.

Heng on the other hand grew up in a Christian family and inherited his interpretation of work from his parents, trying to reproduce the profile of the honest Christian entrepreneur also because it was expected by his community. This Christianese vocabulary, instead of just generating a psychological propensity, was also effective as a channel of rhetoric. The justificatory function of beliefs was at times observable among other Christian entrepreneurs. For some of them, like Hop, the motivation to work hard was already present. In the same way Bo, Yi, or Xun were at times led to find a justification for their economic involvement in their Protestant beliefs. Their Protestant beliefs then turned out for many of them to be a way to make sense of their dilemma:

> I was from a Communist family, my father works for the government. My father works for the government. A family that believes in Communism, I grew up believing that there's no God and that we must work hard for the benefit of the nation, life is just a striving. […] I didn't know what

was religion, in church I met many people and decided to follow this way of the Lord. (Hop, Ibidem)

Success at work comes from the fact that your work is acknowledged for his quality. Then faith, for whatever work you are doing. (Bo, Ibidem)

I studied theology, business administration and I don't ask myself which is over or under, I want to meditate the two, some companies don't know the management, I suggest to learn it, I preached this morning about knowing the social, newspapers, web, to understand things. (Yi, Ibidem)

I left a church that I was part because they didn't teach how to manage money [...] I decided to go in another church where I met entrepreneurs and my faith grew [...] one year later the commerce fellowship changed into a traditional church but I thought it was important to maintain this emphasis with business so I created my new commerce fellowship. (Xun, Ibidem)

If you're a Christian and you don't work, people then think that we [Christians] are lazy, we work but we don't take advantage, also to differentiate ourselves from other unbelievers, work is important because we live in this world. You work better imitating but we don't try to imitate, we try to be more honest. (Nuo, Ibidem)

It also comes from following the crowd, if you have a job I notice it and immediately I want to do the same job. If you are rich the other person that looks at you wants to become rich, they copy each other at last. (Shaiming, Ibidem)

In the mind of the Wenzhounese money is very important, they come first, they think that if you have a lot of money you can speak louder, it doesn't matter if you are a good person. Is sad that also in church some people think that way. (Xiu, Ibidem)

In Wenzhou society started to change. They are no more Communists but liberals. Wenzhou is like that also for its trade position. In flat land. There is minimal difference in trade between the Christian and non Christian, we go to church. (Na, Milan, Wenzhou, 14/12/2015)

Nuo, Na and Shaiming still pointed out the role imitation among Chinese people, which led many to embrace the sets of values of

Protestantism simply in order to conform to the standard of other entrepreneurs. A more evident demonstration of this issue came when I interviewed Fang, a Chinese pastor that previously was a successful entrepreneur and who gave me an interesting insight into the relationship between economic and spiritual needs:

> Everyone has his own business, we created from China an association. We came in Italy to make money, then slowly we became believers. [...] I was among the first famous entrepreneurs in China, there is a lot of materialism but a need inside. People believe in Jesus for health, work, money, me on the other hand not for this but for the emptiness and sadness, the internal fulfillment and the external are linked. (Fang, Ibidem)

Fang, as a spiritual leader, reveals here how in many cases religious faith was only a subsequent stage in the migratory process, as the entrepreneur having already opened his business began to turn into the church to find justification and strength for his work ethic. In the case of the second group of entrepreneurs under job-shadowing, the same justificatory role came into the scene. Ho, for example, during the job-shadowing often gave a more direct and materialistic interpretation of the reason for his strong hard work involvement. Yet the role of family values and work seen as a contribution to Chinese society was at the center of his interiorization of his entrepreneurial propensity:

> My father worked very hard for two kids he worked hard, an high quality of work, contributing to society, he had his personal company, if he does it he fells honored, he succeed to work hard, helping the family, helping society, people admire you, they applaud you because you are ambitious. (Ho, Ibidem)

A more elaborate interpretation in cultural terms was given by Chun in reference to his work attitude and the principles of I Ching again:

> When I have difficulties at work I like to read the book of the I Ching. All our culture is based on this book that the emperor wrote. [...] from it comes the principles for living. This helps me because all projects when you develop them they always have a moment of growth but also of fall, and when there is a moment of crisis is not forever, you must be therefore ready for all things. It is a philosophy on which our culture is based upon. (Chun, Ibidem)

Chun as a non-Protestant, when asked about how he reacted to situations of difficulties at work, pointed out the role of I Ching not as a cause of his behavior but as an instrument to move on. By doing so he was justifying his own economic behavior in light of a philosophical principle. In fact, from further ethnographic observations, it became clear that such view was intended to justify rather than really enhance an economic activity that was already in place. Among other entrepreneurs with no affiliation with the Protestant faith, it was possible to find the same justificatory effort. Quan and Ting, for example, showed how behind communist ideology people became instrumentally open to capitalism, justifying their apparent contradiction by appealing to problems in the system. Sheng on the other hand went beyond this and gave a cultural interpretation of such economic propensity through Confucian lines:

> They failed [communist Russia] because they didn't used the capitalistic system of United States. So China abandoned [Communism] because of Confucianism where your culture and identity can be different from mine. We can live and work together. Now this generation of Western countries work with China. Now we compete but the common interest is greater than the conflict. (Quan, Ibidem)

> The Chinese gain less money? He saves money, works 14 hours, 20 hours, works and likes always to work the Chinese, also the culture before the reform we work always, but now no more because of communism but for money. The Chinese think to be communist but they are not! (Ting, Ibidem)

> Hard work in China comes from the mentality, the Confucian mentality of farmers where everybody know that to survive in China they must work, save money and maintain the family. [...] Since we are identified as Chinese entrepreneurs they give us the connotation then we make it count something. (Sheng, Ibidem)

> People are competitive and jealous, if your neighbor has more you want more, if you are poor they don't respect you, if you are rich they respect you. It doesn't has to do with things but with culture, it comes from culture, they look for respect therefore they want to go out of poverty. (Mei, Ibidem)

> Our Chinese tradition pushes us to work like that, we have thoughts for money: the one who has more money is respected, we try to be better. (Jiao-Long, Ibidem)

> I don't know why in Wenzhou they are like that, they want to do it by themselves, to make money, for me it is a cultural thing, it is like the Jews, they want to do things by themselves. (Biming, Ibidem)

> We from Wenzhou are able to be bosses but also to be independent or sleep in the pavement, it is a different heart, we succeed in bearing different situations. It comes from our ancestors, parents, grand-parents, so this culture is inherited. (Zan, Ibidem)

This same imitation process observed in both groups of entrepreneurs is said by Jiao-Long, Biming and Zan to have its roots in a cultural economic propensity in Wenzhou. The truth, however, is that behind this cultural interpretation there is still an effort in trying to justify their economic propensity.

I am saying all this because it is necessary at this stage to make a methodological note and look at the evidence seen so far through different lens. Each of the elements responds to a need that in social theory has been defined as the process of identification and recognition. Going beyond the methodologic individualism of the Weberian interpretation of beliefs with which I started this research, it is important at this point also to consider the intentions of the actors and to look at the 'reception', identification and recognition of their actions by those that take part in them as well as those that observe them (Pizzorno 2007; Sciolla 2008). Authors in disagreement with the classical methodological approach of Weber suggest instead to look through the perspective of the production of culture and the theory of markets in economics (Azarian 2005). Rejecting sociological dogmatism of the past, I still intend to defend the idea of an empirical social scientist. Yet I realize the need to look also at the social logics behind one's action.

According to this perspective, specific expectations from the side of the actor do involve his need of identification. This does not just imply an individualistic intrinsic intention as in the neoclassical model or just a generic structuralistic instance as in analytical sociology. When like in my case a community of reference is involved, circles of recognition are very elaborate. For example, Chinese entrepreneurs as a specific group may view something as appropriate and in their economic action their judgment on the action is as important as the intention behind it. I mean to see this as a constitutive aspect of the social action, not just an instrumental one (Azarian 2005).

Others have postulated, on a mere political and instrumental level (Hirschman 2013), that all economies have a moral component. This is what Stark calls 'worth', in its double connotation of economic and moral good (Stark 2011). Beliefs, being part of the moral good, are designed to give meaning to social actions. These beliefs sometimes differ from what the individual actually does, yet they still serve for recognition and creating identity (Barbera and Negri 2015). Recognition is a key element even in the day-to-day economic transactions of those Chinese entrepreneurs. This specific element has been called by some scholars the 'economy of conventions', where a set of recognitions are central for the understanding of the economic action (Chicchi 2006).

I mention all this to point out a change of focus that took place at the end of my research. We must bring to mind the changes that capitalism itself has undergone from the times of Weber. Those same transformations in capitalism therefore had a consequent impact in the ideological changes associated with an economic activity (Boltanski and Chiapello 2005). The spirit of capitalism from which I started my reflection therefore inevitably faced some changes. These changes need to be taken into account if we are to come to a final verdict on things. There has been a historical shift in capitalism, from the first bourgeois spirit to a more 'globalized' spirit of capitalism. The ideology that justifies capitalism today is different from the times of Weber. The spirit of capitalism is then now less based on an ethical motivation and more related with a generic call to look for the common good of society. In light of this common good, individuals and organizations are involved in this process of 'justification' and legitimation of their enterprises in terms of the 'common good' (Boltanski and Chiapello 2005).

More neutral concepts as *goodwill* become a potential substitute to the Protestant foundations of what has been transformed into a spirit of global capitalism. Goodwill can be defined in this context as the sentiments of friendship and the sense of diffuse personal obligation which takes place between individuals engaged economic exchange. Literature has already observed the power of this shift in action for the Asian context, namely in Japan (Dore and Sacco 1983). This element of goodwill invites entrepreneurs to share both good and bad times in business, and ethics become institutionalized, part of a national culture. All of those elements reduce risk through relational contract and allow greater investments among firms (Dore and Sacco 1983). My final take here is that it is hard to say however, how such an all-encompassing concept can in and of itself guarantee efficiency, economic success, as well as the presence of many other crucial elements for the growth and promotion of market capitalism (Dore and Sacco 1983).

Yet it is true that at times behind the words of those Chinese entrepreneurs things are presented in terms of legitimizing the 'right actions' to perform in order to make profit in terms of the common good. Such rhetoric is characterized by a vocabulary framed by the community, whether Protestant or not. In their routines, observed during my job-shadowing, entrepreneurs tended to legitimize their behaviors through those rhetorics and the effect was a motivation to success.

In this sense we must be aware that at times entrepreneurs, Protestant or not, did engage in some form of justification logic. Ideas initially alien, or even hostile, to capitalism, such as communism, religion, lineage and culture, were incorporated by Chinese entrepreneurs to defend and justify themselves in light of a challenge. The cultural and religious aspects were embodied in the form of procedures (Lizardo and Strand 2015). If, for example, the Protestant entrepreneur used certain practices of recognition, he knew that he was to be accepted by others. Therefore the need for such stress on the religious aspect of work. The imperative for profit accumulation in this case, even if permeating every ideological aspect, it also demonstrated that work still possesses a meaning and still testifies to the presence of a spirit of capitalism, even if its features are changed (Boltanski and Chiapello 2005).

8.2.2 Evidence from Outsiders

As a final section I want to turn here to reflect briefly about the surrounding environment of those Chinese entrepreneurs I observed in the diaspora. What was the perception of entrepreneurship in the surrounding environment beyond the Chinese context under my analysis? When analyzing the economic success of a specific group of people, it is still important to consider the surroundings which may favor or penalize their economic success. I already mentioned the environment of Chinatown but here it is important to also reflect on what relationship there was between the Chinese businesses and the local entrepreneurship in the diaspora.

In order to understand better the weight of the Chinese propensity toward hard work, I briefly chose to take into consideration also the counterpart of non-Chinese entrepreneurs. In addition with the interviews to the outsiders that I have already mentioned in previous chapters, some occasional job-shadowing was done in stores close to Chinatown, but owned by non-Chinese local entrepreneurs. For example, in several occasions I have observed a café close to Chinatown. This is more of a suggestion, rather than a complete explanation of how non-Chinese entrepreneurs compare with Chinese entrepreneurs. It is not my intention to be exhaustive on this counterpart of small businesses, but only to make a brief final reflection on what would happen to this analysis if we were to compare what was said with the counterpart of a business owned by a local non-Chinese entrepreneur.

The little time at my disposal limited the possibility for a complete description or comparison. The typology of business chosen for this kind of comparison was almost identical to the Chinese entrepreneurs. While these businesses were geographically close to Chinatown, the prices were doubled and the place was almost empty. There were some regular clients, but in this case they were extremely annoying, almost scaring away new clients. The owner was an old local owner, dressed in a very informal dressing, very slow in his work.

The interior design was more refined if compared with the Chinese stores. Clients were usually locals and only rarely Chinese, despite the fact that it was next to Chinatown. The relationship with clients was warmer and more conversational than the Chinese counterpart. The owner had the ability to relate with his own culture. The store had visits from sellers. This gave the café an easy way to make business, also through providing all kinds of food services. This was easier, being a service by locals for locals.

I am not here equating what randomly observed in this café with all local small businesses. I am not denying the possibility of the counterpart with a successful small business. Yet what I want to briefly point out here with this example is how in two almost identical contexts of business, business strategies and daily operations were radically different. There is a Chinese way to approach business, which is totally different from how business is done in the west. Generally speaking, the economic context of Italy and of Milan during the times of my observations was not at its best. Many businesses were forced to fire their own workers and small businesses in particular were forced to close or sell their business. Guozhi and many other Chinese business owners took over local businesses that were bankrupt and they were able through hard work to let them flourish in the midst of an economic crisis.

On the other hand, it is also true that the local counterpart offers a good example of unintended cultural similarities. In the same way as the Chinese context of Wenzhou, the local context of small businesses was characterized by a strong orientation toward family. Just as Chinese business was often started and ran through family networks of reciprocity so did the locals. Furthermore, small business entrepreneurship was always very important to the Italian economy just as in the case of Wenzhou. At first, Chinese small businesses were opened for a Chinese clientele only but later they took over local small businesses with clients of all kinds. If at first there was a general suspicion toward migrants, later the Chinese community began to hold a more respectable role in the eyes of the local society in their diaspora. This was true even during the context of economic crisis that took place while I was doing my research. Chinese entrepreneurs began to be seen as hard-workers by locals, potential business partners, instead of just competitors.

This small comparison does support the idea of a Chinese propensity to hard work and economic success. Some may argue that there might be a *Chinese common denominator* in their propensity to hard work, especially for the case of Wenzhou. Many other factors are responsible of this, in particular geography and historical origins. Also, the economic reforms, together with the internationalization of the Chinese market. This remains valid regardless of being Protestant or not. Local workers in the diaspora doing the same job do not display the same hard work mentality and diligence. In other words, a set of values, beliefs or ideas, clustered here within the encompassing concept of *ethos* (not just in its Protestant connotation) are able to contribute to successful entrepreneurship. My conclusions will now determine to what point it is possible to clearly identify the nature, origins and impact of such Chinese version of the Protestant *ethic*.

References

Azarian G. R., 2005, *The General Sociology of Harrison C. White. Chaos and Order in Networks*, London, Macmillan.

Barbera F., Negri N., 2015, 'Rituals as Mechanisms', in *Paradoxes, Mechanisms, Consequences: Essay in Honor of Mohamed Cherkaoui*, edited by G. L. Manzo, Oxford, Bardwell Press.

Boltanski L., Chiapello E., 2005, *The New Spirit of Capitalism*, London-New York, Verso.

Ceccagno A., Rastrelli R., 2008, *Ombre Cinesi? Dinamiche Migratorie della Diaspora Cinese in Italia*, Carocci, Roma.

Chicchi F., 2006, *Per un'analisi critica dell'Economia delle convenzioni: alcune brevi riflessioni sul suo statuto teorico e sul suo rapporto con la sociologia del lavoro*, Milano, Franco Angeli.

Dore R., Sacco M., 'Goodwill and the Spirit of Market Capitalism', in *British Journal of Sociology*, Vol. 34 (1983), pp. 459–482.

Hirschman A. O., 2013, *The Passions and the Interests: Political Arguments for Capitalism Before Its Triumph*, Princeton, Princeton University Press.

Leong F. T. L., Huang J. L., Mak S., 'Protestant Work Ethic, Confucian Values, and Work-Related Attitudes in Singapore', in *Journal of Career Assesment*, Vol. 22, No. 2 (2013), pp. 1–13.

Lizardo O., Strand M., 'Beyond World Images: Belief as Embodied Action in the World', in *Sociological Theory*, Vol. 33, No. 1 (March 2015), pp. 44–70.

Murphy J., 1999, *Secrets of the I Ching: Get What You Want in Every Situation Using the Classic Book of Changes*, New York, Prentice Hall Press.

Pizzorno A., 2007, *Il Velo della Diversità. Studi su Razionalità e Riconoscimento*, Feltrinelli, Milano.

Redding G. S., 'The Spirit of Chinese Capitalism', in *Journal of International Business Studies*, Vol. 27 (Third Quarter, 1992), p. 572.

Sciolla L., 'La forza dei valori', in *Rassegna Italiana di Sociologia*, Vol. 49, No. 1 (Jan-March 2008), pp. 89–115.

Stark D., 2011, *The Sense of Dissonance: Accounts of Worth in Economic Life*, Princeton, Princeton University Press.

CHAPTER 9

Conclusions

The time has come now to conclude my research, by interpreting the data from the field and propose here a final analysis. While I made mention of the practical influence of the Protestant set of values on business, what I was mainly able to identify is their subjective interiorization, the self-perception of them in the entrepreneurial process. Although this step in qualitative analysis represents already in and of itself a valid goal, through future research it may be possible to explore systematically the same phenomenon elsewhere. This could allow the comparison of both actions and perceptions among even more groups and see any effectual difference.

When I started this book, I stated what at the beginning I thought to be the expected results. After having gone through the fieldwork however it is clear that a direct correspondence of the original thesis without any adjustment is (*a*) impossible. The field has demonstrated the concomitant presence of intervening elements (*c*) which made my original thesis true only in part. So, in light of the empirical findings here presented, and in accordance with similar observations from other scholarly works done in the past, the more legitimate conclusion that the reader can draw from this book is that Weber was indeed going in the right direction but came to the wrong conclusions (*b*). Mainly the study points clearly to the necessity of an adjustment of Weber's original claims in light of this fieldwork and other contemporary findings that seem to go in the same

O. Palombaro, *Christianity and Capitalism in China*,
https://doi.org/10.1007/978-981-97-3549-5_9

direction. It is assurance about salvation rather than anxiety about salvation that produces confidence in the Protestant believer, which in turn impacts self-efficacy and leads to economic success.

At the beginning of this book, I was pointing out how risk-propensity was a key element in literature, when considering entrepreneurship and economic success. Empirical cases such as Enlai and others, show how autonomy and independence are indeed viewed as key values in the culture of Wenzhou. In the same way, Delun and other cases under job-shadowing showed the readiness to embrace challenges typical of the entrepreneurial type. The field pointed out the crucial role of the belief in perpetual assurance of salvation (PAS) for what the literature defines as 'over-confidence' and 'endemic optimism'. In particular 'over-precision', the excessive certainty over the accuracy of one's belief was predominant. All these aspects mentioned by literature can be clearly applied to the case under my analysis. Furthermore, when it comes to evaluating the role of risk-taking, risk-management and risk-propensity in entrepreneurship, job-shadowings clearly showed that Protestant believers in general tended to have a stronger source of emotional and personal support, which was instead weak or absent among the people of the second group case-control of non-Christian entrepreneurs. When faced with financial risk or for example dealing with tough situations or bad clients, the entrepreneurs of the first group were more able to maintain an emotional balance and personal strength. The case-control, or the second group of entrepreneurs on the other hand, resulted to be more stressed and propense toward a general inability to manage cumulated situations of economic risk.

When it comes to evaluating innovation, second chiefest point which characterizes entrepreneurship, I pointed out how the cases under my analysis offered a clear affirmative answer to the theoretical premise. Five out of the six individuals under my job-shadowing (exception made for Ho) responded positively to the profile of the entrepreneur expressed in the literature. Delun as a leading figure held many of the elements proper of this definition of innovation. In the field I was able to notice how Delun often tended to break the static equilibrium, combining factors in a new way and creating different forms of production and business. During the period of my job-shadowing, from a café Delun was able to open 3 different creative innovative businesses. The innovative approach of Delun was also notorious in trying to solve the problem of unemployment in the diaspora through a more integrational approach, if compared with others.

Like Delun, many other cases were the theater of imprudent financial choices, which nevertheless remain characteristic of the entrepreneurial profile. I did not observe any significant difference between the two groups on search for efficiency, importance of teamwork or ability to build relationships.

The continuous exploration of new unknown sectors for cases like Delun, Enlai or Heng was also connected to their identity as second-generation migrants. This was noticeable by comparing the outlook and appearance of those new stores of Heng or Delun with the 'traditional' way of doing small businesses among first-generation migrants. Another important source of innovation was the role of e-commerce among Chinese entrepreneurs both in the motherland and in the diaspora, like in the cases of Minzhe, Lei, Chun's wife and others. In some cases, like Heng's, the proportions of this involvement were significant even on an international scale. Particularly interesting was the creative relationship with the local counterpart of business in both samples, like with Guozhi, Delun or Chun.

Concerning the main thesis of this book, the application of the original theoretical model into the field presents some challenges. In the final analysis, it is possible to see the presence of almost all of the elements of my theorem and therefore to allow the legitimate application of this model to the specific case of Wenzhou in contemporary China through evidence from the diaspora. I showed how several of the *assistants to the preconditions* of the model where present in the field of Chinese entrepreneurs in the diaspora. Some of those components were not covered in detail, yet for example the *role of Sacred Scriptures* was clearly evident in the rationalization of practices and ethical standards among for example Zhenzhen, his constant preaching, connected to his business, or even in Guang and his daily reading of Scriptures in the workplace.

I was also able to point out how the *Boss-Christian phenomenon* present among Chinese entrepreneurs both in Wenzhou and in the diaspora goes back to the forms of inner-worldly asceticism described by Weber. This became clear throughout the job-shadowing of Delun: how his emphasis on personal integrity in all things was derived among other things from the Calvinist teachings of Dr. Stephen Tong or from the application of the ethical rules of his Christian association to his personal business. In the same way, in the words of Ling, Guang, Wing, it was possible to see the range of actions of such a principle. Many times, both during the job-shadowing and during the interviews, it was clear how Protestant members regularly involved in church activities and with a strong faith, were also doing exceedingly well in their business and did not see any contradiction between business and their beliefs. On the other hand, members supposedly 'on the edge', distant from church life, saw a strong contradiction between faith and their work and were not doing as well financially.

The idea of 'calling' and 'vision from God' (*Yi Xiang*) reported by literature for the case of Wenzhou was clearly reflected also in the business led in the diaspora. I quoted cases like Hop or Jun that expressed such awareness or even the biographical experiences of Deming in finding his 'job-calling', Enlai and his being in tune with 'God's schedule'. Even more persuasive was the journey of business callings of Bai or Xun, where the strong connection between faith and this sense of calling for business reached the entirety of the interpretation of their personal achievements and success. As it is also clear from the chart, other elements were found in the field modifying what I previously expected to find approaching the field. In particular, recurrent was the stress on the Calvinistic desire to *glorify God* in everything entrepreneurs were doing. This belief had a strong impact in legitimizing and giving a sense of profound purpose for every kind of jobs.

Connected to this, the role of *house churches* was present in its structure even in the diaspora. I pointed out this role in business by mentioning the circles of favors and finances connected with the house church for example with Xiu and his leadership role in a commerce fellowship, as well as through other examples even with the job-shadowing of Delun or Minzhe. Also, I mentioned how the multiplication strategy of house churches was often applied to business and how countless cases of business partnership among church members represent the turning-point of many migrants who joined the diaspora. Yet the field also showed how house churches, in the same way as the *role of sects* in Weber, go far beyond their role as a network. The emphasis on the control of the conduct was witnessed among many examples, such as Delun or Hop. In this it was very beneficial to consider the connection between church leadership and tendencies toward economic success as in Zhenzhen and his brother Shu or even Shing.

When it comes to establishing the role of the main element of this book (belief in PAS), it was possible to see plainly how such belief is still present and how it plays an active role. The influence of such belief in enhancing confidence and a state of peace was clearly displayed by many of the cases under investigation. Furthermore, the results from the questionnaire on the Self-efficacy scale showed a strong connection between self-efficacy and the belief in PAS, especially among young Protestant small business owners from the city of Wenzhou. The role of this belief was very crucial in many situations of risk and challenge at work. Looking at the personal reconstructions of the entrepreneurs, another unexpected element that often was mentioned was the role of prayer. In one sense those specific findings show that a 'spirit of capitalism' emerges not always necessarily as a consequence of Protestantism, but wherever it emerges someone would expect it to emerge for the exact same reasons. And some of those exact same reasons were clearly present in the field as empirical findings show.

Yet, as it will be clear from the following chart, such interpretation remains somehow one-sided and needs to be considered also in light of other possible intervening factors that are worth being mentioned here. For this reason, the counterpart of non-Christian entrepreneurs from the case-control group under my investigation complicated the simple picture described above. Going beyond surface statements and in light also of the dark side of some stories from the interviews, it is important to consider the possibility of a *Wenzhou Profit-oriented mentality* beyond just Protestantism. At first, the field almost immediately witnessed to the possibility of the intervening role of communism (*Communism explanation*), apart from the mere exaltation of work. Yet communism is no longer held as a belief by the majority of the Chinese population involved in business. In the same way, the cliché of a *constriction explanation*, which could relate this hard work propensity to some form of Stakhanovism, is to be put into question. Especially in light of the context of the second generation of migrants and the changes in Chinese entrepreneurship, a constriction or even a *minority explanation* loses its validity. Furthermore, being an ethnic migrant minority or experiencing exhortation to work hard, in and of themselves do not guarantee in any way the achievement of economic success, which is the main quest of this book (Table 9.1).

The results for the second group of entrepreneurs can be summed up in two major intervening influences that may lead to an adjustment of my initial theoretical model for the case of Wenzhou. The first major influence that came out of the data for both samples were networks (*Network explanation*), which in the case of Protestants went under the name of *house churches* and for the case of non-Protestant entrepreneurs simply changed its name to 'associations', 'circles of friends', lineage or family.

Table 9.1 Synthetic table representing the dynamics of the model for the case of Wenzhou in light of the results from ethnographic observations and the interviews

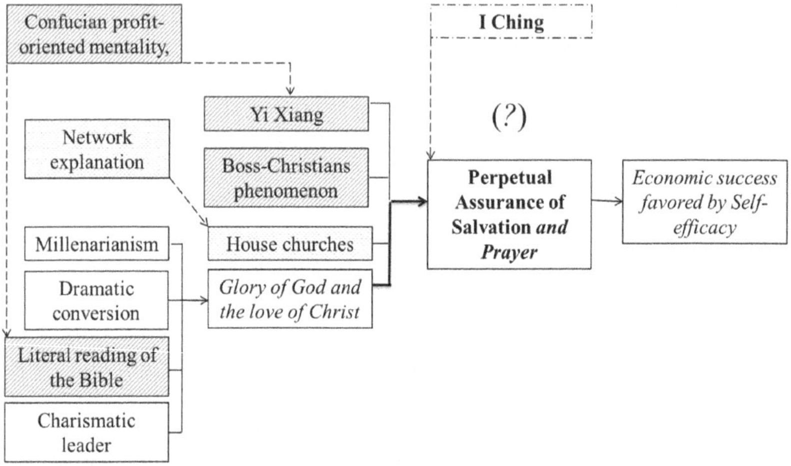

In other words, it is clear that regardless of the specific religious label, network does play a role in business among both categories of Chinese entrepreneurs. This was clearly witnessed among networks of a specific kind for business among the same individuals: house church, family and lineage, etc. … Cases of business partnerships like Delun and Bingwen or Minzhe, Fai and Enlai, based on their commonality of faith, go toward this direction. However, from Delun and Heng we see the overlapping of church and lineage networks for businesses. The house church as a network was also observed, for example at the main storehouse in Milan, with deep ramifications for business connections. A counterpart of this was the widespread chain of businesses called AUMAI. Particularly interesting was to see how networks play their role as emergency channels, especially in situations of economic risk and crisis, giving an essential help in the initial stages of a business, providing information, partnership and crucial resources. It must be noted though, that such type of influence varies on the basis of what kind of network (associations, church membership, migrant community, informal entourages, family, circles of friends, personal connections, etc.).

The field showed that not all those examples of networks play a role in business and their function was not always effective. For example, some associations which supposedly were intended to promote business among Chinese entrepreneurs actually were considered to be more of a burden than a help. Every network has its costs and constraints. In the Chinese context, it functions in an exclusive manner, bringing traditions that especially for the first generation of migrants actually hinder innovation. In fact, when it comes to business multiplication and evaluating the financial weight of networks for business success, it was possible to see that regardless of the type of network, what was crucial was the presence of a specific Chinese principle of relationships: *Guanxi*. The principle of obliged reciprocity was present in cases such as Ning, Jahao, Peng, Delun, Yan, Yi, Na's parents and many others.

So it is not enough to be part of a network of any kind, and that somehow could give access to sources for those small business owners capable to achieve economic success. It is only a particular configuration of network therefore that plays an active role in business, one that involves what in literature is defined as 'circle of recognition' (Barbera & Negri, 2015). In this case the interactions between actors in the network have structurally equivalent nodes and their connections become representations of state of being and belonging, acquiring the value of rituals. This was observed in the field especially for the case of church membership or certain types of associations. The house church networks in particular are able to generate and reproduce their own organizational schemes that in literature are called 'disciplines': stable modes of action displayed in order to support a collective identity and allocate social roles accordingly (Barbera & Negri, 2015). Furthermore, however I also pointed out that there is still a substantial difference in the way that networks operate in the two samples. For the second group the network operates with the function of guaranteeing the *survival* of a specific business, whereas in the case of the house churches I pointed out that the main function, beside the provision of a network, remains the control of the conduct, a stress on Charisma and a strive for affirmation, which pushes the individual toward economic success.

Another major influence that came out of the data as a potential expression of a Wenzhou's profit-oriented mentality was the role of Confucianism (*Cultural explanation*). Particularly it has been noticed how some values proper of Confucianism (stress on diligence and education) may play a parallel function to that of the *Beruf*, the inner-worldly asceticism and the role of Sacred Scriptures for the case of Wenzhou's Protestant entrepreneurs. Such emphasis on ambition was noticed in cases of new generations of entrepreneurs like Ho or Hop and the pressures of their families for achievement in their profession. This does not mean however that those reported similarities in Confucianism are a precise and rigorous reproduction of the several preconditions present in Protestantism. Nor does it mean that these are able to bring an equal outcome in business.

The absence of a systematic set of values and of a religious identification large scale, as the one that I was able to find in Protestantism, limits by necessity the extent of such comparison. Furthermore, not only the degree of identification with Confucianism in Wenzhou is generally low, and when present it expresses itself just in the form of a slogan, without the strong identity proper of Protestantism, but also, such Confucian values already existed long before the advent of today's capitalistic spirit and were not by themselves able to bring these economic changes. On the contrary, other Confucian values were actually considered in the historical analysis of Weber as the cause for the absence of rational capitalism (such as segregation and aristocracy). An effort to try to find in Confucianism an all-encompassing cultural category for such Chinese entrepreneurial spirit, must be therefore considered as misleading since it does not clearly identify what is at stake here. Some principles of Confucianism may nevertheless survive, sometimes unconsciously, like in Sheng's strife to accumulate money, in the devotion to luck through symbols of economic success, but they must be considered more as cooperative rather than substitutive to the model.

Even counting those two main intervening influences, the belief in PAS that I have analyzed before, finds no effective substitute for the case of the second group of entrepreneurs. An exception may be made for the '*I Ching*', connected to the previous point of Confucianism (*Cultural explanation*), which remains however open to question, since it remains a principle circumscribed to few cases. One of them clearly reported was the one of Chun in his business. To say it in clearer words, the Protestant ethic displayed by a series of beliefs, especially the belief in PAS, can lead to an economic success favored by the self-efficacy connected to it, taking into account the role that networks and some Confucian values already exerted in the area of Wenzhou. Giving the difference in self-efficacy observed in the results from the questionnaires, the distinctiveness observed through job-shadowing and the significant information collected from the interviews, allows to make a case for the centrality of a Protestant ethic. Particularly such ethic is valid for what concerns the belief in PAS for the case of Wenzhou. In order to link those findings on the micro level with the macro dimension of the rise of capitalism in contemporary China further qualitative studies may find support through other geographical areas and with a more systematic overview, today still missing. Another critical point for drawing conclusions from this research consists in the long distance between the historical study of Weber and the particular case under my analysis. This gap may therefore affect the extension of the results that someone may draw.

Lastly, even if through this study I was able to identify clearly each factor under analysis in the field, questions remain on the intensiveness of their impact. As I showed throughout this book, the belief in PAS among Chinese entrepreneurs tends to play a crucial role in displaying self-efficacy, especially in situations of risk and difficulty. With which intensity this metaphysical concept permeates the work of the entrepreneur remains still open to debate, which may again limit the conclusions that can be drawn. This has to do mainly with how this belief, together with the preconditions observed, can actively lead to economic success. Further studies and investigations may lead to re-define the elements expressed in the model. What emerged from the data in any case is an undeniable commitment toward an internalized belief that is more than a formal declaration, if considered inside the proper relationship with other statements and within the general structure of the model. When compared with the results for the second group, I was able to see a consistent difference in the way work is internalized by the entrepreneur. I noticed the absence of a purpose-driven activity, but I also noticed the potential impact of some intervening factors in my model (mainly *Network explanation* and *Cultural explanation*).

The possibility of the presence of a *Wenzhou profit-oriented mentality* that would be able to invalidate the role of the Protestant ethic for the case of Wenzhou cannot rely simply on those two factors that by themselves may be able to push toward hard work but are not able to provide an alternative consistent explanatory interpretation for the achievement of economic success. A Wenzhou profit-oriented mentality does indeed exist today. In both cases under my analysis however, I pointed out how such orientation is originated by cultural and social factors and not by mere economic factors. This in and of itself is already an achievement. Through the transformation of Wenzhou, from being a fishing poor city into a business capital worldwide, Protestantism does not work as a universal condition for such change, yet it may be conceived still as a necessary one. I mean that it might not be totally absurd to think of the Protestant ethic, expressed through the Protestant revivals of Wenzhou, as a sort of small little fuse that, together with many other external factors, slowly set in motion the genesis of a 'Wenzhouren spirit of capitalism'. Later on, such spirit by a law of imitation is scattered and is now present in Wenzhou as well as its common citizens with no link at all with the Protestant faith.

The field however also pointed out the possible presence of a justification logic that instead of identifying the belief as a cause for certain behaviors was functioning more as a justificatory instrument for their business. Some interviews and job-shadowings in fact pointed to this possibility, also taking into account more recent theoretical contributions on the topic. The justification logic can reveal the subjective interiorization of why success matters to the eyes of the entrepreneur, beside the actual reason for it. Having said that, the Chinese *ethos* does not simply disappear nor does it lose its significance, it changes its influence. Instead of influencing the behavior only through some psychological connotation, it might also serve as a rhetoric tool in order to legitimize and motivate the economic activity toward success.

Therefore, we may legitimately say that successful entrepreneurship involves specific social, cultural and even religious aspects that move beyond mere business strategies. As a scholar once said, in order to be intentionally successful rarely the *homo oeconomicus* is able to control uncertainty without resorting to the symbolic worth contained in his actions, becoming therefore, even unintentionally, *homo sociologicus* (Barbera & Negri, 2015). Furthermore, according to my results, value-driven entrepreneurs, as opposed to need-driven entrepreneurs, possess the necessary confidence to overcome economic risk and are more able to enhance economic success. Success in a condition of economic crisis like the one I witnessed in Italy, becomes possible only through specific values. The case of Chinese entrepreneurs teaches that success in a crisis is for the one creatively exploiting it, not for the one desperately fleeing it. This is the degree of hypothetical conclusion that some may reach, without ending up with some over-statements. I trust that the reader by now has properly understood that the goal of this analysis was not to support a deterministic application of the theoretical argument for the case of China. But, taking into consideration several potential intervening critical dimensions, this study interestingly enough points out to some unexpected degree of confirmation in the validity of the theoretical model.

Ethos is therefore at stake. Certain ethics seem to make a real difference in business even for the accomplishment of economic success. The motivations for an individual, when derived from radical forms of morality, can have an impact on his actions. Such is the case of salvation viewed by the Protestant Reformation as entirely the gift of God's grace, or with the Lutheran idea of calling in secular pursuits, and most of all through the Calvinistic idea of the Sovereignty of God impacting the creaturely existence at every point, in a community where the 'glory of God' will be realized (Wogaman, 1993). These ethical premises, and many others, see the Calvinist idea of stewardship as religious basis for every active economic life deferring consumption and amassing capital for further economic investments, have an immense influence in shaping the subsequent history.

But what could be the place of these ethics in a secular society? Prescriptive behavior, duty, obligation, distinction between right and wrong, justice and injustice, responsibility and irresponsibility are disregarded by secular authorities, yet society does not cease to be concerned with ethics. A fundamental peculiarity of religious ethics is the relationship with an objective and personal source of conduct: God. I started this book by pointing out the neglect of the 'God factor' in sociology. Sociology as a discipline started as a rejection of the metaphysical stage in favor of the positive stage of science. By doing so, however, conventional analysis in the discipline of sociology of religion failed in recognizing their own biases. Labeling any theological explanation as irrelevant or fruit of rhetoric is as limiting as the opposite case of an uncritical defense of a religious position only on the ground of theological claims. Hopefully, through this analysis the reader has been offered a third way that can make justice to the influence of *Theos* in society, while guarding against an uncritical reception of things. Like under the wall of Berlin, academia today is forcing an unnecessary compartmentalism between sacred and profane, between God and scientific investigation, between metaphysics and empiricism. I have only tried to open a small breach in this giant wall, by testifying that *ethos* is at stake even in business, and even today. The Judeo-Christian ethics particularly address the whole being and they have as their end practices and a responsive behavior (Hughes, 1983).

Moral guides not only respond in situations of crisis but also train the person to transform the crisis into success (Reuschling, 2008). A case of profound social and economic transformation such as the one of contemporary China may show therefore how, against all odds, business ethics and principles coming from a long path of sociology of religion, can contribute real significant added value for both contemporary society and future sociological theories. The conclusion of this study testifies to the reasons why ethics still matter in today's secularized society.

References

Barbera F., Negri N., 2015, 'Rituals as Mechanisms', in *Paradoxes, Mechanisms, Consequences: Essay in Honor of Mohamed Cherkaoui*, edited by G. L. Manzo, Oxford, Bardwell Press.

Hughes P. E., 1983, *Christian Ethics in Secular Society*, Michigan, Baker Book House.

Reuschling W. C., 2008, *Reviving Evangelical Ethics. The Promises and Pitfalls of Classic Models of Morality*, Michigan, Brazos Press.

Wogaman P. J., 1993, *Christian Ethics. A Historical Introduction*, Louisville, Westminster John Knox Press.

Further Reading

ANS (Amity News Service), 1997, *How Many Christians Are There in China*, Available at http://is7.pacific.net.hk/~amityhk/96_4_spe.htm.

Baechler J., 1975, *The Origins of Capitalism*, Oxford, Blackwell.

Barbera F., Negri N., 2015, 'Crypto-Rational Choice or Complex Mechanisms?', in *Sociologica*, (n. 2, 2014), il Mulino, Bologna.

Baxter R., 1678, *A Christian Directory*, London, Robert White.

Beeke J. R., 2011, 2007, *Meet the Puritans: With a Guide to Modern Reprints*, Grand Rapids, Reformation Heritage Books.

Bressan N., 2013, *L'Imprenditoria Cinese in Italia. Due Casi Studio: la Ristorazione Cinese a Milano e il Distretto del Porfido a Trento*, Università degli Studi di Trento.

Burkett L., 1989, *The Complete Financial Guide for Young Couples. A Lifetime Approach to Spending, Saving and Investing*, Wheaton, Victor Books.

Burkett L., 1975, *How to Manage Your Money. An in-Depth Bible Study on Personal Finances*, Chicago, Moody Press.

Bush R. C. Jr., 1970, *Religion in Communist China*, Nashville, Abingdon Press.

Buss A., 'The Concept of Adequate Causation and Max Weber's Comparative Sociology of Religion', in *The British Journal of Sociology*, Vol. 50, No. 2 (1999), pp. 317–329.

Calvin J., 1991, *La Divina Predestinazione*, Torino, Claudiana.

Calvin J., 1845, *On the Christian Life*, Grand Rapids, B. Eerdmans Publishing Co..

Cao N., 'The Church as a Surrogate Family for Working Class Immigrant Chinese Youth: An Ethnography of Segmented Assimilation', in *Sociology of Religion: A Quarterly Review*, Vol. 66 (June 2005), pp. 183–200.

Cavalli L., 1968, *Max Weber: religione e società*, Bologna, Il Mulino.

Ceccagno A., 2003, *Migranti a Prato. Il distretto tessile multietnico*, Milano, Franco Angeli.

Chakrabarty, D., 2000, *Provincializing Europe: Postcolonial Thought and Historical Difference*, Princeton, Princeton University Press.

Chang L. T., 2009, *Factory Girls: From Village to City in a Changing China*, Tantor Audio, Old Saybrook.

Chao J., 1997, *A History of Christianity in Socialist China, 1949–1997*, Taipei, China Ministries International Publishing Co.

Chao J., 1981, 'Cong huaren liaohui fazhan shi kan jiaohui zengzhang' (Church Growth in the History of Chinese Churches), in *Jindai Zhongguo yu Jidujiao lunwen ji* (Essays on Modern China and Christianity), Taipei, Yuzhouguang Press, pp. 345–362.

Chau A. Y., 2006, *Miraculous Response. Doing Popular Religion in Contemporary China*, California, Stanford University Press.

Chen N. N., 2003, 'Healing Sects and Anti-Cult Campaigns', in *Religion in China Today*, pp. 199–214.

Chen Y., Wang H., Yan S., "The Long-Term Effects of Protestant Activities in China," in *Journal of Comparative Economics* Vol. 50, No. 2 (June 2022), pp. 394–414.

Chiang A. C., 'Religion, Proverbs and Economic Mentality', in *American Journal of Economics and Sociology*, Vol. 20, No. 3 (Apr. 1961), pp. 253–264.

Chiapello E., Boltanski L., 2014, *Il Nuovo Spirito del Capitalismo*, Milano, Mimesis.

Chunguang W., Béja J. P., 'Wenzhou ren zai Bali: yizhong dute de shehui rongru moshi' (The Wenzhounese in Paris: A Unique Model of Social Integration), in *Chinese Journal of Social Science*, Vol. 6 (1999), pp. 106–119.

Cipriani R., 2009, *Nuovo manuale di sociologia della religione*, Roma, Borla.

Cohen J., 'Rational Capitalism in Renaissance Italy', in *American Journal of Sociology*, No. 85 (1980), pp. 1340–1355.

Cologna D., 2000, *Chinese Immigrant Enterpreneurs in Italy. Strenghts and Weaknesses of a Ethnic Enclave Economy*, London, Routledge, pp. 262–284.

Cologna D., 2005, 'Differential Impact of Transnational Ties of Chinese Migrants from Zhejiang Province in Italy on the Socio-Economic Development of Their Districts of Origin', in *Asian Pacific Migration Journal*, Vol. 14, No. 1–2 (2005), pp. 121–147.

Cologna D., 2008, *Deconstructing Milan's Chinatown Problem*, Barcelona, CIDOB Foundation.

Corbett M., Corbett J. M., 1999, *Politics and Religion in the United States*, New York, Garland.

Corona M., Del Bello D., 2009, *I Puritani d'America*, Roma, Aracne.

Covell R. R., 1995, *The Liberating Gospel in China: The Christian Faith Among China's Minority Peoples*, Grand Rapids, Baker Books.

Cunfu C., Tianhai H., 'The Emergence of a New Type of Christians in China Today', in *Review of Religious Research*, Vol. 46, No. 2 (2004), pp. 183–200.

Dana L., (Eds.), 2010, *Entrepreneurship and Religion*, Cheltenham, Edward Elgar Publishing Inc..

De Feo M., 1970, *Introduzione a Weber*, Bari, Laterza.

De Marco P., (et alii), 1995, *Identità europea e diversità religiosa nel mutamento contemporaneo*, Edap, Firenze.1

Dean, K., 2003, 'Local Communal Religion in Contemporary South-east China', in *Religion in China Today*, pp. 32–52.

Derman J., 'Max Weber and Charisma: A Transatlantic Affair', in *New German Critique*, No. 113 (Summer 2011), pp. 51–88.

Diamond N., 1996. 'Christianity and the Hua Miao: Writing and Power', in *Christianity in China: From the Eighteenth Century to the Present*, Stanford University Press, pp. 138–158.

Dizikes P., 'Faith and reason. Was Christianity the Engine of Western progress?' in *The Boston Globe* (December 25), 2005.

Doepke M., Zilibotti F., 'Social Class and the Spirit of Capitalism', in *Journal of the European Economic Association*, Vol. 3, No. 2–3 (2005), pp. 516–524.

Dow T. E. Jnr., 'An Analysis of Weber's Work on Charisma', in *British Journal of Sociology*, Vol. 29, No. 1, (March 1978).

Duilmen R., 'Protestantism and Capitalism: Weber's Thesis in Light of Recent Social History', in *Telos*, Vol. 78 (1989), pp. 71–80.

Edwards J., 2006 [ed. orig. 1754], *Freedom of the Will*, Ed. Paul Ramsey, Vol. 1–2, Yale.

Eisenstadt S. N., 'Max Weber: On Charisma and Institution Building', in *The British Journal of Sociology* (1970), pp. 458–460.

Eisenstadt S. N., 1968, *The Protestant Ethic and Modernization*, New York, Basic Books.

Elvin M., 'Why China Failed to Create an Endogenous Industrial Capitalism: A Critique of Max Weber's Explanation', in *Theory and Society*, Vol. 13, No. 3 (May 1984), pp. 379–391.

Fanfani A., 1940, *Cattolicesimo e protestantesimo nella formazione storica del capitalismo*, Milano, Einaudi.

Fanfani A., 1933, *Le origini dello spirito capitalistico in Italia*, Milan, chap. 6.

Fayou M., 1998, *A History of Wenzhou Christianity*, Hong Kong, Alliance Bible Seminary Press.

Ferrarotti F., 1965, *Max Weber e il destino della ragione*, Laterza, Bari.

Finke R., Stark R., 1992, *The Churching of America, 1776–1990: Winners and Losers in our Religious Economy*, New Brunswick, Rutgers University Press.

Forcese D. P., 'Calvinism, Capitalism and Confusion: The Weberian Thesis Revisited', in *Sociological Analysis*, Vol. 29, No. 4 (Winter 1968), pp. 193–201.

Franklin B., 1903, *Poor Richard's Almanack*, B.E. Smith, Century [ed. orig. 1733].

Froese P., 2004, 'After Atheism: An Analysis of Religious Monopolies in the Post-communist World', in *Sociology of Religion*, Vol. 65 (2004), pp. 57–75.

Gautier M. L., 1997, 'Church Attendance and Religious Belief in Post-communist Societies', in *Journal for the Scientific Study of Religion*, Vol. 36, No. 2 (1997), pp. 289–297.

Gernet J., 1985, *China and the Christian Impact: A Conflict of Cultures*, Cambridge, Cambridge University Press.

Gerstner J. H., 1960, *The Theology of the Major Sects*, Ann Arbor, Twin Books Series.

Getz, G. A., 1987, *When the Job Seems Too Big*, Ventura, Regal Books.

Giordan G. (a cura di), 2006, *Tra religione e spiritualità. Il rapporto con il sacro nell'epoca del pluralismo*, Milano, Franco Angeli.

Goldsmith M. M., 'Mandeville and the Spirit of Capitalism', in *Journal of British Studies*, No. 1 (Autumn 1977), pp. 63–81.

Goldstein S., 'Socio-Economic Differentials Among Religious Groups in the United States', in *American Journal of Sociology*, No. 74 (May 1969), pp. 612–631.

Goody, J., 2010, *The Eurasian Miracle*, Cambridge, Polity Press.

Gramling R., Forsyth C. J., Mooney L., 'The Protestant Ethic and the Spirit of Cajunism', in *Journal of Ethnic Studies*, Vol. 15 (1987), pp. 33–46.

Granovetter M. S., 'The Strength of Weak Ties', in *American Journal of Sociology*, Vol. 78 (1973), pp. 1361–1381.

Greeley A. M., 1964, 'The Protestant Ethic: A Time for a Moratorium', in *Sociological Analysis*, Vol. 25 (Spring 1964), pp. 20–30.

Guiso L., Sapienza P., Zingales L., 'People's Opium? Religion and Economic Attitudes', in *Journal of Monetary Economics*, Vol. 50 (2003), pp. 225–282.

Hamilton G., 2006, *Commerce and Capitalism in Chinese Societies*, London, Routledge.

Hill C., 'Protestantism and the Rise of Capitalism', in *Essays in the Economic and Social History of Tudor and Stuart England* (1961), pp. 15–39.

Holton R. J., 'MaxWeber, Rational Capitalism and Renaissance Italy: A Critique of Cohen', in *American Journal of Sociology*, Vol. 89 (1983), pp. 166–180.

Howland D., 'The Dialectics of Chauvinism: Minority Nationalities and Territorial Sovereignty in Mao Zedong's New Democracy', in *Modern China*, Vol. 37, No. 2 (2011), pp. 170–201.

Hsu P., 2014, *China's Quest for Liberty: A Personal History of Freedom*, South Bend, St. Augustines Press.

Hsu P., 'Why Beijing's Largest House Church Refuses to Stop Meeting Outdoors', in *Christianity Today* (April 2011), Carol Stream.

Hudson W. S., 1949, 'Puritanism and the Spirit of Capitalism', in *Church History*, Vol. 1 (1949), pp. 3–17.

Human Rights Watch/Asia, 'Continuing Religious Repression in China' (June 1993), 'China: Persecution of a Protestant Sect' (June 1994), and 'China: State Control of Religion' (October 1997).

Hunter A., Don Rimmington, 'Religion and Social Change in Contemporary China', in *All Under Heaven*, pp. 11–37.

Hunter A., & Kim-Kwong C., 1993, *Protestantism in Contemporary China*, Cambridge University Press.

Introvigne M., 2009, *Storia della riforma*, n. 23, Trento.

Introvigne M., 'Max Weber aveva torto. Una recensione di «The Victory of Reason» di Rodney Stark', in *Cristianità*, gennaio- febbraio 2006, n. 333, p. 5–10.

Italian Chamber of Commerce, 'In Arrivo l'Anno del Toro', in *Camera di Commercio di Milano* (Jan. 2009), Milan, pp. 1–2.

Jianhua M., 'The Development of Rural Christianity in China and Its Challenges', in *Chinese Theological Review*, No. 13 (1999), pp. 65–71.

Joas H., 1996, *The Creativity of Action*, Chicago, University of Chicago Press.

Johnson B., 'Max Weber and American Protestantism', in *Sociological Quarterly*, Vol. 12 (Autumn 1971), pp. 473–485.

Jonassen C. T., 'The Protestant Ethic and the Spirit of Capitalism in Norway', in *American Sociological Review*, Vol. 12, No. 6 (Dec. 1947), pp. 676–686.

Kahn J., 'China's Christians Mix Business and God: Wenzhou Church Thrives on New Capitalists Wealth', in *The Wall Street Journal*, 16 June 1995.

Kangsheng D., 2001, 'Xin Zhongguo Zongjiao Yanjiu 50 Nian' (50 Years of Religious Research in New China), in *Annual of Religious Research* (1999–2000), pp. 38–57.

Kippenberg H. G., 1997, *Die Entdeckung der Religionsgeschichte. Religionswissenschaft und Moderne*, München, C. H. Beck.

Kirven R., *Destination: Excellence*, Worthington, GCI.

Krech V., 2011, *Wo bleibt die Religion?: Zur Ambivalenz des Religiösen*, in Der Modernen Gesellschaft (Sozialtheorie), Auflage.

Kristof N. D., 'Christianity Is Booming in China Despite Rifts', in *New York Times* (7 Feb. 1993), p. A16.
Ku Ch., 2010, 'The 'Spirit' of Capitalism in China: Contemporary Meanings of Weber's Thought,' pp. 19–45.
Lachmann R., 1989, 'Origin of Capitalism and the State in Western Europe', in *Annual Review of Sociology*, Vol. 15 (1989), pp. 47–72.
Lambert T., 1999, *China's Christian Millions*, London, Monarch Books.
Lambert T., 1994, *The Resurrection of the Chinese Church*, Wheaton, IL, OMF/ Shaw Publishers.
Lang G., 1998, 'Religions and Regimes in China', in *Religion in a Changing World*, Praeger, Westport, pp. 149–158.
Laurence B., *The Practice of the Presence of God*, Grand Rapids, Spire.
LeMond J. G., 'A Brief History of the Church in China', in *Word and World*, Vol. 17 (1997), pp. 144–153.
Leung, K. L., 1999, *The Rural Churches of Mainland China Since 1978*, Hong Kong, Alliance Bible Seminary Press.
Li Z., 'China Denies Church Demolition Is Persecution of Christians', in *CNN International* (April, 2014), Atlanta.
Lin-Liu J., 2005, 'At Chinese Universities, Whispers of Jesus', in *Chronicle of Higher Education* (June 10), p. 40.
Lipset S. M., Bendix R., 1959, *Social Mobility in Industrial Society*, Berkeley, University of California Press.
Locke J., 1982 [ed. orig. 1690], *Due Trattati sul Governo e altri scritti Politici*, Torino, UTET.
Locke J., 2000, *Scritti Etico-Religiosi*, Torino, UTET.
Lortz J., Iserloh E., 1990, *Storia della riforma*, Bologna, Il Mulino.
Love J. F., 1987, *McDonald's. Behind the arches*, Guernsey, Bantam Press.
Luther M., 1967, *Scritti religiosi*, Torino, UTET.
Luther M., 2002, *The Small Catechism*, Fort Wayne, Project Wittenberg.
MacDonald W., *Think of Your Future*, Kansas City, Walterick Publishers.
MacKinnon M., 'Calvinism and the Infallible Assurance of Grace: The Weber Thesis Reconsidered', in *The British Journal of Sociology*, Vol. 39, No. 2 (Jun., 1988), pp. 143–177.
Maclnnis D. E., Xi'an Z., (eds.), 1991, *Religion Under Socialism in China*, Armonk, NY, Sharpe.
Madsen R., 1995, *China and the American Dream: A Moral Inquiry*, Berkeley, University of California Press.
Manser M. (Eds.), 1999, *Concise Chinese-English, English-Chinese Dictionary*, Oxford University Press.
Marshall T. H., 'Capitalism and the Decline of the English Gilds', in *Cambridge Historical Journal*, Vol. iii, No. i (1929).

McCotter J., 1983, *God's Revealed Plan for Your Finances*, Silver Spring, Great Commission.

McCotter J., 1984, *The Secret of Success*, Silver Spring, Great Commission International.

Means R. L., 'Protestantism and Economic Institutions: Auxiliary Theories to Weber's Protestant Ethic', in *Social Forces*, Vol. 44, No. 3 (Mar., 1966), pp. 372–381.

Meinhold P., 1994, *Manuale delle Religioni*, Brescia, Queriniana.

Melton G. J., 1993, *Encyclopedia of American Religions*, Washington DC, Gale Research Inc..

Merton R. K., 1962, *Puritanism, Pietism and Science*, Glencoe Illinois, The Free Press, pp. 33–66.

Miller D., 1997, *Reinventing American Protestantism*, Berkeley, University of California Press.

Milton J. Y., 1961, *Sociologia della religione*, Torino, Paolo Boringhieri.

Molloy S., 'Max Weber and the Religions of China: Any Way Out of the Maze?', in *The British Journal of Sociology*, Vol. 31, No. 3, (Sept. 1980), pp. 377–400.

Muratorio B., 1980, *Protestantism and Capitalism Revisited, in the Rural Highlands of Ecuador*, The Journal of Peasant Studies, Taylor & Francis.

Nelson B., 1973, 'Weber's Protestant Ethic: Its Origins, Wanderings and Foreseeable Futures', in *Beyond the Classics?*, New York, Harper and Row, pp. 71–130.

North G., 1986, *Honest Money: Biblical Principles of Money and Banking*, Dominion Press.

North G., 1986, *Sinai Strategy: Economics and the Ten Commandments*, Institute for Christian Economics.

Nuccio O., 2003, *Addio all'«Etica protestante». Umanesimo civile ed individualismo economico nella letteratura italiana: da Albertano ad Alberti*, Roma, Casa Editrice Universitaria degli Studi La Sapienza.

Oberg B. B., (Eds.), 1996, *The Papers of Benjamin Franklin*, New Haven, Yale University Press.

Offenbacher M., 1900, *Konfession und soziale Schichtung: Eine Studie uber die wirtschaftliche Lage der Katholiken und Protestanten in Baden*, Tubingen, Paul Siebeck.

Otsuka H., 1976, *Max Weber on the Spirit of Capitalism*, Tokyo, Institute of Developing Economies.

Overmyer D. L., (ed.) 2003, 'Religion in China Today', in *The China Quarterly special issues*, Cambridge, Cambridge University Press.

Pace E., 2007, *Introduzione alla sociologia delle religioni*, Roma, Carocci.

Parsons T., 'Capitalism in Recent German Literature: Sombart and Weber', in *Journal of Political Economy*, Vol. 37, No. 1 (Feb., 1929), pp. 31–51.

Parsons T., 1963, 'Introduction', in *Max Weber, The Sociology of Religion*, Boston, Beacon Press.

Parsons T., 1947, 'Introduction', in *Max Weber, The Theory of Social and Economic Organization*, New York, Oxford University Press.

Parsons T., 1967, *Societies: Comparative and Evolutionary Perspectives*, Englewood Cliffs, Prentice-Hall.

Parsons T., 1937, *The Structure of Social Action*, Glencoe, Free Press.

Pas J. E., 1989, *The Turning of the Tide: Religion in China Today*, Oxford, Oxford University Press.

Pellicani L., 2006, *La genesi del capitalismo e le origini della modernità*, Marco Ed.

Persico R., 'Il Logos ti fa ricco', in *Tempi*, No. 49/50 (Dec., 2006), pp. 46–47.

Peters T. J., Waterman R. H. Jr., 1984, *In search of Excellence. Lessons from America's Best-Run Companies*, New York, Warner.

Petullà M., 2004, *Vero uomo. L'urto antropologico di Gesù*, DePa Communication, Gioia Tauro.

Poggi G.,1984, *Calvinismo e spirito del capitalismo*, Bologna, Il Mulino.

Pomfret, J., 2002, 'Evangelicals on the Rise in Land of Mao Despite Crackdowns, Protestant Religious Groups Flourishing in China', in *Washington Post* (Dec. 24), p. AO1.

Potter P. B., 'Belief in Control: Regulation of Religion in China', in *The China Quarterly*, Vol. 174, No. 2 (2003), pp. 317–337.

Poupard P. (Eds.), 1990, *Grande Dizionario delle Religion*, Paris i, Cittadella-Piemme.

Qingpeng L., 1999, *Zhongguo de Youtairen: Shenmi de Wenzhou Ren* (Jews of China: The Mysterious Wenzhouness), Beijing, Jingji Ribao Chubanshe.

Ricca P., Tourn G., 2010, *Le 95 tesi di Lutero*, Torino, Claudiana.

Riesebrodt M., 'The Promise of Salvation: A Theory of Religion', in *American Journal of Sociology*, Vol. 116, No. 4 (January 2011), pp. 1384–1386.

Rives J. B. (eds.), 1999, *Tacitus: Germania*, Oxford University Press.

Roulleau-Berger, L., 2012, (eds.) *Sociologies et cosmopolitisme méthodologique*, Toulouse, Presses universitaires du Mirail.

Samuelsson K., 1961, *Religion and Economic Action: A Critique of Max Weber*, New York, Harper and Row.

Schlozman, K. L., Brady H., Nie N., 'Race, Ethnicity, and Political Resources: Participation in the United States', in *British Journal of Political Science*, Vol. 23 (193), pp. 453–97.

Schnitger, M., 1995, *Max Weber. Una biografia*, Bologna, Il Mulino.

Schwarzer R., Jerusalem M., Hahn A., 'Negative affect in East German migrants: Longitudinal Effects of Unemployment and Social Support', in *Anxiety, Stress and Coping An International Journal*, Vol. 6, No. 1 (1993), pp. 57–69.

Shaeffer F., 2009, *How Should We Then Live? The Rise and Decline of Western Thought*, New York, Paperback.

Sharot S., 'Beyond Christianity: A Critique of the Rational Choice Theory of Religion from a Weberian and Comparative Religions Perspective', in *Sociology of Religion*, Vol. 63, No. 4 (2002), pp. 427–454.

Simmel G., 2007, 'A Contribution to the Sociology of Religion', in *American Journal of Sociology*, pp. 359–376.

Singer M., 'Religion and Social Change in India: The Max Weber Thesis, Phase Three', in *Economic Development and Cultural Change*, Vol. 14 (1966), pp. 497–505.

Smith H. W., 1994, *The 10 Natural Laws of Successful Time and Life Management. Proven Strategies for Increased Productivity and Inner Peace*, New York, Time Warner.

Sombart W., 1932, *L'apogee du capitalisme*, Paris, Introduction.

Soothhill W. E., 1907, *A Mission in China*, Edinburgh, Oliphant, Anderson and Ferrier.

Sprenkel van der O. B., 'MaxWeber on China', in *History and Theory*, Vol. III (1963), p. 348.

Stanley Mooneyham W., 1979, *China. A New Day*, New Jersey, Logos International.

Stark R., 1968, *American Piety*, University of California Press.

Stark R., 2004, *For the Glory of God: How Monotheism Led to Reformations, Science, Witch-Hunts, and the End of Slavery*, New Jersey, Princeton University Press.

Stark R., 2014, *How the West Won: The Neglected Story of the Triumph of Modernity*, Delaware, Intercollegiate Studies Institute.

Stark R., & Finke R., 1992, *The Churching of America 1776–1992: Winners and Losers in Our Religious Economy*, New Jersey, Rutgers University Press.

Steele R., 1684, *The Tradesman's Calling*, London.

Stokes R. G., 'Afrikaner Calvinism and Economic Action: The Weberian Thesis in South Africa', in *American Journal of Sociology*, Vol. 8 (1975), pp. 62–81.

Strickmann M., 2005, *Chinese Poetry and Prophecy. The written Oracle in East Asia*, Asian Religions & Cultures, Stanford University Press.

Sweezy P. M., 1942, *The Theory of Capitalist Development*, New York, Oxford University Press.

Tagliabò C., 2001, *Max Weber e lo spirito del capitalismo*, n. 128, Milano.

Tamney J. B., Burton R., Johnson S. D., 1989, 'Fundamentalism and Economic Restructuring', in *Religion and Political Behavior in the United States*, New York, Praeger, pp. 67–82.

Tawney, R. H., 'Bibliography: Studies in Bibliography. II. Modern Capitalism', in *The Economic History Review*, Vol. 4, No. 3 (Oct., 1933), pp. 336–356.

Tourn G., 2008, *La predestinazione nella Bibbia e nella storia*, Torino, Claudiana.

Trevor-Roper H. R., 1968, *The Crisis of the Seventeenth Century*, Harper & Row.
Troeltsch E., 1958, *Protestantism and Progress*, Beacon Press.
Troeltsch E., 1931, *The Social Teaching of the Christian Churches*, 2 vols., London [ed. orig. 1912, *Die Soziallehren der Christlichen Kirchen und Gruppen*, Tiubingen].
Uhalley S. Jr., Wu X. (eds.), 2001, *China and Christianity: Burdened Past, Hopeful Future*, Armonk, NY, Sharpe, pp. 195–216.
Vala C. T., 2009, 'Pathways to the Pulpit: Leadership Training in 'Patriotic' and Unregistered Chinese Protestant Churches', in *Making Religion*, Stanford University Press, pp. 126–150.
Van Der Veer P., 2012, *Governing Difference: Inequality, Inequity and Identity in India and China*, pp. 721–734.
Van Der Veer P., 'Religion, Secularism and National Development in India and China', in *Third World Quarterly*, Vol. 33, No. 4 (2012).
Veblen T. B., 1899, *The Theory of the Leisure Class*, New York, Macmillan.
Wang J., 'The House Church Movement: A Participant's Assessment', in *Word and World*, Vol. 1, No. (19977), pp. 175–182.
Weber M., 1952 [ed. orig. 1917–1919], *Ancient Judaism*, Translated by Hans H. Gerth and Don Martindale, Glencoe, Ill., Free Press.
Weber M., 1978, *Economy and Society: An Outline of Interpretive Sociology*, California University Press.
Weber M., 1949, *The Methodology of the Social Sciences*, Free Press.
Weber M., 1991, *The Protestant Sects and the Spirit of Capitalism*, London, Routledge [ed. orig. 1906, Die protestantischen Sekten und der Geist des Kapitalismus].
Weber M., 1951 [ed. orig. 1916], *The Religion of China*, Translated by Hans H. Gerth. Glencoe, Ill., Free Press.
Whyte M. K., 'Paradoxes of China's Economic Boom', in *Annual Review of Sociology*, Vol. 35 (2009), pp. 371–392.
Whyte B., 1988, *Unfinished Encounter: China and Christianity*, London, Fount.
Williams A., 1983, *A Simple Plan for Financial Independence*, Atlanta, Parklake Publishers Inc.
Wright Mills C., Gerth H. H., 1946, *From Max Weber*, New York, Oxford University Press.
Xiaoxin W. (Eds.), 2009, *Christianity in China. A Scholars' Guide to Resources in the Libraries and Archives of the United States*, New York, M. E. Sharpe.
Yang F., 2004, 'An Economics of Religious Shortage: Communist China in Transition', in *Society for the Scientific Study of Religion Annual Meeting*, Kansas City (Oct. 22–24).
Yang F., 2004, 'Between Secularist Ideology and Desecularizing Reality: The Birth and Growth of Religious Research in Communist China', in *Sociology of Religion, A Quarterly Review*, Vol 65, No. 2 (2004), pp. 101–119.

Yang F., 'Chinese Conversion to Evangelical Christianity: The Importance of Social and Cultural Contexts', in *Sociology of Religion: A Quarterly Review*, Vol. 59, No. 3 (1998), pp. 237–257.

Yang C. K., 1960, *Religion in Chinese Society*, Berkeley, University of California Press.

Yang F., Lang G., 2011, *Social Scientific Studies of Religion in China. Methodology, Theories and Findings*, Leiden, Brill.

Zamagni S., 2008, *L'etica cattolica e lo spirito del capitalismo*, Working Paper n. 49, Bologna.

Zanotto P., 2008, *Cattolicesimo, protestantesimo e capitalismo*, Milano, IBL.

Zaret D., 'From Weber to Parsons and Schutz: The Eclipse of History in Modem Social Theory', in *American Journal of Sociology*, Vol. 85 (1980), pp. 1180–1201.

Zhiming Y., (et alii), 1997, *Soul Searching: Chinese Intellectuals on Faith and Society*, Wheaton, China Horizon.

Zuo J., 'Political Religion: The Case of the Cultural Revolution in China', in *Sociological Analysis*, Vol. 52, No. 1 (1991), pp. 99–110.

SPRINGER NATURE

GPSR Compliance

The European Union's (EU) General Product Safety Regulation (GPSR) is a set of rules that requires consumer products to be safe and our obligations to ensure this.

If you have any concerns about our products, you can contact us on ProductSafety@springernature.com

In case Publisher is established outside the EU, the EU authorized representative is:

Springer Nature Customer Service Center GmbH
Europaplatz 3
69115 Heidelberg, Germany

The manufacturer's authorised representative in the EU is Springer Nature Customer Service Centre GmbH, Europaplatz 3, 69115 Heidelberg, Germany. If you have any concerns regarding our products, please contact ProductSafety@springernature.com

Printed and bound by CPI Group (UK) Ltd, Croydon, CR0 4YY
01/10/2026
02225854-0012